DATE DUE

GAYLORD   PRINTED IN U.S.A.

THE
RISE AND FALL
OF
MODERN MEDICINE

THE
RISE AND FALL
OF
MODERN MEDICINE

James Le Fanu

CARROLL & GRAF PUBLISHERS, INC.
NEW YORK

Copyright © 1999 by James Le Fanu

All rights reserved

First Carroll & Graf edition 2000

Carroll & Graf Publishers, Inc.
A Division of Avalon Publishing Group
19 West 21st Street
New York, NY 10010-6805

Library of Congress
Cataloging-in-Publication Data is available.
ISBN: 0-7867-0732-1

Manufactured in the United States of America

For Frederick and Allegra

Contents

PART 1: THE RISE

PART 2: THE END OF THE AGE OF OPTIMISM

PART 3: THE FALL

Part 4: The Rise and Fall –
Causes and Consequences

ACKNOWLEDGEMENTS

The arduousness of writing has been more than compensated for by the privilege of meeting so many of those who participated in the great events recorded in this book. To them; to the sympathetic souls whose interest has been more important than they realise; to the librarians at the Royal Society of Medicine and the Wellcome Institute for the History of Medicine; to my wife Juliet; to my agent Caroline Dawnay, publisher Philippa Harrison and editor Andrew Gordon; and to Vanessa Adams for her prodigious secretarial skills, my thanks:

Dr Digby Anderson, Lord Annan, Bryan Appleyard, Mr John Ballantyne FRCS, Sir Douglas Black, Professor Nicholas Black, Sir Christopher Booth, Dr Thomas Boulton, Professor John Bunker, Dr Bruce Charlton, Mr Bill Cleland FRCS, Sir John Dacie, Dr Ann Dally, Dr Anthony Daniels, Professor Norman Dennis, Professor C. J. Dickinson, Sir Richard Doll, Professor Deborah Doniach, Professor Israel Doniach, Professor R. S. Downie, Sir John Ellis, Professor Peter Ellwood, Professor Renee Fox, Mr Michael Freeman FRCS, Professor David Galton, Dr John Glyn, Mr James Gow FRCS, Professor John Hampton, Dr Myles Harris, Sir Donald Harrison, Dr I. D. Hill, Professor A. V. Hoffbrand, Dr Arthur Holman, Mr John Hopewell FRCS, Dr David Horrobin, Professor Bryan Jennett, Professor Trevor Jones, Dr Michael Joseph, Dr Leo Kinlen,

Dr Ghislaine Lawrence, Professor John Marshall, Dr William Marshall, Dr Robert Matthews, Professor James McCormick, Professor Kenneth Minogue, Dr G. Misiewicz, Professor John Moorehead, Mr E. P. O'Donoghue FRCS, Professor Peter Openshaw, Mr Nicholas Parkhouse FRCS, Professor Michael Patton, Sir Stanley Peart, Mr Elliot Philipp FRCS, Mr Michael Powell FRCS, Dr David Pyke, Mr Gordon Rees FRCS, Professor Lesley Rees, Dr Henry Rollin, Dr Rupert Sheldrake, Professor Peter Skrabanek, Professor Alexander Spiers, Professor Gordon Stewart, Mr John Studd FRCOG, Professor Raymond Tallis, Dr Tilli Tansey, Dr Wendy Taylor, Professor Tom Treasure FRCS, Mr Patrick Trevor-Roper FRCS, Dr John Wade, Sir David Weatherall, Dr Mark Weatherall, Professor Simon Wesseley, Mr Adrian While FRCS, Dr Elizabeth Whipp, Mr John Wickham FRCS, Sir Michael Woodruff, Dr Nigel Yeatman.

'The Lord hath created medicines out of the earth; and he that is wise will not abhor them.'

ECCLESIASTICUS 38:4

INTRODUCTION

The history of medicine in the fifty years since the end of the Second World War ranks as one of the most impressive epochs of human achievement. So dramatically successful has been the assault on disease that it is now almost impossible to imagine what life must have been like back in 1945, when death in childhood from polio, diphtheria and whooping cough were commonplace, when there were no drugs for tuberculosis, or schizophrenia, or rheumatoid arthritis, or indeed for virtually every disease the doctor encountered; a time before open-heart surgery, transplantation and test-tube babies. These, and a multitude of other developments, have been of immeasurable benefit, freeing people from the fear of illness and untimely death, and significantly ameliorating the chronic disabilities of ageing.

This post-war medical achievement is well recognised, but much less appreciated is the means by which it was brought about. For the previous 2,000 years doctors had sought in vain for the 'magic bullets' that would alleviate their patients' suffering and then, quite suddenly and without warning, they came cascading out of the research laboratories just as if medicinal chemists had hit the jackpot (as they had). Or again, in 1945, desirable objectives such as transplanting organs or curing cancer were rightly perceived as being unattainable, as there was simply no way of overcoming the biological problems of the rejection of foreign tissue or the selective destruction of cancer cells. But these and many other obstacles were surmounted. The past fifty years have been a unique period of prodigious intellectual ferment that, quite naturally, invite investigation.

There is a problem, however, in knowing where to start. The scale of the therapeutic revolution has been so vast that any comprehensive history would necessarily run to several volumes. Decisions had to be made about not only what to include and what, regretfully, to leave out, but also how to go beyond a simple chronological account to illuminate themes of more general significance. The compromise I have chosen is illustrated opposite. This list of the major events of this period identifies 'ten definitive moments' which are considered in depth in a prologue that is necessarily longer than is customary. The rationale of this selection is not of immediate concern but several themes are easy enough to identify, including the decline of infectious disease (sulphonamides, penicillin and childhood immunisation); the widening scope of surgery (the operating microscope, transplantation and hip replacements); major developments in the treatment of cancer, mental illness, heart disease and infertility; and improvements in diagnostic techniques (the endoscope and the CT scanner).

Each of these events is a remarkable story of human endeavour in its own right, but when they are assembled together then, as with the dots of the pointillist, a coherent picture should begin to emerge. The value of such an historical perspective is not necessarily obvious. 'Medicine pays almost exclusive homage to the shock of the new,' writes the editor of *The Lancet*, Richard Horton. 'We place constant emphasis on novelty . . . this is an era of the instantaneous and the immediate.'[1] This preoccupation with 'the new' leaves little room for history and indeed medicine has got by well enough with no sense of its immediate past at all. Perhaps the history of twentieth-century medicine is solely of academic interest, an intellectual pastime for retired doctors but of little practical importance?

The Ten Definitive Moments of Modern Medicine

* A 'definitive' moment

1935	Sulphonamides
1941	*Penicillin
	'Pap' smear for cervical cancer
1944	Kidney dialysis
1946	General anaesthesia with curare
1947	Radiotherapy (the linear accelerator)
1948	Intraocular lens implant for cataracts
1949	*Cortisone
1950	* {Smoking identified as the cause of lung cancer Tuberculosis cured with streptomycin and PAS
1952	The Copenhagen polio epidemic and the birth of intensive care
	*Chlorpromazine in the treatment of schizophrenia
1954	The Zeiss operating microscope
1955	*Open-heart surgery
	Polio vaccination
1956	Cardiopulmonary resuscitation
1957	Factor VIII for haemophilia
1959	The Hopkins endoscope
1960	Oral contraceptive pill
1961	Levodopa for Parkinson's
	Charnley's hip replacement
1963	*Kidney transplantation
1964	*Prevention of strokes
	Coronary bypass graft
1967	First heart transplant
1969	The pre-natal diagnosis of Down's syndrome
1970	Neonatal intensive care
	Cognitive therapy
1971	*Cure of childhood cancer
1973	CAT scanner
1978	*First test-tube baby
1979	Coronary angioplasty
1984	*Helicobacter as the cause of peptic ulcer
1987	Thrombolysis (clot-busting) for heart attacks
1996	Triple therapy for AIDS
1998	Viagra for the treatment of impotence

Needless to say, I do not share this view, but rather, taking my cue from T. S. Eliot – 'the historical sense involves the perception not only of the pastness of the past, but of its presence' – maintain it is not possible to understand the present, and in particular present discontents, outside of the context of this recent past. And what is the nature of these 'present discontents'? Any account of modern medicine has to come to terms with a most perplexing four-layered paradox that at first sight seems quite incompatible with its prodigious and indubitable success.

Paradox 1: Disillusioned Doctors

It might be expected that the success of modern medicine should make it a particularly satisfying career, but recent surveys consistently reveal that increasing numbers, especially of younger doctors, are bored and disillusioned. The London-based Policy Studies Institute has found the proportion of doctors 'with regrets' about their chosen career has increased incrementally, decade by decade from 14 per cent of the 1966 cohort to 26 per cent of the 1976 cohort to 44 per cent of the 1981 cohort and to 58 per cent of the 1986 cohort.[2] These findings should not be taken at face value, as spasms of self-doubt may become commoner for any number of reasons. Nonetheless, they would seem to be symptomatic of a genuine – and serious – trend. What has happened to explain why today's young doctors are so much less content than those who qualified thirty or more years ago? It is important to know, not least because those unhappy with their trade may lack the passion necessary to practise it well.

Paradox 2: The Worried Well

The benefits of modern medicine in alleviating the fear of illness and untimely death should have meant that people are now less worried about their health than in the past. But once again, the trend is the reverse of that which would have been expected. The proportion of the population claiming to be 'concerned about their health' over the last thirty years has also increased in direct parallel to the rise in the number of 'regretful' doctors – from one in ten to one in two.[3] And the most curious thing about this phenomenon of the 'worried well' who are 'well' but 'worried' (that they might not be) is that it is not simply symptomatic of privileged life in the West, where 'people don't know when they are well-off', but that it is medically inspired. The well are worried because repeatedly and consistently they have been led to believe their lives are threatened by hidden hazards. The simple admonition of thirty years ago – 'Don't smoke, and eat sensibly' – has metamorphosed into an all-embracing condemnation of not just tobacco but every sensuous pleasure, including food, alcohol, sunbathing and sex. Further, every year brings a new wave of 'dangers', which in 1997 included low-fat milk and margarine, computer screens, head-lice shampoo, mobile phones and much else besides. This is Healthism – a medically inspired obsession with trivial or non-existent threats to health whose assertions would in the past, quite rightly, have been dismissed as quackery.[4]

Paradox 3: The Soaring Popularity of Alternative Medicine

The demonstrable success and effectiveness of modern medicine should have marginalised alternatives such as homeopathy and naturopathy into oblivion. Not so. In the United States there are more visits to providers of 'unconventional therapy' (425 million) than to 'primary care physicians' (388 million). As the efficacy of alternative therapies is not routinely tested in clinical trials (which does not mean they do not work), it is only natural to ask why the public should appear to have so much faith in them.[5]

Paradox 4: The Spiralling Costs of Health Care

The more that medicine 'can do', the higher will be its cost, which will be further compounded by the continuing rise in the numbers with the greatest need – the elderly. Neither of these two factors, however, can begin to account for the massive escalation in the resources allocated to health care. Thus, in the United States, health expenditure over the last decade has soared by over 60% from $800 billion in 1990 to a staggering $1300 billion in 1997. During this time there have been neither the substantial improvements nor wider access for the uninsured that would begin to justify such an increase.[6]

In summary, then, the four-layered paradox of modern medicine that needs explaining is why its spectacular success over the past fifty years has had such apparently perverse consequences, leaving doctors less professionally fulfilled, the public more neurotic about its health, alternative medicine in the ascendancy and an unaccounted-for explosion in health-service costs.

   It is important to keep a sense of proportion about all this. In general, doctors do find fulfilment in their work, and in general people appreciate the benefits of modern medicine, as anyone whose mobility has been restored by a hip replacement or whose spirits have been lifted by an antidepressant will testify. But the same point could be put the other way. It is precisely because medicine *does* work so well that the discontents reflected by these paradoxes are worthy of explanation.

   These are complex matters and there are many reasons for each of these paradoxes, most notably the subversion, by authoritarian managers and litigious patients, of the authority and dignity of the profession. But 'history is a high point of advantage from which alone men can see the age in which they are living' (G. K. Chesterton), and from the high point of advantage of a historical perspective of medicine's last fifty years it is possible to perceive there might also be a single unifying explanation that can readily be seen from the earlier chronology of major events. The crucial factor is the dates, with the massive concentration of important innovations from the 1940s through to the 1970s followed by a marked decline. There has been, as suggested in the title of this book, a 'Rise and Fall', which provides the key to understanding the paradoxical discontents of modern times.

But when this historical account opens, such matters are still a long way off. Imagine, rather, that Europe is in the throes of war, children are still dying from whooping cough and polio, the inmates of mental asylums are lucky to see a doctor from one year's end to the next and curing cancer or transplanting organs seem like unattainable fantasies. And yet there is a terrific sense of optimism in the air. Medicine's greatest epoch has already begun, and the possibilities of science seem limitless.

A LENGTHY PROLOGUE:

Ten Definitive Moments

The history of modern medicine starts sometime in the 1830s, when a few courageous physicians acknowledged that virtually everything they did – bleeding, purging, prescribing complicated diets – was useless. The distinguished medical commentator Lewis Thomas elaborates:

> Gradually over the succeeding decades the traditional therapeutic ritual of medicine was given up . . . [to be replaced by] meticulous, objective, even cool observations of sick people. Accurate diagnosis became the central purpose and justification for medicine and as the methods improved, accurate prognosis also became possible, so that patients and their families could be told not only the name of the illness but also, with some reliability, how it was most likely to turn out. By the time this century had begun, it was becoming generally accepted as the principal responsibilities of the physician.[1]

By the time this history begins, doctors had become very skilled at diagnosing what was wrong – deploying the simple skills of taking a history, conducting an examination and doing a few simple tests on blood and urine – but, the 'therapeutic ritual' having been jettisoned, the cupboard of specific remedies was virtually bare. The efficacy of some of the traditional remedies derived from plants – such as the heart drug digoxin from the foxglove and aspirin from the bark of the willow tree – had been vindicated. Several forms of immunisation of varying effectiveness had been developed for the treatment of the infectious diseases, and the chemical salvarsan had been found to be specifically successful against syphilis. The only other two significant therapeutic developments had been the discovery of vitamins (though vitamin-deficiency diseases were rare enough) and the isolation of hormones such as thyroxine and insulin for the treatment of diseases caused by their deficiency, hypothyroidism and diabetes respectively.[2]

But that was about it. The pattern of human disease had changed little over the previous 2,000 years. The problems of infectious disease – both acute and chronic – dominated medical practice, culling the young either early in infancy or later from the lethal childhood illnesses such as whooping cough and measles. The cause of the diseases that emerged from adolescence onwards – schizophrenia, rheumatoid, multiple sclerosis – were unknown and had no specific remedies. Those who survived into old age were vulnerable to the chronic degenerative diseases of ageing – cataracts clouded their sight, arthritic hips limited their mobility – and succumbed from the age-determined illnesses of the circulatory disorders and cancer.

In general the nation's health had been gradually improving over the previous hundred years, infant mortality rates were in decline and the average lifespan was, albeit modestly, slowly increasing, trends that could plausibly be attributed to social improvements in housing and diet. There were, however, three 'new' diseases that had recently emerged to become major causes of untimely death in middle age: peptic ulcers, heart attacks and cancer of the lung. Their cause was not known and, as ever, there were no effective treatments. The purpose of this book is to describe what happened next, starting with an account of the 'ten definitive moments' – the 'canon' – of modern medicine.

I

1941: PENICILLIN

The discovery of penicillin is, predictably, both the first of the twelve definitive moments of the modern therapeutic revolution and the most important. Penicillin and the other antibiotics that followed rapidly in its wake cured not only the acute lethal infections such as septicaemia, meningitis and pneumonia, but also the chronic and disabling ones such as chronic infections of the sinuses, joints and bones. This in turn liberated medicine to shift its attention in the coming decades to a completely different and up till then neglected source of human misfortune: the chronic diseases associated with ageing such as arthritic hips and furred-up arteries.

Antibiotics transformed doctors' and indeed the public's perceptions of medicine's possibilities. If a naturally occurring non-toxic chemical compound produced by a species of fungus such as penicillin could make the difference between whether a child with meningitis should live or die, it was only natural to wonder whether other ghastly and baffling illnesses might not yield to similar simple solutions. Perhaps cancer might be curable, or schizophrenia might be treatable?

In the public imagination antibiotics came to symbolise the almost limitless beneficent possibilities of science. Yet, this is not entirely merited for, as will be seen, the discovery of penicillin was not the product of scientific reasoning but rather an accident — much more improbable than is commonly appreciated. Further, at the core of antibiotics lies an unresolved mystery: why should just a few species of micro-organisms

5

produce these complex chemical compounds with the capacity to destroy the full range of bacteria that cause infectious disease in humans?

On 12 February 1941, a 43-year-old policeman, Albert Alexander, became the first person to be treated with penicillin. Two months earlier Mr Alexander had scratched his face on a rose bush, a trivial enough injury perhaps, but the scratches had turned septic. Soon his face was studded with abscesses draining pus, his left eye had had to be surgically removed because of the infection and now his right eye was endangered in a similar way. His right arm drained pus from an infection deep in the bone and he was coughing up copious amounts of phlegm from cavities in his lungs. He was, as Charles Fletcher, the doctor who was to administer the penicillin, recalls, 'in great pain, desperately and pathetically ill'. Dr Fletcher subsequently described what happened:

> Penicillin therapy was started every three hours. All Mr Alexander's urine was collected and each morning I took it over to the pathology laboratory on my bicycle so the excreted penicillin could be extracted to be used again. There I was always eagerly met by the members of the penicillin team. On the first day I was able to report that for the first time throughout his illness Mr Alexander was beginning to feel a little better. Four days later there was a striking improvement . . . he was vastly better, with a normal temperature and eating well and there was obvious resolution of the abscesses on his face and scalp and right orbit [eye].[1]

But on the fifth day, 17 February, the supply of penicillin was exhausted. Inevitably, his condition deteriorated and he died a month later. It would, of course, have been much better for Mr Alexander had more penicillin been available, but in a way his death has a metaphorical significance – a reminder to future generations of the crucial transitional moment between human susceptibility to the purposeless malevolence of bacteria (and there can be nothing more purposeless than dying from a scratch from a rose bush) and the ability, thanks to science, to defeat them. 'It is difficult to convey the excitement of witnessing the amazing power of penicillin,' comments Professor Fletcher. Over the next few years he observed 'the disappearance of the "chambers of horrors" – which seemed the best way to describe the old septic wards' in which Albert Alexander and thousands like him had spent their last days. When more supplies of penicillin became available four more patients were treated, including a 48-year-old labourer with a vast carbuncle on his back 4 inches in diameter that vanished 'leaving no scar' and a fourteen-year-old boy 'extremely ill' with a bone infection – osteomyelitis – of the left hip complicated by septicaemia.[2]

More than fifty years later this first description of the use of penicillin has lost none of its power to amaze. Reading it one has the impression of witnessing a miracle, whose origins, as is well known, lay in the chance observation made by Alexander Fleming in his laboratory at London's St Mary's Hospital over ten years earlier. As a microbiologist Fleming's research work involved growing colonies of bacteria on special plates called petri dishes and observing their behaviour in different circumstances. He had, for example, recently shown that a chemical called lysozyme present in tears could inhibit the growth of several types of harmless bacteria. In 1928, returning from his summer holidays, Fleming picked up a petri dish standing in a pile waiting to be washed and noticed how a contaminating mould (later identified as *penicillium notatum*) had inhibited the growth of a colony of staphylococcal bacteria. He then extracted the juice from the mould (which he called penicillin) and showed it was capable of inhibiting the growth of a whole range of micro-organisms. Curiously, however, when other scientists tried to replicate the accidental method by which he had made his discovery – by dropping some penicillium mould on to a plate of staphylococci – they were quite unable to do so.

It was not until 1964, when Fleming's former assistant, Ronald Hare, investigated the matter in detail, that the reason emerged. Hare found that this failure to replicate Fleming's original observation was because the growth of the penicillium mould occurred at a different temperature (20 degrees Celsius) than the staphylococcus, which grows best at a temperature of around 35 degrees Celsius. So what had happened?

Firstly, the penicillium mould that had 'floated through the window' was not a commonly occurring strain but rather a rare one that had wafted up from the laboratory below, where a fellow scientist and fungus expert, C. J. LaTouche, was working. Fortuitously this rare strain just happened to produce large amounts of penicillin. Some spores, it must be presumed, contaminated a petri dish on which Fleming had been growing some colonies of staphylococci. Inexplicably, but essential for his subsequent discovery, Fleming did not, prior to going on holiday, place the dish in the incubator but left it out on the laboratory bench. Consulting the meteorological records for London at the end of July in 1928, Ronald Hare discovered that while Fleming was away there had been an exceptionally cool nine-day period – which would have favoured the growth of the penicillium mould – after which the temperature rose, which would have stimulated the growth of the staphylococcus. The penicillium mould was by now producing sufficient quantities of penicillin, and on his return Fleming noted that the pinhead-sized yellow spots on the plate, each of which represented a colony of the staphylococcus, had an unusual appearance. 'For some considerable distance around the mould growth the colonies were obviously undergoing lysis [dissolution].' Thus, without the 'nine cool days' in London in the summer of 1928, Fleming would never have discovered penicillin.[3]

Fleming was much luckier than he realised, but he was then remarkably indolent in exploring the therapeutic potential of his findings. He used juice extracted from the penicillium mould to treat a colleague's conjunctivitis and found an obscure application in culturing a species of bacteria in the laboratory that was notoriously difficult to grow, but by the following year he had abandoned any formal research into its further clinical use, because of the prevailing view that chemicals were likely to be too toxic to be used to treat infectious diseases.[4] Fleming did not take the matter further because he did not think it worth pursuing, 'a good example of how preconceived ideas in medicine can stifle the imagination and impede progress'.[5]

So the miraculous properties of penicillin had to be rediscovered all over again ten years later by Howard Florey and Ernst Chain in Oxford, which was preceded, interestingly enough, by recapitulation of Fleming's work on the antibacterial properties of lysozymes in tears. Howard Florey had arrived in Britain from his home country of Australia in 1922 and after obtaining a degree from Oxford rapidly ascended the academic ladder. He was prodigiously industrious, very good with his hands and had the knack of attracting others as, or more, talented than himself to work as his collaborators. In 1935 when still only thirty-seven he became Professor of Pathology at Oxford and promptly recruited Ernst Chain, a young German Jewish chemist refugee from Nazi Germany. As Florey's scientific interests included the study of the chemistry of the body's natural secretions, he initially hoped that Chain's chemical talents would be able to elucidate their biochemical structure. 'When Florey and I in our first meeting discussed the future research programme in the department, Florey drew my attention to a very startling phenomenon,' Chain recalled. This was Fleming's observation, made back in 1921, that lysozymes in tears and nasal secretions were capable of dissolving thick suspensions of bacteria, though how they attacked the cell wall of bacteria was unknown. It took only a year for Chain to show that lysozyme was a complex enzyme. While writing up this work for publication, he looked around for other instances of compounds that might destroy bacteria and inevitably came across Fleming's original paper describing the effects of penicillin. By now it should be clear why Chain and Florey were to succeed where Fleming had failed. The skills of a microbiologist like Fleming lay in the observation and interpretation of experiments with bacteria; the skills of a biochemist like Chain lie at a deeper level, in identifying the biochemical mechanisms that underpin the microbiologist's observations. And so just as Chain had so rapidly solved the question of the biochemistry of lysozyme, it was only a matter of time before he would unravel the mechanisms of the action of penicillin and appreciate its real significance.

Nonetheless, at the outset neither Chain nor Florey believed penicillin would have any 'clinical applications' in the treatment of infectious diseases, so the precise sequence of events that persuaded them to change their minds is of some interest. Firstly it seems that Chain was intrigued to find that penicillin was 'a very unusual substance'. It was not, as he had imagined it would be, an enzyme like lysozyme, but rather it turned out to be 'a low molecular substance with great chemical instability'. In brief, he had no idea what it was so 'it was of obvious interest to continue the work'. Secondly, he had the biochemical skills to extract and purify (though not to a very great extent) penicillin, which when tested against bacteria grown in culture proved to be twenty times more potent than any other substance. Thirdly, when penicillin was injected into mice it was apparently 'non-toxic'. This last point was very important, for, as already pointed out, probably the most important reason why Fleming had failed to pursue the possibilities of penicillin was the common belief that any compound capable of destroying bacteria would necessarily harm the person to whom it was given. Finally, in a classic experiment Chain and Florey demonstrated that penicillin could cure infections in mice: ten mice infected with the bacterium streptococcus were divided into two groups, with five to be given penicillin and five to receive a placebo. The 'placebo' mice died, the 'penicillin' mice survived.[6]

After the publication of the results of this experiment in *The Lancet* on 24 August 1940, Florey hoped that one of the pharmaceutical companies would become sufficiently interested to produce penicillin on a large scale for, as he pointed out, a man, being 3,000 times bigger than a mouse, would need a large amount of penicillin if the results in mice were to be replicated in humans. But these were difficult times. The mice experiment had been conducted just as the British Expeditionary Force of 350,000 men had been driven on to the beaches of Dunkirk to be evacuated by an improvised armada of ships that somehow survived the repeated attacks of the German dive-bombers. This shattering defeat, in which Britain lost the equivalent of an entire army, made the prospect of a German invasion almost inevitable and heralded the Luftwaffe's daily assaults on London in the Battle of Britain.

At this desperate moment, when the future of Britain lay in the balance, Florey decided to commit the puny resources of his laboratory in Oxford to making enough penicillin to test in humans. 'The decision to turn an academic university department into a factory was a courageous one for which Florey took full responsibility . . . if his venture had failed it would have been seen as an outrageous misuse of property, staff, equipment and time, and Florey would have been severely censured.'[7]

The hallmark of Florey's university laboratory-turned-penicillin factory was improvisation, the penicillium moulds being grown on hospital bedpans and the precious fluid extracted and stored in milk jugs:

> [In] the 'practical' classroom, the washed and sterilised bed-pans were charged with medium and then inoculated with penicillin spores by spray guns. They were then wheeled on trolleys to what had been the students' 'preparation' room, now converted into a huge incubator kept at 24° Centigrade. After several days of growth, the penicillin-containing fluid was drawn off from beneath its mould by suction . . . The air was full of a mixture of fumes: amyl acetate, chloroform, ether. These dangerous liquids were pumped through temporary piping along corridors and up and down stairwells. There was a real danger to the health of everyone involved and a risk of fire or explosion that no one cared to contemplate.[8]

By the beginning of 1941 there was just enough penicillin for the first trial in humans. On 12 February Charles Fletcher administered the first injection directly into the policeman Albert Alexander's vein, and, as already described, a further four patients were treated over the next few months. Seven university graduates, including two professors and ten technical assistants, had worked every day of the week and most nights for several months to achieve these results. If the work on penicillin were to go forward then much larger quantities were going to be needed. In June Florey travelled to America where eventually four major drug companies took up the challenge of the mass production of penicillin.

At the end of the war, in 1945, Florey and Chain shared, along with Fleming, the Nobel Prize. Their achievement was not just the development of penicillin but rather the clarification of the principles by which *all* antibiotics were subsequently to be discovered. In his acceptance speech Florey spelled out what those principles were: the screening of microbes to identify those which produced an antibacterial substance; the determination of how to extract the substance; testing it for toxicity; investigating its effect in animal experiments; and finally tests in humans.[9]

We now know, though Florey did not when he gave his speech, that penicillin was not just 'a lucky break'. Rather the screening of tens of thousands of species of micro-organisms over the next few years revealed a handful that produced a whole further range of antibiotics (see page 13). Their impact on medicine has already been mentioned, but three further points are worth noting. Firstly, it is necessary to appreciate the comprehensiveness of the antibiotic revolution. There are many different types of infectious illness, from the trivial sore throat to life-threatening meningitis. The bacteria involved behave in different ways, both in how they spread themselves around and how they damage the body's tissues. An attack of meningitis can kill within twelve hours while tuberculosis may take ten years or more. And yet there is not one of the hundreds of different species of bacteria that cause disease in humans that is not treatable with one or other antibiotic.

Secondly, the antibiotic-producing bacteria might seem simple but the mechanism of action of the antibiotics they produce are both very diverse and highly complex. They can interfere with the enzymes and peptides that make the cell wall, blow holes in the lining of the cell, disturb the transport of chemicals across the lining, interfere with the synthesis of the

Dates of the discovery and sources of the more important antibiotics[10]

Name	Date of discovery	Microbe	Source
Penicillin	1929–40	*Penicillium notatum*	Air, London
Streptomycin	1944	*Streptomyces griseus*	A chicken's throat
Chloramphenicol	1947	*Streptomyces venezuelae*	Mulched field, Venezuela
Chlortetracycline	1948	*Streptomyces aureofaciens*	Soil
Cephalosporin C, N & P	1948	*Cephalosporium sp.*	Sewage outfall, Sardinia
Neomycin	1949	*Streptomyces fradiae*	Soil, New Jersey
Oxytetracycline	1950	*Streptomyces rimosus*	Soil
Nystatin	1950	*Streptomyces noursei*	Farm soil, Virginia
Erythromycin	1952	*Streptomyces erythreus*	Soil, Philippines
Novobiocin	1955	*Streptomyces spheroides*	Pastureland, Vermont
Vancomycin	1956	*Streptomyces orientalis*	Soil, Borneo and Indiana
Kanamycin	1957	*Streptomyces kanamyceticus*	Soil, Japan
Fusidic acid	1960	*Fusidium coccineum*	Monkey dung, Japan
Lincomycin	1962	*Streptomyces lincolnensis*	Soil, Lincoln, Nebraska
Gentamicin	1963	*Micromonospora purpurea*	Soil, Syracuse, New York

nucleotides that make up the bacteria's DNA or inhibit the manufacture of proteins in the cell.[11]

Thirdly, despite the complexity and diverse mechanisms by which antibiotics work, the process of their discovery turned out to be astonishingly simple. All that was required, as Florey pointed out in his Nobel Prize speech, was the screening of micro-organisms to identify the handful that could destroy other bacteria and then the identification of the active anti-biotic ingredient. Thus, though antibiotics are commonly perceived as a triumph of modern science, scientists alone could never have invented or created them from first principles. They are, rather, 'a gift from nature', which raises the question of what their role in nature might be.

The most obvious and commonly accepted explanation is that antibiotics are 'chemical weapons' produced by bacteria to maximise their own chances of survival against other organisms in the atmosphere and the soil. This was certainly the view of Selman Waksman, the discoverer of streptomycin for the treat-ment of tuberculosis. Waksman was, by training, a soil micro-biologist and knew more about the ways in which bacteria in the soil interacted with each other than anyone else in the world.

Waksman received the Nobel Prize in 1952 for his discovery of streptomycin, and yet in the following years he came to realise that his original perception of antibiotics as 'chemical-warfare' weapons deployed by bacteria in the soil must be mistaken. He noted the ability to make antibiotics was limited to a very few species and so could not play an important role in the ecology of microbial life. Further, the ability of micro-organisms to produce antibiotics turned out to be highly dependent on the quality of the soil, and indeed they were only reliably produced in the artificial environment of the laboratory. Next, there was no evidence that antibiotics could be found or accumulated where there are many organisms present. And so, if antibiotics did not act as bacterial 'chemical weapons' in the struggle for survival in the soil what did Selman Waksman believe their role to be? They are, he said, a 'purely fortuitous phenomenon . . . there is no purposeness behind them . . . the only conclusion that can be drawn from these facts is that these microbiological products are accidental'.[12]

This is a very difficult concept to accept. It seems inconceivable that bacteria, the simplest of organisms, should have the ability to produce such complex molecules but which then serve no purpose in their survival, but as Leo Vining, a biologist from Dalhousie in Canada observed at a conference in London in 1992, even 'accepting these products [antibiotics] have a role, does not mean that we can readily agree upon or perceive what that role might be'.[13]

The story of penicillin and the other antibiotics that followed is thus very different from that so often presented — and usually perceived — as the triumph of science and rationalism in the conquest of illness. The unusual climatic circumstances that led to Fleming's discovery of the antibacterial properties of the penicillium mould were quite staggeringly fortuitous. The crucial decision that led to its mass production — Florey's resolve to turn his university laboratory into a penicillin factory when a German invasion was imminent — is a triumph of will over reason. Lastly the questions of how, and more particularly why, a handful of the simplest of micro-organisms should have the ability to create these complex chemicals, and of why they should exist at all, is simply not known. This, the mystery of mysteries of modern medicine, will be revisited.

2

1949: CORTISONE

*C**ortisone** – commonly known as 'steroids' – is the second of the two drug discoveries that created the modern therapeutic revolution. Whereas the first, antibiotics, defeated an external enemy – the bacteria that caused infectious disease – cortisone mobilised the body's capacity to heal itself. This concept requires some elaboration. The human body as a robust and self-sufficient organism must be able to heal itself. This is seen most obviously in the recovery after a wound to the skin or a fracture to the bone but it is, of course, a generalised phenomenon much exploited by doctors over the centuries. Given time, rest, warmth and adequate nutrition, many illnesses will simply get better. These self-healing properties of the body are so pervasive that it was natural to infer there must be some physical or spiritual force to guide them. For the anatomist John Hunter it was a 'vital spirit', for the French physiologist Claude Bernard 'homeostasis' and for the physician William Osler the 'vis medicatrix naturae'.*

Cortisone is not by itself the 'vis medicatrix naturae' yet, through its influence on the body's response to stress and inflammation, this naturally occurring hormone cures or ameliorates upwards of 200 different illnesses and so can probably be described as its main component. As with antibiotics, cortisone's discovery was entirely unanticipated, based on a series of fortuitous and coincidental events that stretched back nearly two decades.

The story of cortisone is synonymous with Dr Philip Showalter Hench, Head of the Division of Medicine at the Mayo Clinic in Rochester, Minnesota, a large, powerful man of relentless determination. His speech was very loud, and, because of a severe cleft palate, difficult to understand, but nonetheless he spoke incessantly and in time became a magnificent lecturer.

On 26 July 1948 a young woman of twenty-nine, Mrs Gardner, was admitted under Dr Hench's care. Her rheumatoid arthritis – from which she had suffered for more than five years – had proved to be relentlessly progressive despite every form of available treatment. 'Many joints were stiff, swollen, tender and painful on motion,' Dr Hench observed. 'Her right hip joint had been eroded away so she could only walk with the utmost difficulty and was essentially confined to a wheelchair.' Two months later she was no better and Dr Hench turned to a biochemist colleague, Edward Kendall, who informed him that the pharmaceutical company Merck had just synthesised a quantity of Compound E – now known as cortisone – which is secreted by the adrenal gland. The following morning a small amount of Compound E arrived by airmail in a special-delivery package. 'We began with daily injections of 100mg,' Dr Hench recalls. 'During that day no change was apparent, the patient ventured only once out of her room as walking was so painful.' But two days later, on 23 September, 'when she awoke, she rolled over in her bed with ease and noticed much less muscular soreness'. The following day 'her painful muscular stiffness was entirely gone'. Scarcely able to walk three days previously, she now walked with only a slight limp. Four days later 'she shopped down town for three hours, feeling tired thereafter – but not sore or stiff'.[1]

Over the following three months Philip Hench treated a further thirteen patients, each as severely afflicted as Mrs Gardner, and presented the results to his fellow physicians at a meeting in April 1949.

The lights were turned down and a colour film began flickering on the screen. First came the 'before treatment' pictures in which patients with characteristically deformed joints struggled to take a few steps. Suddenly an electrifying gasp swept through the audience as the 'after treatment' scenes appeared and the doctors saw the very same patients jauntily climbing steps, swinging their arms and legs and even doing little jigs as if they had never been crippled at all. Even before the film ended, the watching physicians had filled the hall with wave after wave of resounding applause. When the lights went up and Dr Hench approached the lectern, he was greeted with a standing ovation.[2]

The origins of this momentous occasion go back twenty years to 1928 and a chance discussion between Hench and one of his patients, a 65-year-old doctor with rheumatoid arthritis, 'one of the most intractable, obstinate and crippling diseases that can befall the human body'. The doctor, who had been admitted to the clinic for investigation of an attack of jaundice, told Hench that the day after his jaundice had appeared, the pain and swelling in his joints 'had begun to diminish', and that he found he could walk painlessly a distance of one mile. Altogether the doctor's jaundice lasted four weeks but his arthritic feet and hands remained free of pain for a further seven months.

Hench realised this temporary remission of rheumatoid arthritis during an attack of jaundice was no mere coincidence when, over the following few years, he came across several other patients who described the same experience. As he noted: 'The therapeutic implications are obvious. It would be gratifying to repeat nature's miracle – to provide at will a similar beneficial effect by the use of some non-toxic accompaniment of jaundice.'[3]

At that time rheumatoid arthritis was thought to be caused by some, as yet unknown, infectious agent and it was thus only logical to presume that further developments in the treatment of the illness – if there were to be any – were likely to come from the discovery of some chemical with anti-infective properties such as the soon-to-be-discovered antibiotics.

Hench certainly had no grounds for believing this chance observation of a jaundice-induced remission might be put to some practical use as he had no way of knowing what the vital agent – which he designated 'Substance X' – might be. Was it a constituent of the bile or an abnormal chemical produced when the liver was damaged? Or was it something outside the liver altogether that was 'activated' by the jaundice? Hench had no alternative other than to seek to replicate nature's 'miracle' by trial and error. He tried everything. He gave his arthritic patients bile salts, diluted bile, liver extracts, even transfused them with blood taken from jaundiced patients – all to no avail. Nonetheless he concluded his dismal litany of therapeutic failure in an article in the *British Medical Journal* in 1938 on an optimistic note: 'It is important for us to identify nature's dramatic, if accidental, antidotes . . . [but] the next step belongs to the future.'[4]

Meanwhile he had made two further very important observations. Firstly, he noted the symptoms of rheumatoid arthritis also improved in pregnancy, which made it much more likely that his Substance X was not specifically related to jaundice but was rather a hormone whose concentration in the blood increased both during pregnancy and when the liver was damaged. Further, jaundice and pregnancy produced a remission not only of rheumatoid arthritis but also of hayfever, asthma and the neurological disorder myasthenia gravis. So, whatever Substance X might turn out to be, it should, in theory, have been able to improve not just the symptoms of rheumatoid arthritis but these other illnesses as well.[5]

The most significant of all the many fortuitous events on the long road leading to the identification of 'cortisone' as Substance X was that while Hench was trying to treat his rheumatoid patients with bile and liver extracts, the completely unrelated research programme of another scientist working in the same hospital – Edward Kendall – would finally provide the answer.

Edward Kendall was the Professor of Physiological Chemistry at the Mayo Clinic. Back in 1914, when he was still only twenty-eight, he had isolated the hormone secreted by the thyroid gland – thyroxine. Since then another hormone – insulin, secreted by the pancreas – had been discovered to cure diabetes and there was naturally enormous interest in other diseases related to hormonal deficiency. These included Addison's disease of the adrenal glands, which sit on top of the kidneys, whose destruction (most often by tuberculosis) causes a progressive illness of weakness and debility leading to death within six months. Patients with Addison's could be treated with a porridgey compound made from adrenal glands taken from cats, but the precise nature of the hormones they secreted was not known. In 1929, the same year as Hench's conversation with his jaundiced patient alerting him to the possibility of Substance X, Professor Kendall set out to identify what these adrenal hormones might be. By 1936 he, along with researchers from other institutes, had isolated several different chemicals which would be known as Compounds A, B, E and F.[6,7]

Hench and Kendall became close friends and 'on innumerable occasions' they conjectured together whether one or other of these compounds A to F might be the mysterious Substance X. There was, however, no financial incentive for any pharmaceutical company to undertake, on such a shaky hypothesis, the laborious task of synthesising these new compounds in sufficient quantities to investigate their therapeutic potential. According to Hench, the possibility they might relieve the symptoms of rheumatoid arthritis was recorded 'in my pocket notebook' and that, for the moment, was the end of the matter.

Then, precisely as happened with the development of penicillin, the exigencies of war created the incentive to carry the research further. Among several investigations by scientists to find out the precise functions of the adrenal gland hormones, Dr Hans Selye of Toronto's McGill University had found they increased the resistance of laboratory animals to the stress of oxygen deprivation.[8] In 1941 US military intelligence agents reported that Germany was buying up large quantities of adrenal glands taken from cattle in Argentina.

This was enough to balloon the rumour that Luftwaffe pilots (boosted with injections of adrenal cortex hormones) were able to fly at heights of over 40,000 feet. The US Air Force promptly instituted a major research programme in every laboratory in the United States and Canada where work had been done on the adrenal extract.[9]

The rumour about Luftwaffe 'super-pilots' was soon scotched, but by then the research programme had developed a momentum of its own, which was a good thing because, as expected, synthesising the hormones proved to be a long and laborious task. It was not until 1948 that Dr Lewis Sarett, working for the drug company Merck, managed, by a complex chemical process, to obtain a few grams of pure cortisone.

When the news of the 1949 meeting where Hench provided the flickering images of patients' 'before and after' treatment leaked out to the press, cortisone was presented as a genuine 'miracle cure'. As the medical correspondent of The Times reported: 'Within a few days of administration, patients were able to get out of bed and walk about, and the pain and swelling of the affected joints disappeared.'[10] No Nobel Prize has ever been awarded more rapidly. The following year Hench and Kendall travelled to Stockholm to receive their award and Hench donated part of his prize money to Sister Pantaleon – the nun who had run his rheumatology ward for twenty-three years – so she could travel to Rome to see the Pope.[11]

Hench, however, was only too aware that cortisone was not a 'miracle cure', but merely controlled the symptoms and inevitably, once the treatment was discontinued, the arthritis would relapse. And then there was the problem of side-effects. When the British rheumatologist, Dr Oswald Savage, visited Hench at the Mayo Clinic in 1950, he found him 'depressed by the increasingly numerous reports of side-effects . . . My generation will never forget the severe complications they produced – the moon face, the perforated and bleeding ulcers, the bruising and crushed vertebrae. It was clear this drug was so powerful it was imperative to use it safely.' What an irony to have spent a lifetime discovering a cure for an untreatable illness only to find it was so powerful as to be virtually unusable![12]

Soon the enthusiasm for treating rheumatoid arthritis with cortisone started to wane. The temporary – albeit apparently miraculous – improvement was being bought, it seemed, at too high a price.[13] And yet, just as cortisone's reputation for treating rheumatoid began to decline, so its absolutely central role in modern therapeutics began to emerge. Choose virtually any illness of unknown cause for which there is no effective treatment, however unpleasant or even life-threatening, give cortisone and see what happens.[14] In a single issue of the *Bulletin of the Johns Hopkins Hospital* in 1950 four separate articles described the effects of cortisone in treating chronic intractable asthma; hypersensitivity reaction to drugs; the serious disorders of connective tissue, systemic lupus erythematosis and polyarteritis nodosa; and eye diseases including iritis, conjunctivitis and uveitis.[15] The results were so uniformly good as to seem repetitive, and differed from those obtained in the treatment of rheumatoid arthritis in two important ways. Firstly, the benefits could be achieved at much lower doses, or by applying the cortisone externally to the skin or eyes, thus minimising the problem of side-effects. Secondly, it emerged that cortisone could in many circumstances carry a patient through a 'crisis', an acute medical problem of relatively short duration – such as an acute attack of asthma – after which the drug could be discontinued.

Cortisone and its derivatives, now collectively known as 'steroids', were (as shown on page 24) to completely transform the treatment of six medical specialties – rheumatology, ophthalmology, gastroenterology, respiratory medicine, dermatology and nephrology (kidney disorders), as well as facilitating the two most remarkable therapeutic developments of the post-war years – organ transplantation and the cure of childhood cancer. Two general points deserve emphasis.

Firstly, as Hench had originally predicted, steroids are effective in a wide variety of different pathological processes including allergy (anaphylactic shock, asthma, rhinitis, conjunctivitis and eczema); autoimmune disorders (the connective tissue disorders, haemolytic anaemia, chronic active hepatitis and myasthenia gravis); life-threatening infectious disease (septic shock, tuberculosis and meningitis); acute inflammatory disorders (polymyalgia, optic neuritis, psoriasis); and potentially lethal swelling of the brain and spinal cord following injury.

Secondly, the precise causes of many of these diseases remain unknown and herein lies the truly revolutionary significance of steroids in that they subverted the common understanding of how medicine should progress. It would seem obvious that a proper understanding of disease would be indispensible to developing an effective treatment, but the discovery of steroids permitted doctors to pole-vault the hurdles of their own ignorance, or, mixing metaphors, the inscrutable complexity of disease was dissolved away in the acid bath of steroid therapy where, in practical terms (at least for the patient) the only really important question – 'what will make this better?' – was resolved by the simple expedient of writing a prescription for cortisone. And yet this 'panacea' – which despite their limitations steroids certainly are – is a naturally occurring hormone, which brings us back to a necessary reconsideration of the functions of cortisone in the body and why it proved to be therapeutically so beneficial in so many different illnesses.

Cortisone plays a crucial role in the body's ability to heal itself – the *vis medicatrix naturae* – through its effects on the process of inflammation. Consider an infected joint, which is painful and swollen because of the damage caused by invading bacteria. The white blood cells secrete powerful enzymes to destroy the bacteria and remove the damaged tissue – this is the 'inflammatory' phase of healing, which is followed by 'resolution', when the debris is removed and new tissue laid down. Thus, during the 'inflammatory' phase, the symptoms of pain and swelling in an infected joint are as much the result of the powerful enzymes secreted by the white blood cells as part of the process of healing as of the infecting bacteria themselves. When, as happens with rheumatoid arthritis, the healing process cannot eliminate the 'cause' (which is not known), the inflammation persists along with its symptoms of pain, redness and swelling, which further damages the tissues of the joint.

Cortisone in several different ways orchestrates and controls

Diseases responsive to steroid therapy

Addison's disease
Anaphylactic shock
Aspiration syndromes
Behcet's syndrome
Bites and stings
Blood disorders
  Cold haemagglutinin disease
  Haemangioma
  Haemolytic anaemia
  Hypereosinophilia
  Hypoplastic anaemia
  Macroglobulinaemia
  Thrombocytopenic purpura
Cancer
  Leukaemia
  Hodgkin's disease
Cerebral oedema
Cogan's syndrome
Congenital adrenal hyperplasia
Connective tissue disorders
  Systemic lupus erythematosus
  Polymyalgia rheumatica
  Polymyositis
  Dermatomyositis
Epilepsy

Eye disorders
  Allergic conjunctivitis
  Iritis
  Uveitis
  Keratitis
  Sympathetic ophthalmia
  Post cataract surgery
  Corneal graft rejection
  Optic neuritis
  Retinal vasculitis
  Scleritis
Gastrointestinal disorders
  Crohn's disease
  Ulcerative colitis
  Haemorrhoids (piles)
  Hypercalcaemia
Infections
  Glandular fever
  Leishmaniasis
  Leprosy
  Meningitis
  Pneumocystis carinii pneumonia
  Septic shock
  Tuberculosis
Kidney disorders

  Lupus nephritis
  'Minimal change' nephritis
  Membranous nephrophathy
  Renal transplant
Liver disorders
  Chronic active hepatitis
  Alcoholic liver disease
  Biliary cirrhosis
  Sclerosing cholangitis, liver transplants
Male infertility
Neurological disorders
  Bell's palsy
  Coma
  Multiple sclerosis
  Myasthenia gravis
  Polyneuropathies
Organ and tissue transplantation
Respiratory disorders
  Asthma
  Sarcoidosis
  Chronic obstructive pulmonary disease
  Fat embolism syndrome

Croup
Acute eosinophilic pneumonia
Pulmonary eosinophilia
Fibrosing alveolitis
Rheumatoid disease and osteoarthritis
Rhinitis
Skin disorders
  Alopecia
  Eczema
  Contact dermatitis
  Infantile eczema
  Atopic dermatitis
  Dermatitis herpetiformis
  Seborrhoeic dermatitis
  Neurodermatitis
  Psoriasis
  Lichen sclerosis
  Pemphigus
  Pemphigoid
  Pyoderma gangrenosum
  Urticaria
Spinal cord injury
Thyroid disorders
Vascular disorders

(From Martindales, *The Extra Pharmacopeia*, 31st edition, Royal Pharmaceutical Society, 1996. Readers are referred to this source for relevant references.)

this inflammatory response and, as the fundamental pathological feature of rheumatoid arthritis is the persistence of
inflammation, so cortisone will, by suppressing it, result in an
improvement in symptoms. Thus Hench's real achievement
was much greater than demonstrating cortisone's effectiveness
in improving the symptoms of rheumatoid arthritis. He opened
the way to the understanding that many illnesses share the unifying feature of being caused by uncontrolled or excessive
inflammation. Put another way, prior to Hench there was no
sense that this vast range of diseases were connected at all and
it was certainly inconceivable they might all be ameliorated by
a naturally occurring hormone.

The therapeutic potency of cortisone could never have been
anticipated, and so it could never have been created from first
principles. It is thus, just like antibiotics, best conceived of as
'a gift from nature' whose discovery was quite fortuitous.

It is only necessary to add that, fifty years later, the means by
which cortisone controls the inflammatory response are still not
clear. It influences the changes in the local blood supply, the
attraction of cells to clear the injured tissue and the proliferation
of healing tissue, but there is as yet no unifying hypothesis of
how these powerful effects work together.

3

1950: STREPTOMYCIN, SMOKING AND SIR AUSTIN BRADFORD HILL

The advent of antibiotics and cortisone created a mood of such excitement and eager anticipation of further medical advance that some form of celebration was called for. Hugh Clegg, editor of the *British Medical Journal*, saw the year 1950, the mid-point of the century, as the perfect opportunity to invite the Great and the Good to look back over recent achievements and anticipate those to come. They duly obliged, and the the first issue of the year opened with a wide-ranging review by Sir Henry Dale FRS. 'We who have been able to watch the beginnings of this great movement,' he concluded inspiringly, 'may be glad and proud to have lived through such a time, and confident that an even wider and more majestic advance will be seen by those who live on through the fifty years now opening.'[1]

But, the mid-point of the century proved to be more than a convenient opportunity to reflect on the past and crystal-gaze into the future. Two apparently unrelated events, each of great significance in itself, occurred later in the year, ensuring that 1950 was literally a watershed separating medicine's past from its future. The first was the demonstration that two drugs, streptomycin and PAS (para-amino salicylic acid), given together over a period of several months, resulted in a 'marked improvement' in 80 per cent of patients with tuberculosis.

The second was the convincing proof that smoking caused lung cancer.

These two events represent what historians of science call 'a paradigm shift', where the scientific preoccupations particular to one epoch give way to or are displaced by those of another. Thus, for the hundred years prior to 1950 the dominant paradigm had been 'the germ theory', in which medicine's main preoccupation had been to find some effective treatment for infectious diseases. Tuberculosis remained the last great challenge. Without doubt the most notorious of all human infections, the tubercle bacillus alone had proved resistant to treatment because its apparently impermeable waxy coat protected it against antibiotics like penicillin. But now, thanks to streptomycin and PAS, it seemed that even this, 'the captain of the armies of death', could be defeated. And just as the threat of infectious diseases started to recede, so it was to be replaced by a different paradigm or preoccupation – the non-infectious diseases such as cancer, strokes and heart attacks. The incrimination of smoking in lung cancer showed that the cause of these diseases might be just as specific as that for infectious illnesses, but rather than a bacterium being responsible, the culprit was people's social habits. If smoking – which was almost universal following the Second World War – caused lung cancer, then perhaps other aspects of people's lives, such as the food they consumed, might cause other diseases.

The ramifications of this paradigm shift were to be of great importance but surprisingly that is not the main reason for its inclusion in the pantheon of 'definitive moments'. Rather it is the manner in which it was brought about. Prior to 1950, the cornerstone of reliable knowledge in medicine was the cumulative wisdom acquired through everyday practice. The notion that the validity, or otherwise, of specific treatments might be objectively tested was hardly ever raised. But the demonstration of the curability of tuberculosis and the role of smoking in lung cancer changed all this, for both relied on statistical methods of proof that soon permeated every aspect of medicine to become the main – indeed the sole – arbiter of 'scientific truth'. This was almost entirely due to the influence of one man, Austin

Bradford Hill, Professor of Medical Statistics at the London School of Hygiene and Tropical Medicine. Bradford Hill was not medically qualified and had no formal training in statistical methods at which, on his own admission, he was 'not very proficient', viewing them rather as being 'common sense applied to figures'. Nonetheless he was to guide statistics to a dominant position within medicine whose subsequent indiscriminate application would eventually exert a most baleful influence.

This intellectual ascendancy of statistics is essentially the story of Bradford Hill's life. He was born in 1897 into a distinguished Victorian family, at least one of whose members in each of the preceding four generations had featured in the *Dictionary of National Biography*, including his father, Sir Leonard Hill, Professor of Physiology at the London Hospital who, *inter alia*, developed a machine to measure the blood pressure and in a series of self-experiments conducted by himself and his junior lecturer, Dr Major Greenwood, showed that 'the bends' in divers, caused by the formation of bubbles of nitrogen in the blood, could be prevented by slow uniform decompression.[2] Powerfully influenced by the stimulating atmosphere of his home life, Bradford Hill decided to follow his father into medicine but, when the time came to enter medical school, Britain was at war with Germany so instead he joined the Royal Naval Air Service as a pilot. In January 1917 he was posted to the Aegean and joined a party of a dozen officers at Charing Cross station to travel by train to the toe of Italy. 'It was on this exhausting, overcrowded and unhygienic journey, I would guess, I picked up the tubercle bacillus,' he subsequently recalled. Based on the tiny island of Tenedos just off the Turkish coast he had a quiet time, other than the occasional flying accident, in the last of which his engine failed at 11,000 feet, leaving him no alternative other than to glide down to the narrow airstrip. 'I misjudged by about 10 yards and landed on the edge of a muddy lake. The plane stood on its nose and broke its propeller.' Within five months he had become seriously ill with a cough and a fever, the tubercle bacilli that had been multiplying in his lungs were identified in his sputum and he was 'invalided home to die'. To his own astonishment, and that of his doctors, he responded to the only two treatments for tuberculosis available at that time – bed rest and an artificial pneumothorax (the introduction of air into the pleural cavity to collapse down the lung and thus slow the spread of the infection). In 1919 he was discharged from hospital with a 100 per cent disability pension (only given to those whose disability is deemed so severe as to preclude them from any further gainful employment), which he continued to draw for the next seventy-four years till his death at the age of ninety-three.[3]

Though Bradford Hill had survived tuberculosis, a medical career was now out of the question. At the suggestion of his father's erstwhile physiology lecturer, Dr Major Greenwood, he opted for a correspondence course in economics at London University, which he obtained with second-class honours. In 1928 Major Greenwood was appointed the first Professor of Vital Statistics at the recently opened London School of Hygiene and Tropical Medicine, and in 1931 he appointed Bradford Hill as Reader in Epidemiology. Thus began their long collaboration.

These details of Bradford Hill's early life illuminate what was to follow. His frustration at being unable to fulfil his childhood ambition of following his father into medicine only heightened his fascination with every aspect of the medical sciences. It may have been the fascination of an outsider, but this was only to his advantage. From this Olympian vantage point he was able to take a detached and critical view of medical developments. He was particularly lucky that his mentor, Greenwood, was that rarity in medical circles, a full-blooded intellectual whose perception of the contribution statistics could make to medicine was driven by his strong historical sense of past achievements, particularly in the field of public health, reinforced by his contact with the mathematical polymath, Karl Pearson (of whom more later), who in his turn had been a protégé of one of the greatest of all Victorian intellectuals, Francis Galton. It is to these roots of medical statistics that we now turn before taking up again the thread of Bradford Hill's career.

★　★　★

For many, statistics are numbers to which complex mathematical formulae can be applied to produce conclusions of dubious veracity and from which all wit and human life is rigorously excluded. Certainly, any single statistic by itself is a dreary thing, but when they are linked together over months and years then patterns begin to emerge and it is possible to see things that previously were hidden. An unarguable event such as death lends itself particularly well to the statistical method, and when the numbers in any town or region are recorded over a brief period it is possible to appreciate that in the aggregate they represent the distinct biological phenomenon of an epidemic. This is the simplest form of epidemiology – literally the study of epidemics – which, nonetheless, has the power to change the world for the better.

This beneficent capacity of statistics was seen most strikingly in the great movement for sanitary reform in the mid-nineteenth century, when William Farr – 'a very great Englishman' in Greenwood's words – was Compiler of Abstracts in the General Register Office. In his thirty-fifth annual report Farr drew attention to the yawning differential in childhood mortality rates between the rich and poor and asked: 'What are the causes? Do they admit of removal? If they do admit of removal, is the destruction of life to be allowed to go on indefinitely?'[4]

The crucial point to inspire twentieth-century epidemiologists was that statistical enquiry, by determining the underlying causes of ill health such as poor sanitation, provided the means for the prevention of disease on a massive scale, so 'statisticians' potentially had an infinitely greater effect in improving the health of the nation than white-coated doctors with their airs and graces.

There was, as already mentioned, a second and very different use of statistics. The mathematical techniques invented by Karl Pearson of University College to interpret biological variations in height, blood pressure or any other physiological characteristic made it possible to infer general rules about groups of people rather than individuals, and were relevant to experiments to test the efficacy of treatments from which it was possible to deduce whether the results were 'significant'.

In an illustrative example famous for its inconsequentiality, Ronald Fisher – a pupil of Pearson's – poured a cup of tea

> and offered it to the woman standing beside him. She refused, remarking that she preferred milk to be in the cup before the tea was added. Fisher could not believe that there would be any difference in the taste and when the woman suggested an experiment be performed, he was enthusiastic. An immediate trial was organised, the woman confidently identified more than enough of the cups of tea into which the tea had been poured first to prove her case.

In his classic book *The Design of Experiments*, published in 1935, Fisher used this example 'to state the terms of the experiment minutely and distinctly; predicted all possible results, ascertaining by sensible reasoning, what probability should be assigned to each possible result under the assumption that the woman was guessing'.[5]

Thus Greenwood's main intellectual legacy, which he was to pass on to Bradford Hill, was essentially two-fold: the historical contribution of statistical methods to elucidating the cause of substantial public health problems; and the importance of conducting properly designed experiments to test whether a new treatment was effective.

In 1945 Greenwood retired and Bradford Hill was duly appointed as his successor. The paradigm shift in which he was to play so important a role was just five years away. Its two components – the trial of streptomycin and PAS in the treatment of tuberculosis and the elucidation of the causative role of smoking in lung cancer – are here described separately, though they were occurring at the same time. Accordingly the rise of power and influence of statistics in medicine began to appear inevitable.

*The Clinical Trial: Streptomycin, PAS and the Cure of
Tuberculosis*

Bradford Hill had personal reasons for being interested in the
treatment of tuberculosis, having himself only just escaped from
being yet another mortality statistic for the disease at the cost of
two years' convalescence and an artificial pneumothorax. In
1946 he joined the Tuberculosis Trial Committee, which had
been set up to evaluate a new drug, streptomycin, that two
years earlier in the United States had been shown to be capable of killing the tubercle bacilli. It had been unnecessary to
formally test whether or not penicillin worked in humans
because the results were immediate and dramatic. But the efficacy of streptomycin in tuberculosis was not quite so
straightforward because the tubercle bacillus, in its waxy shell,
is very resilient and the damage it causes the lungs and other
organs is more chronic. Accordingly, streptomycin had to be
given for several months before there was any obvious improvement. Nonetheless there was no obvious reason at the time
why doctors should not, as they had done in the United States,
give streptomycin to patients and see what happened. If it
worked, that was fine; if not, then nothing was lost. Bradford
Hill was, however, determined that streptomycin should first be
put to the test in a properly conducted trial, comparing the
outcome with those not given the drug. His view prevailed,
but only because of the fortuitous circumstances that streptomycin was extremely difficult to acquire in Britain at that time
and so for the foreseeable future many would be unable to
benefit from it. Bradford Hill resolved to make a virtue out of
this necessity, as he subsequently recalled:

> We had exhausted our supply of dollars in the war and the
> Treasury was adamant we could only have a very small
> amount of streptomycin. This turned the scales. I could
> argue in this situation it would not be immoral to do a
> trial – it would be immoral not to, since the opportunity
> would never come again as there would soon be plenty of
> streptomycin. We could have enough of the new drug to

use in about fifty patients and I thought this was probably enough to get a reliable answer.[6]

Bradford Hill's position was to be more than vindicated, though not by showing whether streptomycin worked (which was in a sense predictable), but for showing that after a while, and for important reasons, it stopped working. Further, the fact that the treatment of tuberculosis was the first (almost) treatment to be formally tested in this way is highly significant. Tuberculosis was after all much the commonest lethal infectious disease in the West. The fact that this new drug was being tested in the context of a formal experiment designed by Bradford Hill would so enhance his authority as to make his position virtually unassailable.

When the Tuberculous Trials Committee in Britain convened, streptomycin was, at the time, the only drug deemed worthy of investigation. Bradford Hill argued persuasively that the manner of that investigation should take the form of a clinical trial in which the decision about who should be given the drug and who should act as 'a control' should be determined 'at random'. And why was this so important? Once again it is necessary to interrupt the narrative to look at the intellectual provenance of the clinical trial, before rejoining Bradford Hill for the *dénouement* of this part of his career.

The principle of the clinical trial could not be more straightforward: a simple experiment where the efficacy of a remedy is tested by comparing the outcome in those given it with that in a similar group who are not. If there is a measurable improvement in those receiving the remedy it can be presumed that it works. If there is not, it does not. The essence of a trial, then, is a comparison of the outcome between two groups. This is a modest enough scientific experiment and scarcely novel, having been used by the Parisian physician Pierre Charles Louis investigating the benefits of bleeding in pneumonia (in which he found 'no apparent difference in intensity or duration of symptoms between those bled and not bled')[7] and famously by the Scottish ship's surgeon James Lind when investigating the merits of several cures, including lemons, for scurvy, whose devastating effect on British naval expeditions had become a major impediment to further expansion of the Empire.[8]

The method of comparison in the clinical trial requires that the treatment be alternated, giving it to one patient but not the next, and so on, allocating patients to the 'treatment' or 'control' group at random. Bradford Hill explained it thus:

> the advantages of this random allocation of patients ensured three things: it ensures that neither our personal idiosyncrasies nor our lack of balanced judgement has entered into the construction of the different treatment groups; it removes the danger that believing we may be biased in our judgement we endeavour to allow for that bias and by thus 'leaning over backwards' introduce a lack of balance from the other direction; and, having used a random allocation, the sternest critic is unable to say that quite probably the groups were differentially biased through our predilections or our stupidity.[9]

This would all seem entirely reasonable and the lucidity of Bradford Hill's prose only makes it seem even more so, but slightly more is going on here than is readily apparent. The logic of Bradford Hill's argument has to be that the detached objectivity of statisticians inherent in the notion of 'randomisation' is more likely to get at the truth than the subjective impressions generated from clinical experience. And as the verdict of the statisticians is the more reliable, doctors must necessarily defer to their authority. There is a false antithesis here, but a very compelling one. Doctors are certainly intimately involved with their patients, and view the outcome of their endeavours in the best possible of rose-coloured lights. But their clinical judgement is not entirely valueless, while the principle of randomisation, it could be argued, requires doctors to abrogate the fundamental notion of trust on which the relationship with their patients is based – that any treatment proposed will be that which, in the doctor's opinion, is in the best interests of the patient. Clearly this is not possible when the decision as to what treatment the patient receives is being determined randomly.

Bradford Hill's views prevailed. From the beginning of 1947 three London hospitals started admitting patients into the first streptomycin trial, in which fifty-five patients were to be given streptomycin for four months, the results being compared with fifty-two 'controls' who were to be 'treated' with bedrest and, if necessary, the collapse treatment of the lung that Bradford Hill himself had undergone almost thirty years earlier. The allocation to 'treatment' or 'control' was determined by a series of random numbers devised by Bradford Hill and placed in a set of sealed envelopes. The 'objectivity' inherent in randomisation treatment was further bolstered by an emphasis on recording the results, such as changes in the chest X-ray, in a way that could not be biased by knowledge of the treatment being received. The radiologist comparing the chest X-rays was unaware whether it came from someone in the treatment or control group. The participants were all young, with an average age of thirty-two, and had the same pattern of the disease, with widespread tuberculosis of both lungs of relatively recent onset.[10]

By the end of six months, twenty-eight of those given the streptomycin were markedly improved and only four had died, compared to fourteen deaths among those unfortunate enough to have been randomly allocated to the 'control' group. This finding, that those given streptomycin 'did better' than those who were not, scarcely justifies the considerable time and energy devoted to the organisation of a randomised trial but, in a way that Bradford Hill could scarcely have anticipated, his insistence that streptomycin be objectively evaluated in this way was to be completely (if tragically) vindicated. There was a fundamental limitation in the use of streptomycin to treat tuberculosis. Patients certainly improved but the requirement that treatment should last several months guaranteed that some of the tubercle bacilli would become resistant to the streptomycin and, when this happened, their condition subsequently deteriorated again.[11] The streptomycin trial had been so intelligently organised that it was a straightforward matter to assess the potential seriousness of this problem of resistance, and the clear statistical presentation of the results brought home the full gravity of the problem – as revealed by an 'update' published three years later, by which time thirty-five of the original fifty-two 'controls' had died, as well as thirty-two of the fifty-five treated with streptomycin.[12]

The authoritative verdict of Bradford Hill's first trial was thus much more compelling than the resolution of the issue of whether or not streptomycin worked. Rather, it made it absolutely clear that streptomycin represented 'a false dawn' where an initial impressive improvement in a patient's condition was followed by a subsequent relapse that was closely related to the development of resistance. From this perspective there could be no greater vindication of Bradford Hill's espousal of the objective evaluation of new treatments over the subjective impression of doctors. To put the same point another way, had streptomycin, like most drugs up till this time, been introduced in the usual haphazard fashion of giving it to patients and 'seeing what happened', doctors would have been so enraptured (as they often are) by the apparent dramatic improvement they would have been blind to the subsequent problems of resistance, and it could have taken years to work out why, despite the initially impressive response to streptomycin, patients nonetheless were still dying from the disease.

Bradford Hill's methodical approach immediately pointed to the next step, which was to repeat exactly the same trial but this time, in the hope of combating the problem of resistance, combining streptomycin with a second drug that had just been discovered, PAS.[13] This second trial started in December 1948 and exactly one year later, long before the study was complete, the organisers took the unprecedented step of issuing an interim communication that they had 'demonstrated unequivocally that the combination of PAS with streptomycin considerably reduces the risk of the development of streptomycin-resistant strains of tubercle bacilli'.[14] With the publication of the full results in November 1950 the benefits of the combination of the two drugs was glaringly obvious: thirty-three of the participants in the first trial had become resistant to streptomycin, compared to only five in the second trial. No longer, as happened at the first trial, did patients respond initially to treatment only to subsequently die several years later from a recrudescence caused by resistance to streptomycin. With streptomycin and PAS the survival rate soared to 80 per cent.[15]

This was not the end of the story. Over the next ten years tuberculosis treatment became ever more refined and successful with the introduction of other drugs, notably isoniazid in 1952 and rifampicin in 1970.[16] It soon became clear that the combination of three drugs was even better than two, and that if given continuously for a period of up to two years then virtually every patient could be cured of the disease. This happy situation persisted until the late 1980s when the difficulties of treating AIDS patients with tuberculosis led to the emergence of tubercle bacilli that were 'multiply resistant' to all antituberculous drugs, raising the spectre that once again tuberculosis would become, as it had been prior to 1950, essentially an 'incurable' disease.

As a final reminder of that time, it is appropriate to recall the fate of George Orwell, who died in 1950 aged forty-seven, just a few months before the results of the combination of PAS and streptomycin were published. Orwell had first been diagnosed as having tuberculosis back in 1938. His condition improved with bedrest and lengthy convalescence in Morocco, but he suffered a relapse in 1946 soon after moving to a remote farmhouse on the island of Jura in the Hebrides, where he had gone to complete the last and greatest of his books, *Nineteen Eighty-Four*. He managed, through the influence of David Astor, the proprietor of the *Observer*, to obtain a small quantity of streptomycin. Initially all went well and a month after starting treatment he wrote to his friend Julian Simons: 'I have been having the streptomycin and it is evidently doing its stuff. I haven't gained much weight but I am better in every way.' He was, however, one of the unlucky ones who developed a strong allergic reaction to the drug in the form of a terrible rash and blisters such that he was no longer able to continue with treatment. His tuberculosis returned and he died in University College Hospital on 21 January 1950 from a massive haemorrhage into both his lungs. The famous literary critic Cyril Connolly wrote subsequently:

The tragedy of Orwell's life is that when at last he achieved fame and success he was a dying man and knew it. He had fame and was too ill to leave his room, money and nothing to spend it on, love in which he could not participate; he tasted the bitterness of dying. But in his years of hardship he was sustained by a genial stoicism, by his excitement about what was going to happen next and by his affection for other people.[17]

Orwell's fate has profound symbolic significance. Like the experience of the Oxford policeman Albert Alexander, who was the first person to receive penicillin, Orwell's brush with streptomycin is a reminder to future generations of the difference that antituberculosis drugs would make to so many people's lives. Orwell died on the cusp of the paradigm shift. Another couple of years and he would have been spared the bitterness of a premature death to live on for several more decades. Who knows what else he might have achieved?

In the aftermath of the brilliant and lucid manner in which tuberculosis had been shown to be a treatable disease, the Randomised Controlled Trial (shortened to RCT) blossomed just as Bradford Hill had hoped to become the standard way of evaluating new drugs. As his protégé Richard Doll observed in 1982: 'Few innovations have made such an impact on medicine as the controlled clinical trial designed by Sir Austin Bradford Hill . . . thirty-five years later the structure, conditions of conduct and analysis of the currently standard trials are, for the most part, the same. Its durability is a monument to Sir Austin's scientific perception, common sense and concern for the welfare of the individual.'[18] A minority were unconvinced. In a letter to the *British Medical Journal*, in 1951, 'a blast of the trumpet against the monstrous regiment of mathematics', a physician from Sunderland, Dr Grant Waugh, comments on

the outbreak in epidemic form of a disease of pseudo-scientific meticulosis. The symptoms of the condition are characterised by: a) evidence of a certain degree of cerebral exaltation; b) an inherent contempt for those who cannot

understand logarithms; and c) the replacement of human-
istic and clinical values by mathematical formulae. The
systemic effects of this disease are apparent; patients are
degraded from human beings to pricks in a column, dots in
a field, or tadpoles in a pool; with the eventual elimination
of the responsibility of the doctor to get the individual
back to health.[19]

Behind the bombast Dr Waugh was making a serious point for,
as will be seen, clinical trials were not infallible and when
improperly conducted could give rise to false conclusions that
could not be rectified by any amount of objectivity conferred
by 'randomisation'. The RCT, however, was to prove utterly
indispensable in the evaluation of the explosion of new drugs
that occurred in the 1950s and 1960s. The thalidomide tragedy
in 1960 forced governments around the world to insist that all
new drugs be formally tested for their effectiveness and safety in
randomised controlled trials as a requirement for the granting
of a product licence. Thus Bradford Hill established the gold
standard by which the merits of modern drug therapy must be
measured.[20]

Epidemiological Proof: The Case of Smoking and Lung Cancer

Bradford Hill's second indestructible achievement in his annus
mirabilis of 1950 was to show that smoking causes lung cancer.
Nowadays this seems so obvious as to be unremarkable, but
back in 1950 it was not, for the simple reason that as a direct
consequence of two world wars in thirty years virtually everyone smoked. Tobacco had proved as much of a solace in the
trenches of the First World War as during the London Blitz
and, when not calming the nerves, 'a smoke' was at least something to accompany the endless cups of tea that filled the long,
empty hours so characteristic of total war when citizens were
unable to pursue their legitimate occupations. It is easy to
appreciate how difficult it could be to show that smoking
caused lung cancer if everyone smoked, because both those

with and those without the disease would be smokers. Indeed, only statistical methods could resolve this question, because statistics can see 'below the surface' of things to identify relationships that would otherwise remain obscure.

It has been noted that lung cancer replaced tuberculosis in a metaphorical sense as part of the paradigm shift from one pattern of disease to another, but lung cancer also replaced tuberculosis in a literal sense in 1950 as for the first time the number of deaths from the disease – 13,000 – exceeded those from tuberculosis.[21] And while the toll of tuberculosis rapidly receded over the next few years under the onslaught of anti-tuberculosis drugs, that of lung cancer soared. There are further interesting comparisons. The tragedy of both diseases was that their victims died young or, in the case of lung cancer, relatively young, in their fifties and sixties. And, just as tuberculosis prior to 1950 was essentially an incurable disease, so was lung cancer. Indeed lung cancer was the more grievous of the two illnesses, as with the very infrequent exception of those in whom the disease was detected early enough to be surgically removed, most patients died within eighteen months. As for the manner of dying, there was not much to choose between the two diseases, both being associated with progressive debility, weight loss and shortness of breath, though pain and other symptoms from spread of the cancer elsewhere in the body were commoner in those with lung cancer.[22] From this perspective it is almost impossible to overstate the importance of Bradford Hill's implication of smoking, as this dreadful, untreatable, escalating disease suddenly became 'preventable' through the simple expedient of people not smoking. And it is almost impossible to overstate just how significant this was for the subsequent development of medicine, as over the next fifty years this example of the 'preventability' of lung cancer was enormously influential in promoting the notion that most cancers and other common causes of death might also be preventable by similar 'lifestyle' changes (as will be explored in detail in the final section of this book).

Bradford Hill's logical inference from statistical data – his demonstration of smoking's causative role in lung cancer –

was a masterpiece. The simplest of all medical statistics are, as already noted, the 'vital statistics' recording the unarguable event of death. When analysed over a defined period, they may display a characteristic pattern such as the rise and fall typical of an infectious epidemic. The collection and interpretation of such vital statistics constitute a form of scientific observation little different in its way to 'observing' the effects of disease in an individual. But statistics in this form can only report what has happened; they cannot produce any insights into why it has happened. For this it is necessary to move from simple observation to performing an 'experiment', which, like the Randomised Controlled Trial, is fairly straightforward and again essentially involves making a comparison. When the various aspects of the lives of a group of people with a particular disease are compared to that of another group without the disease, differences might emerge which, it might be inferred, could theoretically be the cause of the disease being studied.

In 1947 Bradford Hill, along with Edward Kennaway of St Bartholomew's Hospital and Percy Stock, the government's chief medical statistician, were asked by the Medical Research Council to investigate whether smoking might explain the 'startling phenomenon' of the fifteen-fold increase in the death rate from lung cancer in Britain over the previous twenty-five years. They were subsequently joined by Dr Richard Doll, who later recalled the division of opinion that reflected the prevailing views of the time:

Kennaway was particularly interested in the possibility of smoking being a factor, but I don't think anybody else was. Bradford Hill certainly wasn't particularly keen on smoking as a cause, nor was I, while Stock was particularly keen on the effect of general urban atmospheric pollution. I must admit I thought the latter was likely to be the principal cause, though not pollution from coal smoke which was terrible in those days but which had been prevalent for many decades and hadn't really increased. Motor cars, however, were a new factor. If I had to put money on anything at the time I should put it on motor exhausts or possibly on the tarring of roads. But cigarette smoking was such a normal thing and had been for such a long time that it was difficult to think it could be associated with any disease.[23]

There had been earlier attempts to investigate whether smoking might be implicated as the cause of the rising toll of lung cancer, particularly in Germany where Hitler, a fanatical non-smoker, took a personal interest in the matter, considering tobacco to be 'genetic poisoning'. In 1939 Dr Franz Muller of the University of Cologne had shown a clear association between smoking and lung cancer, but these findings were deemed unreliable as a Danish physician subsequently observed: 'I read the paper with scepticism as it had been published under the rule of a fanatical non-smoking dictator.'[24]

The main problem was that 90 per cent of the adult male population were smokers, so clearly it would not be possible to implicate tobacco simply on the grounds of whether someone smoked or not. Rather, it was necessary to identify some biological phenomenon from which it would be reasonable to implicate tobacco. The most obvious is the 'dose-response relationship' – the higher the 'dose' of tobacco the greater the 'response', or incidence, of lung cancer. The statistical method was known as the 'case-control' study where 'every case' of lung cancer was compared with a 'control' who is similar in every way other than suffering from some other disease. Theoretically, then, if the heavy smokers were disproportionately represented among the lung cancer group compared to the controls, one might infer that smoking was the cause of the disease. Though this seems straightforward in principle, in practice it is quite difficult, mainly because it is so difficult to ensure that the 'cases' and 'controls' are truly comparable. The investigation, therefore, had to do much more than record how much a person smoked, rather,

a range of potentially relevant factors had to be taken into account: the age, sex, urban or rural residence, and social class of the subject; occupational history; exposure to air

pollutants; forms of domestic heating; and the history of
smoking including for those who had smoked, the age of
starting and stopping, the amount smoked before the onset
of illness, the main changes in smoking history, the maximum amount smoked, the practice in regard to inhaling
and the use of cigarettes or pipe.

Starting in April 1948, doctors in twenty hospitals in London
notified Doll of any patients suspected of having lung cancer.
Doll would then arrange for a 'lady almoner', as social workers
were quaintly called in those days, to interview both the patient
and two 'controls', one with cancer of the stomach or colon
and one from another of the general medical and surgical wards
with a disease other than cancer. He found that 99.7 per cent
of the lung cancer patients confessed to smoking, compared to
95.8 per cent of those with 'diseases other than cancer'. Such an
observation by itself obviously proves nothing at all, but when
the patients were subdivided into four groups depending on
how much they smoked, ranging from 'one cigarette' to 'fifty
cigarettes' a day, then it is possible to discern a trend of a higher
risk of lung cancer among the heavy smokers (see page 44).
Examining the final set of figures in the table, 4.9 per cent of
lung cancer patients smoked fifty cigarettes a day, twice as high
a percentage as the 2 per cent of controls – a subtle difference
perhaps, but whichever way the smoking habit was investigated, either looking at the amount smoked every day, or the
maximum amount smoked, or the total amount smoked over
the years, and so on, the same pattern emerged: the greater the
amount of tobacco consumed, the higher the risk. For Doll and
Hill the conclusion seemed inescapable: 'It is not reasonable, in
our view, to attribute the results to any special selection of
cases or to bias in recording. In other words, it must be concluded that there is a real association between carcinoma of the
lung and smoking.'[25]
We now know this only too well, but at the time things
appeared very differently. Social habits had been incriminated
in lethal diseases before, most notably drinking alcohol as a
cause of liver cirrhosis, but this is a fate restricted to a minor-

Smoking habits between patients with lung cancer and controls

	Number of patients smoking daily:		
	1 cigarette	15 cigarettes	50 cigarettes
649 lung cancer patients (99.9%)	33 (5.1%)	196 (30.2%)	32 (4.9%)
649 controls (100%)	55 (8.5%)	190 (29.3%)	13 (2.0%)

(From R. Doll and A. Bradford Hill, 'Smoking and Carcinoma of the Lung', *BMJ*, 30 September 1950, pp. 739–48.)

ity of alcoholics. Smoking was different, as virtually everybody 'indulged'. It was an intrinsic part of each and every social occasion and the offering of a cigarette an integral part of social (and often sexual) intercourse. Its incrimination in a lethal disease was thus a matter of the utmost gravity. The director of the Medical Research Council, Sir Harold Himsworth, strongly advised Bradford Hill and Doll that they should delay making their results public, as Doll subsequently recalled: 'Himsworth said the finding was so important he did not think we should publish it until we had found it again' (i.e., repeated the study and found the same results). They duly set to work, this time investigating lung cancer outside London (lest their findings might have been a fluke attributable to some unidentifiable 'London factor'), but this proved unnecessary when a few months later an American study came to exactly the same conclusions.[26]

Doll and Hill promptly published their first study in the *British Medical Journal* on 30 September 1950 and its distinguishing features merit some comment. Firstly, the 'dose-response' relationship between smoking and lung cancer was very subtle and this could readily have been obscured were it not for the rigorous way in which possible sources of bias had been anticipated and eliminated. Secondly, it is impossible to convey, without publishing the paper in full, the lucidity of its exposition, so its weighty conclusion seems unarguable against. Put another way, it is very difficult to appreciate the novelty of their paper. The source of reliable knowledge in medicine had always been in the biological and physical sciences. Now, in the face of considerable scepticism, statistical methods had 'triumphantly' (one justifiably can say) been demonstrated to be capable of providing a new and genuine insight into the nature of disease.

Nonetheless, it would take more than this for people to stop smoking. Bradford Hill looked around for some other way by which the link could be demonstrated and – in a masterly stroke of imagination – invented an entirely new method of investigation. The 'case-control' study he had just conducted was 'retrospective' in that it tried to make sense of something that had happened in the past, how the habits of a lifetime may have contributed to one disease in particular. But if the association between lung cancer and smoking was valid, he should get the same result looking forward, starting with a large number of men and women, asking them pertinent questions about their lives, including their smoking habits, and then sitting back and watching what happened to them over the years. They would die from diverse diseases, but the smokers should die in disproportionate numbers from lung cancer. The elegance of this 'prospective' or 'cohort' study is the simplicity of the open-ended question – what do smokers die of? – to which time will inevitably provide an answer.

Bradford Hill chose as his cohort the 60,000 doctors on the Medical Register, who were likely to be reliable in answering the questions posed to them. There could be no more forceful way of bringing home to the profession the hazards of tobacco – which hopefully would then be passed on to patients – than by incorporating them in this scientific endeavour to provide further proof that smoking caused lung cancer. In November 1951 Bradford Hill wrote a letter to the *British Medical Journal* which was published under the headline, 'Do You Smoke?':

Last week I sent a letter personally to every man and woman on the Medical Register of the UK asking them to help me. I asked them to fill in a very simple form about their smoking habits.

This, I think, is a new method of approach. May I therefore repeat my appeal through your column? If every doctor, whatever his field of work, will spare only a moment or two this research can be founded on a firm basis and in time give, I believe, firm and important answers. I am, etc.[27]

In a short period, a mere two and a half years, Bradford Hill had his answer. Of the 40,000 doctors who replied to the questionnaire, 789 had subsequently died, a mere 36 from lung cancer. But when the smoking habits of the deceased were tabulated (see below), lung cancer was the only disease in which there was a clear dose-response relationship – the more tobacco smoked, the greater the death rate, rising from 0.48 per 1,000 doctors smoking 1g of tobacco daily, to 0.67 for those smoking 15g, to 1.14 for those smoking 25g or more, compared to those who had died from 'all causes', in whom there was no gradient with increase in smoking habit.[28]

Mortality rate per 1,000 male doctors in relation to the most recent amount of tobacco smoked

Cause of death	Number of deaths recorded	Death rates of men smoking a daily average of tobacco of:		
		1g	15g	25g+
Lung cancer	36	0.48	0.67	1.14
All causes	789	13.42	13.48	16.3

(From R. Doll and A. Bradford Hill, 'The Mortality of Doctors in Relation to Their Smoking Habit', *BMJ*, 26 June 1954, pp. 1451–5.)

In 1993 Sir Richard Doll, during a special celebration to mark his own eightieth birthday, summarised the results of the famous Doctor Study forty years on. Almost half – 20,000 – of the doctors who had answered the original questionnaire back in 1951 had died, of whom 883 had succumbed to lung cancer.

There is a memorable simplicity in the final conclusion. Those smoking twenty-five or more cigarettes a day have a twenty-five-fold increased risk of lung cancer compared to non-smokers.[29]

Bradford Hill's twin achievements of 1950, demonstrating the curability of tuberculosis and the preventability of lung cancer, are impressive enough on their own account, but the true significance – which became ever more apparent as the years passed – was even greater. Firstly, as already described, they signified the paradigm shift from medicine's historical pre-occupation with infectious illness to the prevention and treatment of non-infectious illnesses such as heart disease and cancer. And secondly, his demonstration of the power of the statistical methods of both the Randomised Controlled Trial (RCT) in the evaluation of medical treatment and the comparative studies of people's lifestyles for finding the causes of disease had a monumental impact on medical research, keeping thousands of doctors and scientists busy and generating hundreds of thousands of research projects and scientific papers. Bradford Hill was naturally, if, as ever, modestly, conscious of the nature of his legacy, which he discussed in two public lectures fifteen years later in 1965, which might justly be considered his apotheosis: 'Reflections on the Controlled Clinical Trial' and 'The Environment and Disease: Association or Causation?'[30, 31]

We start with 'Reflections'. 'It is not far off twenty years since the MRC published the results of the [first] trial of streptomycin that set off the population explosion of clinical trials,' Bradford Hill observed, adding, 'over the last twelve months alone they have extended from a treatment for herpes simplex to a low-fat diet in myocardial infarction, from drugs in the treatment of alcohol withdrawal syndrome to prophylactic penicillin for comatose patients.' The popularity of the Randomised Controlled Trial (RCT) obviously lay in its unique ability to provide answers to the sort of questions that doctors ask themselves every day – 'Does this treatment work better than that?' – but crucially the questions were posed and resolved in a manner – the experiment – almost synonymous with science itself. The RCT thus came to be seen as the only 'scientific' way of resolving these questions and so almost by definition, superior to any other form of acquiring knowledge, such as 'clinical experience'. In this way the RCT became the 'dominant' discourse of post-war medicine. This, as Bradford Hill acknowledged from his own personal experience, was not necessarily a good thing, as statistics have an equal, or even greater, capacity to variously mislead, obscure or in some other way subvert the truth as to clarify it.

> I am faced with trials [of drug treatment] on such an ill-defined or undefined pot-pourri of patients that I can but hopelessly speculate on who got what, when and usually why. These poorly conducted trials not only tell us nothing but may be dangerously misleading – particularly when their useless data are spuriously supported by all the latest statistical techniques and jargon.

Such aberrations apart, Bradford Hill maintained that there was simply no alternative to the RCT in evaluating new treatments and challenging the efficacy of the old.

Nonetheless there have been dissenting voices, particularly recently, about the validity and especially the trustworthiness of the conclusions from such trials. They are, it is argued, insufficiently sensitive to variations in the range of symptoms of disease and thus the responsiveness to treatment. There have been many instances when they have produced the 'wrong' result, which was subsequently overturned, but not before the powerful influence of the original false verdict had misdirected medicine down a blind alley, often for decades. There is concern, too, about the habit of aggregating the results of many trials to produce a definitive verdict, as if numbers alone could cancel out the falsehoods inherent in poor scientific data. One observer has described this as:

> A new kind of alchemy . . . arcane, esoteric and mesmerising, that promises not to turn base metal into gold but to transmute statistical sow's ears into scientific silk purses.

Regrettably not all those who have followed in Bradford Hill's footsteps have been gifted with the same degree of intelligence or fastidiousness and so sometimes – perhaps even often – the 'clinical wisdom' of doctors assessing the efficacy of treatment based on their own personal experience may, after all, be a better guide to medical practice than 'the objectivity' of the clinical trial.[32]

In the second lecture given by Bradford Hill in 1965, 'Environment and Disease: Association or Causation?', he elaborated with his customary lucidity on the importance of his discovery of smoking as a cause of lung cancer. This had, after all, established a precedent of the utmost importance, which naturally raised the question as to how many other common diseases – strokes, heart diseases, diabetes and so on (the list is virtually limitless) – might similarly be caused by some aspect of the environment or an individual's 'lifestyle' which, if identified and modified, would prevent it.

Possible clues were assiduously sought in thousands of studies looking for 'something' to distinguish patients with a given disease from healthy controls. Inevitably they turned up interesting observations. For example, people with multiple sclerosis are more likely to be cat lovers, and those with cancer of the pancreas drink more coffee than average, and so on. Given the large number of different diseases and the numerous measurable aspects of an individual's lifestyle, it is possible to generate a virtually infinite number of hypotheses about causation.

But how can one be certain that, for example, keeping cats might cause multiple sclerosis (perhaps because of some transmissible virus) rather than, for example, that those with multiple sclerosis might be more likely to keep cats as company? The possibilities of the case-control study for investigating the causes of disease, given the precedent of smoking and lung cancer, are immense, but so is the danger of drawing false inferences and conclusions. How can one tell?

Bradford Hill formulated a set of criteria that must be fulfilled. They are illustrated here with the example of smoking and lung cancer.

(1) The correlation must be biologically plausible: there are cancer-inducing agents in tobacco which, when brought into contact with lung tissue, could cause the disease.

(2) The correlation must be strong: the death rate from lung cancer in cigarette smokers is twenty-five times higher than in non-smokers.

(3) The correlation must reflect a biological gradient: the more cigarettes that are smoked, the higher the risk of lung cancer.

(4) The correlation must be found consistently: thirty-six separate studies examining the relationship between smoking and lung cancer have found a positive correlation.

(5) The correlation must hold over time: as cigarette consumption has steadily increased it has been paralleled by a rise in incidence of disease.

(6) The association must preferably be confirmed by experiment. If smoking causes lung cancer, then the experiment of stopping smoking should reduce the risk, and the longer the time since stopping smoking, the lower that risk will be.

Bradford Hill concluded:

Here then are different view points all of which we should study before we cry 'causation'. None can bring indisputable evidence for or against the cause-and-effect hypothesis [but] what they can do, with greater or lesser strength, is to help us to make up our minds on the fundamental question – is there any other way of explaining the set of facts before us? Is there any other answer equally, or more, likely than cause-and-effect?

There is nothing here other than the application of elementary rules of logic and, as with the concept of the 'controlled trial' and the 'case-control study', the notion is disarmingly simple: scientific hypotheses about the causes of disease require not single facts, but that those facts be internally coherent, that they 'hang together'. If these criteria are not fulfilled, then the theory is, by definition, incoherent and must fall. In the following decade Bradford Hill's cautious and logical views were ignored as epidemiologists claimed to have found that virtually every aspect of people's lives was implicated in some illness or other, generating both anxiety and confusion in the public mind. But that is another story.

4

1952: Chlorpromazine and the Revolution in Psychiatry

*S*erious psychiatric illnesses such as schizophrenia are usually perceived as having 'something to do' with the chemistry of the brain, an abnormality of one or other of the many chemicals (or neurotransmitters) that transfer 'messages' from one nerve to another, and some of whose names may be vaguely familiar – noradrenaline, acetylcholine and dopamine. Similarly modern drugs – such as chlorpromazine – are presumed to work by correcting these chemical abnormalities.

This schematic view of contemporary psychiatry is plausible enough but incorrect, and importantly so, for it conceals the truly extraordinary nature of the therapeutic revolution in psychiatry in the post-war years. In just over ten years – the decade of the 1950s – six entirely new types of drug were introduced into psychiatric practice and remain its mainstay today. But their discovery was not based on a scientific knowledge of brain chemicals, which was at the time extremely primitive. Rather the drugs came first, being discovered for the most part by chance, preceding by several years the identification of their effect on neurotransmitters.

But that is not all, for even though drugs like chlorpromazine and the antidepressants that followed soon after were subsequently found to alter the chemistry of the brain by boosting or blocking the action of different chemicals, the underlying 'problem' – what actually is *happening in the brains of the mentally ill – remains, despite an extraordinary amount of research, unknown. Thus it subsequently became clear that chlorpromazine blocks the activity of the neurotransmitter dopamine, from which one might reasonably infer that, to have such a beneficial effect, schizophrenia must in some way be associated with an excess of dopamine in the brain. But as far as modern science can tell – and there are some fairly sophisticated ways of finding out – the dopamine systems in the brains of schizophrenics appear to be completely normal. The current state of medical knowledge about severe mental illness can thus be summarised as follows: we know that a handful of drugs discovered by accident almost fifty years ago are effective in relieving the symptoms of schizophrenia and depression – but why they work, the nature of the abnormal changes in the brain they correct and especially the causes of psychiatric illness remain a mystery.*

In 1953, as a newly appointed psychiatrist to Fulbourn Mental Hospital just outside Cambridge, Dr David Clark's tasks included a weekly visit to the 'chronic' ward housing the long-stay (many for a lifetime) patients:

I was taken in by someone who had a key to unlock the door and lock it behind you. The crashing of the keys in the lock was an essential part of asylum life then just as it is today in jail. This led into a big bare room, overcrowded with people, with scrubbed floors, bare wooden tables, benches screwed to the floor, people milling around in shapeless clothing. There was a smell in the air of urine, paraldehyde, floor polish, boiled cabbage and carbolic soap – the asylum smell. Some wards were full of tousled, apathetic people just sitting in a row because for twenty years the nurses had been saying 'sit down, shut up'. Others were noisy. The disturbed women's ward was a phantasmagoric place. The women were in 'strong clothes', shapeless garments made of reinforced cotton that couldn't be torn. Many of them were in 'locked boots' which couldn't be taken off and thrown. There was nothing moveable. There were no knives which were taken in and counted up at every meal. The women all had their hair chopped off short giving them identical wiry grey mops. As soon as you came in they'd rush up and crowd round you. Hands would go into your pockets grabbing at you, pulling at you, clambering for release, for food, for anything until they were pushed back by the sturdy nurses, who shouted at them to sit down and shut up. At the back of the ward were the padded cells, in which would be one or two naked women, smeared with faeces, shouting obscenities at anybody who came near. Then there were the airing courts. Grey, big courts, paved with tarmac surrounded by a wall 12 foot high and a hundred men milling around. A few of them walking, some running, others standing on one leg, posturing, the urine running out of their trouser legs. A couple of bored young male nurses standing on 'points duty', looking at them ready to hit anybody who got out of line, but otherwise not doing anything. A scene of human degradation.[1]

In the same year, in a comparable scene of human degradation in Birmingham's Winson Green Hospital, Joel Elkes, Professor of Experimental Psychiatry, was studying the effect of a new drug, chlorpromazine, which had shown promising results in acute schizophrenia but whose effects up until this time had not been assessed in the chronic, 'burned-out', no-hope patients in the back wards. 'Our limited aim,' wrote Professor Elkes, was 'to determine the usefulness of chlorpromazine in the overactive chronic psychotic patient in the crowded disturbed wards of the mental hospital.' Among those given the new drug was a 32-year-old schizophrenic man who had been in hospital for six years:

His behaviour was greatly disturbed by terrifying visual and auditory hallucinations. He referred to them as 'bogies' and, when present, they occupied his whole attention. He spent a great deal of time writing inconsequential sentences, or drawing to 'ward off the bogies', and he would often shout abuse at them, banging the furniture and marching about the ward. His sleep was disturbed and he required sedation nearly every night. Socially he was very withdrawn and solitary. After three weeks on chlorpromazine he gradually became more accessible and friendly. He worked on the ward and took charge of the Christmas decorations. Eventually he was able to attend occupational therapy for the first time since his admission, where he practised his talents for painting. He received no medication apart from chlorpromazine and had only occasional restless nights despite this. Sporadically he would shout at his hallucinations but he said that 'the bogies do not worry him so much'. He relapsed when on placebo tablets.[2]

So here was a man, one of the vast army of the chronically mentally ill in the backwater of the large mental hospitals, who would have been lucky to receive any form of medical attention from one year's end to the next, but who, after only three weeks of taking chlorpromazine was able to 'take charge of the Christmas decorations'. Elkes could not have appreciated the full significance of such a result but in retrospect it is obvious. If a drug can so effectively transform for the better the mental state of someone with chronic schizophrenia, then perhaps asylums and locked wards are unnecessary; perhaps it might even be possible for their inhabitants to return to live in the community. Chlorpromazine 'tore through the civilised world like a whirlwind and engulfed the whole treatment of psychiatric disorders', but to fully appreciate its impact it is first necessary to return to the 'dark before the dawn'.

Within the spectrum of psychiatric disorders it is customary to distinguish the neuroses, such as anxiety and hypochondriasis, from the psychoses, the severe mental illnesses in which consciousness and perception is impaired, such as schizophrenia and manic depression. It is this latter group who filled the mental hospitals in the 1930s and 1940s in their tens of thousands.

Grim the pre-war asylums certainly were, but it is important not to lose sight of the real misfortune of their inmates – the mental suffering caused by the illness for which they had been admitted. Thus the patient with schizophrenia is often fearful, persecuted by frightening hallucinations or the machinations of delusionary others: 'Fear comes suddenly, chilling and shocking and with it uncertainty and new shadows – shadows with movements and hidden life, the life of the small night-time enemies, rodents, insects, marauders.'[3]

But more frightening even than these fearful spectres was the schizophrenic's loss of control or power over his thoughts. This took many forms: mental exhaustion – 'too timid to continue thinking at all'; or bizarre tempos – 'suddenly my thoughts went slower and slower, like a gramophone running down. Next they dashed ahead faster and faster and to my horror I was thinking gibberish'; or the loss of meaning of words and sentences – 'I tried sitting in my apartment and reading; the words looked perfectly familiar like old friends whose faces I remember perfectly well, but whose names I couldn't recall'; and loss of judgement – 'a parody of rational thought may be found but truly critical judgement is entirely lost . . . my con-scious mind is like an information centre whose staff are sick; as more of them become incapacitated so the rest become more severely overworked . . . unconscious impulses, like a band of irresponsible children, take over the telephone exchange and play around with the controls.'[4]

It is only within this context of quite unimaginable mental suffering, where medicine had nothing to offer other than cus-todial care and sedation, that it is possible to understand the rise in popularity in the 1930s and 1940s of what now seem crude and often cruel treatments – insulin coma, electric shock (ECT) and psychosurgery. These became known as the 'phys-ical therapies', for that is precisely what they were – physical assaults on the patient's brain in the hope that the trauma would somehow correct its malfunctioning.

The first was 'prolonged narcosis', introduced in 1920, where patients were put to sleep for several days with a combination of barbiturate drugs.[5] The next, 'insulin coma', required patients to be given large doses of insulin which, by lowering the blood sugar, induced a comatose state from which they would be rescued by a large dose of glucose.[6] Next they were given a drug, cardizol, that caused them to have epileptic fits,[7] and this in turn was replaced by the use of electric shock therapy (ECT) pioneered by an Italian, Ugo Cerletti.[8] The last of the physical therapies – lobotomies, where the brain was cut with a knife – was pioneered by a Lisbon neurologist, Egas Moniz.[9] The apparent effectiveness of the physical therapies in some patients generated an enormous enthusiasm 'untainted by the normal requirements of rational scientific scepticism'.[10] But they were massively overused, frequently in patients who were quite unsuitable.

The rise and subsequent fall of the physical therapies has been described by Dr Henry Rollin, medical superintendent of a large mental asylum on the outskirts of London:

We had to learn the procedure of Deep Insulin Therapy (DIT) – which was far from simple, at times hazardous and occasionally fatal. Buoyed up with enthusiasm, staff morale in the DIT clinics was inordinately high. Not only were we doing real physical doctoring and nursing, but we believed absolutely in the worthwhileness of what we were doing, despite the fact that some of our patients took on a grotesque, bloated appearance as a result of the inordinate amount of weight they gained . . .

We were also instructed in the use of ECT – in those early days given 'straight' – that is without muscle relaxants or intravenous anaesthetics. The great danger of this primitive method arose with the onset of the fit which produced such violent spasms of the muscles that a squad of nurses was trained to exert pressure on the shoulders, hips and legs. Even so, dislocations and fractures of the long bones and crush fractures of the lower dorsal and lumbar vertebrae were by no means uncommon.

So carried along were we by the claims made that we played our part with enthusiasm in the rush to recommend patients even for lobotomy. I was guilty of recommending the operation for twenty or so of my schizophrenic patients and nothing I have done weighs more heavily on my conscience. The basis for my guilt lies in the fact that not only did I not see any lasting benefit in one single case, but the consequences of the operation in some cases was quite appalling – including post-operative epilepsy, cerebral haemorrhage, and probably worst of all post-operative personality change, mainly characterised by disinhibition.

They were heady days for psychiatrists. Optimism rode high, so high in fact that we were convinced that the psychiatric millennium was just around the corner. Rationality eventually re-established itself and we awoke from our wish-fulfilling dream to the realisation that what we had been unwillingly party to was a variation of the oldest variety of play in the repertoire – the emperor's new clothes. By the mid-1950s the deep insulin clinics had been dismantled. The flood of lobotomies was reduced to a trickle . . . ECT, the sole survivor of *le grand siècle*, was now administered with the aid of muscle relaxants . . .[11]

The physical therapies (with the exception of ECT) were killed off not by a psychiatrist or a psychoanalyst or a brain chemist, but by a jobbing French naval surgeon with an inquisitive mind, Henri Laborit. In 1949, while working at the Maritime Hospital in Tunisia, Laborit was investigating ways of treating patients in 'shock' who had low blood pressure. Shock may result from a variety of causes: severe blood loss, a failing heart, overwhelming blood infection or major surgery. The shock arising from blood loss can be counteracted with blood transfusion but the cause – and therefore the appropriate treatment – in other situations was at the time unknown. Laborit's hypothesis, shared by others, was that the trauma of a major operation or overwhelming infection might lead to the release from the cells of chemicals such as histamine (better known as being involved in allergic reactions like hayfever) and that this would produce the fall in blood pressure. If this hypothesis were correct – which it was not – then blocking the release of these chemicals should prevent the development of post-operative shock. Accordingly Laborit gave his patients before and during their operation a cocktail of drugs including the antihistamine promethazine, which blocks the action of histamine (and is similar to the drugs currently used in the treatment of hayfever). Laborit claimed in an article published in 1949 – remarkable for its complete absence of any data – that with this combination 'we have been able to distinctly influence the development of post-operative problems'.[12]

More importantly, though, he made an extraordinarily insightful clinical observation about the effects of the antihistamine promethazine. The main drawback of this group of drugs, recognised since their introduction in 1937, was that they caused drowsiness, so it was not surprising that he should note that they had 'an extremely powerful hypnotic effect', but he also observed that they had 'an appreciable analgesic property' such that he no longer found it necessary to give morphine to deaden the pain following operations: 'Antihistamines produce a *euphoric quietude* . . . our patients are calm, with a restful and relaxed face.' In an interview several years later Henri Laborit elaborated on this observation of euphoric quietude, describing the action of promethazine on the brain as 'disconnecting' its functions, resulting in 'a state of complete calm and tranquillity without depression of mental faculties or clouding of consciousness'.[13]

In 1950 the drug company Rhône-Poulenc, alerted to the possibility that promethazine might be useful in the treatment of psychiatric disorders, initiated a major research programme. The group of drugs to which promethazine belongs are known as the phenothiazines, and Paul Charpentier, the company's chief chemist, set out to synthesise as many variations of its molecular structure as possible in the hope of finding one which had the same, or greater, ability to create a sense of 'euphoric quietude'. The compounds he synthesised were then tested on rats that had learned to climb a rope to avoid an electric shock signalled by the ringing of a bell. One compound in particular, chlorpromazine, left the rats unmoved when the bell was rung.[14]

Hearing of this, Jean Delay and Pierre Deniker, two leading Parisian psychiatrists, were the first to treat a schizophrenic patient, a 57-year-old labourer, Giovanni A., who had been admitted to hospital for 'making improvised speeches in cafés, becoming involved in fights with strangers, and walking around the street with a pot of flowers on his head proclaiming his love of liberty'. After nine days on chlorpromazine he was able to have a normal conversation and after three weeks he was ready to be discharged. This was much better, much quicker, much safer than any response that had been obtained by the physical therapies such as ECT and insulin coma.[15] The news then spread to Britain, where Joel Elkes at Birmingham's Winson Green Hospital – as already described – started to give chlorpromazine to the 'burned-out' cases on the long-stay wards on whom at the time no treatment availed.

Across the Atlantic the experience of another psychiatrist, Heinz Lehmann of the Verdun Boston Hospital in Montreal, a refugee from Nazi Germany, exemplified the difference that chlorpromazine made. When Lehmann had first arrived in Montreal Hospital before the war it was 'a pretty horrible place . . . I was always convinced that psychotic conditions had some sort of biological cause so . . . I kept experimenting with all kinds of drugs including very large doses of caffeine, in one or two stuporose schizophrenics – of course with no results'. He injected sulphur suspended in oil into his patients, 'which was painful', and typhoid antitoxins to produce a fever. 'Nothing helped, I even injected turpentine into the abdominal muscles which produced a huge sterile abscess and marked raising of the white count. None of this had any effect, but all this had been proposed as being of help in schizophrenia.' Then, in May 1953, Lehmann managed to lay his hands on a supply of chlorpromazine:

Two or three acute schizophrenics became symptom-free. Now I had never seen that happen before. I thought it was a fluke – something that would never happen again, but anyhow there they were. At the end of four or five weeks there were a lot of symptom-free patients. By this I mean that a lot of hallucinations, delusions and thought disorders had disappeared. In 1953 there just wasn't anything that ever produced something like this – a remission from schizophrenia in weeks.[16]

Chlorpromazine was the first swallow, and in rapid succession over the next few years four other major groups of drugs applicable to the whole spectrum of psychiatric illness – depression, mania and anxiety states – were introduced in exactly the same way, through a combination of chance, shrewd observation and the screening of chemical compounds. Nor indeed could it have been otherwise, for at the time there was simply no perception of how the brain functioned, nor even an inkling of what abnormalities lay behind mental illness and consequently no idea of how these drugs – which appeared to work so well – worked at all.[17]

Thus in 1955 the Parisian psychiatrists Delay and Deniker, when summarising their experience of treating 1,000 patients, clearly had not the slightest idea of its mode of action. They suggested variously that it might stimulate the sympathetic nervous system, or reduce oxygen metabolism in the brain, or alter the pattern of the brain waves in the same way that occurs during sleep.[18] It was not until 1963 – eleven years after Giovanni A. had first been given chlorpromazine – that it was shown to interfere with the action of the neurotransmitter dopamine. It was thus only natural to infer that the underlying problem in patients with schizophrenia was a neurochemical one. Perhaps their brain contained too much dopamine or dopamine in the wrong place, or the receptors to dopamine in the brain were oversensitive. But this obvious explanation turned out to be incorrect. Neither autopsy studies nor sophisticated scanning techniques have been able to identify or demonstrate any single abnormality of dopamine biochemistry in the brain of schizophrenics (or indeed that of any of the other neurotransmitters).

Similarly, the mechanism of the antidepressant drug, imipramine, led to the hypothesis that depression was caused by an abnormality of adrenaline in the brain. But even though these drugs are certainly highly effective in treating depressed patients, the question of 'what is wrong' remains as unanswered as it is for schizophrenia.[19]

This has, of course, proved more than frustrating to the thousands who have pursued the Holy Grail of a biological explanation for mental illness. The success of chlorpromazine concealed the crucial fact that it is in no sense 'a cure' for schizophrenia. Rather, the essence of the 'euphoric quietude' it induces is that it lessens the agitation, thus making the patient more 'manageable', while the lessening of the intensity of the distress of symptoms may help recovery. An appropriate analogy would be pain relief following an operation. The alleviation of pain will not in itself speed up the healing of the wound but it may, by reducing the patient's stress, promote a more rapid recovery.

This is not an appropriate place to develop this argument further but it opens the way to recognition that schizophrenia and similar psychotic illnesses may at the same time be 'biological', in the sense that (it must be presumed) there is some as yet unknown abnormality of brain functioning, as well as 'psychological', in the sense that schizophrenia can be both exacerbated and ameliorated by changes in the 'outside' world. The notion that chlorpromazine by itself 'emptied the bins' is certainly a myth. Rather, as has been suggested, the hope that chlorpromazine could cure psychotic illness created a climate in which it became acceptable to close the large asylums.[20]

The history of psychiatry in the post-war years exemplifies, in a very dramatic form, how the growth of the possibilities of treating illness could occur in the absence of any substantial understanding of the nature of the problem being treated or indeed why the treatment worked. Human intelligence – such as Henri Laborit's acute perception of the euphoric quietude induced by promethazine – played a role. So of course does 'science', in particular neurochemistry and pharmacology. Nonetheless we are dealing with the triumph of empiricism, where everything else is a mystery. Why should a compound that blocks histamine in the tissues of the body also interfere with an entirely different chemical – dopamine – in the brain in a way that alleviates symptoms of schizophrenia? What is schizophrenia? What is its cause? The map of mental illness, like that of Africa before the arrival of the Victorian explorers, remains a blank.

5

1955: OPEN-HEART SURGERY –
THE LAST FRONTIER

'*A*ny surgeon who would attempt an operation of the heart should lose the respect of his colleagues,' declared the great German surgeon T. H. Billroth in 1893 – and for good reason, as any 'attempt' would necessarily kill the patient. The heart remained out of bounds for surgeons for another fifty years, and tantalisingly so. The heart is anatomically much the most complex organ of the body and thus presents the widest range of possible defects that might be amenable to surgical correction. In the imagination of surgeons the heart was, like Mount Everest to climbers, the last great peak to be scaled. It could not, however, be climbed unless some means were found for taking over the function of the heart for long enough to permit surgeons to get inside to perform their operations, so the most important development in cardiac surgery was not surgical but technical – the heart-lung machine or 'pump'.

In the five years from 1955 to 1960 the pump transformed cardiac surgery into much the largest and most sophisticated of all surgical specialties, whose influence in turn touched many other branches of medicine. It required, for example, the establishment of the first intensive-care units capable of keeping seriously ill patients alive for long periods after surgery. Further, it seemed a most audacious thing in the 1950s, when death was still defined as a cessation of the heartbeat, for doctors to deliberately stop the heart and then restart it. Here, cardiac surgery enhanced still further the public's perception of medicine's apparently limitless possibilities.

'Open-heart' surgery involves 'opening up' the heart so the surgeon can repair defects in the walls between the chambers or replace diseased valves. The term might seem pedantic but in the early 1950s it was necessary to distinguish this type of operation from that which had preceded it, 'closed-heart' surgery, where a surgeon corrected anatomical abnormalities 'blindly' using his fingers or a knife while the heart carried on pumping out blood. The scope of open-heart surgery, where the surgeon can actually see what he is doing, is obviously much greater but requires that, somehow or other, for the duration of the operation the function of the heart – in pushing blood first through the lungs to pick up oxygen and then around the circulation – must be 'bypassed' or simulated by some other mechanism, otherwise known as the heart/lung machine, the pump oxygenator or simply the pump.

First the surgeon splits the sternum and pulls the chest open to reveal the beating heart within. Next the pump is set up. Two large catheters are inserted into the two large veins draining into the heart. These catheters are then connected by plastic tubing, which passes through a machine which pumps the blood from the veins into the 'oxygenator' – a Heath Robinson-type device which acts as a lung where the blood comes into contact with air, giving up carbon dioxide and absorbing oxygen. The blood then exits from the oxygenator through more plastic tubing and is returned to the patient via a large catheter inserted into an artery in the groin.

The idea of the pump was first conceived by John Gibbon in 1931, though almost a quarter of a century elapsed before he was in a position to perform his first open-heart operation. Gibbon's pump was not just any pump. Rather it made possible the most thrilling and eventful epoch in the whole history of surgery or, as one lyrical surgeon put it: 'Gibbon's idea and its elaboration take their place among the boldest and most successful feats of man's mind – the invention of the phonetic alphabet, the telephone or a Mozart symphony. Not a *deus ex machina* but a *machina a Deo*, a promethean fire; levelling from God his secrets to man's understanding; the pulse of the sacred heart; the breath of life.'[1]

The pump transformed the operating theatre into a real the-atre, a spectacle where the drama on the operating table was closely followed by an audience seated in rows behind glass panels looking down at the action. And why was it so exciting? No surgeon before had been able to explore the interior of a living heart, while the technical problems of replacing valves and closing defects in the wall were not only the last but also the most sophisticated challenge a surgeon could hope to encounter.

The drama also lay in the literally life-or-death contest taking place on the operating table. The operations themselves were technically very difficult. The heart, though 'open', was, in the early days, still beating like a slippery eel while its small size in children (little more than a plum) made the job of repairing the defects particularly taxing. There was also the need to operate under the pressure of time, for even though the patient was 'on bypass' the operation had to be done speedily to prevent long-term damage to the heart muscle. Come the end of the operation there was always the possibility that the heart would not recover its normal rhythm and the patient would die, not discreetly in the wards several hours later, but there on the operating table while spectators seated in the gallery with their opera glasses looked on.

There was one further crucial element to this drama in the early days – the competition between the two main pioneers, Walter Lillehai and John Kirklin. It would have mattered less if they had been working in institutions a long distance apart but Walter Lillehai was based at the University of Minneapolis, just west of the Great Lakes, while ninety miles due south, John Kirklin was Professor of Surgery at the internationally famous, massively well-endowed and prosperous Mayo Clinic in the town of Rochester. In the 1950s and 1960s every aspi-rant cardiac surgeon in the world flew to Minneapolis to watch first Walter Lillehai at work, then hired a car or bought a train ticket and travelled south to see John Kirklin. It would have been difficult to avoid making comparisons but Lillehai and Kirklin were also utterly different in personality and style.

Before returning to the origins of open-heart surgery, a

description by the world's first heart transplanter, Christian Barnard, of an event that took place while he was working as Lillehai's surgical assistant, conveys some of the atmosphere of the daily life and (too often) death struggle in the operating theatres in those early days:

> Dr Lillehai was a great teacher . . . all of this was revealed one terrible day when I made an error in preparing a seven-year-old boy who had come to us for the repair of an imperfectly developed ventricular septum – or hole between the two lower chambers of the heart. He was a slender, dark haired boy from South America, and after we had him in position on the table I learnt his father was among those looking down at us from the glass dome above.
>
> My job was to open the chest, expose the heart and then put tapes around two big veins bringing used venous blood to the heart. Once looped, the two veins would be hooked [via the plastic tubing] on to the heart/lung machine when Dr Lillehai arrived. Until he came, I was in charge, assisted by another doctor, Dr Derward Lepley.
>
> There was trouble at the beginning, we opened the chest, exposed the heart and prepared to loop the two veins. The superior vena cava came into position easily. But in putting instruments around the inferior vena cava I found a bit of tissue in front of it. Turning to Dr Lepley, I gave the fatal command: 'Cut that, will you?'
>
> He gave a cut with the scissors, but it was not quite enough. He cut again, and that was it. Blood spurted. We had cut into the heart.
>
> 'Give me an artery forceps – quick!'
>
> I got it and tried to clamp the hole but only tore it further. The blood poured out now in a flood filling the cardiac cavity. The heart continued to beat, pumping its precious liquid, not into its own chambers but rather outside the heart itself. So it went on, like an animal drowning for want of help, until it was almost submerged and I could not see what I was doing.

'Call Dr Lillehai . . . now . . .'

As we sucked away at the blood the heart continued to pour out more of its own life, until the pressure started to fall. At this point the anaesthetist began to call out the awful figures [of the blood pressure].

'It's below 80 . . . 70, now it's 65 . . .'

Frantically I reached my hand into the cavity filled with blood, trying to find the hole in the heart.

'We are still going down . . . it's below 60 now, 53 . . . 42 and still descending . . .' said the anaesthetist. Then he said, 'I've got no reading. Pressure below 35.'

The heart had stopped. Blindly I reached in and began to massage it, hoping to start it again. But it did not respond and each successive squeeze of my hand only drew out more blood. I could not help but look up once, seeing the faces of those in the dome looking down at me including that of the father, his eyes wild with fear. Seeing me, he shook his head as though to say, 'Please say it is not true – say it is not my little boy, say it is not his heart that you have in your hand . . .'

Lillehai came and we connected the patient on the heart/lung machine. The cavity was drained and I saw where we had cut a hole into the left atrium. With the heart still not beating, but the boy held in life by the machine, Dr Lillehai began the operation opening the heart and repairing the leaking wall between the ventricles. After this he closed the hole we had cut into the upper chambers. Through it all I prayed the child would be all right – that when we ceased supporting him with the pump, the heart would again take over and sustain his life.

'All right?' said Dr Lillehai finally. 'Loosen it, let's see what we've got.'

The heart did not start despite massage and direct stimulants to the muscles. More stimulants were tried, but nothing could help. The boy was dead.

'Close the chest,' said Dr Lillehai, leaving the theatre and leaving me with Dr Lepley to stitch up the chest of the boy who only a few hours earlier had been alive and laughing and confident that he would soon be able to run and play with other boys. Now he lay, limp and dead, beneath my hands.

'I'm going,' said Lepley, leaving me to finish the job, beneath the petrified gaze of the father in the dome above. I did not look at him. If I had I would not have been able to continue.[2]

It is helpful in understanding the evolution of open-heart surgery to have a grasp of the workings of the heart, which consists of two sets of chambers – the right and left atria and ventricles lined up side by side. Venous blood from the upper and lower parts of the body drains into the large veins (the venae cavae) and is sucked first into the right atrium (hall) from where it is pumped into the right ventricle, from which it is propelled through the pulmonary valve into the pulmonary arteries, transporting it to the lungs, where it picks up oxygen and gets rid of carbon dioxide. The oxygenated blood then returns from the lungs to the left atrium, is squeezed through a valve into the muscular left ventricle and is then pumped out through the aorta and major vessels to be transported around the body.

With this scheme in mind, the development of cardiac surgery over the last fifty years can then be divided into four epochs. During the first – the 1930s and early 1940s – the heart was left undisturbed, but the large vessels rising from it, the pulmonary artery and aorta, were operated on to provide some relief of symptoms caused by defects within the heart. The second epoch started almost immediately after the Second World War when surgeons, having made an incision in the wall of the heart and with the heart still beating, 'blindly' dilated narrowed valves with a knife or finger.

The crucial transition occurs in the early 1950s when, thanks to the pump, open-heart surgery becomes possible. There are many different defects in the heart that can only be repaired with open-heart surgery, and during the third epoch of cardiac surgery, from the mid-1950s to the early 1960s, surgeons started to repair 'holes in the heart' and replace diseased valves. The fourth and final epoch of cardiac surgery began in the late 1960s with the first heart transplant.

The most important transition was that from the 'blind' and 'closed' operations to the 'open'. It will be illustrated by reference to a common type of heart defect in children – Fallot's Tetralogy – so named after the French physician Etienne Louis Fallot, who described the four (tetra) abnormalities of which two are of clinical importance (see page 70). Firstly, the pulmonary valve between the right ventricle and the pulmonary artery is narrowed, thus reducing the amount of blood that can be pumped from the right side of the heart into the lungs to pick up oxygen. Secondly, there is a hole in the wall between the ventricles through which the non-oxygenated blood from the right side of the heart is 'shunted' into the left, thus bypassing the lungs. The consequence, as can be imagined, is that much of the blood being pumped from the left ventricle out into the main arteries has not passed through the lungs and so is not oxygenated. The child with Fallot's is thus blue (rather than pink), breathless and grows poorly. These 'blue babies' rarely lived beyond ten years of age. With the evolution of cardiac surgery, the results of treating blue babies becomes increasingly more dramatic, culminating in open-heart surgery, where a combination of dilating the narrow pulmonary valve and closing the hole in the heart restores the anatomy to normal.

The first phase of cardiac surgery started with a piece of lateral thinking by Dr Helen Taussig, a specialist in children's heart problems at Johns Hopkins Hospital in Baltimore. The main aorta, as it emerges from the left ventricle, passes in close proximity to the pulmonary arteries. It is thus quite straightforward, in theory, to link the aorta and pulmonary artery together so the non-oxygenated 'blue' blood in the aorta passes back through the lungs to pick up oxygen. Taussig had little difficulty in persuading the Professor of Surgery at Johns Hopkins, Alfred Blalock, about the soundness of her idea and the first operation was carried out on a fifteen-month-old baby boy in November 1944. He did not survive, but two further patients, aged eleven and six, were operated on the fol-

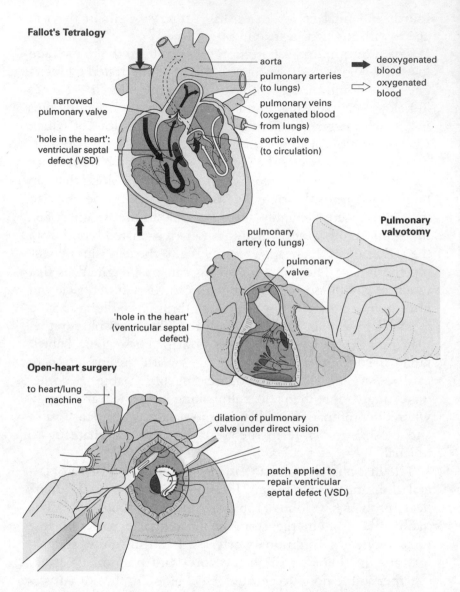

Fallot's Tetralogy

aorta

pulmonary arteries
(to lungs)

pulmonary veins
(oxgenated blood
from lungs)

aortic valve
(to circulation)

deoxygenated
blood

oxygenated
blood

narrowed
pulmonary valve

'hole in the heart':
ventricular septal
defect (VSD)

**Pulmonary
valvotomy**

pulmonary
artery (to lungs)

pulmonary
valve

'hole in the heart'
(ventricular septal
defect)

Open-heart surgery

to heart/lung
machine

dilation of pulmonary
valve under direct vision

patch applied to
repair ventricular
septal defect (VSD)

*The two main anatomical defects of Fallot's Tetralogy are a narrowed pulmonary valve
that limits the amount of blood pumped from the right side of the heart into the lungs,
and a 'hole in the heart' or ventricular septal defect, through which the deoxygenated
blood from the right side is shunted through to the left. During a pulmonary valvotomy, the surgeon dilates the narrowed pulmonary valve through a small incision.
With open-heart surgery, both the pulmonary valve can be dilated and the 'hole in
the heart' repaired, thus restoring to normal the internal anatomy of the heart.*

lowing year.[3] The Blalock/Taussig operation was an instant success and 500 operations were carried out over the following two years. Sir Russell, later Lord, Brock, the distinguished British cardiac surgeon, described the effects of the operation as 'so outstanding that it altered the whole approach to cardiology'.[4] In 1946 Blalock and Taussig toured Europe, demonstrating their operation in Stockholm, Paris and London and generating great excitement as described by Russell Brock:

> Intense interest had already been aroused throughout Great Britain and everyone was eager to hear them. Alfred Blalock and Helen Taussig gave a combined lecture in the Great Hall of the British Medical Association; the huge hall was packed. Dr Taussig delivered her address impeccably, followed by Dr Blalock who presented his surgical contribution. The silence of the audience betokened their rapt attention and appreciation. The hall was quite dark for projection of his slides which had been illustrating patients before and after the operation, when suddenly a search light beam traversed the whole length of the hall and unerringly picked out on the platform a Guy's nursing sister, dressed in her attractive blue uniform, sitting on a chair and holding a small cherub-like girl of two and half years with a halo of blonde curly hair and looking pink and well; she had been operated on at Guy's by Blalock a week earlier. The effect was dramatic and theatrical and the applause from the audience was tumultuous.[5]

This then was the first phase – cardiac surgery without entering the heart. The second phase, 'blind' operations within the heart, followed immediately. The simplest procedure for children with Fallot's is to dilate the narrow pulmonary valve between the right ventricle and the pulmonary artery, thus increasing the volume of blood that is pumped through the lungs. (This would not, of course, completely relieve the symptoms of breathlessness, as some blood would still be 'shunted' through the defect in the ventricle wall from the right to the left side.) Here the surgeon is seeking to restore the natural haemodynamics of the heart, so dilating the pulmonary valve is a more elegant solution than the Blalock/Taussig operation. It does, however, require entering the heart by making an incision in the wall of the ventricle through which the surgeon can introduce a finger or knife, feel around for the narrowed valve and open it up. This operation – a pulmonary valvotomy – was performed for the first time almost simultaneously by Russell Brock at Guy's and Holmes Sellors at the Middlesex Hospital, both in London.[6,7]

Strictly speaking, this was not the first 'blind' operation. Before the war a similar procedure had been attempted on the left side of the heart to relieve narrowing of the mitral valve. In 1923, Elliott Cutler in Boston had inserted a knife through the ventricle of a twelve-year-old girl to dilate her tight mitral valve.[8] Henry Souttar in England repeated the same procedure two years later.[9] Cutler's next few patients did badly and he became so discouraged that he gave up the operation. As for Souttar, he never performed another as his colleagues at the London Hospital were so shocked at his impudence in performing an operation on the heart (though the patient did well) that they never referred him another case. Bill Cleland, Britain's leading heart surgeon in the 1960s, believes it was 'just as well' Souttar was never given the chance to repeat his operation: 'For disaster would surely have ensued . . . there was no blood transfusion service, no antibiotics and appropriate anaesthesia for heart surgery had not been developed.'[10] By 1945, thanks to the necessities of war, these essentials for heart surgery were all available and the heart was no longer seen as a surgical 'no-go area', since an American thoracic surgeon, Dwight Harken, based in England in the final year of the war, had shown it was quite possible to remove bullets and shrapnel from the heart without killing the patient.[11]

Returning to the United States, Harken repeated Elliott Cutler's operation on the mitral valve on the left side of the heart in 1948, while simultaneously, in Britain, Russell Brock and Holmes Sellors were performing the same operation on the pulmonary valve on the right side.[12]

The surgeons however soon realised that operating on the heart was 'different'. Whereas there had been remarkably few complications following Blalock's operations, the same could not be said for those of Harken and Brock. Thus Harken recalls:

> Six of my first ten patients died. This was so devastating that with the tenth patient and my sixth death, I left the operating theatre, insisting I would never do another heart operation. I went home and to bed. The late Dr Laurence Brewster Ellis, my wonderful cardiologist friend and collaborator, drove to our house and asked my wife if it were true that I had said I would never do another heart operation. She confirmed this and he asked if he could see me. She urged him to wait until the next day. The next day, I again insisted I intended to do no more heart surgery, he said, 'I think that would be very irresponsible of you.' I replied, 'What in the world is irresponsible about that? I refuse to kill any more people.' He said, 'You have never killed anybody. I have never sent you a patient who wasn't dying.' I replied that, 'I would not expect any responsible physician to send me another patient.' He replied, 'I am President of the Heart Association and generally regarded as responsible. I would certainly send you patients and I would criticise you if you did not operate. You must have learnt something from those six disasters.' I went back to work and we lost only one of the next fifteen patients.[13]

This pattern of initial disaster followed – if a surgeon kept his cool and carried on – by ultimate success is difficult to explain other than in terms of the 'steep learning curve': with repetition everything gets easier and heart surgery is no exception. The precedent of this pattern was to be important in the next phase of cardiac surgery, in encouraging surgeons to persist even though at times their operating theatres resembled killing fields.

By 1950, these 'blind' operations had reached their intellectual limits and, taking Fallot's Tetralogy as the paradigm of the evolution of cardiac surgery, the next step was to combine dilating the narrow pulmonary valve with repairing the hole in the wall of the ventricle. This could only be achieved by 'opening up' the heart so its interior could be closely scrutinised. The brain is irreparably damaged if deprived of oxygenated blood for five minutes, but the simplest openheart operation takes fifteen minutes. Hence the whole future of cardiac surgery depended on whether or not the ten minutes' difference (at least) could be bridged, and here there were essentially two possibilities. Cooling the body or 'hypothermia' prolongs the length of time the circulation can be interrupted, because cold reduces the brain's requirement for oxygen. The alternative is the pump. In the early 1950s both had their advocates, but the pump ultimately proved to be the better option.

The story of the pump starts in Massachusetts General Hospital in February 1931, when a 28-year-old junior research surgeon, John Gibbon, spent a night sitting by the bedside of a woman who had had a gall bladder operation fifteen days earlier. Both the operation and her convalescence had gone smoothly until she was struck by the most serious of complications of major surgery, a pulmonary embolus, or clot in the lungs. The clot, which originates in the veins of the leg, breaks off and is carried to the right side of the lung to lodge in the pulmonary artery, preventing blood passing into the lung. If the clot cannot be dissolved or removed surgically, the circulation of the blood is effectively interrupted, blood cannot get into the lungs to receive oxygen and the patient dies. John Gibbon subsequently recalled his reflections during his nocturnal vigil:

> My job that night was to take the patient's blood pressure and pulse rate every fifteen minutes and plot it on a chart . . . during the seventeen hours I was by this patient's side, the thought constantly recurred that her hazardous condition could be improved if the blue blood in her veins could be withdrawn into an apparatus where it could pick

up oxygen and discharge carbon dioxide and then pump this blood back into the patient's arteries. At 1 a.m. the patient's condition became worse . . . Dr Edward Churchill [Director of Surgery at Massachusetts General] immediately opened the chest and opened the pulmonary artery with a long incision and removed massive blood clots. All this took place in the space of six minutes and thirty seconds, a fact carefully noted by me, the rather green surgical fellow standing at the head of the table beside the anaesthetist. Despite the rapidity of the operation, the patient died on the operating table and could not be revived.[14]

Gibbon's 'boss' Edward Churchill apparently 'took a dim view' of his young research registrar's idea of 'an apparatus where the blood could pick up oxygen and discharge carbon dioxide'. This was scarcely surprising as, with the exception of a Russian, Professor S. S. Brukhonenko, who had performed some crude experiments with dogs (the development of the pump was to be an anti-vivisectionist's nightmare), no one else had tried to develop such a machine for the obvious reason that the technical problems involved were so vast.

Some notion of how fantastical Gibbon's idea must have seemed to his contemporaries can be gleaned from reflecting on the structure of the lungs. The air sacs, if they were to be dissected out and laid side by side, would cover an area the size of a tennis court. This great space is necessary to accommodate the blood flowing through the lungs that must pass through minute capillaries in the lining of the air sacs, where it absorbs oxygen and gives up carbon dioxide. It was impossible at the time to conceive that a mechanical oxygenator could be built of sufficient size to ensure adequate amounts of oxygen reaching the blood. Further, the blood cells themselves, by being exposed to the mechanical stresses of the pump, were readily fragmented and destroyed.

But as absurd as Gibbon's idea might have seemed to his contemporaries, he would not be dissuaded and 'over the next three years I had this idea constantly in the back of my mind'.

In 1934 Edward Churchill, despite his scepticism, finally agreed to give Gibbon a further year as a research fellow, and he was joined in the laboratory by Mary Hopkins, one of Dr Churchill's technicians, whom he had recently married. It was to be an unusually intimate scientific collaboration. They started by trying to work out the many factors that influenced the circulation of the blood:

> My wife and I experimented on ourselves and on friends. For instance, to find out how constriction and dilatation of the vessels in the extremities could be caused by a slight shift in body temperature, my wife, and I know this sounds odd, would stick a highly sensitive thermometer into my rectum after which I would swallow a stomach tube. She then poured ice water down the tube and measured the effect of this on temperature.[15]

Gibbon's first pump had three main components. He purchased an air pump to impel the blood around the circuit for a few dollars from a second-hand shop in East Boston. Then he used glass tubes (as plastic had not yet been invented) to transport the blood to and from the oxygenator with valves fashioned from a rubber cork to ensure it flowed in one direction. Finally, the oxygenator itself was a rapidly rotating drum whose centrifugal forces flattened the incoming blood to form a thin layer on the inner surface where, being exposed to the air, it took up oxygen.

Gibbon's early experiments were performed on cats, and when they were in short supply he 'would prowl around the local area at night with some tuna fish as a bait and a sack to catch any of the numerous stray alley cats which swarmed over Boston in those days'. The easiest experimental means of testing whether the pump could take over the action of the heart and lungs was to place a clamp around the cat's pulmonary artery, thus interrupting the circulation and diverting the blood into the oxygenator. The experiments themselves were arduous and time-consuming:

We were at the laboratory bright and early. We had to bring
a cat down from its upstairs quarters, anaesthetise it, perform
a tracheostomy and connect the animal up to [a mechanical
ventilator] . . . next the [heart] vessels were exposed and an
open clamp placed over the pulmonary artery. These preparations usually took from four to five hours, so it was
mid-afternoon before we were able to start the critical part
of the experiment . . . the things that were apt to go wrong
were infinite . . . We would terminate the period of [clamp-
ing] of the pulmonary artery, put the cat back on its own
circulation, and see whether it would maintain its blood
pressure at a near normal level. If it succeeded in doing this,
the animal was nursed tenderly for an hour or two . . . then
it was sacrificed, autopsied, the instruments and general
mess cleaned up, and we could go home – a long day.

To the Gibbons' apparent astonishment, the first year's
experiments were not entirely in vain:

I will never forget the day when we were able to screw the
clamp down all the way, completely occluding the pulmonary artery with the pump in operation and with no
change in the animal's blood pressure. My wife and I threw
our arms around each other and danced around the laboratory, laughing and shouting 'Hurray!' That year, then,
marked the first successful demonstration that life could be
maintained by an artificial heart and lung outside the body,
and that the animal's own heart and lungs could again
maintain the circulation.[16]

The pump may have worked but the cat invariably died a
few hours later. It was not until 1939, after a further four years
of experimentation, that they were able to report as 'long-
term survivors' three out of a series of thirty-nine cats who had
survived a year or more.[17]
But then the war came. Though many areas of medical
research benefited enormously from the years of conflict, the

pump was not one of them, as the general opinion still prevailed that the heart was simply 'beyond the reach of surgery'. Immediately the war was over, Gibbon, now Professor of Surgery at the Jefferson Medical College in Philadelphia, started again. His most difficult problem was how to increase the capacity of the pump. It was one thing to keep a cat alive for a few hours and even have a handful of long-term survivors, but a small animal only had a small blood volume. It was quite another to design a machine that would cope with that of humans.

Progress was very slow but by 1948 Gibbon had started experimental heart surgery in dogs, making an incision in the wall of the two ventricles to simulate a 'hole in the heart' and then sewing it up again. Certainly very few of the dogs survived, but aspirant heart surgeons such as John Kirklin realised by now that 'closed' cardiac surgery had already reached its limits and that progress would require a machine such as Gibbon had been developing:

> My fellow residents and I filled pages of notebooks with drawings and plans of how we would repair Fallot's Tetralogy once science gave us a method to get inside the heart . . . at a meeting of the American College of Surgeons in 1948, Dr John Gibbon presented an update on his experimental studies and I can clearly recall his saying that 'we are encouraged and believe some day the heart/lung machine will be a practical affair'.[18]

It seemed as if John Gibbon's hour had finally arrived, but when it came to operating on humans the results were so uniformly disastrous it began to look as if open-heart surgery was, as the sceptics had claimed all along, a fantasy. Gibbon performed his first open-heart operation on a child in 1952 and a further three the following year. Only one survived. The first patient was a fifteen-month-old baby who was thought to have a defect in the wall separating the two atria, but during the operation an entirely different abnormality was found. Gibbon botched the operation and the child died. In May the following year, he performed his only successful open-heart operation, on an eighteen-year-old woman, Cecilia. Her circulation was sustained by the pump for just under half an hour while a hole between the two atria of her heart was closed by continuous silk suture. His next operation was on an eighteen-month-old girl, but 'a cardiac arrest occurred after we had opened the chest'. Her heartbeat was restarted and she was attached to the pump, the abnormality repaired, but 'the heart never recovered normal function'. In his final operation the diagnosis, as with the first, was incorrect: 'The heart flooded with blood . . . you could not get a clear field to work and the flow of bright red blood was so excessive.' They were unable to proceed and the child died. It is clear from Dr Gibbon's own account of these operations that he felt he was out of his depth, with neither the surgical skills nor the psychological stamina to continue. After the panic and helplessness no doubt induced by this last operation, with blood spurting everywhere, he decided to call it a day. Not only did he never again attempt open-heart surgery but there was also the impression that he was deeply discouraged. Though still only fifty-three, his scientific career was over and the account of these operations was the last paper to be published from his research laboratory.[19]

Following Gibbon's misfortunes at the operating table

pessimism was rampant . . . by early 1954 the surgical world had become thoroughly discouraged and disillusioned of the feasibility of open-heart surgery. By this time many of the most experienced investigators had concluded, with seemingly impeccable logic, that the obstacles to success were not with the heart/lung machine. Rather they had come to the general belief that the pump remained a highly lethal procedure, primarily because the sick human heart could not possibly be expected to tolerate the internal incisions and stitchings. It became widely accepted that the concept of open-heart correction, however attractive, was doomed.[20]

Thus the position in 1954 was simple. Either another way must be found to use the oxygenator without killing the patient, or cardiac surgery had reached the end of the road.

The scene now shifted to Minnesota in the middle of the American plains, where Walter Lillehai at the University of Minneapolis and John Kirklin at the Mayo Clinic in Rochester would between them initiate the modern era of open-heart surgery. Within two years of Gibbon's disasters, they had both, with the help of the pump, successfully operated on children with Fallot's. The bridge between Gibbon's experience in 1953 and the rebirth of open-heart surgery had, paradoxically, nothing to do with the pump at all but rather the success of forty-five operations carried out by Walter Lillehai with the help of 'cross circulation', where the patient's blood was passed not through an oxygenator but through a human volunteer. The beauty of cross circulation was that it dispensed with artificial forms of oxygenation of the blood in favour of the most natural and physiological substitute, the lungs of a volunteer. In retrospect it now seems an obvious, not to say ideal, solution, but it was not purposefully planned, emerging instead during an experiment on dogs, during which 'the chance remark was made that it would be very nice if a placenta was available for patients who were in need of open-heart surgery'. (The concept of a 'placenta' refers to the situation where the foetus receives its oxygen from its mother's circulation.) When this new idea was experimentally tried out in dogs by linking together their two circulations, the results were exceptionally good. Not only did they survive but both the dogs operated on and the cross-circulation 'donors' were noted to be up and about within a couple of days.[21]

Lillehai started using cross circulation for open-heart surgery in children on 13 August 1954, when he performed the first open-heart repair of a boy with Fallot's, thus initiating the third step in the evolution of the surgical treatment of this condition. There was no shortage of human volunteers to act as the cross-circulation partner and a 29-year-old man from the child's home town played the crucial role:

> The surgeons linked up the donor and the boy . . . then, as they had feared, [the boy's] weakened heart faltered and stopped. A few minutes later it took up its own beat again

and kept on going placidly throughout the operation. Between the two main chambers of the heart there was a hole a full inch and a quarter wide through which the blood was sloshing. They then looked at and stretched the pulmonary valve and closed the boy's chest. In 14 days he had left the hospital; when he returned it was to tell the surgeons about his baseball games and his cycling runs.[22]

From this auspicious start, Lillehai went on to perform nine further Fallot repairs – four of whom survived – as well as thirty-five other operations involving several types of complex congenital heart abnormalities. This technique of cross circulation, Lillehai later maintained, was the major force to start heart surgery moving again. 'The unprecedented success of the cross-circulation technique in patients with complex defects, and often intractable heart failure, played a crucial role in rapidly dispelling (virtually overnight) the widespread pessimism that had prevailed at that time amongst cardiologists and surgeons concerning the feasibility of open-heart surgery in man.'[23]

It was obvious, however, that the future could not lie with cross circulation, not least because it exposed the healthy donor to an unacceptable risk (although in fact there had been only one serious complication, where the donor had had to be resuscitated). There was thus no alternative other than to return to the pump, and here Lillehai and Kirklin took separate routes. Kirklin thought the principle behind Gibbon's pump to be essentially sound and persuaded the Mayo Clinic to invest heavily in modifying and improving it. In the summer of 1954, Lillehai encouraged a young research worker in his department, Richard DeWall, to resurrect an old idea where oxygen was bubbled into the patient's blood in a reservoir outside the body and then 'debubbled' before being returned.[24]

The psychological barrier of open-heart operations had now been broken. Equipped with their pumps Kirklin and Lillehai dominated cardiac surgery for the next ten years. True to form, their initial experiences were disastrous. All of Kirklin's first five patients died either during or immediately after the operation.

Nonetheless, there was a sense that if they persisted it would 'come right', and it did. The mortality rate fell rapidly to 50 per cent for the next ten patients, and then to 30 per cent, and within a couple of years it had fallen to single figures.

It is necessary to appreciate just how ill these children were. Nowadays babies born with Fallot's are operated on in the first year of life so one no longer sees what Kirklin called the 'pitiful' state of those he operated on. It is well illustrated by one of Lillehai's early cases, a seven-year-old girl whose twin sister had a normal heart. She weighed only 36 pounds compared to her sister's 56 pounds and her cyanosis – the blue tinge of the skin – was 'intense'. She was 'undeveloped and undernourished' and had recently started having convulsive seizures caused by inadequate oxygenation of the brain. Following her operation 'her immediate colour change from intensely cyanotic to pink was dramatic', and by the time she came to leave hospital her clinical appearance was described as 'normal'.

It is difficult to imagine how impressive such results must have appeared at the time and, more astonishingly, how consistently they were achieved. In Kirklin's account of his first seventy operations there is a table listing their subsequent medical conditions. With only very few exceptions it reads: 'Asymptomatic, full activity.'[25]

Soon the repair of Fallot's Tetralogy became routine, and Kirklin and Lillehai turned their attention to even more complex abnormalities such as repositioning the major arteries as they emerge from the heart. Kirklin subsequently recalled the atmosphere of those days:

> I am very proud for the two of us that during this period when we were the only surgeons in the world to perform open-heart surgery and were thus in intense competition with each other that we continued to communicate and argued over our differences, not publicly, but privately in nightclubs and on aeroplanes. Walt was more optimistic than I when we discussed difficult problems. I remember saying to him one day, 'Walt, I am so discouraged with complete atrioventricular canal' [a condition where all four

chambers of the heart communicate and where all the patients Kirklin had operated on up to that time had died]. 'Oh sure,' he said, 'that is a tough one, but we will learn to do well with it.'[26]

By 1960 they had operated on every single 'operable' heart defect in children and turned their attention to replacing diseased valves in adults. Technically these are staggeringly difficult operations, requiring patients to be on bypass for several hours, as the diseased valve has first to be carefully dissected out and the new one sewn into place with hundreds of separate stitches. The results followed precisely the same pattern as the operations in children, with initially a very high death rate of around 90 per cent, either from the operation itself or the failure of the artificial valve to function, as they tore easily and sometimes broke.[27] Donald Longmore, of London's National Heart Hospital, describes the results of these early operations as 'horrendous': 'The commonest post-operative complication was severe multi-organ damage. Moderate cerebral impairment (i.e. brain damage) was for a time almost routine, with cerebral devastation (irreversible brain damage) a frequent occurrence often associated with kidney failure.'[28]

No sooner had surgeons resolved those problems associated with valve replacement than some were turning their minds to what is often considered as the 'ultimate operation', the heart transplant, which was performed for the first time by Christian Barnard in 1967.[29] This looked as if it might be cardiac surgery's armageddon, for in the following year 100 transplants were performed across the world and not a single patient survived. In response to these catastrophic results, a moratorium was imposed on further heart transplants, with only one surgeon, Norman Shunway of Stamford University, carrying on in the face of bitter opposition. But within ten years this too had 'come right'. By the early 1980s 2,000 patients a year in the United States were receiving a heart transplant, with a survival rate of over 80 per cent.

And for all this, ultimately, Gibbon must take the credit. Before his pump, cardiac surgery was essentially limited to one crude 'blind' operation – the dilation of narrowed valves. From 1955 onwards and with increasing competence the surgeons were able to do dozens of different complicated procedures which, by the 1980s, were benefiting tens of thousands of patients every year. No doubt if it had not been Gibbon it might have been someone else, and it is certainly true that there were others involved in building pumps in the late 1940s, notably Viking Bjork in Sweden and Donald Melrose in London. But Gibbon was the first. The challenge he set himself in the 1930s, before he could have imagined what it might lead to, now seems breathtaking. It would be difficult enough to build a pump nowadays from scratch, let alone at a time before the advent of appropriate material such as plastic and with only derisory funds for medical research. Further, Gibbon and his wife were not only alone, but for the best part of twenty years had to contend with the scepticism, indeed active discouragement, of their professional colleagues, who had no faith that their pump would ever be put to practical use.

6

1963: TRANSPLANTING KIDNEYS

*F*ar-sighted surgeons in the post-war years realised transplantation offered much the most elegant solution for those whose kidneys were failing. Dialysis, it is true, provided an artificial means of simulating their function but, nature being so much better than anything man is able to come up with, 'borrowing' a kidney from another person (or the recently dead) is much the better option. Nor indeed are the surgical techniques particularly difficult, as they involve little more than connecting the blood supply of the donated kidney to that of the recipient.

Nonetheless, no matter how elegant or technically feasible transplantation might be, the perspicient surgeons were confronted by an apparently insuperable barrier – how to 'trick' the recipient's immune system into accepting the transplanted organ. For the vital attribute of the immune system is the ability to discriminate between 'self' and 'non-self', so it lives in harmony with the 'self' of the tissues of the body and yet virulently attacks and destroys the 'non-self', infectious organisms such as bacteria and viruses – and transplanted organs. The transplanters were thus presented with an apparently irresoluble dilemma. They could make the recipient more tolerant of 'non-self' kidneys (and so less likely to reject them) by weakening the immune system with drugs or irradiation, but at the price of also compromising its ability to destroy bacteria and viruses, thus exposing the recipient of transplanted organs to the dangers of overwhelming infection.

Success in transplantation was thus qualitatively different from most of the other achievements of the post-war years: whereas the accidentally discovered antibiotics and steroids were 'gifts from nature', which just happened to have quite unanticipated benefits, the early kidney trans-planters had to come to grips with this most fundamental of biological problems – the immune system's ability to discriminate between 'self' and 'non-self'.

The practicality of kidney transplantation was demonstrated by the first successful transplant – between identical twins – in 1953, but this merely bypassed the barrier posed by the immune system and indeed in the ten 'dark' years that fol-lowed every attempt to suppress the immune system in the hope of extending the benefits of the operation to the non-genetically compatible was spectacularly disastrous. It began to seem that transplantation was just a cruel hoax, a technique for killing off the terminally ill in a particularly gruesome manner. And yet the perspicient surgeons were eventually vindicated.

It is not easy to bring together the many strands of medical research involved, but three are particularly significant. This account starts with the work of the British immunologist Peter Medawar, who provided the intellectual framework within which the problem posed by the immunological barrier to transplantation could be understood. Next comes an examina-tion of the practicalities of transplantation developed by Joseph Murray, who performed the identical twin transplant at Boston's Brigham Hospital in 1953. Finally the key that unlocked transplantation – the drug azathioprine – was discov-ered by George Hitchings and Gertrude Elion. All four – Medawar, Murray, Hitchings and Elion – would eventually receive the Nobel Prize.

Peter Medawar: Understanding the Immune System

Peter Medawar was an exotic in the world of biology. Born in Brazil to a Lebanese father and an English mother, he was tall, handsome and gifted, with a felicitous literary style. His contribution to transplantation was two-fold: he was the first to show that the immune system was responsible for the 'rejection' of a transplanted organ; and a decade later he demonstrated that the immune system could be tricked into tolerating transplanted tissues.

In the summer of 1941, Medawar was a lecturer in zoology at Oxford University and, by his own admission, uncertain as to what to do with his life. While sunbathing one afternoon in his back garden with his wife and child he heard the drone of a large bomber overhead. 'The bomber crashed into the garden of a house about 200 yards away and immediately exploded with a fearful whomp!' Amazingly the pilot survived, but with terrible burns covering 60 per cent of his body. After the pilot had been transported to hospital, Medawar continued to take an interest in his fate and a medical colleague – who specialised in the treatment of burns – suggested that he should apply his considerable intellect to working out how best to cover the exposed flesh of burn-injury victims.[1] Peter Medawar tried various methods of eking out the small remaining amounts of normal skin in the form of skin grafts, but soon turned to the crucial question: 'I guessed that if one could use what were then known as "homografts" – that is a graft transfer of skin from a donor – the treatment of war wounds would be transformed.' As he says, 'it was not a very original thought', and others had certainly had the idea before.

Medawar studied the matter further in a large burns unit in Glasgow, where he found that, first time round, the skin 'homografts' lasted for around ten days, but that a second graft from the same donor was rejected immediately. This is very similar to what happens when the body's immune system encounters the measles virus. Following first exposure it takes time to build up antibodies so the virus has time to disseminate through the body to cause the characteristic rash. But, second time round, the immunological system 'remembers' what the virus looks like and promptly generates the antibodies to destroy it. Hence one never gets measles twice. Medawar published the results of his experiments as 'The Fate of Skin Homografts in Man': 'In this paper we propounded the view that skin homografts were rejected by an immunological process – that is to say by the same kind of specific adaptive responses that daily leads to the elimination of bacteria or viruses or other organisms foreign to the body.' So now, at least, those who were interested in transplantation knew the nature of what they were up against.[2]

Peter Medawar stumbled on his second discovery – 'immuno-logical tolerance' – after attending a conference in Stockholm in 1948. There, a fellow delegate asked Medawar whether it was possible to distinguish identical from fraternal twin calves.

'My dear fellow,' I said in the expansive way one is tempted to adopt at international conferences, 'in principle the solu-tion is extremely easy: just exchange skin grafts between the twins and see how long they last. If they last indefinitely you can be sure they are identical twins, but if they are thrown off after a week or two you can classify them with equal certainty as fraternal twins.' I went on somewhat injudiciously to say I would be happy to demonstrate the technique of grafting to the delegate's veterinary staff if he were to get in touch with me.

A few months later Medawar received a letter reminding him of his promise and informing him that the twin calves were all under observation at an experimental farm forty miles from Birmingham.

Without a doubt I was morally committed, so we travelled by car to the farm with the right surgical instruments, drapes and local anaesthetics. The skin grafting presented no difficulty but the results were not at all what we had expected. *All* the cattle twins accepted skin grafts from one another for as long as we had them under observation. Some of these twins must certainly have been non-identical (i.e. fraternal) because they were of different sexes.

So why had Medawar's prediction been proved wrong? He inferred – rightly as it turned out – that something must happen to the immune systems of twin cattle while they were still in the womb together so they could subsequently 'tolerate' each other's tissues. By now at London's University College, Medawar resolved to investigate the matter further: 'Our ambition was to bring about the immunological phenomenon that occurs naturally in twin cattle, to reduce, even abolish, their power to recognise and destroy genetically foreign tissue.' Accordingly he innoculated mouse embryos with 'foreign' cells from adult mice from another strain. Then, after the embryo mice had been born and reached maturity, they were grafted with skin patches taken from the strain of mice to whose cells they had been exposed while in the uterus. Theoretically these grafts should have been rejected in the normal way ten to twelve days later. But they were not. 'We felt we were on to a genuine phenomenon to which we gave the name "acquired immunological tolerance", for we had artificially reproduced the immunological tolerance we had observed between cattle.'[3]

This finding could scarcely be turned to practical use, as Medawar himself acknowledged during a lecture in Oxford several years later when asked by one of the audience – a young surgeon, Roy Calne – whether he could see any clinical application of his studies. He replied, 'Absolutely none.'[4] 'Rather,' he wrote in 1982, 'the ultimate impact of the discovery of tolerance turned out to be not practical but moral, it put new hearts into biologists and surgeons who were working to make it possible to graft kidneys from one person to another.'

Joseph Murray and the First Kidney Transplant

In 1953, a year after Peter Medawar reported on his mice experiments and the phenomenon of 'acquired immunological tolerance', Joseph Murray performed the first successful kidney transplant between identical twins. The close proximity of just over a year might imply some connection between the two events, but there was none. Joseph Murray's first transplant had emerged from a research programme into kidney diseases that had been going on since the war at the Brigham Hospital in Boston, where the two other essential requirements for transplantation besides the solution to the problem of immunological rejection had been developed: kidney dialysis and the necessary surgical expertise.

The first dialysis machine for the treatment of kidney failure was built by the Dutch physician Wilhelm Kolff in 1941, in the extremely adverse circumstances of Nazi-occupied Holland. If the kidneys suddenly fail, as may occur following very severe infection or an episode of shock, they will often recover, usually within a fortnight, if the patient can be kept alive through the two weeks of not passing any urine. This essentially means that some way must be found to remove the accumulating waste materials in the blood, mostly urea. Kolff's initial method involved removing blood from a vein – 50ml at a time – and passing it through a cellophane-wrapped drum, which rotated through a bath of fluid into which the excess urea was absorbed. The 'treated' blood was then replaced back in the arm, and a further 50ml removed, and so on. It was a very time-consuming and laborious process but the results were sufficiently encouraging for Kolff to build a proper dialysis machine. This was not easy for, as Dr Kolff recalled, it was 'quite a problem' to make an artificial kidney 'when nothing could be bought freely and many materials could not be had at all'.

Altogether Kolff treated fifteen patients during the war, only one of whom survived – a 67-year-old woman with acute kidney failure who was actually treated just after liberation. 'It is significant that this patient, at least in our eyes at the time, was not considered to be a very useful member of society,' he recalls. Indeed she was transferred from the local prison where she had been incarcerated for being a Nazi collaborator. After eleven and a half hours of continuous dialysis she emerged from her coma, and according to Dr Kolff 'the first comprehensible words she spoke were that she was going to divorce her husband, which in time she did'.[5]

Kolff then moved to the United States where his dialysis machine so impressed the physicians at the Brigham Hospital that they set up the first formal renal dialysis programme. Dialysis would prove very important for the transplanters. It gave them the experience in dealing with the complex biochemical and haemodynamic problems associated with kidney failure, so they were able to monitor and assess the results of their transplants. Further, dialysis was essential to keep a patient alive while waiting for the operation as well as for ten days or so afterwards, giving time for the transplanted kidney to work.

The second component essential for transplantation developed at the Brigham Hospital during this period was an appropriate surgical technique. Here Joseph Murray refined a method first devised by a Frenchman, Alexis Carrell, following the assassination by an anarchist in 1894 of the President of the French Republic. The anarchist's knife wound had severed the main vein from the liver and Carrell realised the President's death from massive internal bleeding might have been avoided had there been a means of sewing small blood vessels together. The technique he devised was extremely ingenious: 'He sewed three equally spaced sutures round the circumference of each of the cut ends of the blood vessels that he wished to join together. By pulling on all three stitches at once the vessel opened up, its end shaped like a triangle, making the task of joining one end to the other relatively easy. Carrell used very fine thread and sharp round needles coated with Vaseline to seal the holes in the vessels as soon as they were made.'[6] Now that he was able to repair blood vessels, it was an obvious step for Carrell to investigate whether an organ might be transplanted by hitching its blood supply to that of the recipient. In a series of experiments on dogs he removed their kidneys and then retransplanted one of them back.[7] They survived, but not for long which, Joseph Murray inferred, was almost certainly because Carrell connected the kidneys to the carotid artery in the neck:

> Therefore my first aim was to devise a transplant operation which could produce normal renal function indefinitely [where there was no immunological barrier because the dogs were simply being retransplanted with their own kidneys].

By 1954 I had several animals living over two years on solitary, life-sustaining renal autografts (their own retransplanted
kidneys). The key was the implantation of the kidney into
the abdominal cavity of the dog and connecting the ureter to
the bladder. This eliminated the mechanical and infectious
disadvantages of [Carrell's] previous experiments.[8]

Thus, by 1953, 'the stage was set', Murray observed, when
the twins Richard and Ronald Herrick were referred to the
Brigham Hospital. Medical expertise was at hand in the form
of the renal dialysis programme for looking after patients with
severe kidney failure and Murray had a 'proven laboratory
model' for the proposed operation. Richard Herrick was in the
terminal stages of kidney failure caused by an aggressive inflammatory destruction of the kidney known as glomerulonephritis.
He was very ill, his body bloated by the water he was unable to
excrete through his failing kidneys. He was tired and lethargic
because of severe anaemia and was suffering from the
intractable itching arising from the accumulation of waste products in the skin. He was also disoriented and confused. His
admitting doctor was Frank Parsons from Leeds in England,
who was spending time at the Brigham to learn the technique
of dialysis. 'The dialysis went well but it was the most traumatic
one I had ever been in charge of. He constantly spat at me (and
his aim was good) cursing "Bloody limey", but such is the
power of dialysis to correct the confusion [associated with]
kidney failure that the next day he apologised profusely for his
behaviour.'[9] On 23 December 1954 Richard Herrick was given
a kidney from his brother Ronald. 'The kidney functioned
immediately. Richard Herrick's recovery was rapid and complete, exceeding our highest hopes,' Murray recalls.[10] Within a
couple of weeks he was well enough to be discharged from
hospital and promptly married the nurse who had looked after
him in the recovery room after his operation. They had two
children together and Richard Herrick survived another eight
years before dying suddenly from a heart attack.[11]

Murray went on to perform several other 'identical twin'
transplants over the following years. Emboldened by his

success, he sought to widen the scope of transplantation by borrowing kidneys from close relatives, hoping to suppress the inevitable 'rejection' by using X-ray treatment to weaken the recipient's immune system. His results, and that of others who tried, were disastrous. The following decade became known as the 'black years' as every attempt to push the boundaries of transplantation beyond the genetically compatible ended in failure. During this time there were twenty-eight transplants between identical twins, of whom twenty-one survived, but for everyone else it simply did not work. Thus ninety-one patients received a kidney from a blood relative, but only five lived for a year – that is eighty-six healthy people had voluntarily undergone a major operation to donate a kidney only to see the relative to whom they had given it die almost immediately. As for the 120 patients who were given a 'cadaver' kidney from someone recently dead, only one lived longer than a year.[12]

Behind these gloomy statistics lay an even bleaker picture – the manner in which these patients died. One example must suffice – a 21-year-old woman whose kidney failure had been caused by chronic pyelonephritis (kidney infection), who had been given a transplant from her mother. Immediately after the operation she developed severely raised blood pressure and had multiple convulsions. On the fourth post-operative day a considerable amount of urine started leaking from the transplanted kidney, which required a reoperation. Her white blood count then fell. Despite being kept in strict isolation she also developed multiple abscesses. A fortnight later she started haemorrhaging blood, requiring a further reoperation, where it was found that one of her arteries had been eroded by the tube draining her bladder. She then made 'a turn for the worse' because of an acute rejection episode, which it was thought might have been brought on by a further abscess warranting a third reoperation. Her surgical wounds failed to heal and she developed massive bed sores and acute heart failure. These were followed by hallucinations and a drop in blood pressure. After almost six months of this misery she died in hospital.[13]

And then came azathioprine.

*George Hitchings, Gertrude B. Elion and the Discovery of
Azathioprine*

When the bone marrow is unable to make the precursors of the
blood cells the patient succumbs from a combination of anaemia
(due to a lack of red blood cells), overwhelming infection (from
a lack of white blood cells) and haemorrhage (from a lack of
platelets). This is known as aplastic anaemia, for which in 1958
there was no treatment when Dr William Dameshek, Director
of Haematology at the New England Medical Centre in Boston,
speculated that a solution might lie in transplanting some healthy
bone marrow from a close relative. He treated three patients,
suppressing the inevitable immunological rejection with X-ray
treatment. All three patients died rapidly. Dameshek realised – as
the kidney transplanters knew only too well – that some alternative method of immunosuppression was essential. As a
haematologist he also had considerable experience in treating
children with leukaemia, giving them a combination of drugs
including 6-mercaptopurine (6-mp) to provide a temporary
remission from this otherwise invariably fatal illness. The admittedly limited efficacy of this drug was based on its ability to
interfere with the replication of leukaemia cells. Dameshek
wondered whether it might also block the replication of the cells
of the immune system and thus act as an 'immunosuppressant'.

Back in the late 1940s George Hitchings and Gertrude Elion
of the pharmaceutical company Burroughs-Wellcome had
intentionally designed 6-mp as a treatment for leukaemia on
the following principles: DNA (the genetic material in the
nucleus of the cells) is made up of chemicals including purines
which must reproduce itself every time a cell divides. Hitchings
and Elion postulated that one way of stopping a cancer cell
from dividing was to find a chemical similar in structure to a
purine but slightly different, so that when it was incorporated
into the cell's DNA it would 'jam the works' so the cancerous
cell would thus be unable to divide and would die. (The mechanism of action is known as 'competitive inhibition', and had
already been encountered in the discovery of the drug PAS for
the treatment of tuberculosis.)[14]

William Dameshek asked a new recruit to his department, Dr Robert Schwartz, to study the effects of 6-mp with results that turned out to be much more interesting than he – or William Dameshek – could conceivably have anticipated. Dr Schwartz had hoped that at best 6-mp would block the replication of the immune cells and thus generally weaken the immune system and its ability to reject transplanted organs. But 6-mp turned out to be much more specific than this. He found that if rabbits were injected with the human protein albumin and then treated with 6-mp they did not develop antibodies to it, but the rest of their immune system was relatively unaffected. By analogy, if 6-mp were to be given to patients following a transplant this would prevent them from developing antibodies to the 'foreign' kidney but should not impair their ability to produce antibodies to other pathogens such as bacteria. 6-mp thus created a state of 'drug-induced immunological tolerance' similar to the immunological tolerance Medawar had demonstrated when mice embryos had been injected with foreign cells. Thus quite fortuitously Dr Schwartz seemed to have stumbled upon the Holy Grail for which transplanters had been searching for so long – a drug that would allow their patients to tolerate transplanted organs but which would not so impair their immune system as to leave them vulnerable to overwhelming infections.[15]

The transition from Dr Schwartz's small experiment in rabbits to kidney transplants in humans was made by a young British surgeon, Roy Calne. Calne had become interested in the possibility of transplantation when as a 21-year-old medical student at London's Guy's Hospital he had to care for a teenager dying from kidney failure:

'The consultant told me he would be dead in a couple of weeks so I should try and give him two weeks of reasonable comfort while he was dying,' Calne subsequently recollected. 'I knew enough anatomy to realise the kidneys were the kind of organ that you might graft in much the same way that you would graft the branches of a fruit tree or a rose bush, so I asked: "Couldn't he have a kidney graft?"

The consultant physician said: "No. It can't be done." I said, "Why not?" He just said, "It can't be done because it can't be done." One of my friends whispered I'd better not ask any more questions."[16]

Calne qualified with honours and after two years' National Service returned to Oxford in 1958 as a lecturer in anatomy, during which time he attended the lecture given by Medawar, whose verdict on the practical applicability of his research findings – 'absolutely none' – has already been mentioned. Soon after moving to the Royal Free Hospital Calne heard of Schwartz's paper on 'drug-induced immunological tolerance' with 6-mp which, of course, was an entirely different matter. He sought out John Hopewell, a consultant surgeon, who had just established one of the first dialysis units in the country for the treatment of kidney failure. 'One morning I was approached in the quadrangle of the old Royal Free Hospital by a young man [Roy Calne] who told me he was hoping to test the efficacy of 6-mp in combating the rejection of the transplanted dog kidney, and asked if I were interested. I replied enthusiastically.'[17]

Hopewell encouraged Calne to go to the Royal College of Surgeons' experimental research station at Buckton Brown Farm, where over the next few months he showed that giving 6-mp to transplanted dogs improved their survival from around a week to up to six weeks.[18] 'These results were sufficiently encouraging to persuade us to conduct a clinical trial,' Mr Hopewell observed, perhaps rather over-optimistically. The first three human transplants using 6-mp were duly carried out. The first two patients died on the third and eleventh day after their operations without the transplanted kidneys having worked. But the third – who received a kidney from a relative – did survive for a few weeks before succumbing, tragically, from widespread tuberculosis having acquired the infection from his transplanted kidney. An inauspicious but typical beginning.[19]

Soon after Roy Calne went to the United States to join the doyen of all kidney transplanters – Joseph Murray – at the Brigham Hospital. On the way he took time off to visit George

Hitchings and Gertrude Elion at their research laboratory and they provided him with supplies of another chemical similar to but more effective than 6-mp, azathioprine. Three years later, in the summer of 1963, azathioprine brought to an end the 'black years' – suddenly and dramatically.

The occasion was a conference on Human Kidney Transplantation held in the building of the National Research Council in Washington.[20] Virtually everybody involved in transplanting kidneys was present – a mere handful of twenty-five doctors, surgeons and researchers – epitomising, perhaps better than anything else, what a minority pursuit transplantation was at that time. The reasons were obvious enough to those present, as speaker after speaker rose to describe their results. These included Joseph Murray who after the first successful kidney transplant on the Herrick twins nine years earlier had gone on to do seven more. But his transplants between the non-genetically identical had been a different matter. Only one out of a series of twelve who had been immunosuppressed with total body irradiation had survived, most of the other eleven dying within a fortnight. Azathioprine appeared to offer the only glimmer of hope, permitting one 24-year-old transplant patient to return to work as an accountant.[21] Then there were the two transplant teams from Paris – Professor Jean Hamburger and Dr René Kuss – with only one long-term survivor out of twenty-eight transplants between them. The British, Michael Woodruff from Edinburgh and Ralph Shackman from Hammersmith, had not done any better. Roy Calne, by now returned from the United States to London's Westminster Hospital, had treated eight transplant patients with azathioprine but only two were still alive. As one had only received his transplant two months earlier, it was still too early to say whether the drug would have a significant impact on the outcome.

There was one new face at the conference, Thomas Starzl, from the Veterans' Administration Hospital in Colorado. Though he had only been transplanting kidneys for less than a year, he had managed to clock up an impressive thirty-three. 'I felt like someone who had been parachuted unannounced from another planet,' he recalls. When it came to his turn to present his results they were greeted with 'naked incredulity' – twenty-seven of the thirty-three were still alive with functioning kidneys.[22] The 'new boy' had more surviving kidney transplant recipients than everyone else in the world combined. Roy Calne recalls the astonishment of his fellow transplanters and in the evening he along with several others retired to Dr Starzl's hotel room to go through his records. 'He was an obsessional smoker at the time and I recall a pyramid of cigarette butts nearly two feet high. In between smoking, he showed his flow-charts [of his patients' progress] . . . it was the first time I had seen this systematic day-to-day assessment of results and I think that was extremely important . . .'[23]

And how had Thomas Starzl achieved precisely the results that had eluded the veteran transplanters for so long? He too had given his patients azathioprine, but in addition he had treated their episodes of acute rejection with short bursts of very high doses of steroids.[24] By the following morning Calne and the other conference participants had realised there was no secret to Starzl's success. They could all achieve similar results. Almost a quarter of a century later, when Starzl reviewed the long-term results of his first thirty-three transplanted patients, he found fifteen were still alive.[25]

From this moment on kidney transplantation blossomed. It led in rapid succession to liver, heart, bone marrow and lung transplants, though all had their vicissitudes before achieving comparable success rates. There was one further significant development with the discovery of a second potent immuno-suppressant drug – cyclosporine – which emerged as a fortuitous spin-off from a research programme into the antibiotic properties of the fungus *trichodima polysporum*. Cyclosporine transformed the 'narrow tightrope' of immuno-suppression into 'a broad plank', markedly reducing the need for steroids and further improving the survival rate.[26]

7

1964: THE TRIUMPH OF PREVENTION — THE CASE OF STROKES

There is no more certain way of increasing the chances of living to a ripe old age (besides, of course, not smoking) than dropping in periodically to see the family doctor to have one's blood pressure checked and – if it is found to be elevated – taking regular medication to lower it. For, as everyone now knows, if raised blood pressure is left untreated it can burst a blood vessel in the brain to cause a stroke which, if not lethal, can have catastrophic complications including paralysis, loss of the power of speech or many other highly undesirable variations of functional impairment.

The prevention of strokes merits inclusion in the pantheon of the major events of post-war medicine for two reasons. First, strokes are the third most common cause of death, and thus the ability to prevent them is of enormous significance. The second reason is subtler. The need to identify and then treat those with raised blood pressure – or hypertension – expands the scope and influence of medicine enormously. In the past people visited their doctors because they were ill or had some distressing symptoms about which they were concerned. Hypertension changed all this because it usually does not cause any symptoms, so there is no way to know if the blood pressure is elevated other than by visiting the doctor's surgery. Thus the contentment that comes from feeling healthy can be illusory, concealing the damage being wrought by raised blood pressure. We now need doctors not only when we are ill, but also when we feel well.

Hypertension is very common (though how common is a contentious matter) and nowadays much the most frequent reason for people to consult their doctor and take medication is for a condition that previously they would never have known they had. Nor does it stop there. For once it is accepted that identifying and treating hypertension is a good thing then the same principle can be applied to any number of other 'silent killer' conditions that cause no symptoms — such as raised cholesterol levels, or detecting hidden cancers of the breast or cancer of the cervix by screening. The evolution of this type of 'preventive screening' in which doctors screen the healthy looking for disease has led inevitably to the 'mass medicalisation' of society. Now everyone, not just the sick, is a potential patient. And it all started with the successful treatment of hypertension.

The word 'stroke', which for the young carries the gentle resonance of affection and physical comfort, acquires by middle age the much gloomier connotation of its other meaning – a devastating blow. A stroke is a catastrophe. The damage to the brain cannot be repaired so the only rational approach is prevention. Most strokes are caused by raised blood pressure, which either accelerates narrowing of the arteries to the brain or may cause a blood vessel to burst, resulting in a haemorrhage. Logically, then, drugs that lower the blood pressure should reduce the risk of strokes. They do, as first convincingly demonstrated in 1964 by Doctors Michael Hamilton and Eileen Thompson of the Chelmsford Hospital.[1] Their findings were replicated three years later in a larger and more famous study conducted among US military veterans where twenty-seven out of seventy patients whose hypertension was not treated experienced a stroke or heart attack, compared to only two out of seventy patients who were treated. It is hard to conceive of a more powerful verdict on the imperative of treating hypertension.[2]

The therapeutic revolution has had, as already noted, a profoundly beneficial effect on the lives of many people, but the ability to treat hypertension is in a sense a very special case, for the absence of effective treatment prior to the 1960s had a profound effect not just on individuals but on the fate of whole nations. Both the President of the United States, Franklin D. Roosevelt, and the Russian leader, Josef Stalin, had raised blood pressure, with dramatic consequences for world politics in the post-war era. On 12 April 1945 Franklin Roosevelt died of a cerebral haemorrhage which his physician, Admiral Ross McIntire, said had 'come out of the clear sky', as only a few days earlier the President had apparently been 'given a thorough examination by eight physicians including some of the most eminent in the country and pronounced physically sound in every way'.[3] The Admiral was lying; Roosevelt had been diagnosed as having hypertension almost ten years earlier which, by the time of the Yalta conference with Churchill and Stalin in February 1945 (just eight weeks before his death), had caused so much damage to his heart and kidneys that he was 'a dying man'. At this crucial moment in world politics, Roosevelt's ailing health so impaired his political judgement as to produce 'a deadly hiatus' in the leadership of the United States. This led to 'the betrayal of the Poles, the imposition of communist governments in Eastern Europe, the Czechoslovakian coup and – on the other side of the world – the loss of China and the invasion of South Korea'.[4]

In 1953 Josef Stalin also fell victim to a stroke, at the age of seventy-three. Even had there been effective drugs for the treatment of raised blood pressure, Stalin would have been unable to avail himself of them as he had just had his personal physician, Professor Vinogradov – 'the only qualified specialist familiar with his medical problems, including his hypertension' – arrested as part of the 'doctors' plot'. On the day prior to his stroke, Stalin had joked with Beria, the head of the KGB, that unless a full confession was extracted from Vinogradov, Beria's height would be 'reduced by one head'. Stalin did not die instantaneously but lingered on for a few days, conscious but paralysed and unable to speak. 'At the end, his respiration deepened and quickened and his lips and face blackened. He literally choked to death as we watched,' recalls his daughter Svetlana.[5]

Again, like Roosevelt, if Stalin's hypertension had been treatable with appropriate medication the history of the post-war world would have been very different. He could well have lived on for another decade, up to and including the Cuban missile crisis, which might then have had a very different outcome, culminating in the Soviet Union, under his demented leadership, launching a full-scale nuclear war against the United States. One way or another, hypertension has had a crucial impact on the fate of nations and the survival of the human race. So how did hypertension become a treatable disease?

The blood pressure is the pressure generated by the contraction of the heart muscle to pump blood into the arteries and around the circulation. It is determined by two factors. The first is the volume of blood in the arteries (the higher the volume, the greater the pressure needed to pump it round the circulation), and the second is the diameter of the vessels through which the blood travels (the narrower the arteries, the greater the pumping pressure that is required). Hence, prior to the discovery of effective drugs, the two ways of lowering the blood pressure were either to reduce the volume of fluid in the circulatory system or to dilate the blood vessels.

In 1944 Dr Walter Kempner reported that the blood pressure returned to 'normal or almost normal' by reducing the volume of fluid in the circulatory system with a rice/fruit/sugar diet: 'The rice is boiled or steamed in plain water without salt, milk or fat. All fruit juices and fruit are allowed with the exception of nuts, dates, avocados and any kind of dried or tinned fruit. No water is allowed and the fluid intake is restricted to one litre of fruit juice per day.'[6] The problem, as can be imagined, was that the diet itself was so unpalatable that patients could not stick with it. 'It is insipid, unappetising and monotonous and demands great care in its preparation . . . it is quite impracticable for a member of a large household with minimal domestic help . . . its deadly monotony tends to make it intolerable unless the physician can infuse into the patient some of the asceticism of the religious zealot.'[7] Nor indeed, as it subsequently emerged, was Kempner's diet as effective as he claimed, for when other doctors tried to replicate his results they were less successful. 'The change of blood pressure does not exceed the random spontaneous variation to be anticipated,' observed Dr Herbert Chasis of University College Hospital in 1950.[8]

The second approach to treating hypertension – dilating the diameter of the arteries so less pressure is required to push the blood around the body – involved an operation to cut the nerves that control the diameter of the arteries in the legs (a bilateral lumbar sympathectomy). This operation was a major procedure and so was limited to those who were still fairly fit and young.[9]

The limitations of these treatments are self-evident, so in the post-war years research chemists in the burgeoning pharmaceutical industry started to look for chemical compounds that might work in similar ways. The first, pentaquine – a drug originally used in the treatment of malaria – was introduced in 1947, to be followed by several others – hydrallazine, reserpine, guanethidine and methyldopa. All these drugs were, to a greater or lesser extent, effective, but their widespread use was constrained by their side-effects. Most people with raised blood pressure feel completely well, so the prospect of taking drugs that caused variously a dry mouth, constipation, blurring of vision and impotence was unacceptable, even if they might prevent a potentially catastrophic stroke in the future. Hypertension would only become a treatable disease when the drugs used to lower blood pressure interfered so little with the person's life that they would be prepared to take them for long periods. The two that eventually fulfilled these criteria – and thus made preventing strokes a practical proposition – were the diuretic (or water pill) chlorothiazide, which lowers the blood pressure by reducing the volume of blood in the circulation, and the 'beta blocker' propranolol, which theoretically should have raised the blood pressure by narrowing the diameter of the arteries, but turned out to lower it instead.

The story of chlorothiazide's discovery is as follows: soon after the development in the 1930s of the sulphonamides for the treatment of bacterial infection, some patients reported the unusual side-effect of passing large amounts of urine. In 1949, Dr William Schwartz put this side-effect to practical use, giving sulphonamides to three patients with heart failure, in whom the fluid accumulates in the lungs to cause shortness of breath. The daily volume of their urine soared, the fluid in their lungs dispersed and their breathlessness and other symptoms improved. Regrettably, Dr Schwartz observed the drug was 'too toxic for prolonged or routine use'.[10] However, a research chemist, Karl H. Beyer, realised that if he could find a related compound that had the same properties but was non-toxic, it could, by reducing the volume of blood in the circulation, be the long-awaited 'magic cure' for hypertension. The chemistry involved was sophisticated but essentially routine: take the sulphonamide compound, modify it in some way, give it to dogs and see whether it increases the amount of urine they pro-duce. 'It seemed only a matter of time and effort until we found what we were looking for,' which they did in the form of chlorothiazide, 'the best-behaved compound we had ever worked on from the standpoint of safety and efficacy'.[11] When given to ten hypertensive patients, their blood pressure fell back to normal levels within a couple of days. 'Side-effects were mild and infrequent.'[12]

The second drug, propranolol, was almost unique in the annals of drug discovery in being purposefully designed rather being discovered by accident. Its origin and the name of the group of drugs to which it belongs – the 'beta blockers' – lay in the phenomenon whereby the hormone adrenaline has differ-ent effects on different tissues, depending on whether it interacts with an 'alpha' or 'beta' receptor. Its action on the beta receptors in the blood vessels is to cause them to dilate and on the heart is to increase the rate and forcefulness of its con-tractions.[13] In the mid-1950s, the British research chemist (and subsequent Nobel Prize-winner) James Black perceived the enormous therapeutic potential of antagonising this effect (reducing the forcefulness of the contraction of the heart) for the treatment of angina. If he could find a drug that blocked the action of adrenaline on the beta receptors to the heart – a 'beta blocker' – then, theoretically, it should increase the amount of exercise a patient could take before being limited by chest pain.[14]

The drawback of this approach was that the same 'beta blockers' would also antagonise the dilating action of adrenaline on the beta receptors in the arteries, causing them to constrict and become narrower which, as has been noted, would necessarily raise the blood pressure. James Black eventually came up with propranolol which, as he had predicted, markedly reduced the symptoms of angina but which, astonishingly, had the reverse effect on blood pressure than that predicted. Rather than rising, the blood pressure fell.[15] It is not clear precisely who saw that this paradoxical – and quite unexpected – effect could be used in the treatment of hypertension, but as it turned out propranolol worked very well. And so James Black discovered the second 'acceptable' drug for hypertension, albeit for the 'wrong' reasons.

These two drugs, chlorothiazide and propranolol, transformed the treatment of hypertension. Patients with raised blood pressure no longer had to go on the unpalatable rice and fruit diet, or undergo a bilateral sympathectomy to cut the nerves to their legs, or take drugs with unpleasant side-effects. Instead they needed to take, singly or in combination, one or other of these drugs every day. Subsequently further well-tolerated types of drug became available, but the crucial point was that by the mid-1960s hypertension had become a treatable disease.[16]

The very ease with which hypertension could now be treated posed another problem. Drug treatment reduces the incidence of strokes almost to zero, but the situation is much less clear-cut in those whose blood pressure is only marginally elevated, so-called 'mild' hypertension. The question then as to what level of blood pressure merited treatment fuelled a decade-long public and often acrimonious exchange between two of British medicine's leading figures: Robert (Lord) Platt, Professor of Medicine at Manchester University, and Sir George Pickering, Regius Professor of Medicine at Oxford. In essence, Platt maintained that hypertension was a specific illness caused by one or several genes, and that it was possible and indeed necessary to distinguish between those with a 'normal' blood pressure and those with an 'abnormal' one, and only to treat the latter group. Not so, responded Sir George Pickering; hypertension was not an 'illness' in the commonly accepted sense of the term, but there was a continuous gradient of risk relating blood pressure to the chance of a stroke. Clearly the higher the blood pressure the greater that risk became, but any cut-off point between those who needed treatment and those who did not, between the 'normal' and the 'abnormal', was arbitrary. Hypertension was thus not an illness but a matter of opinion.[17]

This argument might seem esoteric but its implications are not. If Pickering were right then logically anyone whose blood pressure was higher than that of the 'average' should benefit from having their blood pressure lowered, leading to the claim following one important study that 24 million United States citizens had 'hypertension' that was either 'undetected, untreated, or inadequately treated'. This was clearly good news for the pharmaceutical industry who had sponsored the study, for the prospect of finding 24 million as yet undiscovered patients and treating them with regular medication for life was nothing other than a gold mine. The catch was that the evidence of benefit from treating the millions with 'mild' hypertension was less than compelling.[18]

There are two predictable effects of telling someone his raised blood pressure needs treatment. The first is to make him worry about his health and be more aware of his mortality. Such fears are likely to be hidden and so difficult to measure, but a study of 5,000 steelworkers in 1978 found 'dramatically increased rates of absenteeism where steelworkers are labelled hypertensive'. Those 'labelled' as having raised blood pressure tended to see themselves as being vulnerable to having a stroke, which naturally encouraged their adoption of a 'sick role'.[19] The second predictable adverse consequence is that no matter how relatively free of side-effects chlorothiazide and propranolol (and similar drugs) might be, they still prove unacceptable to a small percentage of those to whom they are prescribed. Both drugs cause lethargy, dizziness and headache in 5 per cent of those taking them and – in men – impotence in 20 per cent and 6 per cent respectively.[20] When these drugs are being taken by millions of people the cumulative burden of these adverse effects is 'not inconsiderable'. Is it worth it?

Back in 1967 the study of US military veterans had had little difficulty in showing in just 140 patients that the treatment of markedly raised blood pressure for only a year could reduce the rate of strokes almost to zero. But the results of treating those with 'mild' hypertension conducted by the Medical Research Council in Britain in the early 1980s were much more equivocal: it was necessary to treat 850 people for one year to prevent one stroke. Thus 849 people out of 850 taking medication in any one year would not expect to benefit.[21]

Despite these very limited benefits from treating mild hypertension, the 'Pickering paradigm' of 'the-lower-the-blood-pressure-the-better' prevailed. Necessarily, when hypertension is defined as any level higher than the average, then surreal numbers of people have to take blood-pressure-lowering medication and indeed hypertension has become much the commonest cause for medical consultation and drug prescription. By 1996 more than one in three Americans between the age of thirty-five and seventy-four were taking medication to lower their blood pressure, generating an annual revenue for the pharmaceutical industry of $6 billion.[22] This trend would now seem unstoppable, even though it now appears that Pickering was wrong and Platt was right. Hypertension is not just a blood pressure higher than 'the average', but a discrete illness with a strong genetic component.[23]

In the 1990s, the same argument was to be repeated, but this time with cholesterol, where again the benefits of treating those with high levels were extrapolated downwards. The notion of 'the lower the cholesterol, the better' prevailed and millions started taking cholesterol-lowering drugs. And so it is that the great – and very desirable – project of preventing strokes by treating hypertension has enormously expanded the scope of medicine from treating the sick to finding, in the majority who are well, 'illnesses' they do not necessarily have, and treating them at enormous cost.

8

1971 : Curing Childhood Cancer

In medicine – as in life – some problems are more complex than others, and science being the art of the soluble it is only sensible to leave the apparently intractable aside hoping, perhaps, that at some time in the future something will happen to open the doors to their resolution. It is, nonetheless, a distinctive feature of post-war medicine that many doctors and scientists attempted, against all the odds, to take on 'the insoluble'. Here the long march in the search for the cure for childhood cancer, and Acute Lymphoblastic Leukaemia (ALL) in particular, stands in a league of its own. Whereas the effectiveness of the other discoveries in the post-war years – such as antibiotics and steroids – were immediately apparent, the anti-cancer drugs were different. They worked, but not very well, prolonging the life of a child by, at the most, a few months. So the cure of ALL, as will be seen, required not just one drug discovery but four quite separate ones combined together. Further, it was not merely sufficient to dispense these drugs and observe what happened; rather, a vast intellectual machine had to be created to assess the outcome of different treatment combinations to reveal the small incremental gains that eventually made ALL a treatable disease. Finally, the patients involved were children and the drugs very toxic. It needed an extraordinary sense of purpose to persist when most doctors believed that inflicting nasty drugs on children to prolong by only a few months a lethal illness was immoral. For all these reasons the cure of ALL ranks as the most impressive achievement of the post-war years.

Acute Lymphoblastic Leukaemia is a malignant proliferation of lymphoblasts (precursors of the white blood cells that are made in the bone marrow), which spill out into the blood stream. Patients – usually children around the age of five or six – died within three months from a combination of symptoms caused by this lymphoblastic proliferation, which packed out the bone marrow, thus preventing the formation of the other components of the blood: the reduction of red blood cells resulted in anaemia, the paucity of platelets caused haemorrhage and the absence of normal white blood cells created a predisposition to infection. The children were pale and weak and short of breath because of the anaemia, they bruised easily because of the low platelets and the slightest injury could precipitate a major haemorrhage into a joint or even the brain. It was, however, their vulnerability to infection that posed the greatest risk, as they were defenceless against the bacteria that cause meningitis or septicaemia. The 'inevitable' could be postponed for a month or two, with blood transfusions to correct the anaemia and antibiotics to treat these infections. But so dismal was the prognosis that some doctors even disputed whether these supportive treatments should be given. Professor David Galton of London's Hammersmith Hospital summarises the prevailing pessimistic view at that time: 'Children were sent home as soon as they were discovered to have the disease. Even blood transfusions might be withheld on the grounds that it only kept the child alive to suffer more in the last few weeks.'[1]

From the first attempts to treat ALL in 1945 it took more than twenty-five years before a truly awesome combination of chemotherapy (or 'chemo') with cytotoxic (cell-killing) drugs and radiotherapy were shown to be capable of curing the disease.[2] The origins and rationale of this treatment will be considered in detail later but in broad outline it took the following form. The treatment started with a massive assault on the leukaemic cells in the bone marrow, with high doses of steroids and the cytotoxic drug, vincristine, lasting six weeks. This was followed by a further week of daily injections of a cocktail of three further cytotoxic drugs: 6-mercaptopurine (6-mp), methotrexate (MTX) and cyclophosphamide. Next came two weeks of radiation treatment directly to the brain and five doses of MTX were injected directly into the spinal fluid. This regimen, which eliminated the leukaemic cells from the blood stream in 90 per cent of the children, was called 'remission induction' (i.e. it induced a 'remission' of the disease) and was followed by 'maintenance therapy', two years of continuing treatment to keep the bone marrow free of leukaemic cells – weekly injections of the cocktail of three cytotoxic drugs already mentioned at lower doses, interspersed every ten weeks by 'pulses' of the 'induction' regime (steroids and vincristine) for fourteen days.

It is impossible to convey the physical and psychological trauma this regime imposed on the young patients and their parents. Each dose of treatment was followed by nausea and vomiting of such severity that many children were unable to eat and became malnourished, and stopped growing and ceased to put on weight. Then there were the side-effects caused by the action of the drugs, which not only poisoned the leukaemic cells but also the healthy tissues of the body: the children's hair fell out, their mouths were filled with painful ulcers, they developed chronic diarrhoea and cystitis. It is not for nothing that chemo has been described as 'bottled death'.[3]

This terrible burden of physical suffering would be just acceptable were it to result in a cure, but there was absolutely no certainty that this would be the case. Prior to the introduction of this particular regime of treatment in 1967, a survey of nearly 1,000 children treated over the previous two decades found that only two could be described as having been cured – having survived for more than five years – and one of these subsequently relapsed and died. This left an overall cure rate of 0.07 per cent.[4] Looking back now, it seems astonishing that those responsible for devising this highly toxic regime, Dr Donald Pinkel and his colleagues at St Jude's Hospital in Memphis, should have imposed it on these desperately ill

children, not least because of the profound scepticism of his
professional colleagues that 'success' – a major improvement in
the prospects of survival – was achievable. This ambivalence is
well caught by the contribution of a fellow specialist, Dr Wolf
Zuelzer, a paediatrician at the children's hospital in Michigan,
in his contribution at an international conference on
leukaemia: 'The side-effects of treatment outweigh those
directly attributable to the disease,' he observed, and after
reviewing recent progress he could only express the hope that
'others might find grounds for greater optimism than I have
been able to distil from the facts now at hand'.[5] But unknown
to Zuelzer the 1967 protocol of treatment devised by Pinkel
would indeed produce the 'cures' that many had begun to
think might elude them for ever, improving the cure rate from
0.07 per cent to over 50 per cent. 'We conclude from the
results of this study that complete remission of childhood ALL
is significantly prolonged by intensive combination chemotherapy. The toxicity and infection encountered are significant but
certainly not prohibitive in view of the results obtained,' Pinkel
observed in 1971, and everyone agreed. The following year,
when he gave the annual guest lecture at the Leukaemia
Research Fund in London, he outlined to an 'entranced audience' of doctors from all parts of Britain the clinical studies
co-ordinated at St Jude's over many years.[6] 'There is now no
place for the palliative treatment of leukaemia,' The Lancet commented in an editorial. 'Dr Pinkel's results are impressive, not
least for the methodical manner in which seemingly intractable
problems have been solved at every stage.'[7]

To properly appreciate Pinkel's achievement, it is necessary to
clarify the fundamental problems of treating cancer. When a
malignant tumour is limited to one part of the body – say the
breast or the gut – it can be removed and, with luck, cured,
either by surgery or radiotherapy. But when the cancer is dispersed – as with acute leukaemia (and the same applies to any
cancer that has spread or 'metastasised') – the only hope lies in
drug treatment, which can selectively kill the cancer cells wherever they might be. This would be relatively straightforward
were the cancer cells different in some special way that could be

interfered with, thus making it possible to kill them while leaving the healthy cells untouched. But though cancer cells are indeed different from normal ones, it has never been possible to turn those differences to therapeutic advantage. Rather, all drugs that kill cancer cells interfere with their DNA, which necessarily means they will also interfere with the DNA of normal cells. Nor indeed, as was once thought, do cancer cells divide and multiply more quickly, which would at least make them more vulnerable to drug treatments. The problem was aptly summarised by Professor W. H. Woglom, a distinguished cancer researcher, back in 1945: 'Those who have not been trained in chemistry or medicine may not realise how difficult the problem really is. It is almost, not quite, but almost as hard as finding some agent that will dissolve away the left ear but leave the right ear untouched.' In the thirty years following Woglom's disheartening analogy, hundreds of thousands of chemicals were investigated for their anti-cancer activity of which a handful, thirty or so, were found to be of any value. Virtually all owe their origins to chance observation or luck.

The first, starting at the beginning, was nitrogen mustard. At the outbreak of the Second World War, it was anticipated that the Axis powers, Germany and Japan, would resort to chemical warfare – and the use of mustard gas in particular – on a massive scale. Alarmed at the prospect, the US military authorities set up the Chemical Warfare Service to find an antidote. The immediate incapacitating effect of mustard gas is to cause a severe watery inflammation of the eyes (conjunctivitis) and painful blistering of the skin. Its lethality, however, results from its effect on the bone marrow, where it destroys developing blood cells, leaving its victims vulnerable to haemorrhage and overwhelming infections. These effects had first been documented at the close of the First World War and were to be confirmed in 1943 when a German raid on the US fleet in Bari harbour on the Italian peninsula sank a ship – the *Harvey* – with 100 tonnes of mustard gas on board.[8] In a medical report compiled on those exposed to the gas, Colonel Stewart Alexander of the US Medical Corps observed 'the effects upon the white blood cells was most severe – on the third or fourth day the count began to drop in a steep downward trend'.[9]

But if nitrogen mustard kills off the white cells in the bone marrow, might it not also reduce the malignant proliferation of white cells that occur in patients with leukaemia or lymphoma? As part of the US military research programme, two young scientists, Alfred Gilman and Louis Goodman of Yale University (later to become famous for their classic text book *The Pharmacological Basis of Therapeutics*), decided to give nitrogen mustard to 'one lone mouse' with an advanced lymphoma (cancer of the lymph glands) and 'after just two administrations of the compound the tumour began to soften and regress to such an extent it could no longer be palpated'.

'The results of this experiment,' Gilman recalled twenty years later, 'were sufficiently encouraging to consider a therapeutic trial in man.' And so the first cancer patient to be treated with chemotherapy was Mr J.D., a 48-year-old silversmith with a lymphosarcoma. He had massive swelling of the lymph nodes around his face, making chewing and swallowing impossible; in his armpits, such that he was unable to bring his arms down to his side; and within his chest, blocking the return of the blood to the heart causing his head and neck to swell.

The research programme with nitrogen mustard was classified as 'Top Secret', so neither Mr J.D. nor his doctor were allowed to know the nature of the chemical with which he was to be treated. The entry on his chart simply read 'o.1mg per kg compound X given intravenously'. The treatment lasted ten days in all, by which time the massive swellings had evaporated and 'all signs and symptoms due to the disease disappeared'. A month later the tumour recurred, requiring a further course of therapy. He lived on for another two months, 'his death hastened by the untoward effect of the drug on his bone marrow', i.e. the nitrogen mustard, besides killing off the lymphoma cells, had also destroyed the platelets and white cells in the bone marrow. This experience accurately anticipated the results of cancer chemotherapy over the next twenty years, producing at first a short-lived remission but culminating in death, either from recurrence of the disease or the toxicity of the drug.[10]

Nonetheless, this was a more auspicious beginning than might at first appear. First the spectacle of dying patients – such as Mr J.D. – being rescued from their imminent demise by a drug that appeared to 'melt away' the tumour is emotionally very resonant, comparable to watching a miracle take place before one's eyes – albeit a temporary one. The significance of even a short remission should not be overlooked. Professor David Galton recalls that when the poet Michael Roberts developed leukaemia in the late 1940s, his wife, Janet Adam Smith, sought the help of a friend, Alexander Haddow, head of Britain's leading cancer research institute, who just happened to have a supply of the 'latest drug', aminopterin. Following treatment, Michael Roberts had nearly three good months, but when the relapse came he deteriorated very rapidly. Haddow was worried that the extra three months might have been a burden, more of a misery than a benefit, but Janet Adam Smith told him that the brief remission had given them some of the best days of their lives.[11]

The second feature of Mr J.D.'s treatment concerned the drug itself. Nitrogen mustard turned out to be 'far too toxic' even for the treatment of cancer, but modification of its chemical structure led to a whole group of anti-cancer drugs appearing in the next decade, including thiotepa (1950), chlorambucil (1953), melphalan (1953) and cyclophosphamide (1957). But the third and most significant consequence of Mr J.D.'s three-month remission was that his experimental treatment had been carried out under the auspices of the Director of the Chemical Warfare Service, Cornelius 'Dusty' Rhoads. At the end of the war, when the Service was closed down, Dr Rhoads realised the experience gained by the scientists and doctors he had employed could be put to best use within an organisation specifically created to conduct research into the treatment of cancer.[12] He persuaded the philanthropists Alfred Sloane and Charles Kettering to put up the money and in 1948 the Sloane–Kettering Institute was founded, lavishly equipped with more than 100 laboratories. Here, under Dr Rhoads's leadership, the ex-employees of the Chemical Warfare Service came together and over the following twenty years the pursuit of a 'cure' for cancer became serious science. That cure in the form of Pinkel's results of his treatment of ALL at St Jude's Hospital in 1971 was still twenty-six years away. The intervening years can be divided into three phases. During Phase I, several more anti-cancer drugs were discovered. Phase II started in the mid-1950s, by when it had become clear how difficult it was to assess the relative value (if any) of these new drugs without their systematic evaluation on a major scale through the means of 'the clinical trial'. In Phase III, starting around 1962, the new drugs and the methods of evaluating them were combined for 'the final push'.

Phase I: The Discovery of Anti-Cancer Drugs

Aminopterin: The next important anti-cancer drug after nitrogen mustard was aminopterin, introduced in 1948 by Sidney Farber, Professor of Pathology at Harvard Medical School and the 'godfather of cancer treatment'.

Its origins were as follows. In 1933 a British physician working in Bombay, Dr Lucy Wills, identified a particular type of anaemia in textile workers which she attributed to their grinding poverty and grossly deficient diet. The anaemia, she found, could be reversed by the consumption of Marmite, which is made from purest yeast which, she inferred, must contain some as yet unidentified vital nutritional factor or vitamin.[13] This was identified as folic acid ten years later.[14] In 1945, when virtually every newly discovered compound was being tested for its potential as an anti-cancer drug, Sidney Farber gave this newly discovered vitamin to patients with a variety of advanced cancers. It had no effect, except in seven patients with leukaemia in whom regrettably it had the reverse effect of that intended, accelerating their demise. 'Post-mortem studies of the bone marrow showed acceleration of the leukaemic process to a degree not encountered in 200 autopsies of children who had not been given folic acid,' he wrote.[15] Farber, rather than being downhearted, made an inspired, imaginative guess that may seem obvious now but certainly was not at the time: if the vitamin folic acid made leukaemia worse, then a chemical that antagonised it might have the originally desired effect of treating the disease. He turned to Dr Y. Subba Row of the pharmaceutical company Lederle, who had worked out the chemical structure of folic acid, and asked if it were possible to make a compound that was similar to folic acid, but sufficiently different that it could act as a 'false' building brick and thus block the vitamin's action on the leukaemic cells. Subba Row duly obliged and produced a series of such compounds. Farber gave one of them, aminopterin, to sixteen children with acute leukaemia, ten of whom showed 'clinical evidence of improvement'.[16] Three years later in 1949 aminopterin was superseded by a more effective variant known as methotrexate.

Steroids: In 1949 Philip Hench of the Mayo Clinic reported the apparently miraculous effect of cortisone in patients crippled with rheumatoid arthritis, and which was subsequently found to be effective in so many other illnesses. It was only natural for Farber to try it in children with leukaemia. In 1950 he reported the first case of a five-year-old boy who, having failed to improve with aminopterin, went into remission with an injection of ACTH that stimulates the adrenal glands to increase the amount of naturally occurring steroids in the body.[17]

Antibiotics (actinomycin): If steroids could induce remission in leukaemia, then there was every reason to try the second main pillar of the therapeutic revolution – antibiotics – especially those that had been put aside as being too toxic. In the early 1950s Selman Waksman, the discoverer of streptomycin, provided Farber with a related compound, dactinomycin, which was used to treat a boy dying from Wilm's tumour of the kidney with metastases in both lungs. He died within three weeks but 'post-mortem examination revealed what was at the time unique in our experience – the metastasis had disappeared and in many areas of the lung had been replaced by a fibrous material'.[18] Actinomycin C, as the drug became known, was subsequently shown not only to cure Wilm's tumour but also to be effective against the cancer of the placenta choriocarcinoma, cancer of the testes and Ewing's sarcoma, a childhood tumour of the bone. Nor was this the end of the antibiotic contribution to anti-cancer therapy, for ten years later two others – daunomycin and bleomycin – were found to be effective against other cancers.[19]

6-mercaptopurine: 6-mp emerged from the immensely successful collaboration between George Hitchings and Gertrude Elion over four decades, when they synthesised drugs that interfered in one way or another with DNA by acting as false building blocks for one of its main constituents, purine. It ranks as one of the most significant of all drug discoveries, not only inducing and maintaining remission in leukaemia and other cancers but, a decade later, was found to be a powerful immunosuppressant, thus making kidney transplantation feasible.[20]

The Rest: Virtually all the other anti-cancer drugs were 'stumbled upon', either emerging from screening programmes of chemicals or by accident. In 1954, serum taken from guinea pigs was noted to cause regression of tumours in mice and rats and the active ingredient L-asparaginase was identified eight years later.[21] In the West Indies a tea made from the leaves of the white-flowered periwinkle, *vinca rosa*, was reputed to help patients with diabetes. Doctors at the University of Western Ontario, hoping this might lead to an alternative to insulin, were disappointed to find that it had no measurable effect on reducing the blood sugar, but the more they increased the dose, the more their experimental animals died from multiple abscesses caused, they discovered, by a precipitous fall in the white blood count. The same thought occurred to them as had struck the early investigators of nitrogen mustard, that anything that destroys white blood cells might antagonise their malignant proliferation and thus might be a useful treatment for leukaemia. And so vincristine was discovered, which as will be seen, played a particularly important role in the final cure of leukaemia.[22] Finally, there was the most circumstantial and fortuitous discovery of all – platinum. When investigating whether electricity might influence the growth of bacteria, Barnett Rosenberg of Michigan State University placed samples of the bacterium *E. coli* in a bath of water and electrocuted them by a current passing between two platinum electrodes. When the bugs were examined after a couple of hours it was obvious they had ceased to divide (there was no 'pinching of the waist') but their growth was unimpaired and they had formed into long filaments up to 300 times their normal length. This was such an extraordinary phenomenon that it was only natural to find out what might be responsible. Rosenberg eliminated the obvious possibilities – the electric current itself, the temperature and acidity of the bath – concluding finally that the platinum on the electrodes must be responsible.[23] Cisplatin – a chemical derivative of platinum – was subsequently shown to interfere with DNA prior to the division of the cell, and thus to be a potent anti-cancer agent, especially against tumours of the testes and ovaries.

Phase II: Evaluating Anti-Cancer Drugs

The common theme running through the discovery of these cancer drugs was that there was no common theme. Their origins were so bizarre that it was only natural to wonder how many more there might be waiting 'out there' and perhaps the most potent of all was still to be found, including the 'magic bullet' that would miraculously cure cancer just as antibiotics had miraculously cured infectious diseases. It seemed only sensible to rationalise the process and test every conceivable chemical. Accordingly in 1954, the United States Congress made the funds available to the National Cancer Institute for the creation of a Cancer Chemotherapy National Service Center, which over the next decade was to screen 82,700 synthetic chemicals, 115,000 fermentation products and 17,200 plant products – 214,900 in total – for their anti-cancer potential. Further, the need to test these anti-cancer drugs led to the formation of 'an extraordinary clinical trials network': the establishment of a unique co-operative venture where standard protocols for the treatment of leukaemia and lymphoma were drawn up comparing one combination of drugs with another.[24]

Phase III: The Final Steps

By the late 1950s the situation appeared, at least in retrospect, quite hopeful. There were now several drugs, each of which individually could induce a remission in leukaemia, albeit only a short-lived one. Next, thanks to the largesse of Congress, the NCI was now flush with funds. All that was needed for the answer to fall out was the setting up of clinical trials using appropriate combinations of drugs. There were in addition some straws in the wind of cancers – albeit quite unusual ones – that could be cured by a single anti-cancer drug including the cancer of the placenta, choriocarcinoma, and a childhood cancer common in East Africa, Burkitt's lymphoma.[25]

Needless to say, this was not the prevailing view at the time. Chemotherapy seemed to have achieved very little other than prolonging the miserable lives of children for a few more months. For all anybody knew, the chemotherapy approach might be a complete red herring and the 'answer' might lie elsewhere. Leukaemia in mice had been shown to be caused by a virus, so perhaps the thrust of medical research should be towards identifying a similar infectious cause among humans. Indeed, the future direction of chemotherapy was not at all clear; the greater its even very limited success, the more intractable the problem seemed to be. First there was the issue of drug resistance, where a drug that 'first time round' induced a remission turned out to be completely ineffective when given on the second or subsequent occasions. Somehow the leukaemic cells must acquire the means of counteracting its anti-cancer effects – but how? The only possible solution – that had proved necessary in the antibiotic treatment of tuberculosis – was to use several drugs at once, but this would lead to unacceptable levels of toxicity. Next, and even more seriously, some children were now living just long enough to die from a complication that had never been seen before – the leukaemic cells infiltrated the brain and surrounding tissues with predictably dire results, rapidly leading to coma and death. The brain, it emerged, was a 'sanctuary' within which the leukaemic cells could hide protected from the anti-cancer drugs, which were unable to cross from the blood into the brain.[26] Thus, the anti-cancer drugs would also have to be injected directly into the spinal fluid and the brain would have to be irradiated if these 'protected' leukaemic cells were to be eliminated.[27] Even were a child to be subjected to all this there was no guarantee, not even an odds-on chance, that he or she would survive for long enough to make it worthwhile. In such circumstances it is scarcely surprising that the pioneers perceived themselves to be professionally isolated, with many paediatricians openly critical of their experimental therapies: 'We were viewed as being either malicious, or having a screw loose,' recalls Dr Alexander Spiers of London's Hammersmith Hospital.[28]

Beset by all these difficulties, two groups of doctors played a decisive role in 'the final push'. At the National Cancer Institute, Drs Emil Freireich and Emil Frei III provided the intellectual framework with which to proceed. They had found two or more drugs were better than one and, crucially, their toxic effects could be controlled by 'supportive therapy' with blood transfusions and adequate antibiotics. In addition, the cytotoxic drugs turned out to have different effects: steroids and vincristine were relatively non-toxic but the remission they induced did not last as long as those following treatment with the more toxic methotrexate and 6-mp. Perhaps there might be some way of exploiting this effect?[29]

Then there was Dr Sidney Farber and his protégé Dr Donald Pinkel at St Jude's Hospital, the two physicians who had treated more children with leukaemia than everyone else in the world. They were sustained in their difficult task by the perspective that

> the greatest mental peace is obtained by the realisation that a group of doctors and nurses are doing everything that can be done in the light of available knowledge. The needs of the family are met by a policy of complete truth and the only promise that is made is based upon the hope that the next step forward may come in time. [When] the atmosphere is one of guarded optimism based upon actual

achievement, fear is more easy to dispel and to be replaced by a courageous handling of problems.[30]

The breakthrough, when it came, turned out to be philosophical rather than practical: the theoretical demonstration by Dr Howard Skipper of the Sloane–Kettering Institute of how childhood leukaemia should in principle be curable, which transformed the psychological perspective of all involved. For if, as Skipper predicted, 'curing' children of leukaemia was an attainable goal then the dreadful problem of toxicity became less significant. The ends, the cure, justified the means, any means of getting there, even if it required the intensification of treatment to the point where some children would necessarily die from the drugs they were given rather than from their leukaemia.

Skipper had been thinking about cancer for a long time. Like so many of his colleagues his career started in the Chemical Warfare Service, whose Director, Cornelius Rhoads, in his post-war role as head of the Sloane–Kettering Institute, had recruited him to set up an outpost of the Institute in Birmingham, Alabama. Once Skipper had posed the question to himself – What does it take to cure leukaemia? – the answer was obvious: every cancer cell had to be destroyed, as even if a single one were left behind it would double and double again and within a few months there would be more than enough to cause a relapse. The obvious way of killing off the last surviving cancer cell would be to give drugs in sufficient doses and quantities to wipe it out. Skipper, however, perceived that the problem was more subtle than this. The drugs they were using would not eliminate an absolute number of cancer cells each time they were given, but only the same percentage, with significant implications.[31] Consider a combination of drugs capable of killing 99 per cent of leukaemic cells. If there were 1,000,000 leukaemic cells in the bone marrow then, following the first course of treatment, their numbers would fall by 990,000 to just 10,000. But even when the number of leukaemic cells is down to 100, exactly the same dosage of drugs would only knock out the 99 cells and still leave one remaining. This turned out to be an instance of a well-known

biological phenomenon – 'first order kinetics' – best illustrated
by the following analogy:

> Imagine a little boy standing outside a hen house in which
> a thousand eggs were scattered at random. The boy has an
> unlimited supply of small nails. He runs back and forth, and
> without aiming at anything in particular, throws the nails
> through the chicken wire. What would be expected to
> happen? Most of the nails would probably strike the wire
> and fall outside. Of the few that go directly through, each
> egg is likely to be struck many times before it is broken but
> sooner or later it will receive a fatal blow. Then suppose
> that by the time the boy has thrown a bushel of nails, nine
> hundred of the thousand eggs have been broken. The nails
> continue to come in as thick and fast as ever but each nail
> has a smaller chance of breaking an egg because there are
> only a tenth as many eggs. Each egg, however, gets hit just
> as often as it did before and so we may expect the second
> bushel of nails to break about ninety of the remaining one
> hundred eggs. And so on.[32]

If the law of 'first order kinetics' was correct, then the prevailing method of inducing a remission with one drug or a
combination of drugs, and then reducing the dosage to cut
down the danger of drug toxicity, was clearly wrong. Skipper's
theoretical view argued the contrary. Once remission had been
induced then the dose of drugs had to be maintained at as
high a level as possible because the fewer the leukaemic cells
there were in the body the more difficult it was to kill them.
Armed with this theoretical perspective Freireich and Frei at
the NCI fashioned the vital drug protocol: relatively non-toxic
vincristine and steroids (prednisone) would be used first to
induce a remission, but the leukaemia cells would then be hit
again and again with methotrexate and 6-mp, with treatment
continuing for two to three years in the hope of eliminating
'the last surviving cancer cell'.

In Memphis at St Jude's Hospital, Dr Pinkel went one step
further by also giving radiotherapy to the 'sanctuary' of the

brain and methotrexate directly into the spinal fluid in the hope of eliminating any leukaemic cells that might be residing there. He started this new regime in 1962 but the dose of radiation he chose failed to prevent relapse.[33] He responded by doubling the dose and that did the trick, reducing the incidence of relapse in the brain twenty-fold. With this he was able to report, as already described, that the prevailing 'cure rate' of leukaemia (children surviving more than five years) of 0.07 per cent in 1962 had leaped to more than 50 per cent.[34] Nor was that the end. For the next twenty years, yet further improvements emerged from the rigorous analysis of new drug protocols where various combinations of drugs were juggled around in endless combinations, eventually pushing the cure rate up to 71 per cent.[35]

The cure of ALL is proof of the power of science to solve the apparently insoluble. But science can certainly not claim all the credit, for many aspects of the cure of ALL remain frankly inexplicable, as Pinkel himself acknowledged in a lecture in 1979.[36] Firstly, and obviously, ALL could not have been cured without the anti-cancer drugs developed between 1945 and 1960 but these, with the exception of 6-mp, were in one way or another all discovered by 'accident'.

Secondly, there is the question of their mode of action. Here Donald Pinkel, perhaps surprisingly, comments on 'the scant knowledge of how anti-leukaemic drugs work in humans'. Virtually all interfere with the DNA of the cell and therefore the ability of the cancer cell to divide. In the early days, when it was thought that leukaemic cells divided more rapidly than normal cells, this provided an obvious rationale for their anti-cancer activity. But, in fact, leukaemic cells divide more slowly than normal cells, which makes it difficult to understand precisely how they work. There are, of course, various other possibilities. The self-repair mechanism of cancer cells can be defective, making them less able to correct the damage to their DNA caused by the anti-cancer drugs.[37] But there is also a suggestion that some of the drugs might have some 'unknown' anti-cancer activity quite separate from interfering with DNA. As one doctor observed: 'I am not convinced the action of various drugs is indeed restricted to the reproductive mechanism of the cells.

Anyone who has seen the rapid shrinkage of leukaemic infiltration and the explosive destruction at the microscopic level must keep an open mind on the question.'[38] Finally, Dr Pinkel was frankly sceptical that medical treatment alone could explain the cure of ALL. He speculated instead that 'leukaemic therapy in children may suppress the lymphocytic proliferation of ALL until the bodies' own control mechanism becomes operative'.

Following the eventual success of the long march towards a cure of ALL, there was every reason to be optimistic about the future. 'The next ten years will be wonderful ones for cancer therapy,' Sidney Farber told *Newsweek* columnist Stewart Alsop – himself a leukaemia survivor – 'the time could come quite soon when the beast will be tamed . . . surely it is worth a major national effort to speed the coming of that time.'[39] The 'major national effort' materialised immediately in the form of President Richard Nixon's 'War Against Cancer'. Nixon, keen to outflank potential presidential candidate Senator Ted Kennedy, proclaimed in his State of the Union message in 1971: 'The time has come when the same kind of concerted effort that split the atom and took man to the Moon should be turned towards conquering this dreaded disease. Let us make a total commitment to achieve that goal.' And so two days before Christmas 1971 he signed a Congressional bill that would over the next decade increase federal funding for the National Cancer Institute from $400 million to nearly $1 billion dollars a year.

Cancer research was now awash with funds. There was certainly much to do to improve on the results already achieved by Donald Pinkel and to apply the chemo approach to other cancers known to be sensitive to drugs: lymphomas, rare childhood cancers like osteosarcoma, leukaemia in adults, and testicular cancer.[40] The results were certainly impressive, but the problem was these cancers only represented a tiny fraction of the total, less than 1 per cent. If the 'War Against Cancer' was to be won, this form of treatment also had to be applied to all those with the much commoner types of cancer of the lung, breast, gut, the so-called 'solid' tumours that arise from 'solid' organs, which had (or might) spread or metastasise throughout the body.

Confronted by this challenge, bright young doctors flocked to join the newly created speciality of oncology, but there was never the slightest possibility they would achieve similar results. These solid tumours are biologically entirely different from the treatable cancers like ALL. Their causation is intimately bound up with the inevitability of ageing (the risk of getting cancer increases incrementally with each passing decade), so it was as unrealistic to suggest they might be curable on a large scale as it would be to say that ageing itself was curable.

Further, solid tumours respond poorly – if at all – to the anti-cancer drugs. This 'resistance' – which contrasts so markedly with the 'sensitivity' of leukaemic cells – can be attributed to their different origin. Most solid tumours arise from tissues that are exposed to the outside world, such as the larynx, lung, stomach or colon. These tissues must be robust and plentifully endowed with mechanisms to eliminate toxins to which they are exposed, which obviously include cytotoxic drugs. 'Sensitive' cancers by contrast – such as those arising from the blood – are contained within the body and so, not requiring mechanisms to protect themselves against toxic exposure, are unable to defend themselves against the onslaught of anti-cancer drugs.

It is a reflection of the enormous optimism generated by the ALL breakthrough that these clear limitations to the applications of chemo to the solid tumours were scarcely recognised. There was, on the contrary, more than enough money from the NCI to pay for legions of researchers to investigate the effects of treatment in clinical trials, just as they had done so successfully with ALL and there were more than enough oncologists to test out these new treatments on the solid tumours.[41] Two factors fuelled this enthusiasm for chemo. First it offered hope – or rather the appearance of hope – to patients with advanced cancer and was at least 'something else that could be done which might make a difference'. And if it did not work, the doctors could reassure themselves with the argument that they had not quite yet got the magic formula right, the correct combination of drugs given in the correct dosage to crack this particular cancer.

The results were predictably appalling, with those receiving chemotherapy dying more rapidly and with a much worse quality of life than those receiving no therapy.[42] The blindness of oncologists to what they were doing is well exemplified by a 1983 report claiming that chemo was no more toxic to the elderly than to the young, so they should receive chemo at maximum doses. Curiously the author of this report, Dr Colin Beg of Harvard University, felt it unnecessary to make any reference to the results of treatment, where only 20 per cent of elderly cancer patients have any response to treatment (i.e. 80 per cent do not) and the duration of survival with treatment was on average only six months.[43] In Britain Tim McElwain of London's Royal Marsden Hospital commented on 'the confusion of busyness with progress . . . with nasty drugs being thrown at unfortunate patients with very little evidence of gain'. The remorseless litany of failure generated two very different responses on either side of the Atlantic. In the United States the oncologists remained bullish, making exaggerated and readily refutable claims about the benefits of chemotherapy. In Britain, by contrast, where there was no financial incentive for doctors to prescribe chemo and therefore to justify its use, there was more a mood of self-doubt and soul-searching. In 1984 Professor J. S. Malpas of St Bartholomew's Hospital described oncology 'as a child of much promise of which much was expected . . . which it could be said has failed to live up to expectations'.[44]

Indeed it was not until the mid-1990s that modest improvements of around 10 per cent in survival in patients with some types of solid tumour provided at least some justification for the widespread use of chemotherapy.[45]

9

1978: THE FIRST 'TEST-TUBE' BABY

The burgeoning prestige of medicine in the post-war years was grounded not only in its substantial achievements, but the perception that some of those achievements – such as heart transplants and 'test-tube' babies – verged on the miraculous. And it was extraordinary to be able to remove a man's ailing heart and replace it with another, and to facilitate the act of procreation and thus fulfil for the infertile the deep human need to have children.

It is thus only logical to infer that those responsible must be very clever and the possibilities of what medicine could achieve – given sufficient funds – must be limitless. The reality as seen repeatedly with the 'definitive' moments of post-war medicine was rather different. The achievements did not arise from a profound understanding of the nature of medical problems but, more often than not, from chance or luck or some technological development. And the same is true for the events leading up to the birth of Louise Joy Brown, the first 'test-tube' baby conceived by 'in vitro fertilisation', usually shortened to IVF.

Fertilisation 'in vitro' means 'in a glass tube' to distinguish it from fertilisation 'in vivo' – in the living body. IVF might seem to be an amazing scientific breakthrough, but is little more than a sophisticated piece of plumbing for women with blocked fallopian tubes, whose eggs cannot pass from the ovary down into the uterus to be fertilised by the husband's sperm. The solution to overcoming the blockage – at least in theory – is obvious: obtain an egg from the ovary, add the husband's sperm, then pop the fertilised conceptus back into the uterus through the cervix with the help of a piece of plastic tube. With luck, it will stick. Nature does the rest – the difficult part – where the tiny fertilised egg grows and multiplies to form a foetus made up of billions of cells, each with its own specialised function. Thus the contribution of human agency through the procedure of IVF in initiating the process is important enough, but it cannot bear comparison with the real miracle – the ineffable mysteries of foetal development itself.

This sanguine view of the scientific significance of IVF is not intended to belittle the work of those who did so much to make it happen. Rather the reverse, IVF merits its place in the pantheon of great events of post-war medicine on its own account but also because it illustrates better than anything else the essential attributes and multi-faceted nature of the research from which those 'major events' finally emerged. The first point is how difficult it can be to establish even the simplest facts – that it was indeed possible to fertilise a human egg 'in vitro'. Next there is the crucial role of human personality, and in particular that of its pioneer Bob Edwards, who through the two phases of the development of IVF experienced first nine years and then eight years of bitter disappointment that would have convinced any lesser person to give up in despair. Then there is the essential contribution of the cross-fertilisation of ideas from other disciplines. Bob Edwards did not set out to find a treatment for infertility because of blocked fallopian tubes. His primary interest in the fertilisation of human eggs was the observation of the earliest stages of human development, and this just happened to coincide with the blossoming of research into the use of fertility drugs in women where infertility resulted from a completely different reason – the failure to ovulate, or produce eggs. Thus IVF emerged from the fusion of two quite separate areas of scientific endeavour. Finally, there was, as so often happens, the singular contribution of technological development, in this case the laparoscope, which permitted eggs to be removed from the ovary without the necessity of a major operation. This made IVF a practicable proposition.

Each of these developments warrants closer scrutiny but first, to emphasise why IVF was a definitive moment in post-war medicine, comes a description of the culminating event, the birth of Louise Joy Brown in 1978. The *dramatis personae* in this 'sensational story of the world's first test-tube baby' are Bob Edwards, Reader in Physiology at Cambridge University, and his collaborator Patrick Steptoe, Consultant Obstetrician at Oldham General Hospital; Sheena Steptoe, wife of Patrick Steptoe; and the parents Lesley and John Brown. Just before midnight on Tuesday 25 July 1978, Patrick Steptoe performed a Caesarean on Lesley Brown and delivered Louise Joy, who weighed 5lb 12oz. Meanwhile, elsewhere in the hospital, husband John Brown was sitting in his wife's room with Sheena Steptoe.

A Sister burst in excitedly. 'You may come and see your baby daughter now. A porter will take you along. Your wife is fine.'

'What did you say, Sister?'

'You may go to see your baby daughter as soon as the porter arrives.'

John was speechless. Tears poured down his face. He stood up and banged his clenched fist against a wall. When he regained control, he kissed Sister, he kissed Sheena Steptoe, who was also happily weeping, and ran out of the room. He ran all the way downstairs along the sixty yards of corridor to the operating theatre, followed by the porter and Sheena. There we stood with Louise's cot on a trolley, the baby was lifted into John's arms.

'I can't believe it! I can't believe it!' he cried out. 'I don't know what to say.' He gazed mesmerised at the infant, until someone gently guided the baby back into the cot. Lesley Brown was still peacefully asleep [from the anaesthetic], unable to join in the happy delirium all around.[1]

The powerful emotions elicited by this account are enhanced still further when it is realised that this cameo was the combination of eight bitter years during which Edwards and Steptoe's many attempts at IVF had all ended in failure.

Fertilisation In Vitro

Fertilisation is much the easiest part of IVF: given sufficient numbers of sperm, a mature female egg and the right culture medium success can be almost guaranteed. And yet for thirty years before 1969, when Bob Edwards first showed how it could be done, the fertilisation of human eggs outside the body was thought to be impossible. It is a most curious story.

In 1937 John Rock, the most prominent infertility expert in the United States, anticipated the possibility of IVF in a prescient editorial in the *New England Journal of Medicine*, 'Conception in a Watch Glass' – commenting 'what a boon for the barren woman with closed [blocked] tubes' such a treatment would be.[2] His article was inspired by the work of a colleague, Gregory Pincus of Harvard University – later to become internationally famous for his role in the development of the oral contraceptive pill – who claimed to have performed IVF in rabbits by taking an egg from one rabbit, fertilising it and then replacing it in another unmated rabbit to produce offspring.[3]

Clearly Rock's next step was to see whether he could achieve in humans what Pincus had claimed to have shown in rabbits. Here Pincus had made another important contribution, having shown that human eggs – within a couple of hours of being removed from the ovary and placed in an appropriate medium – began to show the changes in the nucleus indicating they were mature and thus receptive to fertilisation.[4] So, in the six years from 1938 to 1944, Rock, with the help of his assistant Dr Miriam Menkin, removed 800 human eggs from female volunteers undergoing major gynaecological surgery such as hysterectomy and attempted to fertilise them with human sperm. 'On the basis of [Gregory Pincus's] finding we have made numerous attempts to initiate in vitro fertilisation of human ovarian eggs,' Menkin subsequently reported, but the result was 'unremitting failure'.[5] In 1944 she did manage to get one egg to divide to the two-cell stage, which was duly reported in the journal *Science* and generated a lot of correspondence from infertile women:

> Most letters came from relatively young women whose fallopian tubes had been surgically removed. A woman from California wrote that when she was twenty-nine, a surgeon while removing her appendix noted her tubes were 'dried up' – so he removed them. She hoped for 'a modern surgical miracle' that would allow her to have a child. One young woman was devastated when surgery for pelvic inflammatory disease robbed her not only of her tubes and ovaries but of her fiancé as well. He 'wanted children very much,' she wrote. 'We have never married because of this.' Another had thought she was undergoing 'a minor operation' while her soldier husband was overseas to enable her to become pregnant when he returned. Instead she found herself without her fallopian tubes. 'I have never,' she wrote, 'felt this operation was absolutely necessary.' Her husband, as well, was 'deeply grieved about their childlessness'.[6]

But despite the desperate need expressed in these letters Rock and Menkin felt they had no alternative other than to abandon their research project. If it was not possible to predictably fertilise human eggs, there could be no hope it would ever become a realistic treatment for infertility.

There were no further serious attempts at IVF in the immediate post-war years, though in 1951 one of Pincus's scientific collaborators, Min Chang, made an observation that might have explained Menkin's failure: sperm, he argued, first had to be 'capacitated', switched on by a chemical in the fallopian tubes before they were capable of fertilising an egg. 'It is quite clear that fertilisation occurs when the sperm have been in the fallopian tube for six hours, which is perhaps required in humans for a physiological change in the sperm enabling them to achieve fertilising capacity,' he wrote.[7] It was in retrospect such an obvious explanation but it made the possibility of IVF as a treatment for infertility even more remote. The 'capacitating chemical' was not known, so somehow it would be necessary first to place the husband's sperm in a woman's fallopian tube for several hours to allow 'capacitation' to take place. The sperm would then have to be removed and placed with the egg in the hope that fertilisation would occur. Such a procedure was so impracticable it was not surprising that no one bothered to try.

The rebirth of IVF as a treatment for infertility can be traced to a single moment in the library of the National Institute of Medical Research in 1960. Bob Edwards, a young physiologist who had been studying the maturation of mouse eggs 'in vitro', was hoping to extend these observations to human eggs.[8] He was, however, unaware that Pincus had conducted precisely the same studies back in the 1930s.

> One morning, in the quiet of that comfortable library, as I read one particular scientific paper I stopped reading and said quietly, 'Sod it.' I looked up and nobody had heard me. Nobody in the library at that particular moment was aware of my sudden disappointment, for I just learnt that my discovery was not new. The American, Gregory Pincus, the noted developer of the contraceptive pill, had reported the same results when he had worked with eggs of rabbits in a Cambridge laboratory a quarter of century earlier. He had placed them in a culture solution as I had done, and watched them ripening in the same way. But Pincus had gone one step further. He had done the same with human eggs having removed them from small pieces of ovary. He described how they followed virtually the same ripening programme as rabbit eggs. Research scientists like to be first. I am no exception. I sat in the middle of the Institute library momentarily depressed; the novelty of my discovery had suddenly worn thin.[9]

Nonetheless, Edwards reflected, 'it was simply amazing that no one else had followed up this work for over twenty-five years'. And so with help from Molly Rose, a gynaecologist at Edgware General Hospital, he obtained a steady supply of human ovarian tissue, taken from women undergoing surgery, in anticipation of confirming Pincus's findings: that they would ripen over a few hours to a state where they were receptive to fertilisation by sperm. 'I started with high hopes. After three months I began to feel less certain. Dozens of eggs were cultured. I examined them eagerly after three, six, nine and twelve hours, none of them changed their appearance in any way whatsoever. They gazed back at me. They would not ripen, no matter which culture medium I used. After six months my hopes evaporated completely. Pincus was wrong.'[10] The implication of Edwards's findings were important. He had shown that Pincus must have been mistaken in claiming that it took the same time for human eggs to mature in vitro as it took for mouse or rabbit eggs. That was clear, but the puzzle remained – why did human eggs not mature in vitro? Bob Edwards had no explanation other than to infer that humans were just 'too different' from other mammals.

Two years passed, during which Bob Edwards turned his attentions to other matters. Still,

> I could not help but dream now and then of working on human eggs again. One morning, in 1963, driving to Mill Hill it occurred to me that the ripening programme in the eggs of primates such as humans might simply take longer than in rodents. Supposing the nucleus changed after twelve hours and only then the chromosomes would become visible? It was just a hunch but it was worth a last throw.

Again the gynaecologist Molly Rose provided the ovarian tissue from which Edwards was able to extract four eggs.

> All I had to do now was wait, wait. I must not look at them too early. The first one I would examine after 18 hours. After 18 hours exactly, I looked and saw alas the nucleus unchanged, no sign of ripening at all. Failure. Impatiently, I looked at a second egg. It was like the first. I had to

accept that I had drawn a blank, but I had two human eggs left, I would look at one of them again in six hours' time – by then they would have been in the culture medium for twenty-four hours. When I next peered down the microscope I could not help but feel elated. Surely something was beginning to move? Just a suggestion but I must be patient. Four hours passed by slowly, slowly, but when I did examine the final egg I felt as much excitement as I had ever experienced in all my life. Excitement beyond belief, at 28 hours the chromosomes were just beginning their march through the centre of the egg. Fine, clear, absolutely visible, a sight to reward all my past efforts. A living, ripening, human egg beginning its programme just as the mouse eggs had done. There, in one egg in the last of the group, lay the whole secret of the human programme.[11]

Thus human eggs could indeed mature in vitro, they just took longer. When Bob Edwards reported his findings in *The Lancet*, he tactfully omitted any reference to Pincus's work twenty-five years earlier.[12]

Here then, was another reason – besides Min Chang's theory of capacitation – to explain the failure of Miriam Menkin's IVF programme in the 1940s. Taking her cue from Gregory Pincus's claim of rapid maturation of human eggs she had simply added the sperm too early, before the egg was ready to receive them. Thus, theoretically, fertilisation should be possible if the sperm were added to the egg after twenty-four hours, but first they would have to be capacitated by exposure to the unknown chemical in the fallopian tubes postulated by Chang.

Perhaps understandably Edwards failed to anticipate that Chang's theory of capacitation would turn out to be just as erroneous as Pincus's observations. As a result he was to spend another three years engaged in futile research. In 1965 Edwards accepted an invitation to travel to Baltimore, where he tried every conceivable method of capacitation including the addition of small fragments of fallopian tubes to the fertilisation dish, and 'we even tried to fertilise human eggs in the fallopian tubes of rhesus monkeys, collecting the eggs twelve to twenty-four hours later'. Nothing happened. In six months he failed to fertilise a single human egg. Back in England he repeated these capacitation experiments in female volunteers. The sperm were placed in minute chamber pots and inserted into the womb overnight in the hope they would be influenced by the 'capacitation factor'. Again, nothing happened.[13] So once more Edwards had come to an impasse; clearly whatever the mysterious capacitation factor might be, it must be presumed to be crucial to fertilisation of human eggs. Until it could be identified there was no hope of further progress.

Edwards had no alternative other than to turn his attention to other scientific matters until two years later Chang's theory of capacitation was shown to be incorrect. Barry Bavister, a colleague of Edwards in the physiology laboratory in Cambridge, found that if hamster sperm was added to eggs in a culture medium containing sugar, bicarbonate, and a spot of beef protein, they promptly fertilised. And if it worked for hamsters, why not for humans? It did and quite spectacularly so – if the human eggs were left for long enough to mature and sperm were added in the right culture medium, then fertilisation almost invariably followed.[14] It could hardly have been simpler. The thirty years that had elapsed since Dr Miriam Menkin's failed in vitro experiments back in the 1940s are devastating testimony to the harm caused by false ideas in holding back scientific research.

Fertilisation may have turned out to be straightforward, but this only serves to emphasise Bob Edwards's achievement. In any scientific endeavour the decision about which experiment needs to be done must be underpinned by some general philosophical perception of what is likely to work. When Bob Edwards started his investigations in 1960, the philosophical perspective least likely to produce results was that the correct solution was the simplest, because, following Menkin's studies in the 1940s, everyone knew that the fertilisation of human eggs in vitro was staggeringly difficult to achieve, if not impossible. To move from the supposition that the solution – if there was to be one – was certainly going to be complex to the realisation of its simplicity required him to demonstrate that not just one but the two established 'facts' about human fertilisation – Pincus's work on egg maturation and Chang's concept of capacitation – were in error.

Understanding Hormones

As Bob Edwards's lonely struggle continued through the 1960s, major developments were occurring in the understanding of the female reproductive hormones, both to promote fertility with 'fertility' drugs and to prevent conception with the oral contraceptive pill. The hormonal mechanisms that control first ovulation and later, following fertilisation, sustain pregnancy are elegant but complex. Four main hormones are involved. The first two are secreted by the pituitary gland at the base of the brain. These are the Follicle Stimulating Hormone (FSH), so called because it 'stimulates' the maturation of the 'follicle' or egg, and Luteinizing Hormone (LH), which prompts the ripened egg to pop out of the ovary and start its descent down the fallopian tubes. The other two hormones are secreted by the ovary – oestrogen produced by the ripening follicle and progesterone from the remnants of the follicle (the corpus luteum) after ovulation has taken place. All these hormones were identified in the 1920s and the manner in which they interacted – one of the great scientific insights of the twentieth century – was clarified in 1930 by a humble laboratory assistant at the University of Chicago, Dorothy Price. She had been trying to make sense of some apparently inexplicable experimental results from injecting the male sex hormone, testosterone, into rats. From this, she inferred the notion of 'reciprocal influence', which we now know as 'negative feedback', by which the hormones secreted by the ovary influence the secretion of the hormones of the pituitary, and vice versa.[15]

This is now understood as follows. At the beginning of the menstrual cycle the pituitary secretes FSH, which encourages the ripening of the egg-containing follicle in the ovary, which itself starts to produce oestrogen, whose levels begin to rise. This oestrogen 'feeds back' to cut off the secretion of FSH from the pituitary, permitting the LH to surge upward and precipitate ovulation. The follicle, now emptied of its egg, becomes the corpus luteum that secretes progesterone, which prepares the lining of the womb to receive the fertilised egg. If conception does not take place, the progesterone levels fall, menstruation takes place and, in the absence of the negative feedback from the ovarian hormones, the pituitary FSH levels start to rise again, leading to the ripening of the next egg-containing follicle and so on.

The precise mechanisms by which these hormones interact were not fully elaborated until 1966 but already the implications of the 'reciprocal influence' or 'negative feedback' had been exploited for the development of fertility drugs and the oral contraceptive pill. Thus fertility drugs can be obtained from the urine of women going through the menopause for the following reasons: when the ovaries cease to function at the menopause, the levels of the hormones they secrete, oestrogen and progesterone, fall precipitously. There is thus no longer any 'negative feedback' inhibiting the secretion of FSH and LH from the pituitary, which consequently produce vast quantities of these hormones. These are excreted in the urine, from which they can be isolated and given to infertile women to stimulate ovulation. Collectively, the FSH and LH in the urine is known as human menopausal gonadatrophin (literally 'sex organs stimulating') or HMG.[16] Conversely, the pill, containing oestrogen and progesterone, operates on the same principle, but in reverse, exerting 'negative feedback' on the pituitary to stop the secretion of FSH and LH, and thus preventing ovulation.

There is one further important hormone that does not fit directly into this scenario. If the egg is fertilised by the sperm so that conception takes place, it is vital that the lining of the womb remains receptive and is not lost at menstruation. This is initially achieved by the progesterone secreted by the empty follicle, but its function is then taken over by a hormone secreted by the conceptus itself, or more precisely, from the early placenta (or chorion), which is known as human chorionic gonadatrophin or HCG, which is present in large quantities in the urine of pregnant women. As the appellation 'gonad-atrophin' or 'sex organ stimulating' suggests, HCG possesses a very unusual quality. Though its main physiological function is to prevent menstruation and, by maintaining the lining of the womb, permit the early months of foetal growth, it also has, and quite inexplicably, the same physiological effect as the LH secreted from the pituitary in stimulating the ovary to precipitate ovulation.

Thus, women whose infertility results from a failure of ovulation can be treated by fertility drugs derived from these two naturally occurring chemicals – HMG and HCG found in the urine of menopausal and pregnant women respectively. At the beginning of the menstrual cycle, HMG (obtained from the urine of post-menopausal nuns) with its high concentration of FSH encourages the follicle to ripen. Then halfway through the cycle a dose of HCG (obtained from the urine of pregnant women) will, like LH, cause ovulation to take place. This treatment was first suggested in 1954 and introduced in 1960.[17]

Fertility drugs are, of course, used to treat infertility arising from failure of ovulation rather than blocked tubes, but they were nonetheless crucially important in the development of IVF for several reasons. First, their widespread use in the 1960s was associated with considerable publicity, not least because of their unfortunate tendency to induce multiple pregnancies.[18] The treatment of infertility thus became a major issue and must have influenced Bob Edwards into perceiving that his work on the fertilisation of human eggs might have a practical application in the treatment of infertility that resulted from blocked fallopian tubes. Next the fertility drugs were of great practical use in increasing the number of eggs that could be 'harvested' during IVF, which made the whole procedure much more efficient. Lastly they focused attention on the need to understand the precise way in which the female hormones interacted during the menstrual cycle and, as will be seen, particularly on the role of progesterone in sustaining the lining of the womb to receive the fertilised egg.

Laparoscopy

Bob Edwards's work on fertilisation had all been performed on eggs taken from women undergoing major gynaecological operations such as hysterectomies, which involves opening up the abdomen, thus permitting access to the ovaries. Clearly, if IVF were to become a practicable form of treatment, some alternative method of obtaining eggs had to be found. The answer was laparoscopy, which was being introduced into Britain by Patrick Steptoe just as Bob Edwards was having his first success with the fertilisation of human eggs. Rather than a major abdominal operation, laparoscopy only required a small incision below the umbilicus, through which a metal tube was introduced into the abdomen to allow eggs to be removed from the ovary.

Laparoscopy is now so widely used in gynaecology that it is hard to imagine that back in 1967 Patrick Steptoe was virtually the only man in Britain who had any experience with the technique at all. He appreciated its considerable potential in clarifying one of the most difficult problems confronted by gynaecologists – how to sort out the many causes of pain in the pelvis by looking inside to see whether it was the result of an ovarian cyst or an ectopic pregnancy in the fallopian tubes or some other inflammatory condition. Steptoe was also adept at laparoscopic sterilisation in which the fallopian tubes are tied off, and had advocated its use as a means of observing what was happening to the ovaries during the administration of fertility drugs as a way of preventing multiple pregnancies.[19]

In March 1967 Steptoe published a monograph – *Laparoscopy in Gynaecology* – describing its many benefits.[20] It is not quite clear how Edwards, sitting in his laboratory in Cambridge, heard about Steptoe's text, but he was struck by its potential as a means of retrieving human eggs for fertilisation. They had a brief conversation on the telephone and met formally at a conference at the Royal Society of Medicine on 6 January 1968. Robert Edwards recalls the moment as follows:

Sitting in the rows of green chairs facing the raised platform and the lectern were many distinguished gynaecologists and endocrinologists. One of the topics discussed was the disadvantage of the fertility drugs for they led too often to multi-pregnancies. 'If only the ovaries could be inspected easily beforehand,' the speaker continued, 'then we would have advanced warning of multi-pregnancy. We would see how many eggs were growing. Perhaps the new method of laparoscopy could be of use here?'

People lulled in their chairs. It was an august gathering and the chairman had no need to disturb anybody by bringing his wooden mallet down sharply. But suddenly a distinguished-looking gentleman, sitting in front of me, raised to his feet.

'No,' he said dogmatically. 'Laparoscopy is of no use whatsoever. It is impossible to visualise the ovary using that technique. I have tried it.'

He was suggesting it was just a gynaecological gimmick when, at the back of the hall, a thickset, grey-haired man leapt to his feet evidently impatient with the speaker. He did not actually say 'Rubbish' but his remarks were pungent and direct. Forcefully he recounted how, through the laparoscope, not only could the ovaries be seen but also the fallopian tubes and other parts of the reproductive tract. 'Indeed,' he continued, 'the whole abdominal cavity can be inspected. You are hopelessly wrong. I carry out laparoscopy routinely everyday – many times over. It is simple and only takes me a matter of minutes.'

This obviously was the Patrick Steptoe of Oldham General Hospital. I felt immediately, here was a man I could trust and respect and work with. He knew his mind. He was utterly convincing and he offered to demonstrate the slides he had brought along to substantiate his claims. Afterwards in the foyer, near the marble columns of the Royal Society of Medicine, I approached.

'You are Patrick Steptoe,' I said.

'Yes.'

'I'm Bob Edwards.'[21]

About four months later, on 1 April 1968, Bob Edwards made his first trip to Patrick Steptoe's hospital in Oldham with the apparatus, microscopes and culture fluid, to set up his 'research laboratory' (in reality an old storeroom) for the fertilisation of the female eggs, which Patrick Steptoe would retrieve through his laparoscope.

The Long Hard Journey to Success

The second phase of Bob Edwards's involvement in IVF lasted for a decade from 1968 to 1978, the last seven years of which were devoted to trying to achieve a successful pregnancy. It came eventually but the disappointments and frustrations along the way were enormous. During all this time both Steptoe and Edwards knew they must be close to their goal but, for reasons that only became clear in retrospect, they could not make IVF work. Their difficulties were compounded by a further factor illustrated by a map of England, which shows that the 'commute' from Cambridge in the south-east to Oldham in the north-west is a distance of 165 miles as the crow flies. As there were no motorways in the late 1960s, the journey had to be made by ordinary roads. For the best part of a decade, when everything they tried seemed to end in failure, Edwards and his fellow scientist, Jean Purdy, were to make that arduous journey several times a year.

Initially things could not have gone better, and they made substantial progress in the first two years of preliminary research prior to the first therapeutic use of IVF. They started by devising a fertility drug regime to maximise the number of eggs and ensure they would be retrieved at the right time. In the first half of the cycle women were given three doses of HMG to 'bring on' two or three eggs simultaneously. This was followed by one injection of HCG (to mimic the effect of LH) to induce ovulation. Patrick Steptoe then performed a laparoscopy and retrieved as many eggs as possible from the ovary. These were placed in the culture medium, sperm was added and almost invariably fertilisation occurred. The major uncertainty at the beginning was whether eggs fertilised in this way would develop normally, so first they had to be allowed to grow for long enough and then be 'squashed' to allow them to be examined under the microscope for evidence of abnormality. There was none.[22]

As the time approached to start treating the first patients, the problem of conducting an experimental therapeutic programme over such long distances seemed immense. Bob Edwards recalls:

> The years of constant travelling to Oldham were now beginning to take their toll. The days of sojourn in Lancashire played havoc with my family life. All too often I could see Ruth's [his wife's] face cloud over as I had to disappoint the children over some matter or I had to cancel a party at the last moment while I hired a car and dashed northwards complete with equipment and necessities. Jean [Purdy] also had to face similar problems. I always remember returning home on one occasion after a prolonged stay at Oldham and being surprised to discover not only new neighbours in the street but fresh colleagues in the laboratory at Cambridge.[23]

The obvious solution was for Patrick Steptoe to move from Oldham to Cambridge. There was a possible vacancy as an NHS consultant at Newmarket General Hospital, which would have cut Bob Edwards's commuting distance to ten miles. This would, however, require special funds, so they turned to the Medical Research Council for help. Their joint application was rejected on three grounds: 'serious doubts about ethical aspects of the IVF programme'; 'a lack of preliminary studies in primates'; and reservations about the justification of using laparoscopy for 'purely experimental purposes'.

The grounds for rejection may have been particularly ill-informed, but Edwards and Steptoe had no alternative other than to carry on as before, and to start treating patients in the hope that success – which at the time seemed imminent – would alter the MRC's view.

So the commuting started again in earnest. In December
1971, the first patient underwent IVF:

> With a sense of an important occasion Patrick passed a
> cannular [a thin plastic tube] containing the embryo in its
> drop of culture medium through the cervical canal of our
> first hoped-for mother. There was a few seconds' delay
> while the fluid dispersed and the embryo was carried into
> the recesses of the womb. But despite the high hopes of it
> all, this reimplanted embryo did not stick, pregnancy was
> not established and with the tell-tale signs of the beginning
> of her menstrual period we all realised this first attempt of
> IVF had been a failure.[24]

As indeed were all the other attempts over the next six years.
The disappointment of these times is difficult to imagine, not
least because the success of their preliminary research had
shown them that they must almost be there. The validity of
every single step of the process had been confirmed only to be
frustrated by the failure to get the reimplanted embryo to 'stick'
into the lining of the uterus to create a viable pregnancy.
Recording this period Edwards observes: 'One after another
we had to admit at least temporary defeat, had to telephone an
anxious waiting husband and say, "Sorry – we failed again."
T. S. Eliot had remarked on those who are undefeated only
because they go on trying. It was only in that sense that we
were now undefeated.'

In November 1973, Bob Edwards reported their first eight
attempts at achieving pregnancy with IVF had been 'without
success'.[25] A new tack was called for. He inferred that, as the
difficulty was in getting the embryo to stick, then presumably
the lining of the womb was not being adequately sustained by
the progesterone secreted by the corpus luteum in the second
half of the cycle. He decided, fatefully, to 'support' the second
part of the cycle with a progesterone supplement, Primolut.
This did not work either in the ten or more further attempts at
IVF over the following two years. Finally in the summer of
1975, when on holiday, Edwards received a telegram from

Patrick Steptoe: 'Pregnancy test positive. Ring me urgently. Patrick.' 'This pregnancy was a major advance for us,' Edwards subsequently recalled. 'It was decisive for we now knew that the fertilisation of the embryo in vitro and the method of replacement were good.' Sadly the pregnancy turned out to be an ectopic one in the remnants of what was left of the patient's fallopian tube and it had to be removed surgically.[26] Further attempts with the progesterone support in the second half of the cycle were also unsuccessful and it occurred to Edwards that perhaps the reason they had managed to achieve their one and only pregnancy was that the embryo had implanted in the fallopian tubes, whose lining is not extruded like that of the uterus during menstruation. If this was the case, then Primolut was clearly not 'supporting' the lining of the womb as intended and indeed they were later to discover it was actually working as an abortificant, accelerating the loss of the lining of the womb. Little wonder that this phase of IVF research proved so unsuccessful.

There seemed no alternative other than to start all over again. From the beginning of 1976 several approaches were attempted, including changing the types of fertility drugs used, trying to initiate fertilisation in the womb by replacing the egg and the sperm together, and finally dispensing with all supportive medical treatment and seeking to simulate as closely as possible what happens in nature. This last strategy was the one that finally brought success.

The theoretical advantage in using the fertility drugs – HMG and HCG – was that they both increased the yield of eggs and determined the moment of ovulation so that Patrick Steptoe knew when to intervene – thirty-six hours after the HCG injection – in the knowledge the egg would be ripe and thus ready for fertilisation. But perhaps, reflected Edwards, these features of the IVF programme that seemed so essential were actually the problem, interfering in some subtle way with the vital process of implantation. If so, it would be necessary to dispense with them. The prospect of dispensing with fertility drugs would not only reduce the yield of potential eggs but also mean that Steptoe and Edwards's work would now be determined by the natural rhythm of the woman's own menstrual cycle. They did not intervene in the first part of the cycle but let the woman's own FSH ripen the egg-containing follicle in the ovary. After ten days they started to monitor the level of LH in the urine, knowing that when it surged upwards, towards the middle of the cycle, ovulation would take place twenty-four to thirty-six hours later. This then determined the time when laparoscopy could be performed and the egg could be retrieved, which could be at any time, including the middle of the night.

Lesley Brown was the second woman to be treated with this new regime in November 1977, and three other pregnancies followed soon after. Two of these subsequently aborted, one tragically following amniocentesis at twenty-one weeks and the second due to a chromosome abnormality. The considerable adverse publicity had she been born alive – with the false inference that this resulted from her manner of conception – would have done enormous damage to the prospects of IVF.

That left two live pregnancies after ten years of endeavour: Louise Joy Brown, born in July 1978, and in January 1979 a boy, Alistair.[27] The remarkable feature of the ten years of research that culminated in these two live births was that in the end it all turned out to be so simple. The first 'test-tube' baby was thus made possible by four simple pieces of technology: a method of measuring LH in the urine to detect the 'LH surge'; laparoscopy to obtain an egg; a culture medium in which the conceptus would grow for a couple of days; and finally a thin plastic tube for its relocation back in the womb.

Almost immediately following the birth of Louise Brown, the wheel of IVF treatment turned full circle. First other investigators and then Steptoe and Edwards themselves returned to using the regime they had originally started with back in 1971. In 1981, in Australia, Alan Trounson and his colleagues reported four successful pregnancies using the fertility drug Clomiphene to boost the number of 'harvestable' eggs in association with HCG to promote ovulation. These along with several other modifications established the basis of the success of IVF throughout the 1980s.[28]

Thus to their chagrin Steptoe and Edwards realised that their original strategy back in 1971 had been the correct one. Had they persevered rather than 'adding in' Primolut to sustain the second half of the cycle they would almost certainly have been successful much earlier. We know this now, but should not overlook the fact that this 'mistake' exemplifies the essential problem of scientific research. By definition, it involves tapping away at the boundaries of the unknown in anticipation of the breakthrough. Here IVF posed a particular problem because its success rate is naturally low, so it was difficult for Steptoe and Edwards to know when or if their procedure was correct. So, just too hastily, they changed their original technique by adding Primolut, but now their failure was due to an entirely different reason. And so on.

The point here is that scientists never know why something is not working until they come across something that does. Whatever might appear obvious in retrospect never is at the time. This necessarily leads to the second aspect of the scientific achievement – the human side – the moral courage that sustained them during the inevitable disappointments of trying to make sense of the, as yet, unknown. The reward for Steptoe and Edwards was that the two children born at the end of their seven years of travail became 40,000 pregnancies in the following two decades.[29] Further, IVF, it soon emerged, could be extended to treat many other types of infertility as well, including 'unexplained infertility' and male infertility resulting from a low sperm count. Virtually everyone now knows of couples whose lives, which otherwise would have been 'blighted by barrenness', have been immeasurably enriched – thanks to Steptoe and Edwards – by the ability to have children.

1984: HELICOBACTER – THE CAUSE
OF PEPTIC ULCER

*T*his tenth and last definitive moment of post-war medicine seems much the least significant. In 1983 a young Australian doctor, Barry Marshall, reported the presence of an 'unidentified curved bacillus' (a new type of crescent-shaped bacterium) in the lining of the stomach, subsequently named as helicobacter (literally, helix-shaped bacillus) which turned out to be an important cause of several diseases of the upper intestinal tract including gastritis (inflammation of the lining of the stomach), ulcers and stomach cancer. Marshall's discovery may be of considerable interest but is not in the same league as, for example, the decades of endeavour that led to the cure of childhood leukaemia or transplant surgery. Its inclusion in this pantheon requires a brief justification.

The therapeutic revolution of the post-war years had quite different effects on the pattern of disease in the young, the middle-aged and the old. The young were the major beneficiaries of the control of infectious diseases with antibiotics and immunisation. Their serious medical problems now mainly result from either inherited diseases such as cystic fibrosis, problems associated with prematurity, accidents, or allergies such as asthma. At the other end of the age spectrum, the elderly are vulnerable to diseases of the circulatory system and cancer, which are powerfully age-determined (that is, caused by ageing of the body's tissues), or to the 'chronic degenerative' diseases, such as arthritis and cataracts.

To put it crudely, modern medicine has squeezed the major burden of illness to the extremes of life – among the very young and the old – and in general most people from their teenage years up to their fifties or sixties are remarkably resiliently healthy. This brings into focus the singular peculiarity of the illnesses that do occur in the middle years, such as diabetes, rheumatoid, multiple sclerosis, schizophrenia, Parkinson's, and many others. By definition these are not related to age but rather seem to strike out of the blue. The unifying feature of all these illnesses is that their cause is not known.

They must have a cause; there must be some reason why the nerves in someone with multiple sclerosis should be damaged, or the joints in someone with rheumatoid should become chronically inflamed. But, despite prodigious efforts and vast sums spent on medical research, their origins remain profoundly enigmatic.

There is thus a vast ocean of ignorance at the heart of medicine. The causes of the common diseases of middle life are simply not known, and self-evidently, without knowing their cause, they can neither be prevented nor cured. Certainly in some the symptoms can be alleviated by one or other of the drugs discovered in the post-war years, such as chlorpromazine in schizophrenia or cortisone in rheumatoid arthritis, but these are palliative in that they fail to resolve the underlying pathology in the same way that antibiotics get to grips with infections.

Stomach (or peptic) ulcers were yet another of these illnesses of middle life whose cause was unknown, though they seemed to be related to an excess of acid production in the stomach which had been variously attributed to genetic factors, faulty diet and, of course, 'stress'. And then along comes Dr Marshall, who identifies a single type of bacterium as the 'trigger', which not only profoundly changes the nature of understanding of the disease but also the manner in which it should be treated. If this is the situation for peptic ulcers then, by analogy, perhaps there should be a similar singular explanation for the other diseases of middle life.

The discovery of H. pylori *thus illuminates in a striking way the last great intellectual challenge in medicine: finding out the cause of these illnesses. If a bacterium can cause peptic ulcer then presumably other as-yet-unidentified infectious agents might also be responsible for multiple sclerosis or rheumatoid arthritis.*

In the summer of 1984 a 32-year-old Australian doctor, Barry Marshall, swallowed a cocktail containing large numbers of the bacterium helicobacter, which had been obtained from the stomach of a man suffering from dyspepsia.[1] Self-experimentation of this type has a long and distinguished history. Many researchers have in the past exposed themselves to considerable personal danger and discomfort in the pursuit of science. In 1892, at the age of seventy-eight, the German scientist Max von Pettenkoffer, sceptical that the cholera bacillus recently discovered by Robert Koch really was the cause of cholera, swallowed a mixture laced with cholera bacilli taken from the stool of a recent victim. His scepticism, he soon realised, was misplaced when he became acutely ill with profuse diarrhoea and abdominal colic. In January 1930, Dr Gail Dack of Chicago, convinced that − contrary to prevailing opinion − food poisoning could be caused by the staphylococcus, deliberately swallowed a piece of contaminated sponge cake. 'Later on, as he was about to sit down for supper, he suddenly ran from the table to spend an hour in the bathroom. His wife heard him say between bouts of vomiting and diarrhoea, "Oh, this is wonderful!" But Mrs Dack thought otherwise. Believing her husband was about to die, she summoned his partner who came but could offer little comfort other than staying by his bedside until he recovered.'[2]

Marshall conducted his self-experiment for precisely the same reasons as Pettenkoffer and Dack: to prove (or disprove) a theory that bacteria found in association with an illness were actually the cause of that illness. And sure enough, within a week of swallowing his infective cocktail, Marshall developed symptoms of dyspepsia, with vomiting and abdominal discomfort. His friends noted his breath smelled 'putrid'. A colleague passed a gastroscope into his stomach, whose lining appeared red and inflamed, and a biopsy showed inflammatory cells and 'bacilli adhering to the surface'. Marshall started a course of antibiotics and 'his symptoms resolved completely within twenty-four hours'.

The results of Dr Marshall's self-experiment might seem predictable. It is only natural to presume that ingesting a cocktail of infective organisms might have adverse consequences on the lining of the stomach, but that was not the way things were viewed in 1984. The prevailing wisdom maintained, and for good reason, that bacteria simply could not be implicated in diseases of the stomach for the simple reason that they could not survive its high concentration of hydrochloric acid that can burn a hole in concrete, dissolve a lump of meat and destroy 99.99 per cent of all bacteria within half an hour.[3] Marshall's self-experiment showed this to be incorrect. The stomach was not entirely sterile. Some bacteria, like the heli-cobacter, had clearly adapted to living in this hostile environment.

So why had the connection never been made before? It was scarcely for lack of opportunity to observe the presence of these bacteria in the stomach as, since the development of the fibre-optic endoscope in the 1960s, the stomach had become one of the most scrutinised organs of the body. But even though these bacteria must clearly have been present, pathologists examining the specimens apparently did not see them, or if they did they ignored them. Rather, blinded by the dogma that bacteria could not survive in the stomach, the causes of gastritis and peptic ulcer had been attributed to a variety of fanciful explanations.

The stomach lining is protected against the corrosive hydrochloric acid secretions by a layer of mucus on its surface. An ulcer or gastritis is best understood as arising from either an oversecretion of acid or a defect in this mucous protective layer. Certainly two important causes of peptic ulcer are readily explained within this model. The first is the very rare Zollinger-Ellison syndrome, where a tumour of the pancreas secretes a hormone (gastrin) that massively increases the amount of acid produced by the stomach, resulting in intractable ulcers of the upper intestinal tract. The second are drugs like aspirin, which disrupt the mucus layer, exposing the stomach cells underneath to the acidic secretions. The difficulty has always been trying to explain those ulcers – the vast majority – in which neither of these causes apply. Essentially two theories have been proposed – 'personality' and 'stress' – both of which are based on the supposition that chronic anxiety maintains levels of acid secretion 'above the normal range'.

The role of personality in peptic ulcer can be traced back to the psychoanalytic theories of disease of the 1930s and 1940s. In 1935 an American analyst, Franz Alexander, asserted that patients with peptic ulcer were struggling against 'feelings of dependence' on parents and persons of authority. Freudian theory being based on the perverse proposition that everything is the reverse of what it seems, this 'struggle against' is actually a concealed 'desire for' dependence on parents. Thus, according to Alexander, ulcers occurred in those who had reverted to the 'infantile' state of wishing to be fed, 'which serves as a permanent stimulus of the empty stomach and causes its dysfunction'. Alexander clarifies the theory as follows: 'We found in our cases of peptic ulcer a strong regression to the infantile attitude of oral receptiveness and aggressiveness. Furthermore we saw these infantile cravings become thwarted internally by a conflict between oral-receptive and oral-sadistic impulses.' This interpretation, said Dr Alexander, was 'clear and in harmony with our physiological knowledge and explains the observed facts [sic]'.[4] By the 1950s the psychoanalytic emphasis on the individual had shifted towards blaming the parents. Dr Elsa Goldberg from London's Tavistock Institute found that the mothers of those with peptic ulcers were 'striving, dominant and obsessional in the house' while the fathers were 'steady, unassertive and passive'.[5]

While the personality theory emphasised 'internal conflict' as the source of chronic anxiety leading to an increase in acidic secretions, the 'stress' theory focused on external factors and arose from a series of experiments conducted in the 1940s by Stewart Wolf and Howard Wolff of the New York Hospital on an unfortunate employee called 'Tom'.[6] Tom was a 56-year-old Irishman who, at the age of nine, had the misfortune of drinking some extremely hot clam chowder his father had left in a pail in the kitchen, which caused severe burns to the oesophagus. The strictures that resulted could not be dilated so, with Tom unable to swallow any food, the surgeons had no alternative other than to fashion an opening from the abdominal wall directly into the stomach – a gastrostomy – through which he learned to feed himself. Wolf and Wolff placed a thin plastic tube through the gastrostomy to assess the amount of acid secreted by the stomach, which appeared to be related to Tom's moods and emotional states, increasing when he was fearful of losing his job, when depressed after being unable to move from his 'unpleasant neighbourhood' to a more desirable area, when anxious during his step-daughter's investigations for suspected cancer of the bladder, and so on. From these studies they concluded that excess secretion (of gastric acid) occurred in situations that posed a threat to the emotional security of the individual. Here, then, was an apparently scientific explanation that over the next two decades was deemed to be so self-evident that it was merely perverse to challenge it. Stress pushed up the levels of gastric acid in an empty stomach and the result was a peptic ulcer. Many other studies provided apparent independent confirmation, including some cruel and ingenious monkey experiments. The animals were placed in the situation where one of the pair was obliged to assume 'executive' responsibility for avoiding electric shocks to itself and to the second member of the pair. In each pair the 'executive monkeys' developed peptic ulcers; and some even died from perforation of the stomach.[7]

These psychosomatic explanations for peptic ulcer were never formally disproved, but gradually the emphasis shifted to constitutional or genetic factors that might increase the secretion of acid and other hormones. The belief that 'excess acid' was the culprit certainly seemed to be vindicated by the introduction of the drug cimetidine in 1976, which, by reducing the amount of acid in the stomach, allowed ulcers to heal. The fundamental weakness of all these theories is that they failed to offer any explanation as to why any individual should develop a peptic ulcer in the first place. Indeed, there was simply no recognition that there might be some unknown 'initiating factor' to explain the whole process, despite the fact that the changing pattern of peptic ulcer disease over the previous 100 years strongly suggested that an infectious agent must be involved.

Peptic ulcer was rare before the turn of the century but over the next fifty years it had become ever more frequent, affecting approximately one in ten of adult males. Then, suddenly, the rate started to fall quite dramatically, declining by almost 50 per cent between 1960 and 1972.[8] It is clearly impossible to correlate this 'rise and fall' with changes in personality or methods of parenting or stressful types of work, but it rather inescapably points to an infectious cause, belatedly identified by the young Barry Marshall. So how did Marshall stumble on the cause of this common disease that had eluded the medical profession for the previous fifty years?

In 1983 Dr J. Robin Warren of the Royal Perth Hospital in Western Australia observed the presence of 'small, curved bacilli' in biopsy specimens taken from the stomachs of patients with acute gastritis. 'The extraordinary feature of these bacteria is that they are almost unknown to clinicians and pathologists alike,' he reported, 'even though they are present in about half our gastric biopsy specimens in numbers large enough to be seen routinely.'[9] Meanwhile, as a junior doctor at the same hospital, Marshall was looking around for some interesting research project, so Warren suggested he might take a closer look at the patients in whose stomach biopsies he had just noted these 'small curved bacilli'. Warren, it would seem, did not fully appreciate the true significance of his observations and, as Marshall had had no experience in medical research, he could scarcely have anticipated his investigations would lead to some momentous discovery. Marshall's moment of revelation came, quite by accident, when one of the patients whose stomach biopsy specimen had contained the 'unidentified bacilli' reported that, following a course of the antibiotic tetracycline for a chest infection, his symptoms of dyspepsia had improved. Marshall promptly performed a gastroscopy to inspect the appearance of the stomach wall and found the bacilli had vanished. The conclusion seemed obvious. As both the patients' symptoms and the bacteria in the stomach wall had disappeared following a course of antibiotics, then the bacteria must have been the cause of those symptoms.[10]

There was no reason why anybody should share the youthful Dr Marshall's excitement about his observations, but what he may have lacked in experience he certainly made up for with enthusiasm. In the following twelve weeks he performed gastroscopies on a further 184 patients – almost four a day – and, now that he knew what he was looking for, the stagger-ingly high prevalence of helicobacter infections began to become apparent not only in those with gastritis but also, he noted, in 100 per cent of patients with peptic ulcers.[11]

The next step in understanding the properties and behaviour of this unusual bacterium was to grow it – but this proved sur-prisingly difficult. It is standard practice, once bacteria have been inoculated on to a dish of culture medium, to incubate them for forty-eight hours and look for evidence of growth, but nothing happened. The thirty-fifth attempt was interrupted by a five-day Easter holiday, and unintentionally the culture dishes were incubated for a further three days. When the microbiologists returned from their break they found that the culture plates were studded with small colonies of helico-bacter.[12] Now, with abundant helicobacter available, Marshall could undertake the crucial self-experiment to show heli-cobacter were not just 'associated' with inflammatory changes in the stomach wall but were the actual cause of that inflam-mation. If they were the cause, then logically antibiotic treatment should be curative. There already was – as men-tioned – a highly effective treatment for peptic ulcers in the form of cimetidine, which reduces the quantity of acidic secre-tions and with less acid around the ulcer heals, but within a year of stopping treatment, the ulcers tend to recur.[13] By contrast antibiotics should, by eliminating the helicobacter, ensure that once the ulcer was healed it stayed healed. And so it turned out: in a study of fifty patients with 'intractable' peptic ulcer reported in *The Lancet* in 1990, those in whom helicobacter was eradicated with antibiotics had 'no ulcer relapse'. By contrast, in those treated with standard anti-ulcer medication but without antibiotics, 89 per cent had a further ulcer within the year.[14] Rather than taking acid-suppressant drugs for years, patients with peptic ulcers now only had to take a seven-day course of antibiotics. There could be no more powerful illus-tration of the importance of knowing 'the cause' of a disease.

Nor indeed was that the end of the story. It soon became clear that helicobacter was not only implicated in gastritis and peptic ulcer but almost certainly responsible for up to two-thirds of cases of stomach cancer[15] and that a rare type of lymphoma of the gut associated with helicobacter was curable with antibiotics alone.[16] By the end of the 1980s every gut specialist in the world was looking for and finding helicobacter in their patients' stomachs and curing their ulcers with antibiotics. There was now no escaping the scale of their earlier collective self-deception, for not only had they failed to see these bacteria even though they were present in virtually all their patients, but they had systematically misinterpreted the many clues pointing to the fact that peptic ulcers must be caused by an infectious organism.

And how did the helicobacter protect itself against the corrosive effect of hydrochloric acid in the stomach? It turned out to be a very unusual organism, with a streamlined spiral shape propelled by a tail moving it very rapidly through the acidic secretions to find sanctuary in the mucous layer of the stomach wall. Though it does not directly penetrate the cells of the stomach wall to cause an ulcer, it does produce a range of toxins that, by causing inflammation, generate the fluids and debris that are believed to be its main source of nutrition. Helicobacter is thus perfectly adapted to its unusual environment and, once installed, persists probably for life.[17]

Still, the precise mechanisms by which it causes ulcers and gastric cancer is not clear. Helicobacter is only found in the stomach, yet the type of ulcers with which it is most clearly associated occur in the duodenum, the part of the gut that links the stomach to the small intestine. Further, though helicobacter infection increases the risk of stomach cancer from between three- and six-fold, again exactly how remains to be elucidated. It has been suggested that chronic infection can, over a long period of twenty years or more, induce early cancerous changes in the stomach wall, which along with other factors eventually result in a malignancy. The details of how helicobacter causes disease may still be obscure, but this does not detract from its significance. Helicobacter has provoked another 'paradigm shift' in changing scientific understanding, not only of the diseases with which it is directly associated, but of all diseases.

Prior to the discovery of helicobacter the three main stomach diseases – gastritis, peptic ulcer and stomach cancer – were believed to be separate entities, each with their own plausible explanations, so stress-induced excess acid led to peptic ulcers, or pickled foods or salt or nitrate fertilisers in some way damaged the lining of the stomach wall to cause cancer.[18,19] But these theories were a mere 'façade of knowledge', incapable of providing any useful insights as to how these illnesses might be prevented or cured. And then along comes Marshall, for whom the reverse of the standard cliché applies: chance favoured his unprepared mind. It was precisely because he was young and inexperienced that he was able to think the 'unthinkable' that peptic ulcer might be an infectious disease. And in the aftermath of his self-experiment everything fell into place. Helicobacter offered both a unifying biological explanation for all the important diseases of the stomach, while simultaneously making treatment and prevention a practical proposition, as in curing peptic ulcers with antibiotics and immunising against helicobacter to prevent stomach cancer. There could be no more striking instance of the contrast between a coherent biological explanation that opens up the possibility of genuinely effective treatment and pseudo explanations – whether psychological or dietary – that blame patients for their disease and leaves them impotent to do anything about them.

Nor indeed do the implications of helicobacter stop here. Its discovery necessarily raises the question how many of the other diseases of unknown causation, such as multiple sclerosis or rheumatoid arthritis or diabetes, might also have a biological cause that will make them amenable to curative treatment in a similar way. This issue will be returned to.

PART I

The Rise

MEDICINE'S BIG BANG

In an influential essay, 'Science: the Endless Frontier', published in 1946, the American physicist Vannevar Bush described science as 'a largely unexplored hinterland' that would provide the 'essential key' to the economic prosperity of the post-war years. He himself had participated in 'the greatest mobilisation of scientific power in the history of the world', the Manhattan Project, which at a cost of $2 billion had built from scratch in under five years the first atomic bomb, which had been dropped with such devastating effect on the Japanese cities of Hiroshima and Nagasaki. This awesome power unleashed by atomic fission would, predicted Bush, soon cease to be a 'jealously guarded military secret', becoming instead 'a source of limitless energy' in the service of peace and industrial progress.

Vannevar Bush's optimistic anticipation of science's 'endless frontier' was to be repeatedly vindicated over the following twenty years. In 1948 the invention of the transistor increased the calculating power of computers a million-fold to usher in the Electronic Age. Five years later in 1953 Francis Crick and James Watson's identification of the structure of DNA unlocked the mysteries of the genetic code. In 1961 Yuri Gagarin's orbit of Earth launched the Space Race that would culminate eight years later in the first Moon landing. Even when compared to such momentous events, the post-war therapeutic revolution was the most momentous of all, a multitude of discoveries in diverse scientific disciplines stretching over a period of three decades. And its 'definitive moments' already described were only the headlines. For a proper sense of the scientific ferment that underpinned these achievements, it is necessary to imagine the thousands of chemists in their laboratories synthesising and testing millions of chemical compounds, or to reflect on the time and energy expended by similar numbers of physiologists, endocrinologists and neurochemists in making sense of, for example, the subtle hormonal regulation of the pituitary gland, or the mode of action of neurotransmitters in the brain.

The phenomenal scale of the post-war medical achievement calls out for explanation. What inspired it? And sustained it? Why did it happen when it did? What can it teach us in general about the nature of scientific solutions and the origins of scientific innovation?

The most striking impression of the ten definitive moments is how little they have in common. The paths to scientific discovery are so diverse and depend so much on luck and serendipity that any generalisation necessarily appears suspect. The relative ease with which Howard Florey rediscovered the therapeutic potential of penicillin could not be more different from Philip Hench's twenty years' relentless failure in pursuit of Substance X, which quite fortuitously turned out to be cortisone. Nor again is there much in common between the two 'definitive' surgical moments – open-heart surgery and transplantation. Open-heart surgery is technically very difficult and would never have happened without the innovation of the pump. Transplantation, by contrast, is technically quite simple, but would have been inconceivable without the fortuitous discovery of azathioprine's capacity to induce immunological tolerance. This diversity of discovery is perhaps best illustrated by the contrast between the experiences of Bob Edwards and Barry Marshall. Bob Edwards first had to demonstrate that not one but two accepted truths about human fertilisation were in error before even starting on the major project of in vitro fertilisation, which then frustratingly took seven years to be realised. By comparison, Barry Marshall had it easy. His discovery of the significance of helicobacter in peptic ulcer depended on his complete lack of any experience of medical research, which allowed him to 'think the unthinkable' – that it might be an infectious disease.

Nonetheless, diverse as these paths of innovation might appear, they are clearly 'of a piece', carried along by a strong undercurrent of ideas and events among the most important of which was the war. It is a truism that the urgency of conflict accelerates the pace of innovation and several of the definitive moments were forged by the necessities of wartime.

The search for an antidote to chemical weapons led Alfred Gilman and Louis Goodman to inject nitrogen mustard into a mouse with a lymphoma and observe that the tumour 'regressed to such an extent it could no longer be palpated'. Again, military intelligence reports of rumours that Luftwaffe pilots boosted by injections of adrenal hormones were able to fly at heights of over 40,000 feet stimulated the US National Defense Research Council to initiate the arduous research programme that culminated in the synthesis of cortisone.

The influence of the war can be detected in two other ways closely related to Vannevar Bush's concept of the 'endless frontiers' of science. Bush, as a major participant in the Manhattan Project, had seen at close hand what state funding and the central direction of research could achieve. The same lesson was not lost on government in the post-war years and the notion of massive state investment in research as a basis of future prosperity was readily extrapolated to health, which led in time to the vast billion-dollar-funded organisations such as the National Institute of Health and the National Cancer Institute.

But, more important still, the Allied victory in 1945 released a surge of pent-up utopian energies. The limitless possibilities of science would build 'a better world', whose form, according to Vannevar Bush, 'is predestined by the laws of logic and the nature of human reasoning'. The builders of this new world would include 'men of vision who can grasp in advance just what is needed for rapid progress, who can tell by some subtle sense where it will be found and have an uncanny skill in bringing it into the light'. Nowadays such unbridled optimism seems naïve, even embarrassing. But it alone can explain why, during this period, doctors and scientists seemed quite prepared to take on what at the time appeared quite insoluble problems. If the possibilities of science were truly limitless then everything was possible, including the cure of childhood cancer, transplanting organs and open-heart surgery.

Taken together, these war-related therapeutic innovations contributed to the creation of 'a critical mass', when a high level of activity in many fields of medical research sparked off a chain reaction of further developments. This internal dynamic can be conveniently divided into six separate themes. The first two, and the concern of the rest of this chapter, were the coincidental discovery of antibiotics and steroids and the 'interconnectedness' of medical research. The remaining four, examined in the remaining chapters of this section, are: the rise of 'clinical science' in the 1940s as the dominant ideology of medicine; the fusion of chemistry with capitalism to give rise to the pharmaceutical revolution; the contribution of technology; and 'the mysteries of biology'.

It is obvious now that the post-war medical achievement was built on the twin pillars of antibiotics and steroids or, to revert to the earlier metaphor, they were the fuse that lit the chain reaction of post-war medical innovation. There is no difficulty in recognising the crucial role of antibiotics but the claim that cortisone was equally important might be considered more contentious. Certainly, the therapeutic effect of antibiotics and steroids were very different but crucially they were also complementary: antibiotics in their assault on infections, the commonest known cause of disease; steroids by proving so useful in many diseases whose causes were and remain unknown. They were both effective in specific diseases – penicillin against pneumonia, steroids in the treatment of rheumatoid arthritis – but they also transformed whole categories of illness. Antibiotics effectively eliminated the vast burden of misery caused by chronic infections – of the bones and joints that so preoccupied orthopaedic surgeons, or of the ear, sinuses and upper airways that had kept ENT surgeons so busy, or of the female reproductive organs that had been such an important cause of infertility and maternal mortality. As for steroids, they established in a way that had never been clear before that apparently quite distinct diseases – asthma, eczema, chronic active hepatitis, myasthenia gravis, polyarteritis, optic neuritis – nonetheless shared the common feature of arising from uncontrolled and excessive inflammation.

Nor was that all. Antibiotics and steroids changed the everyday practice of medicine, but they also offered positive proof of the notion, already alluded to, that 'the possibilities of science' were limitless and that one day apparently insoluble problems would be overcome. And indeed they were instrumental in bringing this about: steroids provided the crucial breakthrough – along with azathioprine – in overcoming the immunological rejection of transplanted organs in 1963, and they were also one of the four drugs of the protocol with which Dr Donald Pinkel achieved his 50 per cent cure rate of leukaemia in 1971. Antibiotics provided a source of several important anti-cancer drugs and also made transplantation possible by protecting immunocompromised patients against the threat of overwhelming infection.

This contribution of antibiotics and steroids to the success of transplantation and cancer therapy illustrates the second feature of the 'internal dynamic' of the post-war medical achievement, which for want of a better term might be described as the 'interconnectedness' of medical research, the way in which developments in different scientific disciplines came together at particular moments to propel the therapeutic revolution onwards.

In the development of IVF four quite independent lines of research combined to culminate in the birth of the first test-tube baby: embryology, the study of human fertilisation in the early stages of foetal development; endocrinology, the elucidation of the mechanism of action of the female reproductive hormones; radioimmunoassay, the technique that allows minute quantities of hormones in the blood to be measured accurately; and optics, essential for the design of Patrick Steptoe's laparoscope, through which he aspirated eggs from the ovary. When the definitive moments of post-war medicine are viewed separately they seem diverse and independent of each other, but their interconnectedness lies at the heart of the cumulative progressive nature of medical advance.

This Olympian view may seem to provide reason enough for the rise of medicine in the post-war years. But it is not, for as soon as one starts to scrutinise these events in greater detail, a whole new level of explanation becomes apparent. The first was the displacement of the traditional philosophy of medical practice with the revolutionary new creed of 'clinical science', where the best interests of the patient become – in the name of progress – secondary to the scientific scrutiny of his illness. The second and without doubt much the most powerful single factor of all was the stunning success of the exploitation by the pharmaceutical industry of medicinal chemistry, which increased within a few years the number of useful drugs from a handful to several thousand. The third, predictably enough, was the liberating power of technology – the pump, dialysis and endoscopy – in 'opening up' new territories to medical intervention. Finally, however, we are left with the curious phenomenon that the origins of several of the most significant achievements remain to this day inscrutable biological mysteries that lie beyond the range of rational explanation.

2

CLINICAL SCIENCE – A NEW
IDEOLOGY FOR MEDICINE

Throughout the thirties a radical and dynamic new ideology – clinical science – began to permeate the leading medical institutions on both sides of the Atlantic. The clinical scientist sought to extend the intellectual range and rigour of medical practice by systematically investigating the sick and scientifically evaluating the effects of experimental treatments. In the United States the rise of clinical science is epitomised by the Mayo Clinic in Rochester. The medical staff of thirty at its inception in 1914 has grown almost twentyfold with two hundred medical staff engaged primarily in research, supported by a small army of nearly eight hundred post-doctoral fellows. Several of the achievements of the Mayo Clinic have already been alluded to including Hench and Kendall's discovery of cortisone and John Kirklin's pioneering open heart surgery in the post-war years. I have chosen, however, to focus on the Postgraduate Medical School in London which best illustrates the history of the intellectual forces that gave rise to clinical science, and how they differed from that which had gone before.

On 13 January 1935, King George V visited the Hammersmith Hospital in west London, formerly known as the Workhouse Infirmary, situated next door to one of Britain's largest prisons, Wormwood Scrubs. This location had been chosen as the site for the British Postgraduate Medical School, the first institution in the country committed to 'training specialists and the promotion of medical research in the advance of medical knowledge'. It was a 'glittering gathering'. The King was met by the chairman of the board of governors, Sir Austen Chamberlain, brother of the future Prime Minister, Neville, as well as 'the most distinguished medical men of the day resplendent in their academic regalia'. The King expressed the wish 'that the school with its happy union of ward and laboratory, joining students and teachers alike from all parts of our Empire . . . may prosper under God's blessing.'[1]

But no sooner had the School become established than the outbreak of war threatened to close it. 'The advance of medical knowledge' had to give way to more urgent priorities. Most of the medical personnel of the School were seconded elsewhere, leaving behind a 'skeleton staff' to run the hospital, whose responsibilities now extended to looking after civilian casualties from the Blitz. And yet the research conducted in these straitened circumstances by the 'skeleton staff' that remained behind, John (later Sir John) McMichael, Sheila (later Dame Sheila) Sherlock and Eric (later Professor Eric) Bywaters, ensured the style of medicine epitomised by the School – 'clinical science' – would in the following twenty-five years sweep all before it. This is best illustrated by describing their research in some detail.

Eric Bywaters, writing in the *British Medical Journal* in March 1941, described 'a specific and hitherto unreported syndrome' in civilian air-raid casualties who had been dug out of their homes with crush injuries to their limbs. He described this syndrome as follows:

> The patient has been buried for several hours with pressure on a limb. On admission he was in good condition except for a swelling of the limbs and some local anaesthesia . . . a few hours later the blood pressure falls with pallor, coldness and sweating. The blood pressure can be restored by multiple transfusions of plasma and occasionally blood [but] anxiety now arises concerning the circulation of the injured limb which shows all the changes of incipient gangrene.

The patient's urine output starts to fall, the kidneys fail resulting in coma and 'death occurs suddenly usually within a week'. Bywaters suggested this 'hitherto unreported syndrome' be called 'crush syndrome', which he correctly inferred resulted when debris from the crushed muscle clogged up the kidneys, for which, as there was no treatment for kidney failure, there was nothing to be done. The most striking aspect of Bywaters's paper is the manner in which this new syndrome is reported – the meticulous day-by-day recording of the patient's steady deterioration in which the blood pressure, haemoglobin, urine volume, level of urea and other biochemical measurements are all noted. Indeed, Bywaters's paper was the most detailed scientific monitoring of the biochemical changes prior to death from kidney failure that had ever been reported.[2]

Sheila Sherlock's research addressed another problem thrown up by the war: the difficulty in identifying the cause of jaundice in servicemen and particularly distinguishing between the three main causes, infective hepatitis (now known to result from the hepatitis A virus), blood transfusion hepatitis (now known to be caused by the hepatitis B virus) and hepatitis arising as a complication of the treatment of venereal disease with arsenic. This too, as with Bywaters's research, was in a sense 'academic' as there was no treatment for any form of hepatitis, but perhaps if specimens of liver were removed by a sharp needle through the abdominal wall (liver aspiration, now known as liver biopsy) and were examined under the microscope, this might reveal some valuable information? Sherlock performed liver aspiration on 126 patients, of whom two died following the procedure, including one who was 'already moribund from subacute liver necrosis, general paralysis of the insane and rectal carcinoma'. She found three patterns of pathological change – 'diffuse' (generalised), 'zonal' (confined to one area) and 'residual fibrosis' (replacement of the liver with fibrous tissue), but there was no correlation between any of these specific patterns and the underlying cause of the hepatitis.[3]

Lastly, John McMichael investigated another military-related medical problem, the haemodynamic changes in the heart following severe blood loss. Here a group of volunteers agreed to have a catheter inserted into a vein in the arm and manoeuvred into the right side of the heart. They were then bled of 1 litre of blood, after which the pressures within the heart were measured through the catheter. Dr McMichael found that the tendency to faint following blood loss arose from a fall in blood pressure caused by dilation of the arteries in the muscles.[4]

Through modern eyes these three research projects might seem straightforward, if of rather limited practical application. Their significance rather lies in the circumstances in which they were carried out. Research of any sort is never easy, but for these doctors to undertake these studies alongside their primary responsibility of looking after patients suggested a certain zeal and desire for knowledge. This zeal is the defining characteristic of the new ideology – clinical science – that was to transform medicine. It is difficult to describe how this philosophy of medicine differed from that of the pre-war years which it supplanted, but some idea can be gleaned from a comparison between two dominant medical figures of the pre-war years in Britain, Lord 'Tommy' Horder of St Bartholomew's Hospital and Sir Thomas Lewis of University College Hospital.

Lord Horder symbolised the pinnacle of achievement to which every consultant in London aspired. He was wealthy and stylish, turning up at St Barts in his Rolls-Royce and sporting a top hat. 'Tommy [Horder] was certainly the greatest clinician of his day, based on vast experience and shrewd judgement. His short squat figure exuded wisdom and humanity.'[5] Born the son of a Dorset draper, his reward for winning every prize at medical school was to be appointed for his first job as the house doctor to Samuel Gee, physician to the Royal Household, whose patronage rapidly propelled the young Horder into the most influential of circles.

Horder's private practice read like a *Who's Who* of the times. It included three Prime Ministers – Andrew Bonar Law, Ramsay MacDonald and Neville Chamberlain; writers – Sir James Barrie, Somerset Maugham, Rebecca West and H. G. Wells; and musicians – Sir Thomas Beecham, Sir Malcolm Sargeant, Sir Henry Wood. And in time he succeeded Samuel

Gee as physician to the Royal Household, becoming medical adviser to first King Edward VII, then George V, Edward VIII, George VI and finally Queen Elizabeth II.[6]

Tommy Horder's success was well deserved. He was very good at what he did which, in the era before sophisticated medical investigations, was making an accurate diagnosis, relying almost exclusively on what are known as 'clinical methods', the ability to infer what is amiss from the patient's history and physical signs elicited at examination. This was traditional doctoring, unencumbered by the trappings of technology, and its essential feature was the human relationship between doctor and patient.

While Lord Horder was attending to the rich and famous, Sir Thomas Lewis, the son of a Welsh mining engineer, was hard at work in the basement at University College Hospital investigating the many different types of irregularity of the heart beat with the help of the newly invented electrocardiogram. This was extremely arduous and complex work, involving thousands of recordings of the heart, which Lewis then investigated further by conducting experiments on dogs, placing electrodes into their hearts to identify the precise manner in which the electrical impulses spread. The distinguished cardiologist, Paul White, subsequently recalled what it was like:

> Lewis stopped for a brief moment to greet me, as he stood in his cutaway morning coat at the operating table in the laboratory massaging the heart of a dog with one hand . . . On several occasions I walked along Oxford Street with Lewis back to his lodgings and then returned to the laboratory. Night after night for weeks we measured the time intervals of the electrocardiograms of cats and dogs down to a ten-thousandth of a second under various experimental conditions. He taught me how to burn the midnight oil . . . he was one of the best teachers I have ever had, a hard task master with a brain as sharp as a razor.[7]

This work culminated in 'a truly magnificent volume', *The Mechanisms and Graphic Registration of the Heartbeat*, 529 pages long with 400 figures and more than 1,000 references.

As a young man Lewis had come under the influence of the leading physiologists of the day, one of whom, E. H. Starling, summed up what was to become the main difference between the Lewis and Horder methods of practising medicine: 'This is what I regard as the University spirit, not simply diagnosing a patient and deciding what to do for him in order to earn our fee, but what we can get out of his case in order to do better next time.' Lewis's biographer, Arthur Holman, elaborates:

> All Lewis's research had this factor of applying the experimental method to clinical problems and over the years he variously called this 'progressive medicine', 'experimental medicine' until he eventually adopted the phrase 'clinical science'. He had a passionate belief that clinical science was just as good as any other science, and it would be established as a University discipline . . . one has to remember that in the 1930s in Britain, the concept of a full-time lifelong career in clinical research was distinctly unlikely . . . when he started his campaign, full-time research was regarded rather as a refuge for those unable to withstand the strains of a consultant's life.[8]

The science in question was essentially the application of the methods of physiological investigation to man. For 200 years physiologists had been cutting up animals, investigating how their hearts beat and their nerves worked. Now, in the form of clinical science, precisely the same approach was to be applied to patients. Its appeal was obvious. Horder's medicine of 'clinical methods' could not progress. It could be refined and added to, but essentially its knowledge base was grounded in the autopsy room of the late nineteenth century. Clinical science, by contrast, appeared to have apparently limitless possibilities of investigating, as Lewis did, the abnormal rhythms of the heart, or as among his youthful protégés, such as McMichael, what precisely happened to the circulatory system following a substantial loss of blood. This was 'new' knowledge, out of which might come 'better' understanding of disease and perhaps even 'better' treatments. This at least was the view that had inspired

Thomas Lewis and a handful of others and had culminated in 1935 in the opening of the Postgraduate Medical School at the Hammersmith.

But John McMichael was to take Lewis's concept of clinical science one small but definitive step further, which probably more than anything else explains what a truly radical departure it was to become. In December 1943, at a meeting at London's University College Hospital chaired by Thomas Lewis, McMichael presented the research he had been conducting, where catheters were inserted into the heart to measure the fall in pressure following blood loss. At the end of the presentation Lewis described his work as 'startling' and strongly hinted that he should abandon it. 'The study sent shock waves through medical London, as many physicians regarded the technique as unethical, even immoral.'[9]

The rubicon crossed by McMichael at this meeting requires some elaboration because it is so essential to subsequent developments. The technique of manipulating a catheter into the chambers of the heart would rightly be considered 'as asking for trouble', not to say life-threatening, as it could potentially precipitate a fatal disturbance of the heart rhythm. Further, the knowledge gained from McMichael's experiment could reasonably be described as 'trivial', certainly from a therapeutic perspective, as the treatment of the low blood pressure because of haemorrhage simply requires the replacement of blood. The precise mechanism by which the blood pressure actually falls, measured so precisely by the catheter placed inside the heart, is irrelevant.

This, it seems, was not Lewis's idea of clinical science, but here was the rub. If clinical science was to progress it certainly could not place internal constraints upon itself, but must be capable of always pushing at the boundaries of the technically feasible. Here, then, is the decisive moment when the focus of medicine shifts from the Horder view of a professional contract – where the doctor's sole concern is the best interests of the patient as an individual – to one where the welfare of the patient is subordinated to the progress of science. In this new world, patients become 'interesting clinical material' on whom the ambitious young doctor performs his experiments with a view to publication in a prestigious medical journal. Here is how one young doctor puts it: 'A lot of the research you do is of no benefit to patients, and there is a real possibility you can do them harm. So, in order to do research you have got to close your eyes to some extent, or at least take calculated risks with those on whom you run the experiments.'[10]

Whatever reservations Lewis might have had about his protégé McMichael's aggressive experimental approach, time and again, as medical progress accelerated, it was to be vindicated. Thus, coincidental with McMichael's experiments on fainting in 1944, Alfred Blalock performed the first 'blue-baby' operation to correct the congenital defect Fallot's Tetralogy that in a few years would lead to the triumph of open-heart surgery. Surgeons obviously had to know in advance the precise nature of the anatomical defect they were operating on, and the only way this could be done was by using McMichael's technique of introducing a catheter into the heart, through which a dye could be injected to illuminate the anatomical defect within. Similarly Sheila Sherlock's 'liver aspiration' may not have been of much benefit to any of those who underwent it but, soon after the publication of her paper, she was being referred dozens of cases of jaundice. With the accumulating experience of their management, she rapidly became the world's leading expert in liver disease. As for Eric Bywaters, his meticulous study of 'crush syndrome' might have seemed pointless as all his patients died, but at the end of the war his knowledge about kidney failure attracted to the Hammersmith others like Wilhelm Kolff, whose dialysis machine would in time be able to save those who would otherwise have died from this 'previously unreported syndrome'.

In the ten years following the end of the war, the situation where 'research was regarded as a refuge for those unable to withstand the strains of consultant's life' was completely reversed. Now the ambitious doctor's only hope for advance was as an investigative scientist in the mould of John McMichael. Under his leadership the Postgraduate Medical School became the dominant medical institution in the country, driven forward by an extraordinarily optimistic belief in medical progress. The many achievements of those who passed through the Hammersmith during this time encompassed an exhilarating range of medical research, including investigating the 'new' antibiotics, the 'wonder drug' cortisone, the treatment of childhood leukaemia and the study of thyroid function with radio isotopes. From Hammersmith the gospel of clinical science spread outwards, so that before long every teaching hospital had adopted its tenets.[12]

The contribution of clinical science to the post-war medical achievement was to create an atmosphere within which it was possible to believe that the most difficult of problems might eventually be soluble.

There is one further critical but neglected aspect of its legacy. It is now very difficult in retrospect to understand how the pioneers in the early years of treatment for childhood leukaemia or the 'black' years of renal transplantation carried on despite the enormous suffering they inflicted and the high mortality rate from their interventions. Why did they persevere? This is a complex question but part of the answer lies in *Human Guinea Pigs* by Maurice Pappworth, published in 1967.[13] Pappworth came from Liverpool where he trained under Lord Cohen, who, like Tommy Horder, was a brilliant clinician. In time Pappworth became the standard-bearer of the tradition of clinical methods and coached several generations of young physicians to pass their postgraduate exams on principles set out in his book *A Primer of Medicine*, in which he consistently emphasised the superiority, when making a diagnosis, of clinical skills over the tests and investigations vigorously promoted by the clinical scientists.[14]

Pappworth opened his *Human Guinea Pigs* by citing the views of Sir William Heneage Ogilvie, senior surgeon at Guy's: 'The science of experimental medicine is something new and sinister, for it is capable of destroying in our minds the old faith that we, the doctors, are the servants of the patients whom we have undertaken to care for and the complete trust that they can place their lives or the lives of their loved ones in our care.'[15]

This 'sinister' aspect of clinical science, where patients become 'human guinea pigs', Pappworth illustrates with numerous examples of experiments on infants, pregnant women, the mentally ill, prisoners, the old and the dying. They are variously cruel, dangerous or purposeless. Here the cardiac catheterisation popularised by John McMichael becomes in the hands of a group of doctors from Birmingham a superior form of torture, in which patients must sit on a bicycle with a mask on their face and catheters coming out of their arms to permit the pressure within their hearts to be recorded. Not a pleasant experience, but as Pappworth points out, the crucial point is that all these patients were seriously ill, suffering from anaemia, an overactive thyroid, or various forms of obstructive lung disease. Not only would they not have benefited from these experiments, but neither would anyone else, because the knowledge acquired usually had little value, other than providing the opportunity for those conducting the experiments to further their career by writing the results up in a scientific journal.

Human Guinea Pigs outraged academic physicians and Pappworth paid a heavy price. He was ostracised by the medical establishment and denied the Fellowship of the Royal College of Physicians right up until a year before his death. This was the inevitable reverse side of the coin of clinical science, where the necessity for doctors to perform experiments as a requirement for their own advancement led to the sort of degenerate scientism that was the antithesis of the Horderian concept of a 'personal' relationship between doctor and patient. Nonetheless, this medical ruthlessness was an indispensable requirement when it came to pushing forward the boundaries of medicine. The ideology of clinical science encouraged a sort of emotional disconnectedness, without which the pioneers would never have persisted with their experimental therapies.

3

A CORNUCOPIA OF NEW DRUGS

The newly qualified doctor setting up practice in the 1930s had a dozen or so proven remedies with which to treat the multiplicity of different diseases he encountered every day: aspirin for rheumatic fever, digoxin for heart failure, the hormones thyroxine and insulin for an underactive thyroid and diabetes respectively, salvarsan for syphilis, bromides for those who needed a sedative, barbiturates for epilepsy, and morphine for pain. Thirty years later, when the same doctor would have been approaching retirement, those dozen remedies had grown to over 2,000. The medical textbook he had bought as a student – the first edition of Cecil's *Textbook of Medicine*, published in 1927 – had, by the time he purchased the fourteenth edition in 1960, changed out of all recognition, as its chief editor Paul Beeson subsequently observed:

In going through the first edition, one cannot fail to be impressed by the paucity of available drugs. Many medicines used in 1927 have simply disappeared, such as strychnine, the arsenicals, tincture of capsicum, tincture of ginger, dilute hydrochloric acid, boric acid, and bromide preparations. Only about thirty drugs mentioned in the first edition are still in use today.

Dr Beeson then proceeds to enumerate the therapeutic cornucopia of new drugs that are mentioned in the fourteenth
edition. They include:

> . . . 86 anti-infective agents, 5 antihistamines, 10 synthetic
> steroids, 35 other hormone preparations, 9 drugs affecting
> blood coagulation, 13 anti-epileptic drugs, 31 cytotoxic or
> immunosuppressive agents, 18 analgesics, 11 sedatives, 39
> drugs affecting the autonomic nervous system, 15 nutrients,
> 11 diuretics and 7 new preparations for the treatment of
> poisoning.[1]

In parallel with this massive increase in the range of treatments our doctor was now able to prescribe, his perception of
the role of medicine had utterly changed. He would have been,
when qualifying in the 1930s, a 'therapeutic nihilist', not only
aware there was little to offer his patients, but doubtful that
there ever would be. He had, after all, spent time in the autopsy
room and seen the terrible ravages of disease on human organs,
against which no remedy could prevail. As the great William
Osler, Regius Professor of Medicine at Oxford from 1905 to
1919 had expressed it: 'We work by wit and not by witchcraft,
and while our patients have our tenderest care and we must do
what is best for the relief of their sufferings, we should not
bring the art of medicine into disrepute by quack-like promises
to heal or by attempts to cure "continuate and inexorable
maladies".'[2]

Osler's profoundly influential views were themselves the outcome of the struggle, going back to the 1830s, to purge from
the practice of medicine dubious and unproven remedies. For
Osler the purpose of medicine was not to make people better,
which was unrealistic, but rather to correctly diagnose what was
amiss and to give a prognosis as to the likely outcome of the illness. Thus pneumonia he described as being 'a self-limiting
disease, which can neither be aborted nor cut short by any
known means at our command. The young practitioner must
bear in mind that patients are more often damaged than helped
by the promiscuous drugging that is only too prevalent.'

Our doctor had watched this intellectually rigorous but nihilistic view of medicine's possibilities melt away almost before his eyes, as every year brought new and extraordinary drugs to treat the previously untreatable. He had long since ceased to be a therapeutic nihilist, now his expectation – and that of his patients – was that for virtually every ill, there should be a pill.

So what transformed the paucity of remedies of the 1930s into the cornucopia of the 1960s? It is natural to assume there must have been some scientific development to make it possible for scientists to design chemicals that could correct the defects of functioning caused by disease. But that is not what happened. Rather, as illustrated time and again in the account of the definitive moments of post-war medicine, the consistent manner in which drugs were discovered happened by accident in any number of forms: Alexander Fleming's chance observation of the unusual appearance of the bacteria on a culture plate, which led to penicillin; Philip Hench's surprising discovery of the astonishing effects of cortisone in rheumatoid arthritis; or Henri Laborit's astute perception of the 'euphoric quietude' in his surgical patients, which led to chlorpromazine. Alternatively drugs used to treat one condition were 'accidentally' found to relieve another, or 'accidentally' found to have side-effects that could be turned to therapeutic advantage. Even drugs that emerged from screening programmes were 'accidental', because it could not have been anticipated which few out of the hundreds of thousands of chemicals tested might prove to be effective against tuberculosis or cancer. Indeed, the origins of virtually every class of drug discovered between the 1930s and the 1980s can be traced to some fortuitous, serendipitous or accidental observation. It could not have happened any other way, for the following reasons.

It is obvious that drugs, being chemicals, must work by interfering in some way with the chemical composition of cells, either the constituents of the walls that surround them, the process of manufacturing proteins within them, or perhaps the chemical transmitters that connect the function of one cell to another. Clearly then, if a chemist were to intentionally design a drug for the treatment of some illness he would have to know at a cellular level the defect that, hopefully, his chemical would correct. For this he would have to know something about the microscopic world of the cell but – and it is astonishing – during the period of the therapeutic revolution the knowledge of how the cell worked was virtually non-existent.

If the impetus for the therapeutic revolution could not come from the understanding of the chemistry of the cell and how it might be changed by drugs, then it had to come from the other side of the equation – the chemistry of the drugs themselves. Here the situation was very different. By the 1930s chemistry was a highly sophisticated science, in which it was possible to determine the composition of any chemical, the varying amounts of carbon, hydrogen, oxygen and sulphur it contained, its structure and how the molecules were bound together, and above all how one chemical could be changed into another.

In essence, the therapeutic revolution started with a 'lead' – a chance observation that some chemical seemed to have some effect on a diseased state. Then the research chemists played around with it, the fecundity of chemistry being such that it is possible to synthesise literally thousands of related compounds from a single lead. Then it was time to experiment, giving the chemicals to those suffering from an illness (or an animal 'model' in which it is simulated) to see what happens. The range of chemical variations is so vast that even if there is little understanding of what is wrong at a cellular level or how a synthesised chemical might put it right, the likelihood is that sooner or later one is going to hit the jackpot.

This is not to suggest that this process is 'unscientific'. On the contrary, science is involved at every stage. Chemistry is a sophisticated science and the methods for synthesising new chemical compounds require great skill and ingenuity. The investigation and assessment of the effect of chemicals in altering symptoms of disease requires a rigorous and systematic scientific method, but the crucial point remains that the identification of the original 'lead' could only come about by accident.

Thus the therapeutic revolution of the post-war years was not ignited by a major scientific insight, rather the reverse: it was the realisation by doctors and scientists that it was not necessary to understand in any detail what was wrong, but that synthetic chemistry blindly and randomly would deliver the remedies that had eluded doctors for centuries. This is certainly different from the conventional way in which medical progress is believed to have occurred, but is well illustrated by the career of the chemical that started the therapeutic revolution in the first place – the sulphonamides identified by the German chemist Gerhard Domagk in 1933.

In 1927 the chemical company Bayer had appointed Domagk as Director of Research with a brief to investigate whether synthetic dyes might have antibacterial properties that could be used to treat infectious diseases.

The principles of his research programme were as follows. His colleague Josef Klarer synthesised new chemical dyes, which he then passed to Domagk, who tested them in mice that had been experimentally infected with different types of bacteria that caused meningitis, gonorrhoea, puerperal fever and so on. It was a typical piece of systematic German research. Domagk did all of his own post-mortem dissections and microscopic examination of the animals' organs, during which time he was accessible to no one, took no telephone calls and received no visitors. 'We dissected until we could no longer stand on our feet, and looked through microscopes until we could no longer see.'

Domagk's first four years of research – up until 1932 – were 'not particularly encouraging'. And then came prontosil, a red dye that had originally been synthesised in the hope it would be valuable for colouring leather. In December 1932 Domagk conducted his standard experiments on two groups of mice infected with the streptococcus. The group given prontosil survived, the control group died.[3] Domagk did not publish the results of these experiments for another two years but in 1933 he had direct personal experience of prontosil's effectiveness in humans when his four-year-old daughter developed a fulminating skin infection of the hand, for which the only treatment up till then had been amputation. She was cured by prontosil.

Within a few months of Domagk's publication of the result of his mice experiments in 1935, scientists at the Pasteur Institute in Paris discovered the therapeutic effects of prontosil in killing bacteria had nothing to do with its chemical properties as a dye; the active component rather was a chemical to which the dye was linked, known as a sulphonamide.[4]

And so by this circuitous route the sulphonamides were discovered. It is appropriate to pause for a moment before following their dizzying career to reflect on the difference they made to the treatment of infectious diseases and in particular the three caused by the streptococcus bacterium: puerperal fever in women following labour, erysipelas (the skin infection suffered by Domagk's daughter) and scarlet fever. In Britain in the 1930s over 1,000 women died every year from puerperal fever, where the traumatised vaginal tissues became contaminated by streptococcal bacteria that then gained entry to the blood stream, causing blood poisoning, collapse of the circulation and death within a few days. After Domagk discovered prontosil, Dr Leonard Colebrook, Director of Research at Queen Charlotte's Maternity Hospital in London, managed to get hold of supplies of the drug and treated thirty-eight women within a few months, thirty-five of whom were cured. His comments on the cases convey some of the astonishment he felt at this new treatment. Thus one 36-year-old woman with a fulminating infection of the womb is described as being 'very ill, debilitated and delirious. After admission her condition deteriorated until she was given prontosil. Spectacular improvement.'[5] The curative power of prontosil had a dramatic effect on the mortality graph of puerperal fever, which fell like a stone from 2.5 per 1,000 live births in 1937 to less than 0.5 three years later.

It was the same story with the skin infection erysipelas, a particular hazard for doctors and nurses. 'Most large hospitals have records of tragic deaths [among their staff] from this cause. In each of the cases of which I have personal knowledge, infection was through a finger prick or scratch during attendance on a septic patient . . . there was an acute cellulitis [skin infection] of rapid onset, spreading to the arm, the onset of septicaemia was heralded by high fever and rigor.' The decline in mortality from erysipelas paralleled that of puerperal fever. Nor was that all, for the sulphonamides were also effective against 'strep sore throats', which had just been implicated as the cause of rheumatic fever attacking the joints, kidneys and heart valves to cause respectively arthritis, kidney failure and heart failure from diseased valves. Sulphonamides saved the life of Franklin Roosevelt's son, and Winston Churchill when he contracted pneumonia in Carthage in December 1943.[6]

It is scarcely necessary to emphasise what an extraordinary phenomenon the sulphonamides represented. But this is only the beginning of the story of their contribution to modern medicine. They were, up until the discovery of penicillin, the only effective drugs against infectious disease and, besides being widely prescribed, were naturally a focus of great scientific interest. Consequently a whole series of other quite unanticipated therapeutic benefits soon became apparent.

1939: Donald Woods of London's Middlesex Hospital discovered the structure of sulphonamides to be very similar to another chemical, PABA, an important constituent of the vitamin folic acid. Humans obtain their folic acid from their diet but bacteria have to manufacture it for themselves. Hence sulphonamides worked, Woods inferred, by being a 'false building-block' and thus 'jamming the works' – the bacteria when trying to make their own folic acid utilised sulphonamide rather than PABA and as a result they died. The phenomenon is called 'competitive antagonism'.[7]

In the United States George Hitchings and Gertrude Elion, inspired by Woods's conception of 'competitive antagonism', applied (as described in 'Curing Childhood Cancer') the same principle to purine – a component of DNA – in the hope of finding the 'false building-blocks' that would prevent cells from dividing and which might then be useful in the treatment of cancer and similar disorders. Over the next twenty years, this approach led to, *inter alia*, drugs for leukaemia (6-mp), the immunosuppressant azathioprine that made transplantation possible, allopurinol for the prevention of gout, and the most successful drug for the treatment of viral illnesses – acyclovir.[8]

1940: In the following year patients receiving large doses of sulphonamides reported the unusual side-effect of passing inordinate amounts of urine (as already described in 'The Triumph of Prevention') – because, it eventually transpired, the sulphonamide blocked an enzyme in the kidney. Several serious medical conditions result from increased fluid in the tissues, including the breathlessness of heart failure and the water-logging of the tissues of kidney failure, while others, such as raised blood pressure and the blinding condition glaucoma, benefit from fluid reduction. There was at the time no effective treatment for any of these conditions, but this unusual side-effect encouraged the chemists to start playing around with the sulphonamide molecule, leading in rapid succession to the discovery of the powerful drug for lowering the blood pressure (bendrofluazide), diuretics or water pills (frusemide) for the treatment of heart and kidney failure, and acetazolamide for the treatment of glaucoma.[9,10]

1941: F. V. McCallum at the Johns Hopkins Medical School in Baltimore observed that a variant of sulphonamide markedly increased the size of the thyroid gland in rats. Investigating the matter further, he found that a chemical, thiourea, blocked the synthesis of thyroxine, leading to its logical therapeutic use as a treatment for an overactive thyroid or thyrotoxicosis.[11] In the same year, another sulphonamide was found to prevent the growth of the leprosy organism in mice. This in turn led to the rediscovery of another sulphonamide, dapsone, which remains the mainstay of anti-leprosy treatment.[12]

1942: Marcel Jabon of the Medical Faculty at Montpellier University observed that a derivative of a sulphonamide used for the treatment of typhoid fever made some patients extremely ill by lowering their blood sugar. This raised the possibility that they might be of use in the treatment of diabetes (in which the blood sugar is raised), leading to a group of drugs, the sulphonylureas, which, along with insulin, remain an important treatment for this condition.[13]

1946: A further variant of sulphonamides was discovered to be weakly effective against malaria, which led to the introduction of proguanil, still used in the prevention of this terrible illness.[14]

Now it is possible to get a sense of how synthetic chemistry was going to transform medicine. We start with a simple compound made of sulphur, hydrogen, nitrogen, carbon and oxygen atoms 'accidentally' discovered by Domagk, which revolutionised the treatment of a whole range of infectious illnesses. Then, over the next twenty years, the same sulphonamides were responsible in one way or another for treatments for hypertension (thus reducing the incidence of stroke), diabetes, heart failure, glaucoma, thyrotoxicosis, malaria and leprosy. Further, the discovery of their mode of action opened up, through the work of Hitchings and Elion, a vast new field of therapeutics, leading to treatments for cancer, gout and viral illnesses.

The fortuitous, serendipitous and accidental nature of drug discovery is amply illustrated in many of the definitive moments already discussed. It could not have happened any other way, as scientific understanding of disease was much too limited to provide an intellectual basis for the purposive design of drugs. Regrettably it is simply not possible to begin to describe in any detail the way in which this cornucopia of new drugs transformed every aspect of medicine. Some idea of the extraordinary scale of this phenomenon can, however, be gleaned by referring to the table on page 185.

There was one final ingredient necessary for the full promise of the application of chemistry in medicine to be realised – the capitalist mode of production. The lessons of the discovery of the sulphonamides, antibiotics and cortisone were not lost on the pharmaceutical industry. The potential market for these drugs was so vast, the profits to be made from just one discovery so enormous, that they started to invest massively in research, recruiting every chemist they could lay their hands on. The potential of synthesising new chemical compounds seemed virtually limitless, and the whole process was best achieved by placing it on an industrial footing. This was a high-risk venture with no guarantee of return on the investment – as there was no predicting where the next discovery might come from – but 'risk' is what capitalism is all about. The dynamics of the therapeutic revolution owed more to a synergy between the creative forces of capitalism and chemistry than to the science of medicine and biology.

The atmosphere of optimism and energy driving the therapeutic revolution forward is illustrated by events at the drug company Upjohn soon after Philip Hench's revelation of the therapeutic benefits of cortisone. Its cost, because of its method of extraction, was still extremely high, so vast financial rewards would go to the drug company that found a cheaper way of manufacturing it:

> Top members of the research division mapped out a massive seven-pronged programme aimed at finding practical new methods of producing cortisone on an industrial scale. One group would work on a modification of the method of producing cortisone from bile-acids employed by Merck [who had originally provided the cortisone used by Philip Hench]. A second would make an effort to synthesise cortisone from simple raw materials, such as coal tar chemicals. A third team would work on the chemical conversion of an easily obtained steroid made by yeasts to cortisone, the fourth would seek to prepare the hormone from a steroid compound extracted from the root of the green helibore. A fifth group of researchers would look into the possibility of obtaining the hormone from steroids made by the adrenal cortex gland with the aid of enzymes. Another group would see whether micro-organisms might be enlisted in carrying out a particularly difficult step in the cortisone synthesis. And as a final measure, Upjohn would take part in an expedition to Africa, one of six sent by pharmaceu-

The golden age of drug discovery, 1940–75

	Infectious diseases	Cancer	Psychiatry	Rheumatology	Circulatory disorders	Endocrinology	Other: neurology (N), haematology (H), gastroenterology (G), respiratory (R) illnesses
1940	Penicillin Streptomycin PAS Chloramphenicol Tetracycline Cephalosporin	Antibiotics Cortisone Methotrexate 6-mp	Lithium	Antibiotics Cortisone Methotrexate	Lignocaine Hydralazine Acetazolamide	Carbimazole Stilboestrol Vasopressin	Antibiotics Cortisone Vitamin B12 (H) Vitamin K (H)
1950	Nystatin Erythromycin Vancomycin Kanamycin Amphotericin B Griseofulvin Metronidazole	Thiothepa Chlorambucil Melphalan Cyclophosphamide Actinomycin 5-FU	Chlorpromazine Imipramine Marsilid Meprobamate Haloperidol	Phenylbutazone Hydroxychloroquine Cyclophosphamide	Clofibrate Methyldopa Disopyramide Spironolactone Chlorothiazide	Chlorpropamide Phenformin HRT	Bisacodyl (G) Factor VIII (H) Primidone (N) Ethosuximide (N) Isoprenaline (R)
1960	Fusidic acid Lincomycin Gentamycin Ethambutol Clotrimazole Trimethoprim Rifampicin Amantadine Idoxuridine	Daunomycin Bleomycin L-Asparaginase Vincristine Cisplatin	Diazepam Chlordiazepoxide	Indomethacin Ibuprofen Penicillamine Allopurinol Mefenamic acid	Propranolol Verapamil Frusemide Cholestyramine Clonidine Amiloride	The 'Pill' Bromocriptine HCG Clomiphene Tamoxifen	Azathioprine L-dopa (N) Carbamazepine (N) Naloxone (N) Sodium valproate (N) Carbenoxolone (G) Salbutamol (R) Sodium chromoglycate (R) Chlormethiazole (G)
1970	Carbenicillin Interferon		Fluoxetine Clozapine	Diflunisal Piroxicam	Captopril Nifedipine Amiodarone Dipyrimadole		Cyclosporin Metoclopramide (G) Cimetidine (G) Cheonodeoxycholic acid (G)

tical companies and government agencies, in search of the famous lost strophanthus vine, whose seed was reported to contain a substance from which cortisone might be made easily – if the vine could be found and cultivated. Well over half of the three hundred people in the research division were thrown into the cortisone fray. It was the biggest research gamble the company had ever undertaken.[15]

Compounding this frenetic activity was what can best be called the multiplier effect. The more chemicals that were synthesised and the more drugs that were produced, so the greater the chance for the 'accidental' observation, whether in the laboratory or on the ward, that would draw attention to other useful therapeutic avenues to explore. The consequence can be seen in every new edition of the *Pharmacopoeia*, as by the 1960s over 100 new drugs were being registered each year. But this process could not go on indefinitely. Sooner or later the chemists must run out of new chemicals to test – and then what would happen?

4

TECHNOLOGY'S TRIUMPHS

Technology, along with drug discovery, shares the prize for the massive expansion of medicine in the post-war years. They are similar in that both provided empirical solutions to the problems of disease without the necessity for a profound understanding of its nature or causes. They differ, however, in that the manner of technological innovation is almost the precise opposite of drug discovery for, whereas most drugs were discovered by 'accident', technological solutions are, by definition, highly intentional, specific answers to well-defined problems.

Many medical problems proved highly amenable to technological solutions, which subdivide into three categories: Life-sustaining, Diagnostic and Surgical (see next page). The life-sustaining technologies of the intensive care unit, and particularly the ventilator machine, which ensured adequate oxygenation of tissues, could keep people alive during an acute illness until their physiological functions recovered. Dialysis and the heart pacemaker extended this principle to keeping alive for many years those with chronic illnesses, such as kidney failure or potentially lethal abnormalities of heart rhythm.

Next, the new methods of diagnostic technology permitted doctors to scrutinise every nook and cranny of the body. The brain, thanks to the CT and MRI scanners, can now be seen with a haunting clarity, while the foetus that previously grew

Three forms of medical technology

LIFE-SUSTAINING[1]
Intensive care	Dialysis
Ventilator	Pacemakers

DIAGNOSTIC[2]
CT scanner	PET scanner
MRI scanner	Angiography
Ultrasound	Cardiac catheterisation

SURGICAL[3]
Joint replacement	The pump
Intraocular lens implant	Operating microscope
Cochlear implant	Endoscopy

hidden from view within the womb can, thanks to ultrasound, be observed virtually from the moment of conception.

Finally, the surgical technology of the pump (as already described), and joint replacements, created respectively the entirely new specialty of cardiac surgery and transformed the scope of orthopaedics.

The significance of these technological innovations needs no elaboration. But the most important of all, in the comprehensiveness of its effects, was optics. The Zeiss operating microscope and the endoscope allowed surgeons not only to 'see more' but also 'do more' and in the process had a major impact across the whole range of surgical disciplines: ENT surgery, ophthalmology, neurosurgery, plastic surgery, replantation surgery, gynaecology, orthopaedics and abdominal surgery.

The Operating Microscope

The possibilities of the operating microscope are best conceived by thinking of a household pin whose head is slightly less than 1 millimetre or ¹⁄₂₀ inch in diameter. Then imagine the pinhead is an artery that has to be sewn on to another artery of the same dimensions. It can't be done. But if the same pinhead-sized arteries are viewed through an operating microscope and

magnified twenty-fold then, to the surgeon's eye, both ends
now appear to be an inch in diameter, and with delicate instruments they can be sewn together. Welcome to the world of
microsurgery.[4]

Microsurgery effectively started in 1954, when the German
optics company Zeiss produced the first binocular surgical
microscope. Among the first to see its possibilities were the Ear,
Nose and Throat (ENT) surgeons, for reasons that are readily
apparent when leaning over the surgeon's shoulder to watch an
operation on a patient whose deafness is caused by hardening of
the bones of the middle ear. Peering down the ear canal, the
eardrum is readily identifiable as a curtain of tissue. The surgeon takes a knife and cuts away its lower half and then lifts it
upwards like a tent flap to expose beneath the three small bones
of the middle ear, the most distant of which, the stapes (so
called because of its physical resemblance to a rider's stirrups) is
in close proximity to the organ of hearing, the semi-circular
canals of the inner ear. In otosclerosis, as this patient's condition
is called, the stapes becomes immobile and is unable to transmit
the vibrations of sound from the eardrum. The surgeon duly
mobilises the stapes by drilling a minute hole through its centre
and dropping through a piston whose movements can now
transmit the vibrations. It requires little imagination to appreciate how this and similar delicate operations, performed deep
within the ear, can only be reliably accomplished with an operating microscope.[5]

Next came the ophthalmologists with their immensely successful Intraocular Lens Implant for cataracts which, along with
Charnley's hip replacement, is one of the great 'mass' operations developed in the post-war years. In 1948 Harold Ridley,
ophthalmic surgeon at St Thomas's Hospital, had a flash of
inspiration when a student remarked, after observing him
remove a cataract: 'It is a pity the lens cannot be replaced by an
artificial one.' Ridley was stimulated by this apparently naïve
remark to recall his experience from a few years earlier when
treating eye injuries in fighter pilots during the Second World
War. To his surprise, the fragments of glass from the aircraft's
shattered windscreens that had pierced the eyes had caused

little damage. Perhaps, Ridley speculated, the eye was some sort of 'privileged sanctuary' that could tolerate foreign objects such as splinters of glass. If so, it would indeed be possible to replace the lens clouded by cataract with a plastic one. His review of his first twenty cases two years later was modestly optimistic, though he did note that 'in some the persistence of exudate on the lens surface still partially obstructed vision, but it is not beyond hope that all will become clear in due course'. His medical colleagues took a different view as his former house surgeon observed: 'It needed great fortitude to face up to the loud criticisms of his colleagues and the frank disbelief at his results.'[6]

Ridley's very high failure rate discouraged others, but the advent of the Zeiss operating microscope in the 1950s and a newer, lighter implant improved results so dramatically that 80,000 lens implants are now performed routinely each year in the United Kingdom. 'Without the Zeiss microscope, ocular surgery as it now is would be unimaginable,' and that includes not just cataracts, but operations for the relief of glaucoma, for detachment of the retina and on 'the vitreous', the jelly-like substance that maintains the shape of the eyeball.[7]

The operating microscope was also indispensable for operations involving very small blood vessels, which proved essential in three further surgical specialties: neurosurgery, plastic surgery and the replantation of amputated limbs. The first successful replantation operation was performed in Boston in 1962 on a twelve-year-old boy, run over by a train which completely amputated his arm. Eight years later he was arrested by the police 'after using his replanted hand to steal from a store'. The Chinese became particularly adept at this type of surgery, with a report from Shanghai's Sixth People's Hospital of the first hand replantation in 1963 on a 27-year-old man who subsequently became a table-tennis champion.[8] In neurosurgery, the repair of bleeding blood vessels and aneurysms in the brain had always carried a very high mortality rate but in the first forty repairs done with the aid of the operating microscope there was not a single fatality. 'The importance of the introduction of magnification has completely changed virtually all procedures done within the specialty. The pioneers created a new world through their attention to anatomical detail and technical manoeuvres.'⁹

Finally, in plastic surgery microsurgery revolutionised skin grafting for severe burns, replacing the standard technique invented by Sir Harold Gillies in 1917, when confronted with the problem of reconstructing the face of a sailor severely burned in the Battle of Jutland. 'This poor sailor was rendered hideously repulsive and well nigh incapacitated by his terrible burns. The structure of the nose, lips, eyelids, the ears and neck were burnt and his hands were contracted into frightful deformity. How a man can survive such an appalling burn is difficult to imagine until one has met one of the survivors from such a fire and realised the unquenchable optimism which carries them through almost anything.' Gillies dissected a skin graft out from its donor site on the sailor's chest except for one end − 'the pedicle' − and then rolled it into a tube and swung it in the direction of the burns on the face, and reattached it. The graft's blood supply was maintained by the pedicle until the replanted end had acquired its own blood supply, at which point the graft could then be separated from the pedicle, the tube unrolled and used to cover the mouth and nose.

Gillies was the 'father of plastic surgery' and he trained the following generation just in time for the next major conflict to produce horrifying burns − the Battle of Britain, in 1940. British pilots tumbled out of the air over Kent and into beds at East Grinstead Hospital under the care of one of Gillies's pupils, Sir Archie McIndoe. There they became one of McIndoe's 'guinea pigs', so called out of respect for the surgeon under whose care they sometimes remained for two years. Twenty or more separate operations were sometimes necessary, in which pedicles were swung from the arm and shoulder and chest upwards to the face to repair its ravaged appearance. The result was never perfect, though with the passage of time it became more acceptable.¹⁰

Then, quite suddenly, in 1972, these techniques became redundant with the first report of a microsurgical 'free skin flap transfer'. Instead of raising a 'tube pedicle' and waiting for it to acquire a new blood supply, the full thickness graft was taken from a part of the body that could afford to lose it – which in the first reported case was the groin – and transferred to the site requiring grafting, the ankle. The minuscule blood vessels of the graft were then connected – with the aid of the operating microscope – to those of the donor site, the arterial clamps were removed and 'there was immediate perfusion of the graft as evidenced by its colour. After 17 days the sutures were removed and a few luxuriant pubic hairs were noted growing on the ankle. The donor site had completely healed.'[11] The significance of this development scarcely needs to be spelt out as two years of surgery involving up to twenty operations were telescoped down into one procedure.

In summary, the Zeiss operating microscope transformed the practice of ENT, ophthalmology, neurosurgery and plastic surgery. Simultaneously the endoscope, by allowing the visualisation of the internal structures of the body, was having a similar effect on an entirely different range of specialties, including gynaecology, orthopaedics and abdominal surgery.

The Endoscope

There are many ways of 'seeing' beneath the skin to find out what is amiss in the inner recesses of the body, from the simple chest X-ray to the total body CT scan, but if the intention is not just to see but also to do something as well, such as cauterising a blood vessel bleeding into the stomach, then there is no alternative other than to use an instrument through which the site of the bleeding can be seen with the human eye and down which a cauterising device can be passed. These instruments are known as 'endoscopes' – derived from the Greek prefix *endo* – 'within' – and the verb *skopein* – 'to observe' – not merely in the sense of 'looking at something' but also to 'observe with intent'.

There are two types of endoscope, each with its own optical requirements. When the intention is to 'observe with intent' a hollow organ such as the stomach, colon or bladder, the endoscope must be fully flexible, able to look in all directions and contain an aperture down which a biopsy's forceps or a cauter-ising device can be passed. When, however, the intention is to inspect a closed cavity such as the abdomen to perform some procedure on the female reproductive organs or the gut, then a rigid endoscope is required down which instruments can be passed and whose optics must be of such high quality that it is possible to see what is being operated on with intense clarity.

The origins of both types of endoscope stretch back to the late nineteenth century, but they never achieved widespread use because their optical systems were deficient. Thus the gastro-scope for inspecting the inner lining of the stomach was only 'semi-flexible' so only a partial viewing could be obtained, while the visualisation of the inside of the abdomen as seen down the laparoscope was much too poor to permit any sort of operative intervention. And that was the situation up until Harold Hopkins – a lecturer at Imperial College in London – solved both problems, first with the fully flexible fibreoptic endoscope in 1954 and then five years later with the Hopkins rod-lens system, which improved the quality of the laparo-scopic image eighty-fold.

Harold Hopkins was born in 1918, the son of a Leicester baker. After graduating in physics and mathematics in 1939 from the university of his home town he worked briefly for a firm of optical instrument makers. He spent his war years as a scientific research officer attached to the Ministry of Aircraft Production and in 1947 joined the staff of Imperial College, London, where he stayed for twenty years before moving to Reading University as Professor of Applied Physics. 'Harold Hopkins was an outstanding physicist, he had a fertile mind, steely determination and ferocious curiosity. His intellect was motivated by a constant belief in the power of fundamental physics.'[12] It is not possible to describe precisely how Hopkins came to make his two remarkable contributions (not to men-tion, at the request of the BBC in 1947, how he devised the first 'zoom lens') as this type of technical scientific creativity is not amenable to exposition. The following account therefore is limited to the events leading up to and the consequence of his achievement.

At a dinner party in 1951 Hopkins found himself sitting next to Hugh Gainsborough, a gastroenterologist from St George's Hospital, who complained to him about the 'inadequacies' of the gastroscopic instruments then available. Even the most sophisticated, the semi-flexible gastroscope, he told Hopkins, required great skill and expertise, caused considerable discomfort to the patient and the field of vision was limited, leaving 'blind spots' at the apex of the stomach and at the entrance to the duodenum. This seriously limited its diagnostic usefulness and the doctor could never be entirely sure that he had not 'missed something' to account for the patient's symptoms. What was needed, suggested Dr Gainsborough, was a gastroscope whose tip could be manipulated in several different directions so that the lining of the stomach could be visualised in its entirety.

Reflecting on this problem Hopkins, it would seem, was reminded of an experiment conducted by the great Victorian scientist, John Tyndall, who showed that light, which usually travels in straight lines, could, in special circumstances, go round corners. In 1870, at a demonstration held before the Royal Society in London, Tyndall used an illuminated vessel of water to show that when a stream of water was allowed to flow through a hole in the side of the vessel, light was conducted along the curved path of the stream. This effect can be simulated with curved glass. Indeed glass-blowers in Ancient Greece and Renaissance Venice had constructed beautiful glass objects made of thin cylinders, along which light could be conducted from a lamp beneath with magical effect.

Hopkins speculated that if tens of thousands of very narrow flexible glass fibres were collected in a bundle they should be able to transmit light round corners, and whatever was illuminated should be transmitted back up the bundle to be viewed by the observer. He spent three years on the project publishing the details in *Nature* in January 1954. So was born the fibreoptic endoscope.[13]

Hopkins, as an optical physicist, was not in a position to apply the principle of fibreoptic endoscopy for medical use, but a young South African, Basil Hirschowitz, a research fellow in

gastroenterology at the University of Michigan who was 'frustrated at the inadequate visualisation and difficulty' of the
gastroscopes in use at the time, read Hopkins's article in *Nature*
and immediately arranged a vacation. He flew to London to see
Hopkins at Imperial College, finding him 'warm and friendly
and most modest and generous'. Hopkins's instrument was very
much a prototype, being less than a foot long and thus quite
unsuitable for practical use, but 'the definition was good
enough' so Hirschowitz returned to the United States to turn it
into a practical instrument.[14] 'The apparatus for making the
glass fibres was assembled from odds and ends in the physics
department – no more than $250 being spent on the equipment.
The principle was to melt the end of a vertically held rod of
glass in an eight-inch-long tubular furnace to draw out a fibre
from the smelt.' The fibre was then wound on to a drum (originally a circular 2lb box of Mother's Oats), with 200,000 fibres
having to be oriented so the ends were exactly the same and
stayed that way. This was difficult and very time-consuming
work posing many technical problems, the most insuperable of
which was 'cross talk' – when two fibres are in close contact,
light jumps from one to the other, and if this occurs often
enough the image is lost. Somehow the glass fibres had to be
insulated from each other, a problem solved by Hirschowitz's
collaborator Larry Curtiss. 'When he first proposed to melt a
rod of optical glass inside a tube of lower refractive index glass
and pull the two together into a composite fibre, all the wise
men in the physics department laughed at him. Fortunately he
persisted and produced the fibre on which today's fibreoptics is
based – a glass-coated glass fibre.' Dr Hirschowitz's first view of
the potential of Larry Curtiss's method of insulation was 'on a
dark late December afternoon when a single fibre was used to
transmit a white spot of light 25–30 feet from one room into the
next. We knew that the problems of insulation and excessive
light loss were solved. From then on it was purely a matter of
applying and developing the process – we were home free.'

Within six weeks Dr Hirschowitz had the first modern fibreoptic gastroscope in his hands. 'I looked at this rather thick,
forbidding but flexible rod, took the instrument and courage in

both hands and swallowed it over the protest of my unanaes-
thetised pharynx.' Within a few days he had passed the
instrument into his first patient, the wife of a dental student
with a duodenal ulcer. The new gastroscope was everything
and more that Hirschowitz could have hoped for, rendering the
conventional semi-flexible gastroscope 'obsolete on all counts'.
The illumination was two and a half times better and the whole
of the inner lining of the stomach could be visualised.

Hopkins's fibreoptic instrument changed the practice of
medicine in multiple ways, falling into two categories – the
diagnostic and the therapeutic. With the fibreoptic endoscope,
the doctor could travel much further and deeper than ever
before into previously uncharted territory. Thus the gastroscope visualised not only the lining of the stomach but could be
passed through the pylorus into the duodenum, which in turn
gave access to the pancreas and biliary system. Coming from
the other end, the fibreoptic colonoscope could be manipulated all the way up the colon to a site where it joins the small
intestine. The furthest reaches of the lung and bladder became
equally accessible. The technique of using the endoscope was
readily acquired and so it could be used in a routine way to
investigate the cause of any symptom that might arise from
any of these structures. Bleeding from the gut, for example,
could be investigated by the most reliable and direct means –
inspecting the lining to identify what was amiss. Further, once
the bleeding was identified it could be biopsied and the tissue
examined under the microscope, permitting an accurate
diagnosis that would then have a major influence on treatment.

The difference that fibreoptics made to improving the accu-
racy of diagnosis was paralleled by its therapeutic potential
permitting, for example, a bleeding artery in the stomach to be
cauterised or a polyp in the colon to be ensnared without the
need for major surgery.[15]

Hopkins's second optical innovation came in 1957, six years
after the dinner party that had led to the fibreoptic endoscope.
This time, however, Hopkins was sought out by a Liverpool
urologist, Jim Gow. During the war Gow had served in the
North African campaign, which culminated in the Battle of El

Alamein. Among the German booty seized by the victorious
allied forces, he spotted a Leitz cystoscope, a metal instrument
for examining the interior of the bladder, which he appreciated
was the most sophisticated of its kind in the world. Gow duly
appropriated it in anticipation of specialising in urology once
the war was over. Gow's main hobby was photography, which
he combined with his professional work as a urologist by taking
photographs of the bladder through the appropriated Leitz cystoscope as an aid to diagnosis, particularly for documenting the
response of tumours to treatment.[16] Regrettably the results
were not very satisfactory: 'It was apparent after many attempts
that not only was the optical system inadequate but also the
illumination was insufficient.' Jim Gow turned for help to the
physics department at Liverpool University, who suggested he
should contact Harold Hopkins in London.

Though initially reluctant, Hopkins agreed to evaluate the
optics of the Leitz cystoscope and calculated that 'the transmission would have to be increased by a factor of fifty-fold to
obtain enough light' for Jim Gow's purposes. The most that
could be hoped for from design refinements of the instruments
currently in use was a two-fold improvement. Clearly if the difference was to be bridged the whole optical system of rigid
endoscopes would have to be considered.

The Leitz model contained along its shaft a group of lenses
every few centimetres, acting as a relay system, conveying the
image down the barrel to the eye piece where it was magnified.
Hopkins decided to turn these conventional optics on their
head. Rather than an endoscope consisting of a tube of air
interrupted by thin lenses of glass, his contained a tube of glass,
interrupted at intervals by thin lenses of air. The Hopkins rod-
lens endoscope had a total light transmission eighty times
greater than the Leitz system it replaced. Now Jim Gow's photographs of the interior of the bladder had the same clarity as
any conventional photograph taken outdoors on a sunny day.[17]

And with such a brilliant view, suddenly it was obvious that
there was much more that could be done down an endoscope
than just the taking of photographs. In particular the laparoscope inserted into the closed cavity of the abdomen would,

like the fibreoptic endoscope, obviate the need for many forms of surgery. First a small incision is made in the abdomen, just below the umbilicus, through which the laparoscope is slipped. The surgeon or gynaecologist then starts to look around to identify different organs – the ovaries, the fallopian tubes, the liver, the small intestine and so on. Having identified the structure he wishes to operate on, he then passes instruments down through the laparoscope and the patient is saved from what would previously have been a major operation.

The gynaecologists were the first to appreciate the potential of the new approach. In Germany Kurt Semm at Kiel started with sterilisation operations, passing down through the laparoscope an electric cauterising device that he used to close off the fallopian tubes. Over the next twenty years he performed the full range of gynaecological operations down the laparoscope, treating ectopic pregnancies, ruptured ovarian cysts and injured fallopian tubes.[18] In Britain, Bob Edwards's collaborator, Patrick Steptoe, used the laparoscope to obtain maturing eggs from the ovary, which, once removed and fertilised, made possible the birth of the first test-tube baby.[19]

The influence of the laparoscope on surgery of the gut and liver came about more slowly. In 1983 the first gall bladder was removed through the laparoscope, transforming an operation that previously involved a major abdominal incision and ten days of convalescence into a 'day surgery' procedure. Three years later a computer chip television camera was attached to the end of a laparoscope, inaugurating the era of 'keyhole' or 'minimally invasive' surgery. As with gynaecology, a wide range of operations that previously required open incisions in the abdomen – hernia repairs and the removal of malignant growths and parts of the spleen, stomach and colon – could now be performed so expeditiously and with so little trauma that the patient could often return home the same day.[20]

And so it went on. Orthopaedic surgeons used the endoscope to look inside and repair traumatic injuries, especially to the knee and shoulder.[21] ENT surgeons found that chronic sinusitis could be cured by improving the circulation of air with an operation through an endoscope at the back of the nose.[22] Even the removal of a kidney, which previously left a vast scar in the flank, could now be performed endoscopically.[23]

Harold Hopkins was a genius. The impact of his modern endoscopes – along with the operating microscope – is clearly very important in its own right, but also illustrates the cardinal feature of the technological contribution to post-war medicine. Surgeons had, it is true, been practising various forms of endoscopy since the turn of the century, but it remained a province of a few enthusiasts and the results were unreliable. Hopkins's two optical innovations meant that now anyone could become an endoscopist, so the number of patients who could benefit increased vastly. The contribution of technological innovation has thus been not only to enlarge the scope of medical intervention, but also, by simplifying the complex, to enlarge its range as well. This, as will be seen, can be something of a two-edged sword. Technology can make medical intervention almost too easy, leading to inappropriate investigations and treatment.[24]

5

THE MYSTERIES OF BIOLOGY

Momentous events have multiple causes. The excavation of the origins of the rise of modern medicine reveals explanations at many different levels. All those considered so far – the war, clinical science, the cornucopia of new drugs and technology's triumphs – were clearly essential, but there are two further layers, readily overlooked, that can rightly be described as the foundations. The first are the human, moral qualities necessary for scientific innovation. There is always a difficulty in describing the process of scientific discovery because in retrospect it so often appears to have been quite obvious. But those who chip away at the boundaries of the unknown have a very different perspective, because they can never know in advance whether their research will be successful or a futile dead end. And when, as with Donald Pinkel's search for a cure for childhood cancer, or Bob Edwards's research on in vitro fertilisation, that research stretches over decades, it requires great strength of character to persist, often, as has been noted, in the face of repeated failure and the open hostility of colleagues.

They also, of course, had to be intelligent and clear-sighted, but with a few exceptions, such as Harold Hopkins, they were not geniuses. This brings us to the second of the neglected foundations of the rise of modern medicine – the 'gifts' from nature. No amount of moral fibre, scientific creativity or natural

200

intelligence could have elaborated, from first principles, antibiotics, or steroids, or azathioprine, or indeed virtually any of
the cornucopia of discoveries of medicinal chemistry. They
were rather 'gifts from nature', profounder and more complex
than human knowledge at the time, and even now, can
comprehend.

We turn first to that mystery of mysteries, antibiotics and the
bacteria and fungi that produce them. The common perception
of antibiotics (as described in 'Penicillin') is that of chemical-
warfare agents, produced by one microbiological species to
maximise its chance of survival by destroying others and which,
quite fortuitously, were found to be effective against a full range
of infectious disease in humans. This was certainly the principle
which inspired Selman Waksman to investigate the actino-
mycetes species of bacteria in the soil from which so many of the
antibiotics that are commonly in use today were derived. But as
has also been noted, Selman Waksman, within a few years of
receiving the Nobel Prize for his great discovery of streptomycin, realised his chemical-warfare theory must be wrong, and
for several reasons. Antibiotics, he pointed out, could not play a
central role in the microbes' struggle for survival, because only a
handful of species were capable of producing them. More specifically, he had been unable to demonstrate the presence of
antibiotics in the soil in sufficient quantities that would allow
them to destroy other bacteria. Even if they were to do so, the
other competing bacteria in the soil had the capacity to become
rapidly resistant, as indeed has been found in the treatment of
human infections. Further, he noted: 'Specific nutrients characteristic for each organism are a *sine qua non* requirement for the
production of antibiotics, but such nutrients are never found in
proper combination or in sufficient concentrations to enable the
antibiotic-producing organisms to dominate their environment.'
For these and other equally cogent reasons, Waksman concluded
that antibiotics are a 'purely fortuitous phenomenon . . . there is
no purposefulness behind them'.[1]

Such a view is so heretical, so contrary to the prevailing
scientific view that there is a reason and necessity for everything, it must be presumed that Waksman was wrong. But this

apparent purposelessness of antibiotics is not exceptional, being only one example of a generalised phenomenon in biology – 'secondary metabolism' – that is hardly ever alluded to, precisely because it strikes at the heart of the claims of scientists to fully understand the natural world. This observation clearly requires some clarification.

Every living organism on the face of the Earth, from bacteria to humans, shares certain chemical features. Their cells are made of the same type of large molecules, proteins, fat and carbohydrates, and the 'energy' that drives them to fulfil their functions and reproduce are based on the same sort of chemical reaction. These chemical necessities of life are known as primary metabolites. But, in addition, bacteria and plants in particular also produce an enormous range of other chemical secondary metabolites (including antibiotics), which are not essential for sustaining life but are rather the distinguishing feature of the organism. Thus the cells of a potato are made up of primary metabolites and water and cellulose, but what makes a potato a potato is a cocktail of over 150 chemical secondary metabolites, including arsenic, alkaloids, nitrates, tannins and oxalic acid. Precisely the same applies to every grass, fruit, vegetable, flower, fungus and micro-organism – they are all vast chemical factories, manufacturing secondary metabolite chemicals in abundance. Indeed, there are over 20,000 known secondary metabolites, but with so many species still uninvestigated, the true number is probably several times greater.

These secondary metabolites have always played an important role in human affairs, forming the basis of the hundreds of natural dyes such as English woad and Tyrian purple and the fragrances jasmine, rose and sandalwood. They provide the mind-bending chemicals such as cocaine, cannabis and morphine and therapeutic drugs such as aspirin (from the bark of the willow tree), digoxin (from the foxglove) as well as the anti-cancer drugs like actinomycin and vincristine, and many others, including antibiotics. More importantly than all this, they account for the diversity of the natural world, the colours and fragrances of flowers, the taste and texture of fruit and vegetables.

It is possible, in some instances, to infer the role of some of these secondary metabolites in the survival and propagation of the plant or organism that produces them, either in discouraging predators or, as with the scent of flowers, encouraging bees to pollinate. But for the most part, they appear to be, just like antibiotics, 'a fortuitous phenomenon . . . there is no purposefulness behind them'. In this context antibiotics are not 'the mystery of mysteries' that initiated the therapeutic revolution, but only one example of a much greater mystery that lies beyond the comprehension of contemporary science. Why do living organisms produce in such abundance so many complex chemicals that are not necessary to sustain life?[2]

The second pillar of the therapeutic revolution, cortisone (secreted by the adrenal gland), was also a 'gift from nature' but of a very different sort. The small adrenals that balance on top of the kidneys secrete many hormones that control the amount of water in the body. They metabolise sugar to provide the energy that drives the chemical reactions in the body, as well as being the essential precursor for the all-important sex hormones oestrogen and testosterone. But their crucial role in the control of inflammation – mediated by cortisone – was not appreciated until Philip Hench treated his first patient, Mrs Gardner, so miserably afflicted with rheumatoid arthritis: 'The most unusual thing about this historical discovery was its unexpectedness,' observes one commentator, citing another expert on the adrenal gland who, when asked whether an extract from the adrenal gland might be useful in the treatment of inflammation, had replied, 'I cannot imagine anything more unlikely.'[3]

The discovery of the value of cortisone in both rheumatoid arthritis and upwards of 200 other illnesses was thus just as much an unexpected revelation as antibiotics. But this is only to scratch the surface of the extraordinary nature of the discovery, for then one has to go on to ask *why*, or rather *how*, does cortisone exert its influence on the cells involved in the inflammatory reaction. This requires a closer look at how cells work, which is best conveyed by imagining a single cell that has been magnified several million times:

On the surface of the cell we would see millions of openings, like the portholes of a vast space ship, opening and closing to allow a continuing stream of materials to flow in and out. If we were to enter one of these openings we would find ourselves in a world of supreme technology and bewildering complexity. We would see endless corridors branching in every direction away from the perimeter of the cell, some leading to the central memory bank in the nucleus and others to assembly plant units. The nucleus itself would be a vast spherical dome inside of which we would see, all neatly stacked together, the miles of coiled chains of the DNA molecules. A huge range of products and raw materials would shuffle along the corridors in a highly ordered fashion to and from all the various assembly plants in the outer regions of the cell.

We would wonder at the level of control implicit in the movement of so many objects, all in perfect unison. We would see that nearly every feature of our own advanced machines has its analogue in the cell: artificial languages and their decoding systems, memory banks for information storage and retrieval, elegant control systems regulating the automated assembly of parts and components, proof-reading devices utilised for quality control, assembly processes involving the principle of prefabrication and modular construction. What we would be witnessing would be an object resembling an immense automated factory carrying out almost as many unique functions as all the manufacturing activities of man on Earth. However, it would be a factory which would have one capacity not equalled in any of our most advanced machines, for it would be capable of replicating its entire structure within a matter of a few hours.

It is astonishing to think that this remarkable piece of machinery, which possesses the ultimate capacity to construct every living thing that ever existed on Earth, from a giant redwood to the human brain, can construct all its own components in a matter of minutes and is of the order of several thousand million million times smaller than the smallest piece of functional machinery ever constructed by man.[4]

Put like this it is only natural to wonder how this 'remarkable piece of machinery' came into existence in the first place. Of more immediate concern is to work out how a single molecule of cortisone alters the function of the cell in a way that will dampen down the inflammatory response.

First, the cortisone molecule must pass through one of the millions of portholes on the external surface of the cell where it finds and docks with another molecule, its receptor. Together they pass down one of the avenues or conduits leading to the nucleus into which they pass and somehow, inexplicably, find among the closely packed coils of DNA the particular section that codes for one or other of the many proteins involved in the control of inflammation. The cortisone molecule, with its receptor, somehow stimulates the relevant section of DNA to produce a replica of itself called messenger RNA (mRNA), which then passes back out of the nucleus into the main part of the cell. The mRNA finds a protein factory called a ribosome into which it feeds itself like a tickertape, providing the instructions to construct the relevant anti-inflammatory protein which is then conveyed to the outer wall of the cell and expelled to enter the general circulation.

Simultaneously, other cortisone molecules will be acting on other parts of the DNA in other types of cells to produce other anti-inflammatory proteins which are also involved in dampening down the inflammatory response. In all, cortisone either increases or decreases the production of up to twenty different proteins, the overall effect of which is far too complex to begin to describe (and indeed has never been properly worked out), but which has the effect of relieving the red, painful swollen joints of patients with rheumatoid arthritis, or reducing the life-threatening narrowing of the airways that occurs in an acute attack of asthma, or alleviating a multitude of other grievous conditions.

Back in 1948, when Philip Hench gave the first cortisone injection to Mrs Gardner, there was absolutely no conception of the way in which the cell worked or how it could stimulate the production of these anti-inflammatory proteins. Self-evidently then, cortisone could never have been synthesised from first principles, because those principles in 1948 were not known. It could only have been 'a gift from nature'.

And in this, cortisone was quite unexceptional, because precisely the same applies to virtually each and every one of the cornucopia of new drugs, each of which exerts its effect by entering the cell, latching on to a receptor, travelling to the nucleus and influencing the manner in which DNA codes for certain proteins. The therapeutic revolution is thus best conceived of as a massive game of roulette in which research chemists synthesised chemicals in their tens of thousands and then blindly tested them in the hope of a lucky break, when one or other would just happen to initiate the process already described. It was in this way that virtually all the drugs for the treatment of psychiatric illness, rheumatological disorders, heart disease and leukaemia were discovered.

It is now possible to see how those like Howard Florey and Philip Hench, and so many others like them, were able to achieve so much without the need to be scientific geniuses. They just happened to be around at the crucial moment when it became possible to exploit the therapeutic potential of these complex and potent chemicals without having to create them in the first place or even know how they worked. The chance discovery and exploitation of these 'mysteries of biology' is the bedrock that underpins the rise of modern medicine and, as will be seen, also accounts for its fall. There is, after all, likely to be a limit to the number of nature's gifts that can have a major impact on disease, so there is a ceiling to the 'roulette' approach to drug discovery. Sooner or later the rate of innovation must slow down, with the transition from a 'cornucopia' to a 'dearth' of new drugs.

But that is not all. It is perhaps predictable that doctors and scientists should assume the credit for the ascendency of modern medicine without acknowledging, or indeed recognising, the mysteries of nature that have played so important a part. Not surprisingly, they came to believe their intellectual contribution to be greater than it really was, and that they understood more than they really did. They failed to acknowledge the overwhelmingly empirical nature of technological

and drug innovation, which made possible spectacular breakthroughs in the treatment of disease without the requirement of
any profound understanding of its causation or natural history.
And, as will be seen in the following chapters, when this
expectancy that medicine can solve any problem comes into
conflict with a decline in therapeutic innovation, then false
ideas, and claims to knowledge not possessed, are likely to
flourish.

PART 2

The End of the Age of Optimism

THE REVOLUTION FALTERS

'I know, from life and from history, something you have
not thought of: often, the outward, visible, material signs
and symbols of happiness and success only show themselves when the process of decline has already set in. The
outer manifestations take time – like the light of that star up
there – which may in reality be already quenched when it
looks to us to be shining its brightest.'

Thomas Mann, *Buddenbrooks*

By the close of the 1960s medicine's astonishing progress
over the previous quarter-century was building to a climax:
the travail of incremental progress towards a cure for childhood cancer was finally coming to fruition, while the
experience gained from open-heart surgery and transplanting
kidneys had culminated in that supreme technical achievement
of the heart transplant. It takes time, of course, for important
new developments to 'feed through' to become a part of everyday practice – a generation of doctors must acquire the
appropriate skills and further refine and improve on them.
Predictably then it was the decade that followed – the 1970s –
when the full potential of the post-war therapeutic revolution
would be realised, as shown by the rising numbers of hospital
specialists in Britain during this decade.

The expansion of the range of treatments required the creation of four entirely new categories of specialist: gastroenterology (the gut), endocrinology (hormones), medical oncology (cancer) and clinical pharmacology (drugs). The numbers of kidney specialists increased almost four-fold to cope with the rising demands for dialysis and transplantation; the number of cardiologists almost doubled primarily because of the widening range of treatments for coronary heart disease; the number of haematologists quadrupled to treat the now curable leukaemias and lymphomas and other cancers of the blood; the number of psychiatrists almost doubled because mental illness was now a treatable disorder, and so on.[1]

Medicine had matured into a highly sophisticated enterprise, with the intellectual energy and resources to deal with the whole range of human illness.

And yet just as medicine's dramatic upward spiral started quite suddenly after the war, it was, by the close of the 1970s, almost equally suddenly coming to an end. For, as Thomas Mann has his hero observe so acutely in his great novel *Buddenbrooks*, the light of the stars we see shining brightly in the heavens has taken millions of years to reach us, by which time the energy that originally generated it has become exhausted. Similarly, the light of medicine's success that was now shining so brilliantly was generated by the scientific endeavour of the previous thirty years. Where were the new ideas, the fresh shoots of research and innovation that would maintain that momentum?

Several apparently disconnected events combined to suggest that the apparently relentless onward and upward march of medical progress had come up against some invisible barrier. Thus in 1978, Colin Dollery, Professor of Clinical Pharmacology at the Postgraduate Medical School, chose as his title for the prestigious Rock Carling Fellowship monograph *The End of an Age of Optimism*. The Postgraduate Medical School, it will be recalled, had in the post-war years been the nursery for the revolutionary new creed of 'clinical science'. Dollery had joined the staff in 1960 as John McMichael's protégé, investigating the drugs that would very soon, by making hypertension a treatable disease, permit the prevention of strokes. Simultaneously, in the same hospital, cardiothoracic surgeon Bill Cleland was performing the first open-heart surgery in Britain and Ralph Shackman was doing the first kidney transplants. In his monograph, Professor Dollery wistfully recalls these momentous times and then turns his attention to the realities of 1978:

> Problems seem larger, and solutions to them more elusive . . . the morality and cost-effectiveness of scientific medicine has been challenged . . . many people, including some of the most senior of the medical research hierarchy, are pessimistic about the claims of future advance. The age of optimism has ended.[2]

Why was the 'age of optimism' coming to an end?

In the following year James Wyngaarden, in his presidential address to the Association of American Physicians in Washington, DC, suggested an explanation encapsulated in the title of his speech 'The Clinical Investigator as an Endangered Species': 'There has been a declining interest in medical research amongst medical students and young doctors for several years,' he claimed, 'clearly visible to the heads of professorial departments who increasingly find the recruitment pool smaller each year.' This trend, said Wyngaarden, could be clearly seen in the falling numbers of traineeships awarded by the National Institute of Health to doctors wishing to undertake postdoctoral research. Over the previous ten years it had declined by a half from a peak of 3,000 in 1968 to a mere 1,500.[3]

A year later came the first recognition that the great bastion of the post-war therapeutic revolution, the pharmaceutical industry, was also in trouble. There was 'A Dearth of New Drugs', the editor of the prestigious science journal *Nature* observed.[4] In a more detailed analysis, Dr Fred Steward of Birmingham's Aston University observed that the rate of introduction of New Chemical Entities (NCEs), i.e. genuinely new drugs, had dropped off sharply from over seventy a year in the 1960s to less than twenty in the 1970s. 'The identification of many biologically important chemicals starting after the war may have created for a period a fruitful basis for innovation but has subsequently showed diminishing returns,' he observed. Nor was it just proving harder to come up with genuinely new drugs. An analysis of the most recent NCEs found only a third that seemed to offer even 'moderate therapeutic gain'.[5]

The significance of these events is not difficult to grasp. The main pillars of the post-war medical achievement – clinical science, medicinal chemistry, and, as will be seen, for rather different reasons, technological innovation – were in trouble. The implications were obvious. The relentless rise of the post-war years was coming to an end. This pivotal moment in the history of post-war medicine has until now hardly been commented on. Clearly it merits further examination.

2

THE DEARTH OF NEW DRUGS

When, in 1995, Richard Wurtman of the Massachusetts Institute of Technology reviewed the record of the previous fifty years of drug innovation, he observed: 'Successes have been surprisingly infrequent during the past three decades. Few effective treatments have been discovered for the diseases that contribute most to mortality and morbidity.' Whereas the number of New Chemical Entities (NCEs) were running at around seventy a year throughout the 1960s, by 1971 they were down to less than thirty a year, a position from which they have never recovered. Nonetheless, even thirty new drugs a year might still seem a respectable rate, as cumulatively they would be expected to have a significant impact on many illnesses. But it is not that simple. Many of the 'new' drugs introduced since the early 1970s were just more expensive treatments for diseases already taken care of by older and cheaper medicines.[1]

The common explanation for this decline in innovation was the tightening of safety regulations in the aftermath of the thalidomide disaster. It is difficult nowadays to imagine just how non-existent such regulations used to be. The Parisian psychiatrists, Delay and Deniker, started treating their schizophrenia patients with chlorpromazine within months of it having been synthesised by the pharmaceutical company Poulenc. As for its most important derivative, the antidepressant imipramine, only a few weeks elapsed between its synthesis and first administration to patients, without any toxicity tests, any study of its pharmacology in the body or any formal clinical trials. But imipramine was one of the last drugs introduced in this way. In 1966 reports started appearing, first in West Germany and Australia and then from around the world, of children being born without arms and legs whose mothers had been prescribed the sleeping pill thalidomide early in pregnancy. Missing limbs are a very prominent deformity and the pictures of thalidomide victims as they grew up over the next twenty years acquired in the public imagination a sort of symbolic significance, a metaphor of the negligence and avarice of the pharmaceutical industry.[2]

The momentum to introduce legislation requiring stricter testing of new drugs became unstoppable. This naturally made the whole process of innovation much more complicated and therefore expensive and, claimed the pharmaceutical industry, unnecessarily so. It is never possible to be absolutely certain whether the results of toxicity tests of drugs on animals are necessarily applicable to humans, so in order to at least give the appearance of thoroughness – as inevitably some drugs will cause unexpected side-effects – the regulatory authorities insisted the pharmaceutical industry produce enormous quantities of data. This was a prolonged business. By 1978 the 'development time' for each new drug had increased to around ten years, while the 'development costs' had escalated from $10 million in the 1960s to $50 million in the mid-1970s to a staggering $300 million by the 1990s. Inevitably this acted as a disincentive to innovation and, it is alleged, several useful drugs were 'lost' on the way, having failed one or other of the required toxicity tests. This close correlation between the rise in regulation and decline in the rate of innovation is self-evident, and one has to presume that over-regulation had, if not exactly killed off the golden goose, certainly reduced her production of golden eggs.[3]

There was, however, an equally important explanation for the 'dearth of new drugs'. The most extraordinary aspect of the post-war therapeutic revolution is how it occurred in the

absence of the most basic understanding of disease processes –
of what, for example, was happening to cause the airways to
constrict during an attack of asthma, or the functioning of the
neurotransmitters in the brains of patients with schizophrenia.
This ocean of ignorance had been bridged by the facility with
which pharmaceutical research chemists could synthesise
chemical compounds in their millions which could then be
investigated for any potential therapeutic effect.

But the pharmaceutical companies realised that sooner or
later they would start to run out of new chemicals to test in this
way. From the mid-1960s onwards there was a hope that it
should be possible to replace this rather crude method of drug
discovery with something altogether more elegant and 'scientific'. Certainly pharmaceutical researchers now knew much
more about the biochemical workings of the cell and had identified many of the chemical transmitters in the brain and
elsewhere by which one cell communicated with another. So,
it seemed much better, rather than stumbling around in the
dark hoping to chance upon some unexpected discovery, to
exploit this newfound knowledge and deliberately design drugs
to fulfil a defined function. This approach was not exactly new.
George Hitchings and Gertrude Elion had discovered a whole
string of drugs such as azathioprine by purposefully designing
drugs to interfere with the synthesis of DNA. But it was Sir
James Black's two classic discoveries, first of propranolol (which
blocked the beta receptors in the heart thus relieving the symptoms of angina), and then of cimetidine (which blocked the
histamine receptors in the gut, thus reducing the amount of
acid secretions and allowing ulcers to heal), that convinced
many that the future lay with 'designing drugs'.[4]

In a curious paradox, this 'scientific' approach to drug discovery has turned out to be much less fruitful than was hoped,
particularly when compared to the blind, random methods it
was intended to replace. The philosophical rationale was that if
the problems of human disease could be explained at the most
fundamental level of the cell and its genes and proteins, it
should then be possible to correct whatever was wrong.
Though intuitively appealing, this approach presupposes that it

is actually possible, given the complexity of biology, to 'know' enough to be able to achieve this. By contrast, the earlier mode of drug discovery, blind and dependent on chance as it might be, did at least allow for the possibility of the unexpected. Or, put another way, this scientific approach to drug discovery could never have led to penicillin or cortisone.

It would be wrong to suggest the scientific road to discovery from the mid-1970s onwards has not produced some genuinely useful drugs. Its successes include, most recently, a vaccine against the chronic liver infection hepatitis B and 'triple therapy' for the treatment of AIDS.[5] But the current list of the top ten big 'blockbuster' drugs – the ones that generate the billions of dollars of revenue that sustain the industry's profitability – features, for the most part, new or more expensive variants of the antibiotics, anti-inflammatories and anti-depressants that were originally introduced twenty or more years ago.[6] They might well be more effective, have fewer side-effects or be easier to take, but with the occasional exception none can be described as making a significant inroad into previously uncharted therapeutic areas in the way that the discovery of chlorpromazine, for example, transformed the treatment of schizophrenia. There was enormous optimism that biotechnology might generate a further cornucopia of new drugs, but, again with the occasional exception, these compounds – insulin, growth hormone, factor VIII – turned out to be no better therapeutically than those they have replaced. They are certainly a lot more expensive.

The most striking feature of many of the most recently introduced drugs is that there is considerable doubt about whether they do any good at all. Thus, there was much hope that the drug finasteride, 'scientifically designed' to block the metabolism of testosterone and thus shrink the size of the prostate, would reduce the need for an operation in those in whom the gland is enlarged. This would indeed have been a significant breakthrough but, as an editorial in the *New England Journal of Medicine* observed, 'the magnitude of the change in symptoms [of patients] is not impressive'.[7] Similarly, a new generation of drugs for the treatment of epilepsy based on interfering with the neurotransmitter, GABA, were dismissed by an editorial in the *British Medical Journal* as having been 'poorly assessed' with no evidence that they were any better than the anti-epileptic drugs currently in use.[8] New treatments for multiple sclerosis and Alzheimer's disease appear to offer such marginal benefits that their 'clinical cost-effectiveness falls at the first hurdle'.[9]

Frustrated at the failure to find cures for serious diseases like cancer and dementia, the pharmaceutical industry has been forced to look elsewhere for profitable markets for its products. This explains the rise of so-called 'lifestyle' drugs whose prime function is to restore those social faculties or attributes that tend to diminish with age: Regaine for the treatment of baldness, Viagra for male impotence, Xenical for obesity and Prozac for depression. The pharmaceutical industry may have blamed the 'dearth of new drugs' on over-regulation but the problem seems to run much deeper. It should still have been able to come up with genuine breakthrough drugs irrespective of the new stringent regulatory requirements, but despite investment in research on a scale greater by orders of magnitude than that of the halcyon days of the 1950s and 1960s, they have not materialised. This dispiriting analysis is vulnerable to the charge of oversimplification, but it is confirmed by the one truly objective measurement of the fortunes of the pharmaceutical industry – its performance in the market place. Thanks to the 'blockbuster drugs', the industry remains profitable, but the twin pressures of massive research costs ($12 billion was spent by the top ten companies in 1994 alone) and the imminent prospect that the patent protection on many of the more profitable products will expire around the time of the millennium has undermined the viability of many previously gilt-edged companies, leaving them no alternative other than to submerge their identity in a rash of massive billion-dollar mergers: Glaxo with Wellcome, SKF with Beechams, Upjohn of the United States with Pharmacia of Sweden, Sandoz with Ciba, and so on.[10] Reflecting on this merger mania, John Griffin, formerly director of the Association of the British Pharmaceutical Industry, has observed: 'These companies are "ideas poor", resorting to finding new uses and novel delivery systems for established active products whose patent expiry is imminent . . . real innovations are very obviously not coming from those companies involved in merger mania, whose management currently appears unable to think radically or constructively.'[11]

The contrasting fortunes of the pharmaceutical industry before and after the 1970s are underpinned by the profound paradox of an apparent inverse relationship between the scale of investment in research and drug innovation. Recognising this, the pharmaceutical industry in the early 1990s decided to reorient its approach to drug discovery, using automated techniques to screen millions of chemical compounds for their biological activity, hoping to identify the 'lead compounds' that might have the sort of genuinely novel therapeutic effect that could form the basis for new drugs. This reversion – albeit with techniques much more sophisticated than in the past – to the process by which the important drugs of the 1940s and 1950s were discovered, is obviously highly significant, though whether it will 'deliver the goods' remains to be seen.[12]

3

TECHNOLOGY'S FAILINGS

Fire was the 'original technology', acquired for man by
Prometheus, who had stolen it from the gods. Zeus was not
amused and directed that Prometheus be bound to a rock with
chains, to be visited there daily by an eagle who fed off his liver.
The punishment may seem a bit harsh, but in one sense Zeus
was right: technology is double-edged. It confers prodigious
powers, yet such power can also be enslaving, controlling the
actions of those who possess it.

Technology was out of step with the major trends of the End
of the Age of Optimism. The 1980s were an important decade:
for diagnostic imaging (with important developments in CT
and MRI scanning, ultrasound and similar techniques)[1]; for
'interventional radiology' (with angioplasty, the dilation of narrowed arteries with plastic catheters)[2]; and for ever more
sophisticated methods of endoscopy, culminating in the remarkable technical achievement of Minimally Invasive Surgery.[3]

Nonetheless, against the background of these innovations,
the general and probably correct perception of medical technology is that it is out of control. The discussion that follows
examines the consequences with three examples in ascending
order of seriousness: firstly 'overinvestigation' (the overuse of
diagnostic technology); secondly, the false premises, and
promises, of foetal monitoring; and lastly, the role of intensive
care in needlessly prolonging the process of dying.

The Misuse of Diagnostic Technology

The ever-perspicient Peter Medawar, Nobel Prize-winner for his contribution to transplantation, observed that when people spoke about the 'Art and Science' of medicine they invariably got them the wrong way round, presuming the 'Art' to be those aspects that involved being sympathetic and talking to the patient, and the 'Science' to be the difficult bit of interpreting the results of sophisticated tests that permits the correct diagnosis to be made. The reverse is the case, argued Medawar. The real 'science' in medicine is the thorough understanding of the nature of a medical problem that comes from talking at length to the patient, and performing a physical examination to elicit the relevant signs of disease. From this old-fashioned style of medicine it is usually possible to infer precisely what is wrong in 90 per cent of cases. By contrast, the technological gizmos and arcane tests that pass for the 'science' of medicine can frequently be quite misleading. The logic of Medawar's argument leads to the playful paradox that the more tests that doctors can do, the less 'scientific' (in the sense of generating reliable knowledge) medicine becomes. And throughout the 1970s doctors did 'do' more tests, twice as many at the end of the decade as at the beginning, resulting in the description of an entirely new syndrome of 'medical vampirism', where so much blood was taken for tests from patients while in hospital that they became anaemic, requiring in some instances a blood transfusion.[4] 'The comforting, if spurious, precision of laboratory results has the same appeal as a lifebelt to the weak swimmer,' an editorial in *The Lancet* noted in 1981, before going on to enumerate the several reasons why doctors performed so many unnecessary tests: there was the 'just-in-case test' requested by junior doctors 'just in case' the consultant might ask for the result, and the 'routine test' whose results hardly ever contributed to the diagnosis, and the 'ah-ha test' whose results were known to be abnormal in certain conditions and which were ordered 'to advertise the cleverness of the clinician'.[5]

This fetishisation of technical data was part of a more generalised phenomenon where the modern physician had become a doctor with technically specialised diagnostic skills. Thus it was no longer sufficient for the gastroenterologist to know a lot about gut diseases; he had also to be skilled in passing the endoscope down into the stomach and up into the colon. Nor was it sufficient for the cardiologist to rely on his traditional skills with the stethoscope, as he also had to acquire the necessary manipulative skills of the 'catheter laboratory', passing catheters into veins and arteries to measure the pressures within the heart.

There is, of course, no reason why gastroenterologists or cardiologists should not possess these skills, but they can easily become an end in themselves, a means of gathering information that might be gleaned by simpler means. There is, for example, little difficulty in establishing the diagnosis of a peptic ulcer by the traditional clinical methods of taking a history and examining the patient, but for the modern gastroenterologist any patient with stomach pains merits an endoscopy to visualise the ulcer, as well as a further endoscopy after treatment to see if it had healed. This inappropriate use of investigational techniques was, argued one of their number, Michael Clark of St Bartholomew's Hospital, a sign of intellectual degeneration. 'The young men of the 1960s became gastroenterologists because it was an expanding speciality with an intellectual challenge to understand more about the gut and apply this to clinical practice,' he wrote, 'but the young gastroenterologist of today is only happy if he can learn another endoscopic technique: the excitement of the 1960s has been replaced by the decade of the Peeping Tom.'[6]

The great virtue of endoscopy for the gastroenterologists was that it earned them a lot of money and indeed in the United States, the endoscope and 'catheter lab' generate 80 per cent of the specialist's income. This phenomenon of 'over-investigation' – the performing of large numbers of tests in patients whose medical problems are quite straightforward – may seem a fairly trivial matter, but it is costly and, more seriously, it introduces an alien element into the medical encounter, downgrading the importance of wisdom and experience in favour of spurious objectivity.

Foetal Monitoring: Technology and a Shot in the Foot

The success of technology in so many fields of medicine encouraged doctors to believe there must be a technical solution to every problem; that, for example, foetal monitoring during labour would prevent death or damage to the baby. The argument was as follows: the shift from home to hospital deliveries had coincided with a decline in both maternal and infant mortality rates, from which one might quite naturally infer that, thanks to medical intervention, childbirth was becoming ever safer for both mother and baby. Nonetheless, babies still died during labour (approximately 3,000 a year in the United States) while several times that number (approximately 15,000) were born with severe forms of brain damage, such as cerebral palsy. Such misfortunes, it was legitimate to presume, arose because the foetus was deprived of oxygen during the stress of labour, so further medical intervention to determine when it was 'distressed' might act as a red-alert system, prompting an emergency Caesarean to avert disaster. 'Since the stress of labour is clearly capable of causing foetal death, it seems not unreasonable to assume that labour may also be a factor in producing brain damage,' observed two protagonists of this view, obstetricians Edward Quilligan and Richard Paul of the University of Southern California in 1974.[7] The inference was indeed 'not unreasonable', and appeared to be supported, they pointed out, by crude experiments on monkey foetuses which, while still within the womb, were deprived of oxygen by separating the placenta from the side of the mother's uterus. Following birth, they were killed and their brains examined, apparently revealing a particular pattern of damage 'identical to that seen in human subjects who are afflicted with cerebral palsy'.[8]

Two technological developments in the late 1960s would, it was hoped, by improving on the traditional methods of assessing 'foetal distress', alert the obstetrician to the possibility the foetus was being deprived of oxygen and thus prevent the catastrophe of cerebral palsy. The first was a monitor strapped to the mother's abdomen to give a continuous read-out of the heart rate of the foetus, providing objective evidence of rapid 'accelerations' or 'decelerations' that can occur when the foetus is in trouble. Secondly, soon after labour had begun and just as the baby was starting its descent down the birth canal, a needle was placed in its scalp, through which small quantities of blood could be removed and its acidity measured, a useful warning sign that the baby was being deprived of oxygen and thus vulnerable to brain damage. Clearly the initial costs of purchasing the necessary equipment and training the nursing staff would be considerable – estimated at around $100 million for the United States – but, argued Quilligan and Paul, this would be offset by financial savings – estimated at $2 billion – in the long-term care of brain-damaged children if their numbers were to be reduced by a half by foetal monitoring technology.[9]

Throughout the 1970s, obstetricians, convinced by these compelling arguments, introduced foetal monitoring on a wide scale only to elicit a strong backlash from the 'natural childbirth' movement representing the interests of pregnant women. The problem was that no matter how plausible the arguments might be in its favour, foetal monitoring has a seriously adverse impact on many women's experience of labour. The mother's mobility has to be severely restricted for the monitor readings to be reliable, requiring her to lie prone on her back for long periods. Meanwhile she might have one arm connected up to an intravenous drip, while a cuff is strapped to the other to keep an eye on her blood pressure. She is in effect immobilised. Such irksome restraint imposed by foetal monitoring is also unphysiological and, by denying the mother the opportunity to move around freely and adopt different positions, prolongs labour unnecessarily.

And so to the crucial question, did it work? Yes, claimed Quilligan and Paul, markedly reducing complications during labour, albeit at the cost of a considerable increase in the numbers of births by Caesarean section, as the monitor tended to be 'oversensitive' producing readings suggesting the baby was in distress when it was not.[10]

The more that time passed, the less convincing these results seemed to be. Foetal monitoring was not quite the exact science its protagonists had claimed, failing (it emerged) to detect 84 per cent of the babies who suffered some degree of oxygen deprivation during birth, while 'conversely most of the infants who were thought to be in foetal distress were vigorous'. By the early 1980s the *British Medical Journal*, in marked contrast to its enthusiastic endorsement of the aspirations of foetal monitoring a decade earlier, had become disillusioned by its many technical difficulties. 'The foetal heart rate pattern correlates poorly with the acid–base balance (the acidity of the blood obtained through the scalp needle) . . . foetal outcome depends not only on the correct interpretation of data but also on appropriate action by the staff in the obstetric unit.'[11]

The vogue for foetal monitoring would, like other medical fashions, probably have slowly withered away, were it not for the intervention of the lawyers. The drawback of foetal monitoring, which was not well appreciated when it was first claimed to prevent 'adverse outcomes' such as cerebral palsy, is that when children are born so affected it is 'not unreasonable' for the parents to assume negligence on the part of the obstetrician for failing to act on the evidence of an 'abnormal' heart reading (and in court virtually any reading, in the hands of a hostile expert witness, could be shown to be 'abnormal', undermining the original claims that it provided an objective assessment of the child's progress).

This is clearly a most invidious situation. The birth of each and every 'less than perfect' child can, with the help of a clever lawyer, be blamed on the negligence of the obstetrician in charge. Their only defence is to deny the rationale upon which foetal monitoring had originally been conceived, that oxygen deprivation at birth is a common and preventable cause of brain damage – which it is not. While the maternal and foetal mortality rates have fallen continuously from the 1950s onwards, the number of cases of cerebral palsy had remained virtually unchanged. This could only mean that the majority of cases – probably 90 per cent – of cerebral palsy cannot result from events occurring during childbirth, but must be caused by some abnormality of the development of the brain much earlier in pregnancy. The whole episode had been 'a catastrophic misunderstanding', according to one obstetric journal, where the expectation that foetal monitoring could prevent brain damage in children was based on 'false analogy and assumptions'. Obstetricians had 'shot themselves in the foot'.[12]

The most curious aspect of this saga is that right from the beginning dispassionate observers had warned obstetricians of the 'false assumptions' behind foetal monitoring, and indeed these should have been clear to obstetricians themselves. They would have known from their personal experience that not all babies consequently shown to have cerebral palsy had experienced particularly difficult or complicated labours but the profession was seduced into thinking otherwise by the promise of the power of technology to provide solutions.[13]

Technology and the High Cost of Dying

The third and most significant type of misuse of technology is the use of life-sustaining technologies to prolong the process of dying. The principles of intensive care and artificial ventilation pioneered in the Copenhagen polio epidemic of 1952 to keep children alive long enough for the strength of their respiratory muscles to recover may save thousands of lives a year but they had also, by the mid-1970s, become diverted into a means of prolonging – at enormous cost – the pain and misery of terminal illness. Thus a United Press Agency bulletin describing General Franco's final illness in 1975 reported:

> At least four mechanical devices are being used in the battle for General Franco's survival. A defibrillator attached to his chest shocks his heart back to normal when it slows or fades; a pump-like device helps push his blood through his body when it weakens; a respirator helps him breathe and a kidney machine cleans his blood. At various times in his 25-day crisis General Franco has had tubes down his windpipe to provide air, down his nose to provide nourishment, in his abdomen to drain accumulated fluids, and in his digestive

tract to relieve gastric pressure. The effort in itself is remarkable considering he has had three major heart attacks. He has undergone emergency surgery twice, once to patch a ruptured artery to save him from bleeding to death, the second time to remove most of an ulcerated and bleeding stomach for the same reason. He has taken some four gallons of blood transfusion. His lungs are congested . . . his kidneys are giving out and his liver is weak. Paralysis periodically affects his intestines . . . he suffers occasional rectal bleeding. Blood clots have formed and spread in his left thigh. Mucus accumulates uncontrollably in his mouth.[14]

General Franco, being an important man, might have been expected to have received preferential treatment, but this account of his dying days is little different from that of thousands of patients who have had the misfortune to spend their last moments on a modern-day intensive-care unit, where, as one organ system fails after another, its function must be taken over by some technological means in the increasingly unlikely anticipation of eventual recovery. This is a costly business. By 1976 one half of medical expenditure in the United States was incurred in the last sixty days of a patient's life. 'The furore over the high economic costs of dying parallels concern over its high emotional cost,' observed Muriel Gillick of the Hebrew Rehabilitation Center for the Aged in Boston, commenting on a report in the *New York Times* that showed 'a significant segment of the public believes that doctors cruelly and needlessly prolong the lives of the dying [for reasons] of avarice and a passion for technology, which leads them to use procedures to excess, unmindful of the suffering they may inflict on patients.[15]

The fault was certainly not all on the doctors' side who, pressurised by relatives or fearful of subsequently being charged with negligence, felt they had little alternative other than to demonstrate that 'no stone had been left unturned'. Paralleling the Church's last rites, medicine too now had its last rite – the compulsory period on the ventilator without which a patient was not allowed to die in hospital. Thus an analysis of the outcome in almost 150 patients severely ill with cancer who had been admitted to the intensive-care unit of one hospital in southern Florida over a two-year period found that more than three-quarters of those who had survived to go home had died within three months.[16]

Such misuse of intensive-care facilities is a telling sign of the degree to which medical technology has spiralled out of control. There was nothing that could be done about it. By 1995, twenty years after General Franco's grisly demise, expenditure on intensive care in the United States had escalated to $62 billion (equivalent to 1 per cent of the nation's GNP), one-third of which – $20 billion – was being spent on what had euphemistically come to be known as PIC or Potentially Ineffective Care.

The portrayal of the three forms of 'inappropriate' use of technology may seem unnecessarily bleak, but it is merely the mirror image of the transforming power of the technological innovation so essential to the post-war therapeutic revolution. The culprit is not technology itself, but the intellectual and emotional immaturity of the medical profession, which seemed unable to exert the necessary self-control over its new-found powers.

4

The Clinical Scientist as an Endangered Species

'The clinical scientist as an endangered species', as identified by James Wyngaarden in his presidential address to the Association of American Physicians in 1979, is the third and last indication of the End of the Age of Optimism. The number of doctors awarded traineeships for postdoctoral research by the National Institute of Health, Dr Wyngaarden had noted, had declined by half over the previous decade, with the obvious implication that doctors qualifying in the 1970s were less enthusiastic about research than earlier generations. This he attributed, at least in part, to 'the seductive lure of the high incomes that now derive from procedure-based specialty medicine'. And what does that mean? Specialists like gastroenterologists and cardiologists had, as described in the previous chapter, acquired unique skills or 'procedures' such as endoscopy or cardiac catheterisation, for which they were able to charge a lot of money in private practice, or, as Wyngaarden described it: 'A high proportion of young doctors who in the past have been willing to delay economic gratification and indulge a curiosity in research now exhibit the "young physician-Porsche syndrome".' There may be an element of truth in the allegation that this generation of doctors, the first to have been untouched by the scientific idealism of the post-war years, may have preferred to graze in the lucrative fields of private practice, deploying their newly acquired skills in endoscopy and catheterisation rather than pursuing the intellectual excitement of the research laboratory. There is, though, another much more important reason why young doctors found research a less attractive option: the revolution of clinical science as initiated by Sir Thomas Lewis and carried on by John McMichael and his contemporaries had become exhausted.

There are many forms of medical research – synthesising new drugs, inventing new technologies, experimenting on animal models of disease, and so on – but the distinguishing feature of clinical science is that it is practised by doctors with a unique access to the 'experimental subjects' – patients with illnesses. Most clinical science involves observing or measuring in some way the phenomena of disease in a living person, rather than on a dead one in the autopsy room, usually with some special technique. Thus, in the post-war years at the Postgraduate Medical School, John McMichael used the cardiac catheter to measure pressures within the heart while Sheila Sherlock used the liver biopsy needle to take specimens of the liver from jaundiced patients to make a more accurate diagnosis. Much of the dynamic of clinical science can be accounted for by new methods of measuring some aspects of human physiology, ranging all the way from the imaging techniques of the CT and MRI scanner for delineating the internal organs, to the ability to measure minuscule levels of hormones and chemicals in the blood in different disease states. The therapeutic revolution added a further major dimension to clinical science, because every new drug or new technology was 'experimental', so there were considerable opportunities for the clinical scientist to evaluate its effects.

There was certainly much to do. These were uncharted waters, there was little competition from others, as only doctors could do clinical science, while the wards and out-patients were packed with 'clinical material', the dreadful euphemism for patients whose interesting diseases merited investigation. The bright young doctor only had to collect twenty or thirty patients with one illness or another and encourage them to come to the laboratory, where he could measure something or try out some new treatment, whose effects he could measure. The results could then be written up and published in a medical journal.

This is not to belittle clinical science, which certainly expanded knowledge and understanding of the physiological processes of disease, but such a 'phenomenological approach', as it is called because it involves the observation of the 'phenomena' of disease, obviously has intellectual limits. There comes a time when there is no more useful knowledge to be gained from doing yet more catheter studies on children with congenital heart disease, or from performing yet more biopsies on patients with jaundice. This saturation of clinical science's potential for further observational studies just happened to coincide with the decline in therapeutic innovation. By the late 1970s clinical science was in serious trouble.

This decline in its fortunes, which would explain its lack of appeal to young doctors, can be illustrated in two ways. The first is to compare the contents of medical journals before and after the End of the Age of Optimism. The January 1970 issue of the Journal of the American Medical Association is clinical science 'writ large' with articles on the role of dialysis in acute kidney failure, hepatitis as a complication of blood transfusion in patients who have had open heart surgery, and the description of a test to identify patients whose raised blood pressure is due to a tumour of the adrenal glands. There are a couple of unusual cases histories including the description of torsion of the testes while still in the womb, and a potentially confusing form of metabolic abnormality in patients with diabetes. The correspondence section is similarly concerned with clinical matters including reports of allergic reactions to local anaesthetics and weakness of the upper arm due to damage to the nerves from prolonged carrying of a rucksack. Thus, virtually everyone, both specialist physicians and family doctors, reading this issue of the *Journal of the American Medical Association,* would have found much of general interest directly touching their everyday practice.[2] From the mid-seventies onwards, the proportion of space in the medical journals devoted to clinical science fell rapidly. By the 1990s its contents were so different as to be virtually unrecognisable.[3] The January 1999 issue of JAMA, for example, features a massive statistical analysis of 'structural interventions to increase physical activity' and a 'cost effectiveness' study of methods to increase the sensitivity of cervical smears. There is an article on the difficulties of providing essential drugs in poor countries while the correspondence columns discuss firearm related homicides in young men, the role of alcohol in Russian mortality statistics and a call to 'action' on drug safety. Sandwiched between these discursive pieces there are just two short articles directly related to clinical practice — the discussion of the best form of contraception for a forty year old woman and the treatment of PMT in the older woman.[4]

The second illustrative example of this marginalisation of clinical science from its previous pre-eminent position within medicine's intellectual life is reflected in the changing fortunes of its major research institutions, and in particular in Britain the brief and troubled life of what was intended to be its flagship, the Clinical Research Centre, founded in 1970. The CRC was attached to a brand-new district hospital – Northwick Park – in Harrow, North London, for the specific purpose of studying common clinical science-style medical problems such as bronchitis, heart disease and strokes. 'The opening of a lavishly equipped hospital and research centre is inevitably an occasion for congratulations,' commented the *British Medical Journal* a month before its official opening by Her Majesty The Queen. And lavish it certainly was. The capital cost was three times greater than that of a standard hospital. Besides the usual complement of consultant staff there were 134 research posts spread across fourteen research divisions. 'This was a substantial and essential investment in medical care which it is hoped should enable the Medical Research Council to retain its place as a leader in international medical research.'[5]

But this 'lavish' palace of disease, with facilities for research that would have been inconceivable to preceding generations, did not prosper. Perhaps it was ill-conceived to try and create a research institution *de novo* in this way. The Centre rapidly achieved white elephant status with its high running costs and its abysmal research record became a major embarrassment. Just over a decade later, in 1986, the decision was made to close it down following the report of a committee which found 'little prospect of creating the unity of purpose essential for the future development of high-quality clinical research'.[6]

Comparisons with the achievements of an earlier epoch are inevitable. The important developments in medical research at the Postgraduate Medical School and elsewhere from the 1940s through the 1960s were carried out on a shoestring budget with a fraction of the funds and other resources available to those working at the CRC. There can thus be only two explanations for the disparity in its 'research productivity'. Either those involved were less intelligent and committed than the preceding generation – which seems unlikely. Alternatively the intellectual context within which they were working must have changed so that clinical science had lost its capacity to make substantial contributions to the major problems posed by disease.

Almost a Dead End

It would be absurd to suggest that medical progress had completely ground to a halt by the end of the 1970s. Several of the 'definitive' moments were still to come, including the discovery of helicobacter as the cause of peptic ulcer, and the role of clot-busting drugs in saving lives following heart attacks. The 1980s would also see the flowering of the new methods of Minimally Invasive Surgery, as well as modest improvements in survival from cancers of the breast and colon.[7] And, most importantly of all, the 1980s were a very necessary period of 'fine-tuning' of the innovations of earlier decades, defining much more precisely the value and indications for their use.

And yet the verdict of the End of the Age of Optimism is inescapable. The therapeutic revolution was faltering. Medicine, like any field of endeavour, is bounded by its concerns –

Sir Alexander Fleming points to the discovery that made him famous. The circular penicillium mould has inhibited the growth of the streaks of bacteria on the agar plate.

Sir Ernst Chain in his flat in Oxford. A prodigiously talented biochemist, he was recruited by Howard Florey in 1936 to work in the Department of Pathology, where he identified the chemical structure of penicillin.

Sir Howard Florey, as President of the Royal Society – the highest honour to which a scientist can aspire. In the immediate aftermath of Dunkirk, when Britain's future lay in the balance, he committed the puny resources of his department to manufacture sufficient quantities of penicillin for use in humans.

Selman Waksman (left) in front of a vast fermentation plant for the production of the antibiotic streptomycin, used in the treatment of tuberculosis.

Philip Hench (right), standing next to Edward Kendall in the laboratories of the Mayo Clinic. Together they discovered the therapeutic benefits of cortisone (steroids).

Sir Austin and Lady Bradford Hill, admiring the view from a Scottish mountaintop. Sir Austin's monumental dual achievement was both to propose statistical methods for evaluating the efficacy of drug treatment and to prove the causative role of environmental factors (such as tobacco) in disease (such as lung cancer).

John Gibbon with his wife and life-long collaborator, Mary Hopkins, and their heart/lung machine or pump – 'one of the boldest feats of man's mind'.

The pump allowed John Kirklin of the Mayo Clinic (below left) and Walter Lillehai of the University of Minneapolis (below right) to repair the many complex anatomical defects of the heart.

Howard Hopkins, inventor of both the fibre-optic and rigid rod-lens endoscope, which permitted doctors not just to 'see more' but also to 'do more', and in the process transformed the practice of virtually every branch of medicine.

Sir James Black celebrates the announcement of his Nobel Prize for the discovery of the beta blocker propranolol and the anti-ulcer drug cimetidine – two of the most therapeutically and commercially successful drugs of the post-war years.

Donald Pinkel devised the protocol of cytotoxic drugs and radiotherapy for the successful treatment of Acute Lymphoblastic Leukaemia (ALL) in children.

TOPHAM PICTUREPOINT

Sir Peter Medawar, 'an exotic in the world of biology', identified the immunological mechanisms of rejection that had to be overcome if transplantation were to be a viable option for the treatment of failing organs such as the kidney.

For forty years, from the mid-1940s onwards, George Hitchings and Gertrude Elion investigated methods of blocking the replication of DNA that led to drugs for the treatment of leukaemia, malaria, gout and viral infections as well as azathioprine, the key to successful transplantation.

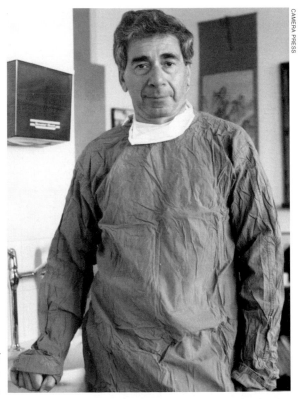

Sir Roy Calne pioneered the use of immunosuppressant drugs in kidney and liver transplants.

POPPERFOTO

Lord 'Tommy' Horder, seen here pruning his roses at his country home in Kent, was in the 1930s 'the greatest clinician of his day'. His style of medicine, based on vast experience and shrewd judgement, was challenged by the revolutionary new ideology of clinical science as exemplified by Sir Thomas Lewis, shown below with the electrocardiogram whose recording of the electrical impulses of the heart established the scientific basis of modern cardiology.

COURTESY OF DR. A. HOLLMAN

The full potential of clinical science was realised by the generation of physicians that followed Lewis, based at the newly established Postgraduate Medical School at the Hammersmith Hospital. These included Sir John McMichael (seated, centre), Dame Sheila Sherlock (seated, left) and Professor Eric Bywaters (standing, far right). The experimental methods of the clinical scientists were strongly criticised by Dr Maurice Pappworth (below) in his book *Human Guinea Pigs*, published in 1967.

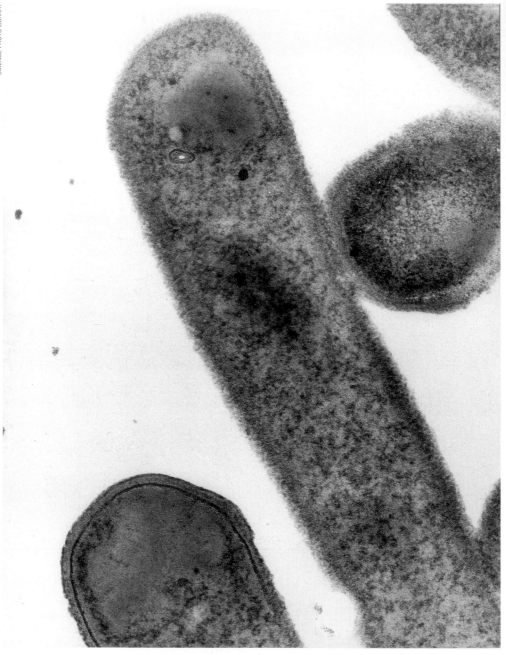

Throughout the 1970s new techniques made it possible to identify and manipulate genes which, it was hoped, would have a profound impact on medicine in three ways. First, genetic engineering would produce novel drugs by splicing genes into bacteria. In this photomicrograph, magnified 40,000 times, the bacterium B. *subtilis* is producing large quantities of a protein for use as a vaccine.

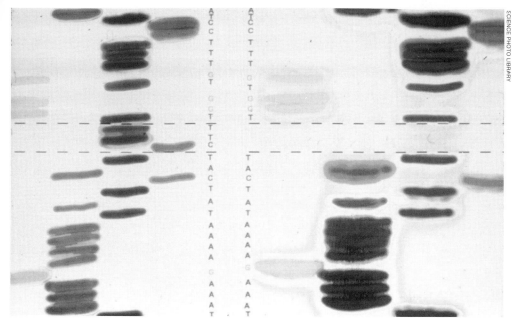

Next, the discovery of the genes involved in human disease opened up the possibility of their prevention by genetic screening. Above, the comparison between the DNA sequence of a patient with cystic fibrosis (on the right-hand side) and a healthy individual reveals a missing CTT sequence – one of over two hundred genetic mutations that can give rise to the disease. Thirdly, doctors sought to replace malfunctioning genes by gene therapy. The child below has severe combined immunodeficiency (SCID), a genetic disease similar to AIDS, and is isolated in a sterile tent to prevent infection. The genetic defect has been corrected by inserting the normal gene into his bone-marrow cells.

From the mid-1970s onwards The Social Theory of disease became increasingly influential, with the claims that most human illnesses were due to an 'unhealthy lifestyle' or external factors like poverty and pollution. Professor Geoffrey Rose was the main protagonist in Britain of the theory that the epidemic of heart disease was caused by the 'Western diet'.

In *The Causes of Cancer*, published in 1981, Sir Richard
Doll, erstwhile collaborator of Sir Austin Bradford Hill,
maintained that almost three-quarters of cancers –
excluding those related to tobacco – were caused by food.

After almost ten years of disappointment, the efforts of Bob Edwards (right) and Patrick Steptoe in developing the techniques of IVF were finally rewarded with the birth of the first 'test-tube' baby in July 1978.

Dr Barry Marshall, despite no experience in medical research, made the stunning discovery that peptic ulcers were caused by the bacterium helicobacter.

the treatment of disease – and so success necessarily places a limit on further progress. From the 1950s onwards it had advanced exponentially through a positive feedback mechanism, where knowledge gained from one area was applied to another, which in turn was applied to another, culminating in an event like transplantation of the heart that depended on half a dozen or more 'definitive moments'. Once that had been accomplished, cardiac surgery had reached its limits, and there was little further for it to go.

But, there is at least one last major 'soluble' challenge left, already illustrated by the discovery of the role of helicobacter in peptic ulcers. There remains a vast ocean of ignorance at the centre of medicine: the causes of virtually all the diseases of early and middle life – multiple sclerosis, rheumatoid, Parkinson's and myriad others – remain completely obscure. It was precisely this search for 'causes' that would become the dominant medical paradigm from the early 1980s onwards, and it is to this we now turn.

PART 3

The Fall

The value of a historical perspective is that it allows for the 'wisdom of hindsight', illuminating matters that were not at all obvious at the time. In retrospect it now seems quite clear that, concealed behind the glory days of medicine in the 1970s when the innovations of the previous decades began to be widely applied, significant trends indicated that the continuous onward march of medical progress was coming to an end.

But that is not all for, again with the wisdom of hindsight, it is possible to see that, simultaneously during the 1970s, the foundations were being laid for an entirely new paradigm to fill the intellectual vacuum left by this decline in therapeutic innovation. This new paradigm emerged quite dramatically in the 1980s driven by two very different specialties that up till now had only played a marginal role in post-war medicine: epidemiology and genetics. They promised to move beyond the empiricism that had driven the therapeutic revolution to identify the underlying causes of disease. The epidemiologists, with their 'Social Theory', insisted that most common diseases such as cancer, heart disease and strokes were caused by the social factors of an unhealthy 'lifestyle' and were thus readily preventable by switching to a healthy diet and reducing exposure to environmental pollutants. As for genetics, or rather 'The New Genetics' as it became known, a few truly astonishing developments in the 1970s had opened up the possibility of identifying the abnormal genes in several diseases. There is a beguiling complementarity between these two very different types of explanation as they represent, in a different guise, the specific contributions of nature (the gene) and nurture (social and environmental factors) in human development.

The rapidity with which this new paradigm filled medicine's intellectual vacuum is striking testimony to the declining power of empirical therapeutic innovation. In the process, however, the claims of the epidemiologists and geneticists were never properly scrutinised at the outset, and there were sound theoretical reasons for doubting their validity. Thus The Social

Theory might seem plausible enough, but Man as the culmination of millions of years of evolution is capable of surviving in the most diverse of circumstances. It would thus seem highly improbable that suddenly, in the middle of the twentieth century, he should have become vulnerable to lethal diseases caused by his 'lifestyle'. Similarly, genetics is unlikely to be an important or modifiable cause of disease as evolution, operating by the laws of natural selection, ensures those unfortunate enough to be born with deleterious genes are unlikely to survive long enough to procreate. As it turned out, both The Social Theory and The New Genetics have proved in their different ways to be blind alleys, quite unable to deliver on their promises. Their failure is 'The Fall' of modern medicine.

I

The Brave New World of The New Genetics

(i) The Beginning

Currently most medical researchers would concede that progress has slowed in recent years, but almost in the same breath will add optimistically that another golden age is 'just around the corner'. The source of this optimism is molecular biology, the science of the molecules within our cells. And what are these molecules? Look down a microscope at a cell and you will see in the centre a dark circle – the nucleus – packed with the molecules of DNA that make up our genes, the code of life. Surrounding the nucleus is the cytoplasm of the cell, filled with other specialised molecules, the 'factories' that transform the messages from the DNA of the gene into the tens of thousands of different proteins, hormones and enzymes of which the human body is made. These molecules are biology's bottom line. There is nowhere further that science can take us so, almost by definition, once we understand the workings of these essential elements of life all will become clear.

This application of molecular biology to medicine is now commonly known as The New Genetics. Its potential is exemplified by the Human Genome Project which, by the early years of the next century, will have spelled out each of the 3 billion molecules of DNA that make up the genes within each

241

nucleus. Every gene codes for a protein, so knowledge of every gene means we will also have knowledge of every protein. It is then only a matter of working out how these proteins are malfunctioning in diseases like cancer or multiple sclerosis to find ways of putting them right. 'Genetic research will have the most significant effect on our health since the microbiology revolution of the nineteenth century,' observes John Bell, Nuffield Professor of Medicine at Oxford. It will, 'like a mechanical army, systematically destroy ignorance,' argues Professor John Savill of Nottingham's University Hospital, and 'promises unprecedented opportunities for science and medicine'.[1]

Almost daily the newspapers trumpet reports of the triumphs of The New Genetics. A selection of headlines from 1997 reads: 'Gene find gives insight into brittle bones', 'Scientists find genes to combat cancer', 'Scientists find secret of ageing', 'Gene therapy offers hope to victims of arthritis', 'Hope of skin disease cure as gene found', 'Cell growth gene offers prospect of cancer cure', 'Researchers encouraged by fibrosis gene trial', 'Four genes linked to child diabetes', 'Gene transplants to fight anaemia', and so on. Even allowing for a certain amount of hyperbole on the part of the headline writers, there is a powerful impression that something really important is happening, though the frequent use of terms like 'hope' and 'prospect' and 'clue' suggest it has not quite happened yet. And will it? The cheque has now been in the mail since the early 1980s, raising the possibility that perhaps this optimism is misplaced.

The validity – or otherwise – for the claim that The New Genetics 'promises unprecedented opportunities' is obviously central to any evaluation of the history of post-war medicine, but the science involved is so arcane it is virtually impossible for anyone other than those directly involved to understand precisely where it is going. The protagonists will naturally wish to 'talk up' the significance of what they are doing while, for everyone else, the belief in its potential might simply rest on the assumption that so complex a matter *must* be important. The only way to try and come to a balanced judgement is to trace the evolution of the principal ideas over the last twenty-five

years and then examine the record of its three practical applications to medicine: Genetic Engineering as a method of
developing new drugs; Genetic Screening as a means of eradicating inherited disease; and Gene Therapy for the correction
of genetic defects.

First, a word of encouragement. Many people are daunted
by genetic terminology but, as will be seen, it is not *that* difficult and the central concepts are so truly amazing that it is well
worth making the effort to understand them.

We begin with a preamble elucidating how the genes work.
This starts in 1953, when James Watson and Francis Crick
famously discovered the structure of DNA to be a spiral staircase (or double helix).[2] The two outer banisters of the staircase
are made up of two strands of sugar molecules – Deoxyribose –
from each of which is suspended a parallel series of four molecules of nucleic acid – Adenine, Guanine, Cytosine and
Thymine (referred to by their initials AGCT) – arranged in
sequence. The chemical bonds linking one chain of nucleic
acid with its parallel chain form the steps of the staircase, hence
DNA or *Deoxyribose Nucleic Acid* (see page 244). This 'staircase structure' is particularly well suited to the replication of
genetic information every time the cell divides, as Watson and
Crick described:

> We imagine that, prior to duplication, the bonds [con-
> necting the two parallel chains of nucleic acids or
> 'nucleotides'] are broken and the two chains unwind and
> separate [the staircase, as it were, splits down the middle].
> Each chain then acts as a template for the formation on to
> itself of a new companion chain, so that eventually we shall
> have two pairs of chains where we only had one before.
> Moreover the sequence of the pairs of nucleotides will have
> been duplicated exactly.[3]

Next, the manner in which the nucleic acids (or nucleotides)
form the 'genes' that code for the tens of thousands of different proteins (enzymes, hormones, etc.) was clarified. Here it is
necessary to appreciate that each protein is made up of a unique

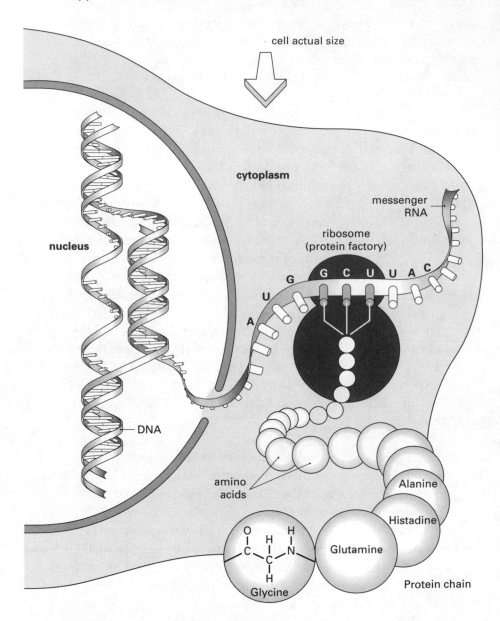

The double helix of DNA consists of two parallel strands of deoxyribose sugar molecules, to which are attached a sequence of nucleotides – AGCT – arranged in threes. The genetic instruction for a protein is conveyed by a strand of messenger RNA (mRNA) that passes out of the nucleus into the cytoplasm, where it feeds its coded instructions into a ribosome or protein factory.

combination of simpler building-blocks known as amino acids, of which there are just twenty. The four nucleotides of DNA by themselves could only code for four amino acids, but if they are arranged in threes (or triplets) – such as CCG or CGC or GCG or similar variants – there are actually sixty-four possible permutations, which is more than sufficient. So a gene made up of ninety nucleotides arranged in threes, will code for thirty amino acids that make up a single protein.

Finally, we need a mechanism by which the 'message' of the gene (the sequence of ninety nucleotides) is turned into the thirty amino acids that make up the protein. The section of DNA that includes the gene unravels and acts as a template for the building of a parallel sequence of nucleotides that is known as messenger RNA or mRNA, because it carries the message of the gene. The mRNA passes through the wall of the nucleus out into the cytoplasm of the cell where it is picked up by a protein-making factory, a ribosome. Like a ticker tape, the mRNA feeds itself into the ribosome, which reads off the first triplet of nucleotides and then pulls in from the immediate vicinity the relevant amino acids for that triplet. It reads off the next triplet and then pulls in another amino acid and so on. So, from a gene made up of a sequence of ninety nucleotides one gets a unique arrangement of thirty amino acids that makes up one protein molecule.

This then, in a grotesquely oversimplified outline, is what Francis Crick described in 1958 as the 'central dogma' of genetics: DNA makes RNA makes protein.[4] The corollary is obvious. The fault or mutation in genetic diseases arises because of a faulty arrangement of the sequence of nucleotides of the gene. This results in a faulty message being transmitted by the mRNA, leading to a faulty arrangement of amino acids, causing the faulty protein, which in the case of the genetic disease cystic fibrosis results in damage to the lung, and in Huntington's Chorea results in degeneration of the nerve cells in the brain.[5] It is impossible to convey the scale of the intellectual problems that had to be surmounted before this mechanism of gene action became clear, nor indeed to describe the sheer sense of excitement experienced by the scientists over the fifteen years that it took to work it all out. Nonetheless it is important to appreciate that as of 1970 this understanding of the workings of DNA had no practical application at all, nor indeed did there seem to be the slightest prospect that it might. The molecular biologists had established this mechanism by which the gene acted – DNA makes RNA makes protein – from experiments on the bacterium *E. coli*, but the 'details' of the individual genes and where they were located within the nucleus remained completely inaccessible, concealed somewhere in the virtually infinite amount of information encoded within DNA, compressed into the virtually infinitely small space of the nucleus. Christopher Wills, Professor of Biology at the University of California, draws an appropriate analogy:

> I have just with some difficulty hefted *Webster's Third New International Dictionary* onto my lap. This is the one that you see in libraries, sitting proudly on its own little lectern. I find there are about sixty letters to a line, 150 lines to a column and three columns to a page. This works out at 27,000 different letters to a page. The dictionary has roughly 2,600 pages adding up to 70 million letters in all. Since there are about 3 billion nucleotide molecules in the human genome, it would take 43 volumes the size of this enormous dictionary simply to list the information that they carry. Let us call each of these volumes a Webster. Each Webster is three and a half inches thick so a human genome's worth of information in the form of 43 Websters would fill a shelf 12 feet long . . . Suppose you took one of these Websters off the shelf and opened it at random, you would be confronted with a grey expanse of featureless type, with no spaces and no breaks into paragraphs. Examined more closely each line would look something like this:

> TTTTTTTTTGAGAGATTTGCTGCTGCT

> There would be, in each volume of this library of 43 books, over a million such lines of type all looking at first glance the same.

In reality, of course, each nucleotide molecule is minuscule compared to the capital letter – C, G, A or T – used to represent it, so stringing together the 3 billion nucleotides of DNA results in a continuous strand only 25mm long. But these 25mm have to be packed into the nucleus of a cell about $\frac{1}{1,500}$ mm across, and in achieving this extraordinary feat,

> the DNA molecules pack over a hundred trillion times as much information by volume as the most sophisticated computerised information system that human intelligence has been able to devise.[6]

It is appropriate to stop here for a moment's reflection. The single-celled conceptus, immediately after fertilisation, contains within its nucleus this trillion times miniaturised forty-three Webster volumes' worth of genetic information, which over the next few months will replicate itself billions of times. Somehow the genes 'know' how to instruct the individual cells, first, to form the basic structure of the foetus with a back and front, head and limbs, and then to instruct the cells to fulfil the specialised functions of a nerve or a muscle or a liver cell, and then to instruct the specialised cells to grow through childhood and adolescence to adulthood and, in this process, to link up and interact with each other to form the functioning organs of the brain, the heart and the liver. This extraordinary potential of the biological information locked within the nucleus of each cell can best be conceived of as the mirror image of the infinite size and grandeur of the Universe.

It is little wonder then that most molecular biologists in 1970, having worked out in outline the mechanism of the action of the genes as reflected in 'DNA makes RNA makes protein', believed they had reached the limits of what they could achieve. There was simply no way of locating within the vast impenetrable haystack of genetic information the individual straws of nucleotide sequences that made up the separate genes. 'The time of the great elucidation has come and gone,' wrote Nobel Prize-winner Sir MacFarlane Burnet in 1969 as 'the great objective' of understanding how the genes work had been completed and 'no one can discover that again'.[7] Or in the words of another molecular biologist, 'at the dawn of the 1970s [only] a handful of cranks in the world thought it was not yet time to wind up fundamental research on DNA. Nobody listened to them or took them seriously.'[8] And yet, amazingly, 'the handful of cranks' were to be vindicated as over the next ten years four technical innovations cracked the apparently impenetrable complexity of the genes wide open.

Cutting the text: The first task was to try to isolate the individual straws of nucleotide sequences within the haystack of the genome to permit them to be scrutinised in greater detail.

Viruses, as the smallest of all organisms, have insufficient space within their cells to make the proteins necessary for their own survival and replication, so they infect organisms larger than themselves such as bacteria (or humans), and 'borrow' their protein-making machinery. Once inside the cell, they incorporate their own genes into those of the bacterium, so it starts producing the proteins necessary for their (the viruses') survival. Anthropomorphically speaking, the bacteria resent being hijacked in this way and in retaliation produce a series of enzymes that immobilise the virus by chopping its genes up into little useless fragments. The first of these 'restriction enzymes', as they are called – or, in popular terminology, 'DNA text- cutters' – was discovered in 1968. A further 150 were identified over the following decade. Thus the addition of a combination of these text-cutters to human DNA cuts the three-billion-long string of nucleotides up into a series of more manageable sequences or, to put it another way, they make it possible to tear pages out of the forty-three volumes of Webster's dictionary.[9]

Photocopying: But these single fragments (or pages) by themselves are still just an incomprehensible string of nucleotides – CGTA etc. etc. etc. *ad*, virtually, *infinitum* – so some means had to be found, as it were, of photocopying them hundreds of times, so that many different scientists can endeavour to work out what they mean. This brings us to the second technique, which exploits another important aspect of bacterial life.

Bacteria are asexual creatures and reproduce themselves by the simple expedient of dividing in two. They can, however, still swap genetic information between each other, thanks to a small circular string of DNA (or plasmid), quite distinct from the DNA of its own genes, which can be transferred like pass-the-parcel from one bacterium to another. In this way bacteria can 'pass around' the genes for resistance to antibiotics, which explains why they can all suddenly become resistant to, say, penicillin. If it were possible to get hold of a plasmid, make an incision in the circle of DNA so that it opens out into a string and insert a fragment of human DNA (obtained by the use of text-cutter enzymes), 'reseal' the plasmid and reinsert it back into the bacterium, then, every time it divides, so would the plasmid. After several divisions it would end up with large numbers of photocopied versions of the human DNA fragment. This was first achieved in 1973 and a couple of years later an industrious Harvard scientist, Thomas Maniatis, had completed a 'library' of DNA sequences covering the whole of the human genome.[10]

Finding the gene: It is all very well chopping up human DNA into little bits and 'photocopying' them, but what one really wants to know is what those bits mean and particularly whether they contain the sequence of nucleotides that make up a gene that codes for a protein. This was the really intractable problem to which the molecular biologists prior to 1970 believed there could be no answer. But they were wrong. In 1970 two Americans, Howard Temin and David Baltimore, discovered quite independently yet another very special enzyme, this time made by a certain type of virus. As this is the really crucial moment, it requires some elaboration.[11]

Consider the hormone insulin, made by the pancreas, which controls the level of sugar in the blood and whose deficiency results in diabetes. The sequence of nucleotides or the section of DNA coding for insulin (the insulin gene) within the nucleus of these pancreas cells will be generating a lot of messenger RNA, that then moves from the nucleus out into the main part of the cell or cytoplasm to be picked up by the protein factory (ribosome), whose reading of the 'triplet code' will ensure the correct arrangement of the amino acids that make up the insulin protein. This is all in line with the central dogma of genetics: DNA makes RNA makes protein. Doctors Temin and Baltimore's momentous discovery was that an enzyme produced by a certain type of virus reverses this process, converting the RNA back into DNA (it 'reverses the transcription', hence the enzyme's name 'reverse transcriptase'). Theoretically, then, if the RNA coding for the insulin protein could be isolated from the pancreas cell, the addition of 'reverse transcriptase' would turn it back into the gene from which it originated, so the straw of hay of the insulin gene can be plucked out of the haystack of the human genome. What a coup!

So is that all there is to it – extract the RNA for a protein from the cell, add reverse transcriptase and you end up with the gene? Not quite. There had to be vast amounts of the relevant RNA in the cell for the process to work, and there were really only two situations in which this applied. First, there is a benign tumour of the pancreas known as an insulinoma, producing vast quantities of insulin, therefore its cells contain abundant insulin RNA, to which the reverse transcriptase could be added to convert it back into the original insulin gene. The second is the red blood cell which, for important reasons relating to its function, contains masses of RNA coding for the haemoglobin protein, which carries oxygen to the tissues. Here, adding the enzyme reverse transcriptase converts the RNA in the blood cells back into the haemoglobin gene. The insulin and the haemoglobin gene were thus the first to be discovered while, as will be seen, the isolation of those genes responsible for genetic conditions such as Huntington's Chorea and cystic fibrosis proved to be much more arduous. Nonetheless, it is easy to appreciate that the discovery of these two genes was profoundly important.[12]

Deciphering the gene: There is one final technical development to complete the quartet that underpinned The New Genetics. In 1977, again almost simultaneously, Frederick Sanger in

Cambridge, England and Walter Gilbert of Harvard University described two quite different methods of working out the precise sequence of nucleotides in any strand of DNA. So now it was possible not just to find the insulin gene but to know the precise sequence of the nucleotides of which it was made up.[13,14]

Thus within the ten years of the 1970s, molecular biologists had moved from a situation where the details of DNA were completely unknown, locked away in the trillion-times-miniaturised forty-three Webster volumes' worth of information, to knowledge of the precise nature of certain genes. It is necessary to acknowledge that this potted description cannot begin to convey the true complexity of the intellectual problems involved and the scale of achievement in their resolution. By 1980 all that was required was a name, something that would encompass the potential of these techniques. In an editorial in the *American Journal of Human Genetics* in 1980 the editor David Comings observed: 'Since the degree of departure from our previous approaches and the potential of these procedures are so great, one will not be guilty of hyperbole in calling it "The New Genetics".' 'The New Genetics' it became.[15]

Now imagine, for a moment, the situation in 1980. Sir Colin Dollery has just written the epitaph for the Age of Optimism, *Nature* is bemoaning the Dearth of New Drugs, and the clinical scientist is becoming an Endangered Species. Then suddenly and quite unexpectedly, like the mounted cavalry, The New Genetics arrives just in time to rescue medicine from this pessimism and despondency. It restores medicine's faith in its future, placing it back on the rails of the relentless upward curve of knowledge that had started back in 1945. It bolsters the public perception of the intellectual status of the profession that, besides everything else, can understand the arcane mysteries of the genes and can pull, like rabbits out of a hat, the gene for this and the gene for that. And most importantly of all The New Genetics restored medicine's status as an intellectual discipline. This was real science of the sort that earned people Nobel Prizes and made genuinely new and important discoveries. There was more than enough to be getting on

with, forty-three Webster-sized volumes of information whose
meaning was just waiting to be clarified. The New Genetics
was 'the new dawn' with the potential to have 'the most significant effect on health since the microbiological revolution of
the nineteenth century'.

There were only two unnoticed flies in the ointment. The
first, already alluded to, is that genes are, for obvious evolu-
tionary reasons, not a particularly important cause of disease in
humans, so the medical applications of this new knowledge was
likely to be limited. Second, despite the elucidating power of
the techniques of The New Genetics, the genes are so obviously very complex as to defy any profound understanding of
how they work. Perhaps Isaac Newton's famous observation
more adequately expresses what might be hoped for: 'I do not
know what I may appear to the world, but to myself I seem to
have been only like a boy playing on the seashore, diverting
myself now and then, finding a smoother pebble than ordinary,
whilst the great ocean of truth lay all undiscovered before me.'

These matters will become clear as we follow the practical
application of The New Genetics to medicine from 1980 to the
mid-1990s, which can conveniently be discussed in three areas.
The first, Genetic Engineering (often referred to as biotechnology), starts with the insertion of the gene for insulin into
bacteria to produce human insulin. It certainly offered the
opportunity for some scientists to become very rich very
quickly, though the therapeutic benefits turned out to be dis-
appointing. Next comes Genetic Screening. There are
approximately 4,000 diseases resulting from a defect in just one
gene – the so-called single-gene disorders. Luckily they are all
very rare, except for a handful including Huntington's Chorea,
cystic fibrosis and the congenital blood disorders such as sickle
cell anaemia. The discovery of the relevant genes opens the way
to the prevention of these disorders by testing the foetus before
it is born and selectively aborting those shown to carry defective genes. And thirdly there is Gene Therapy, where doctors
sought to insert a normal copy of an abnormal gene into a cell
in the hope that, by generating the correct rather than the gar-
bled genetic message, genetic diseases might be cured.

(ii) Genetic Engineering

Genetic engineering may evoke unsavoury images of scientists manipulating DNA but it is only a method for making new types of drugs, and, as such, could not be more straightforward and uncontroversial. The human body is made up of thousands of specialised types of protein – neurotransmitters, hormones, enzymes, and so on. Self-evidently, when one or other of these proteins is deficient or absent then illness will result. Thus diabetes is (probably) the result of viral inflammation of the insulin-producing cells of the pancreas, while haemophilia arises from a defect in the blood-clotting protein, factor VIII. Treatment of these conditions is obvious: replace the 'missing' protein from another source. Thus insulin can be obtained from the ground-up pancreases of pigs and cattle and factor VIII from the concentrated plasma of blood donors. Genetic engineering simply offers an alternative source for these proteins. Once the relevant gene has been discovered – say the gene for insulin – it can be inserted into a plasmid (the ring of DNA within a bacterium), so now a bacterium will make human insulin. That is all. Certainly the 'engineering' – getting the gene into the plasmid and making the bacteria produce insulin in sufficient quantities – is technically highly sophisticated, but there is nothing unsavoury about it.

The concept of genetic engineering positively vibrates with a sense of limitless possibilities, though it is interesting to note that its therapeutic potential is actually limited to the production of proteins like insulin, which could also be obtained much more simply from other sources. This, however, certainly did not prevent scientists and others making great sums of money from the promise that it could achieve much more than this, as illustrated by the first commercially successful medical biotechnology product – insulin. This takes us back to the earliest days of The New Genetics in the early 1970s and two personalities in particular: Herbert Boyer of the University of

Southern California, who discovered the first of the restriction enzymes ('text-cutters') for cutting up DNA; and Stanley Cohen of Stanford University, who had been studying the circular rings of DNA or plasmids in bacteria so useful for 'the photocopying' already described. During a scientific meeting in Hawaii in November 1972, Stanley Cohen heard Herbert Boyer describe his text-cutters and saw the possibilities: 'That evening,' he recalled later, 'at a delicatessen across from Waikiki Beach I proposed a collaboration with Boyer' from which emerged the first successful experiment of The New Genetics. Stanley Cohen used Boyer's text cutters to cut up the DNA from the cell of the African clawed toad, *Xenopus laevis*, which he 'spliced' into a plasmid from the bacterium *E. coli*. He then reintroduced the plasmid back into the bacterium and – lo and behold – the erstwhile amphibian DNA was replicated along with that of the bacterium. Although technically very ingenious, this experiment had no practical applications and it was to be another two years before Herbert Boyer – at least publicly – made the intellectual leap to see where it might lead. 'I think this has a lot of implications for utilising the technology in a commercial sense,' he observed, 'that is, bacteria could be used to make hormones such as insulin.' This was the first indication that the central dogma of genetics was to be rewritten to read 'DNA makes RNA makes protein makes *money*'.

Meanwhile, a 28-year-old venture capitalist, Robert Swanson, anticipating that these new methods of manipulating DNA could prove to be a gold mine – without, it would seem, really understanding what they involved – had been ringing round distinguished molecular biologists trying to set up a meeting. They all declined, until Herbert Boyer agreed to see him 'for a few minutes on a Friday afternoon' in 1976.

> Swanson hadn't really done his homework. He had no idea that in Boyer he was talking to a co-inventor of the very techniques he sought to exploit commercially. He was excited, he recalls, that anyone sounded even vaguely encouraging. On the agreed upon afternoon Swanson dropped by Boyer's laboratory. The two men liked what

they heard from each other and continued the discussion over beer at Churchill's, a local bar. 'After that meeting,' Swanson says, 'we did some thinking, him on the technology side, me on the business side, to see what was possible. We started out with a list of known proteins and looked at which markets were the most interesting.' The decision to plunge ahead in those heady days does not seem in retrospect to have been horribly costly. The businessman (Swanson) and the molecular biologist (Boyer) each coughed up a modest $500 and that $1,000 became the initial operating capital for the new company – Genentec.[16]

Top of the list of 'known proteins' was insulin, whose gene had still not been identified but was imminently anticipated. Then it would only be necessary to replicate the original Cohen–Boyer experiment by introducing the insulin gene (rather than a fragment of toad DNA) into a plasmid, and by reinserting the plasmid into a bacterium to produce limitless quantities of genetically engineered 'human' insulin. Insulin was an obvious choice – with a ready market in the millions of diabetics around the world – with the only drawback that there was more than enough insulin already obtainable from the ground-up pancreases of pigs and cattle. Further, and importantly, the structure of this pig insulin is virtually indistinguishable from that of the human variety, and certainly fulfils its therapeutic purpose of controlling the blood sugar very well. There would thus seem to be little incentive for setting out to make human insulin by means of an as yet untried technology requiring an initial capital investment to the tune of tens of millions of dollars. But the collective genius of Boyer and Swanson was their appreciation that they were selling an idea – that genetic engineering had enormous potential. Their credibility depended on making something that potential investors might have heard of, and everyone knew about insulin. Their great selling point was that their genetically engineered insulin – made by a bacterium – would be 'human' and therefore by implication superior to anything from a pig or a cow. Further – though there was no evidence for their claim – they maintained that the traditional sources of insulin would be insufficient to meet demand in the future, which would then have to be met by their genetically engineered product.

In 1977, the year after the meeting in the Churchill bar, the insulin gene was, as had been predicted, discovered thanks to – as already described – the 'reverse transcriptase' enzyme. And the following year, on 24 April 1978, Boyer reported that he had managed to obtain small amounts of human insulin after 'splicing' the insulin gene into a plasmid of the bacterium *E. coli*. Two weeks later, almost exactly three years since their first meeting, Boyer and Swanson signed a contract with the pharmaceutical giant Eli Lilly for the mass production of genetically engineered insulin. The genetic engineering boom was now under way. When their company, Genentec, was launched on the New York stock market in 1981 – without human insulin or any of its other potential products still having reached the market place – the $35 'asking' price for each share leaped to $89. Howard Boyer's initial $500 investment was now worth – on paper at least – in excess of $80 million.

Stock markets rely on credibility, which is precisely what Swanson and Boyer had set out to acquire by choosing as their first target one of the best known of human proteins, insulin. Their strategy had paid off. In the unprecedented reaction to the flotation of Genentec it is possible to discern what was to be a central feature of biotechnology in the coming years – the credulousness of investors in believing in the commercial possibilities of something they did not really understand. Few, if any, of the punters buying Genentec shares at $89 a piece understood molecular biology well enough to grasp the limits of its therapeutic potential. They could only infer that something big was about to happen, 'big' enough for *Time* to put Herbert Boyer on its front cover:

He looks just like a leftover from the 1960s in his faded jeans and open leather vest, with a can of Budweiser in his hands. Back then he marched regularly in the streets of Berkeley, California taking part in civil rights and anti-war demonstrations but despite his casual look, Herbert Wayne

Boyer is a millionaire many times over, at least on paper. More important, he is in the forefront of a new breed of scientists, entrepreneurs who are leading gene splicing out of the university laboratory and into the hurly burly of industry and commerce.[17]

In a similar vein, James Erlichman, the *Guardian*'s expert on the pharmaceutical industry, observed that 'the rewards for genetic engineers will be immense', a rosy view of the future that reflected the prevailing opinion:

Human insulin is just an introductory skirmish in a far more lucrative commercial campaign. The company that unlocks the secrets of human insulin production on a large and cost-effective scale will have gained the scientific and technical knowledge to repeat the feat, and beat the competition to a host of related and even more profitable breakthroughs in biotechnology ranging from other drugs through to cheap food proteins and 'biomass' energy supplies.[18]

But Genentec's immediate priority was to sell sufficient human insulin to make it profitable, which was not a straightforward matter as there was certainly no sign that the supplies of the considerably cheaper insulin from pigs and cows would be incapable of meeting demand. Two tactics were adopted. First, the intrinsic superiority of human insulin was vigorously promoted on the lines that patients with diabetes, who might have to be injecting themselves with insulin for several decades, deserved 'the best', even if it was structurally very similar and much more expensive. Second, just in case doctors were not getting the message, the drug company Eli Lilly decided to 'phase out' its production of animal-based insulin so it was less readily available.

The general verdict on 'human' insulin might have been that, besides being a triumph for biotechnology, its advantages were more apparent than real, were it not for the quite inexplicable fact that many diabetics found 'human' insulin to provide poorer control of their diabetes than the animal-based form they had used before. The level of sugar in the blood is kept within normal limits by a delicate balancing act between several hormones, so the effect of insulin in lowering the blood sugar is counteracted by others such as adrenaline which, if it falls too low, causes glucose to be released from stores in the liver. In patients with diabetes, this physiological balancing act can never be fully replicated by giving insulin, exposing them to the risk that their insulin injection will drive down the blood sugar too low to cause hypoglycaemia – commonly known as 'hypos' – where they feel faint and hungry and start sweating. If prompt action is not taken to boost the sugar level in the blood (by eating a biscuit or a sugar lump), the diabetic patient slips into a coma, which, if not corrected, can be lethal. With experience, diabetics naturally become very skilled at detecting these premonitory signs of hypos and by taking the necessary steps avoid such potentially serious complications.

The British Diabetic Association, soon after the 'big switch' from animal-based to human insulin, started to receive unsolicited letters from its readers claiming they were experiencing significantly more hypos. The Association duly circulated a questionnaire to all its members, half of whom reported that since they had switched to human insulin they felt 'worse off'. Their main problem was that the premonitory symptoms warning of an imminent hypo seemed to be much less marked and as a result of this 'hypoglycaemic unawareness' (as it became known) they moved from a situation of feeling well to a state of mental confusion, without having had the opportunity of taking the necessary averting action. Further, those diabetics who had insisted on reverting back to using animal-based insulin reported that their 'hypo awareness' returned. It was indeed possible – if difficult to prove – that the new human insulin contributed to an unusually high number of deaths of young diabetics during this period. In 1988, a psychiatrist in London claimed 'personal knowledge' of sixteen cases of sudden death in young diabetics over a six-month period, at least half of whom were known to have recently changed to human insulin. There is no explanation why the allegedly superior genetically engineered human insulin should have had this regrettable side-effect.[19]

Insulin may have been a pyrrhic victory for biotechnology, but Boyer and Swanson had no alternative other than to start with it, because it was the first hormone whose gene had been isolated – in anticipation of generating the capital necessary for this new way of producing drugs which, being so different and so more 'scientific' from that which had gone before, it would seem, could not fail to deliver. But that is certainly not how it has turned out. After almost fifteen years, human insulin is still biotechnology's commercially most successful product, while a mere dozen other biotech drugs have since become available, most of whose contribution to medical progress – like that of human insulin – has been marginal (see page 292). Indeed, as of 1995 there are only two biotechnology drugs that could genuinely be described as representing a significant therapeutic advance: a vaccine against the viral infection of the liver, hepatitis B; and erythropoeitin (EPO), a hormone, secreted by the kidney, which stimulates the production of red blood cells and thus reverses the severe and debilitating anaemia often experienced by patients with chronic kidney failure.[20]

It is testament to the power of the idea of genetic engineering that the limits to its therapeutic potential were not appreciated earlier, but the reason is quite obvious. Biotechnology may be a technically dazzling way of making drugs but it is severely constrained by the fact that the only things that genes can make are proteins, so the only therapeutic use for biotechnology products are conditions where either a protein is deficient and needs replacing (such as the use of insulin in diabetes) or where it is hoped that giving a protein in large enough doses might in some way or other influence a disease, such as cancer.

Genetic engineering by definition cannot come up with the sort of surprises that drove the therapeutic revolution, completely novel chemicals that just happened, like chlorpromazine, to improve the symptoms of schizophrenia, or just happened, like azathioprine, to prevent the rejection of transplanted

Biotech products in use in 1995

DRUG	USES
Human insulin	Diabetes
Interferon alpha	Hairy cell leukaemia; hepatitis B & C; keeping lymphoma, leukaemia in remission
Human growth hormone	Dwarfism
Interferon beta & gamma	Chronic granulomatous disease (decreases infections); multiple sclerosis; hepatitis B & C
Tissueplasminogen activator	Clot-buster drug
Erythropoietin	Treatment of anaemia in kidney failure
G-SCF, GM-CSF	Stimulate white blood cells after cancer chemotherapy
Ceredase	Gaucher's disease
Hepatitis B vaccine	Immunisation against hepatitis B
DNAse	Cystic fibrosis; chronic bronchitis
Interleukin-2	Kidney cancer; melanoma; leukaemia; ovarian cancer
Factor VIII	Haemophilia
Anti IIb IIIa Antibody	Prevent narrowing of coronary arteries after angioplasty

(Adapted from a list provided by Dr Richard J. Wurtman, Department of Brain and Cognitive Sciences, Massachusetts Institute of Technology.)

organs. Further, the technical complexities of biotechnology markedly constrained its innovatory capacity, in contrast to the ease with which medicinal chemists in the 1950s and 1960s synthesised thousands of variations of a single chemical. In 1996, a decade and a half after human insulin launched the genetic engineering revolution, the editor of *The Lancet* mordantly observed that despite the 'millions of dollars poured into biotechnology research worldwide', there is 'very little to show for such investment'. Perhaps, he speculated, a new anti-cancer drug, Marimastat, developed by the firm British Biotechnology at a cost of £150 million, would be the 'breakthrough that the biotech industry has been waiting for'? A month later Marimastat was shown to be no more effective than no treatment at all.[21]

(iii) THE NEW EUGENICS

It is crucial to remember that throughout the 1980s The New Genetics was blossoming out in all directions, and it was this cumulative effect that conveyed the impression that the possibilities of medicine were being transformed. Thus in the same year, 1982, that the molecular biologist Herbert Boyer and the venture capitalist Robert Swanson launched human insulin, Judy Chang and Yuet Wei Kan of the University of Southern California described a technique for diagnosing the blood disorder sickle cell anaemia in the foetus while still in the womb, thus opening the gates to a whole new medical venture: the elimination of genetic disease by prenatal screening and the selective abortion of foetuses found to carry abnormal genes.[22]

Once the gene for haemoglobin (the oxygen-carrying protein in the blood cells) had been identified (with, as will be recalled, the help of the enzyme reverse transcriptase), it became possible to identify specific defects involved in genetic blood disorders. In sickle cell anaemia this takes the form of the substitution of one triplet of nucleotides, GAG, with another, GTG. The messenger RNA then carries this 'faulty' message to the protein factory, the ribosome, which makes the haemoglobin protein, where the amino acid valine (coded for by GAG) is substituted with another glutamic acid (coded for by GTG). This single substitution of the 'wrong' amino acid alters the physicochemical properties of the haemoglobin protein, as a result of which the red blood cell collapses inwards (it assumes a sickle shape). The tissues are therefore deprived of oxygen resulting in 'sickling crises', which the patient experiences as pains in the chest and bones.

Chang and Kan's technique made use of 'text-cutters', which cut up DNA into fragments at the site of a particular sequence of nucleotides. Thus, a restriction enzyme that usually cuts the haemoglobin gene at the GAG sequence will not do so if it is replaced by the GTG mutation, so the resulting fragments of the haemoglobin gene will be of a different size in sickle cell anaemia. In broad outline, this is how they achieved it. First they removed some foetal cells from the amniotic fluid and extracted the DNA within. They then added a text-cutter and passed the DNA through a machine that separates out the resulting fragments. By showing the fragment lengths were different from those obtained from normal haemoglobin, they could thus conclude the foetus carried the sickle cell gene.[23]

In theory this method can be applied to virtually any genetic disease where the gene is known, with the obvious corollary that a 'positive' prenatal diagnosis permits those affected to be aborted, thus the genetic disease will be 'prevented'. In reality, things, as might be expected, turned out to be a bit more complicated, and sickle cell anaemia turns out to be something of a special case. But to appreciate the impact this type of genetic screening might have it is necessary to take a step back and look at genetic diseases in general.

There are more than 5,000 genetic diseases. This might sound high but virtually all are staggeringly rare, being the result of a 'spontaneous mutation' in the DNA a child inherits from its parents. Spontaneous mutations 'just happen'; there are so many and they are so unpredictable that they cannot be 'prevented' by genetic screening, because it would not be feasible to search the DNA of a foetus looking for them. This leaves a handful of commoner genetic diseases – which are, in fact, not very common – for which prenatal genetic screening might be possible. Most of these will be familiar and are caused by the inheritance of a faulty gene from one or both parents. They include the blood disorders such as sickle cell anaemia and thalassaemia; the bleeding disorder haemophilia famously transmitted by Queen Victoria to the royal households of Europe and resulting from an abnormality of the gene that codes for the 'clotting' protein factor VIII; cystic fibrosis, a disease of the lungs that predisposes to chronic infection which destroy the lung tissue leading to respiratory failure; muscular dystrophy, which causes a progressive weakness of the muscles; and Huntington's Chorea, which causes a dementing illness from the forties onwards and whose most famous victim was the American folk singer, Woody Guthrie.

Most inherited genetic diseases are incurable, with the obvious exception of haemophilia which, as pointed out in the previous chapter, can be corrected by transfusions of the missing factor VIII. Their symptoms can sometimes be ameliorated, but they can only be prevented by prenatal genetic diagnosis and selective abortion. Put another way, most of these conditions can be diagnosed quite straightforwardly after birth, but by then the option of 'prevention' is lost as the postnatal equivalent of abortion, infanticide, has not – since the German eugenics programme of the 1930s and 1940s – been permitted in Western countries. The only problem was that besides the haemoglobin gene involved in the genetic blood disorders none of the other genes responsible for these 'common' inherited genetic disorders were known, nor was there any obvious means whereby they could be discovered. And why? The haemoglobin gene had been identified because of the abundant messenger RNA for haemoglobin in the red blood cells; working back with the help of reverse transcriptase, the gene had been discovered. The same, however, did not apply to most of the other inheritable disorders already mentioned, because the defective protein was not known so it was not possible to find the relevant messenger RNA in the cells, and so work back to the gene. Here, then, was an impenetrable impasse to the further development of genetic screening.

The solution to this problem had first been formulated in 1979 and ranks as one of the great intellectual insights of The New Genetics. The principle is illustrated by the discovery of the gene involved in Huntington's Chorea. First it is necessary to obtain the DNA of patients with Huntington's Chorea, by taking blood samples from as many people with the disease as possible. Fortuitously a large community of closely related Huntington's patients were discovered living in a squalid community in primitive tin shacks and lakeside huts on hills on the shores of Lake Maracaibo in Venezuela. Next, text-cutters were added to the DNA, cutting it at specific nucleotide sequences. The resulting fragments were then passed through a machine to separate them out, so producing a distinctive pattern of lengths of DNA generated by the text-cutters. This produced a characteristic DNA 'map' of Huntington's that could then be compared with a map of someone without the disease, in the hope of finding in the Huntington's DNA a distinct fragment that might have included the abnormal gene. This fragment may have been a million or more nucleotides long; the next task was to sequence it, identifying one nucleotide after another, in the hope that somewhere on the way you would come across an area that looked as if it could possibly be the sort of gene that might have coded for the sort of protein that might be involved in the disease.[24]

There is no way of conveying the complexity of this gene hunt other than to observe that it occupied hundreds of researchers in different laboratories around the world for the best part of ten years. By 1995 this monumental effort had identified the genes involved in no less than forty-two different diseases, including those that, by being relatively common, might be suitable for prenatal screening, such as cystic fibrosis and muscular dystrophy.[25]

The blazing publicity that accompanied the report of the discovery of one gene after another could not but fail to convey the impression that sooner or later it would be feasible to eradicate genetic diseases by prenatal screening. But that is not how it has turned out. As with genetically engineered drugs – albeit for different reasons – the impression of progress has not been vindicated by anything resembling the practical benefits originally anticipated.

The genetic screening of foetuses certainly can work most obviously in the rather unusual circumstances where a particular genetic disorder is common in well-defined communities. Thus the abnormal haemoglobin gene involved in the blood disorder thalassaemia (responsible for a very severe form of anaemia) is common in Cyprus, with as many as a quarter of the population being carriers, resulting in fifty-one children being born with the disease in 1974. Ten years later, following the introduction of screening, this figure had fallen to two.[26]

This situation is, however, not typical and certainly cannot be compared to the problem of trying to find, for example, those foetuses carrying the gene for cystic fibrosis out of the tens of thousands of pregnancies in Britain every year, which is why almost ten years after the gene has been discovered, the number of cases a year, 300, remains unchanged. What explains this? First, it is necessary to identify those pregnancies where the foetus might be affected, so, as a preliminary, both parents must be screened early on in the pregnancy to identify those couples where both mother and father are 'carriers'. Prenatal testing can then be performed in these pregnancies and those foetuses found to be carrying the abnormal gene can be terminated. The complexities of this type of prenatal genetic screening are illustrated by a 'pilot' project that has been running in Edinburgh for almost ten years. Over this period 25,000 couples have been tested. In twenty-two both mother and father were carriers and thus the foetus was 'at risk' of having cystic fibrosis. The diagnosis was confirmed in eight of these twenty-two pregnancies and the foetuses were aborted. Despite this massive screening programme, though, several babies with CF were 'missed', because so many different mutations can give rise to the disease.[27]

Clearly this type of mass screening during pregnancy is an enormous undertaking, expensive both in laboratory services and the professional skills of those who administer the tests. Further, like all antenatal testing the process of screening invariably generates much anxiety among parents. It is thus not entirely obvious that it is worthwhile screening 25,000 couples to terminate 0.03 per cent of pregnancies, or as The Lancet cautiously observed in commenting on the results: 'We still have to think whether nationwide screening programmes are what we really want.' And it is a fair bet it will not happen. If this is the verdict for cystic fibrosis, then clearly prenatal genetic screening cannot be considered a valid option for preventing the many other much rarer inheritable disorders.

The practicalities of screening for cystic fibrosis have been discussed at some length because they illustrate so well a recurring feature of The New Genetics – the hiatus between anticipated benefits and reality. The implicit assumption during the race to find the cystic fibrosis and other genes was that as soon as they were discovered it would be rapidly possible to prevent these disorders. But now, almost a decade later, the number of new cases of cystic fibrosis remains almost unchanged, while the substantial costs of screening – with estimates of over £100,000 per case 'prevented' – almost guarantees that this situation will continue.

As the enthusiasm for genetic screening has declined, so the focus has shifted to 'genetic testing', to identify those individuals at high risk of a serious disease in later life, such as cancer and heart disease. When heart disease and cancer 'run in families', they almost invariably occur at a relatively young age and are often very aggressive. The 'cause' in such cases is almost entirely genetic: the mutation of one gene or other involved in, for example, cholesterol metabolism (leading to heart disease); or breast development (leading to breast cancer when young).

Those unfortunate enough to be born into families where several relatives have died young from such diseases naturally want to know what they can do to avoid a similar fate. There are two obvious benefits from a genetic test. Those found to be 'negative', that is, who do not carry the mutant gene, can relax, reassured that their risk of these illnesses is no greater than that of the general population. Those who are found to carry the mutation can take pre-emptive action, either by having regular screening tests, such as mammographies to detect breast cancer early, or indeed submit voluntarily to bilateral mastectomy, followed by reconstruction of the breast with an implant, in an attempt to entirely rid the body of any threat of malignancy from this source.[28]

The gene hunters, following their success in finding the genes for the commoner genetic disorders such as cystic fibrosis, have subsequently turned their attention to finding in a similar way the genes that predispose to cancers that run in families. In 1994 the first breast cancer gene, named BRCA1, generated the usual excitement and speculation associated with every genetic breakthrough. This was followed eighteen months later by the discovery of a second gene, BRCA2. These two breast cancer genes are believed to account for most 'hereditary' cases of the disease, but they are normal, and therefore uninformative, about those that are non-hereditary and make up 95 per cent of the total. Further, as with all genetic diseases, many different mutations of the genes involved have been found, which, as can be imagined, makes the problem of testing considerably more complex.[29]

This leads to the central issue of genetic testing for these common diseases. If the gene for hereditary breast cancer had also been involved in the remaining 95 per cent of cases, one could imagine that perhaps, at some time in the future, it might be possible by genetic testing to predict at birth the probability for any individual of their subsequent risk of developing this type of serious disease in later life. But clearly this is not going to be the case. It may indeed be useful in the minority whose cancers run in families, as it will be useful to know whether the abnormal gene is or is not present. But widespread genetic testing is not an option, not least because it would be foolhardy to volunteer for such tests. The results could seriously and adversely influence the chances of obtaining life insurance, or would so increase the premiums for private health insurance as to make them unaffordable.[30]

In summary then, back in the early 1980s it was quite legitimate to assume that the discovery of the genes involved in disease would, almost by definition, considerably widen the scope of medicine to include the prevention of 'common' genetic diseases, such as cystic fibrosis, while deepening scientific knowledge of the genetic contribution to adult disease in a way that would allow them to be averted or ameliorated. Such assumptions have turned out to be ill-founded. Both goals seem now more unachievable than ever, a curious paradox that will be explained after an examination of the final of the three great promises of The New Genetics – gene therapy.

(iv) GENE THERAPY

Gene therapy is the supreme aspiration of The New Genetics, taking the technical innovations already discussed to their ultimate logical conclusion: the correction of genetic defects by physically changing the genes themselves. In addition, gene therapy in the public consciousness possesses a deeper resonance, evoking the notion that humans might finally acquire mastery over their destiny, their potential no longer constrained by the limitations imposed by the lottery of genetic inheritance.

The immediate prospects for gene therapy lie in the treatment of the same group of diseases caused by a defect in the single gene considered in the discussion of genetic screening, most notably cystic fibrosis and Duchenne's muscular dystrophy (DMD). Indeed much of the attraction of gene therapy is that it offers a positive alternative to the eugenicist ideology that is implicit in genetic screening. How much better it would be to be able to correct the genetic defect in a child with, for example, cystic fibrosis rather than selectively aborting those foetuses found to be carrying the abormal gene!

But how to do it? First, the gene responsible for those diseases that might be suitable for gene therapy must be known and, as we have seen, molecular biologists have been very successful at locating several of them. Next, a copy of the 'normal' gene must somehow be introduced into the abnormally functioning cell, which in children with cystic fibrosis, for example, means the normal gene must be inserted into the cells lining the airways, which are the ones adversely affected by the disease. The most obvious candidate to act as a 'vector' to carry the normal version of the gene into the abnormally functioning cell is a virus, as it has both the capacity to penetrate the cell wall and, crucially, integrates its own genes into that of the host cell's DNA. Clearly, if a virus is to act as a vector it must first be 'disabled', by removing those of its genes which have the potential to damage the cells they invade, and then 'modified', so as to include the normal human gene. The normal gene, it is to be hoped, once incorporated into the genome of the defective cell, will override the action of the abnormal gene and thus restore the cell's functioning to normal. It all sounds – and indeed is – an astonishing piece of science.

The first gene therapy experiment took place in 1990 at the US National Institute of Cancer in Washington, DC. Two girls, nine-year-old Cynthia Cutshall and four-year-old Ashanthi de Silva, were both victims of a very rare genetic disease involving an enzyme, adenosine deaminase or ADA. Their disease – known as ADA deficiency – is caused by a defect in the ADA gene, so that the level of the enzyme in the white blood cells, the T lymphocytes, is reduced to a critically low level such that they can no longer function properly. The T lymphocytes are part of the immune system protecting the body against infection, thus ADA deficiency has the same effect as AIDS, being an immunodeficiency disorder leading to repeated devastating infections. This ever-present threat means those affected with the disease have to live their terrible and abbreviated lives in a plastic bubble isolated from the external world. Few survived beyond four years of age. Their prospects improved markedly following the development of a special preparation of the ADA enzyme that could be directly injected into the veins, thus restoring the competency of the T lymphocytes, but this treatment, at £100,000 a year, is very expensive. It would seem a better and certainly more elegant solution to correct the underlying genetic defect so that the T lymphocytes themselves would start making the ADA enzyme in sufficient amounts.

The more seriously affected of the two children, Ashanthi de Silva, was the first to be treated. On 14 September 1990 her white blood cells, including the T lymphocytes, were removed and exposed to the 'disabled' virus bearing the inserted normal ADA gene. The T cells, now hopefully healthily complete with the normal ADA gene, were then reinfused back into the vein. The entire undertaking was clinically uneventful, and thus began human gene therapy. Four months later it was the turn of Cynthia.

This first foray into gene therapy, albeit for an extremely rare condition, showed that the principles were sound. It was undoubtedly a very impressive technical achievement. Nonetheless, it was certainly not a permanent cure, as the T lymphocytes' lifespan is limited to a few months before being destroyed and replaced by others. Hence the gene therapy had to be repeated several times a year, which naturally makes it very costly. Further, both Ashanthi and Cynthia continue to receive preparations of the ADA enzyme, so it is not possible to discern the specific contribution (if any) of the gene therapy in protecting them against infection and ensuring their continued good health.[31]

Still, the experiment was a start, generating great excitement, as would be expected for any new, elegant, sophisticated form of treatment for a previously intractable disease, but this time with the twist – that put the news on the front page – that for the first time doctors had intervened to change an individual's genetic inheritance. Proposals for further gene therapy experiments multiplied, both for comparable simple gene disorders like cystic fibrosis and Duchenne's muscular dystrophy and for certain types of advanced cancer. 'The concept and techniques of gene therapy have moved from being fanciful to the beginnings of human clinical application,' observed one of its pioneers, Theodore Friedmann of the University of Southern California, a sentiment echoed by Dr French Anderson of the National Institute of Health, who had participated in the ADA experiment: 'Human gene therapy has progressed from speculation to reality in a short time . . . the many clever applications of gene transfer that investigators are discussing ensure that gene therapy will be applied to a broad range of diseases over the next several years,' he observed in the journal *Science* in 1992, though noting that 'only thousands not millions of patients are treatable by current techniques'.[32]

Even this relatively modest expectation of treating 'thousands' has turned out to be hopelessly optimistic. In 1995, just three years after Dr Anderson's prediction, an internal review conducted by the National Institute of Health concluded that gene therapy was not only expensive but useless. At the time the NIH was spending $200 million a year on research into gene therapy, a sum multiplied several times over by commercial firms as investors had poured hundreds of millions of dollars into gene therapy companies in anticipation of 'blockbuster' discoveries. Yet the two authors of the internal review found that 'despite anecdotal evidence of success clinical efficacy has not been definitively described . . . significant problems remain in all basic aspects of gene therapy'.[33] What had gone wrong? Three months before this internal review, the credibility of gene therapy had been undermined by two papers published in the same edition of the *New England Journal of Medicine*, both of which concluded it simply did not work.

The first paper described the results of gene therapy in twelve children with cystic fibrosis.[34] The defective gene in CF results in an abnormal protein in the cells lining the airways, which produces an abnormally sticky mucus that predisposes to repeated chest infections, over time damaging the lung irreparably. To correct this genetic abnormality, each child had a solution instilled in the nose containing millions of modified viruses containing the normal gene. These viruses would, it was hoped, infect the cells lining the airways and thus replace the abnormal gene with a normal one.

The second paper described the results of gene therapy in twelve children with muscular dystrophy, in whom a defective gene leads to the production of an abnormal muscle protein so that, from the age of four onwards, they become gradually weaker. By the age of ten most are wheelchair-bound.[35] The twelve children in this study were given injections of primitive muscle cells containing the normal gene directly into the muscles of one arm.

Neither experiment worked. In the first, an analysis of the cells removed from the nose showed that in only one of the twelve children was there any evidence of transfer of the normal gene, which was minimal, did not last long and was insufficient to correct the underlying defect. As for the twelve boys in the muscular dystrophy experiment: 'There was no improvement in the strength of the muscles that received the injection in any of the patients.' Dr Jeffrey Leiden of the University of Chicago in an accompanying editorial commenting on these two experiments observed how far the results fell short of the goal of 'successful gene therapy', which would require for both conditions 'the delivery and long-term expression of the appropriate genes in large numbers of cells throughout [damaged] tissue'.[36]

The main impediment to success would seem to be 'the vector' – the virus is just not very good at getting the normal gene into the diseased cell – but the problem is actually much more serious. The logic of gene therapy presupposes that the 100,000 or so genes in the cell work independently of each other, so that a faulty gene can be replaced, in a similar way to replacing a faulty car part. But for every gene that codes for a protein, there are others that regulate its actions and yet others that regulate the regulators. The genome can thus be compared to an orchestra, which must produce multiple musical notes in harmony to generate the desired effect. Just as one cannot correct a poor performance of a Beethoven symphony by changing a single note, so one cannot repair a disease like cystic fibrosis just by inserting a copy of a normal gene without also linking it up to all the other genes that regulate it. The gene therapy experiments may have been scientifically very ingenious, but they were bound to fail.

The gene therapists put a brave face on the NIH report, admitting its therapeutic potential had, as Theodore Friedmann put it, 'possibly become greatly exaggerated and that hopes for clinical success had become confused with fact . . . We all conveyed advances in an unrealistically rosy way . . . [with] undeliverable promises.' These were, however, still early days: 'Gene therapy is not a failure, it is simply still too immature to deliver yet on its promises.'[37] Perhaps, but within a few months of the NIH internal review, Nature reported 'the regular stream of proposals for innovative gene therapy experiments has dried up'.[38] For the moment the realistic proposals for gene therapy have been postponed indefinitely. 'The timescale of scientific progress is a long one,' observes George Dickson, Professor of Molecular Cell Biology at London University, who 'envisages ten to fifteen years before [we have] something workable'.[39]

(v) THE END

The New Genetics, in the three distinct but overlapping phases of genetic engineering, genetic screening and gene therapy, has been the intellectual driving force of medicine during this period, generating genuinely novel and brilliant answers to fundamental problems. And yet for all the enthusiasm and excitement and the millions of hours of research endeavour and the tens of thousands of scientific papers and the acres of newspaper coverage, its practical benefits are scarcely detectable. Genetic engineering has turned out to be an expensive method for making drugs that were either – like insulin – already available, or have been shown to be of marginal therapeutic benefit. Genetic screening has had hardly any impact on the prevention of the common inherited disorders, and gene therapy simply does not work. Nor, indeed, is this all, for several other much anticipated benefits of The New Genetics have similarly failed to fulfil the expectations held out for them, most notably the genetic transformation of pigs as a source of organs for transplantation.[40]

The New Genetics begins to appear like a relentless catalogue of failed aspirations. This is profoundly shocking, for as already noted, virtually all doctors and to a greater or lesser degree the public perceive The New Genetics not only as the great scientific success story of the past fifteen years, but also as holding the key to a golden future when everything that is currently obscure will be revealed. This discrepancy between the perceived and the actual achievements of The New Genetics is pivotal to any analysis of the current state of medicine. It poses two related questions: 'Why is there a pervasive belief in the limitless possibilities of The New Genetics?' or, its antithesis, 'Why has The New Genetics failed to deliver?'

First, why the pervasive belief in limitless possibilities? The New Genetics emerged at precisely the right moment to fill the intellectual vacuum created by the End of the Age of Optimism of the late 1970s. Next, The New Genetics was serious science, apparently much more serious than the pot-luck empirical hit-or-miss medicinal chemistry that had generated so many new drugs in the 1950s and 1960s. And, being so serious, it was only natural to expect it would, by pinpointing the relevant genes, find 'the ultimate cause' of common diseases. Then, the possibilities of The New Genetics were vigorously hyped in a way that had never happened before. Commercially, biotechnology pioneers like Robert Swanson were initially selling *the idea* that the technical complexity of making drugs by inserting genes into bacteria must mean they would be genuinely beneficial in previously untreatable diseases, like adult cancer and multiple sclerosis. And with billions of dollars of investors' money at stake, there was every incentive to talk up such possibilities.

This advocacy of the potential of The New Genetics has proved very persuasive with the result that, in the popular imagination, DNA has acquired the reputation of providing the key to understanding the whole of human biology. It is the Book of Man, a Dictionary, a Map or a Blueprint, determining who we are. Logically then, The New Genetics can, by offering an understanding of 'the blueprint', improve our minds and bodies and make us better and healthier people. There is certainly every reason for molecular biologists to project this view of their task, as it is the ultimate guarantee of continuing funds for their research.[41]

It is time now to turn our attention to the other side of the chasm-like discrepancy between the promise and the reality of The New Genetics, to see why it might be that it has so singularly failed to deliver. The first and obvious constraint on the scope of the medical applications of The New Genetics is quite simply that genetics is not a particularly significant factor in human disease. This is scarcely surprising, as man would not be as successful a species as he is (many would argue too successful), were it not that natural selection had over millions of years weeded out the unfit. Consequently there are only a handful of common gene disorders and they themselves are not very common. Further, the contribution of genetics to adult disease such as cancer is limited to a minority of cases and for everybody else it is almost invariably only one of several factors, of which the most important is ageing, an everyday fact of life about which there is not much that can be done.[42]

The second important reason why The New Genetics has failed to live up to expectations is that the genes themselves turn out to be infinitely more complex and elusive than could ever have been imagined. There was a charming and elegant simplicity revealed by the unravelling of the genetic basis for sickle cell anaemia – a defect in one triplet of nucleotides caused the insertion of the 'wrong' amino acid in the haemoglobin protein, thus altering the red cells' physicochemical properties so that it 'sickles'. It seemed, in the early 1980s, that genetics could be understood in terms of such well-defined rules and certainly, if all diseases had been similar to sickle cell anaemia, then everything would have been sorted out in no time. But now we know better. Sickle cell anaemia turns out to be virtually unique in the simple nature of its genetic defect. The behaviour of the genes turns out not to be determined by hard and fast rules, but rather is ambiguous, elusive, contradictory and unpredictable. The central concept that the gene, in the form of triplets of nucleotides, codes for an arrangement of amino acids that makes up a protein has turned out to be deficient in several ways. The first is 'linguistic': any triplet of nucleotides turns out to mean different things in different circumstances. Richard Lewontin, biologist at Harvard University, explains:

> The difficulty in devising causal information from DNA messages is that the same 'words' [nucleotides], as in any complex language, have different meanings in different contexts, and multiple functions in a given context. No word in English has more powerful implications of action than 'do'. 'Do it now!' Yet in most of its contexts 'do' as in 'I do not know' [has no meaning at all]. While this 'do' has no *meaning* it undoubtedly has a linguistic *function* as a spacing element in the arrangement of a sentence. The code

sequence GTA AGT is sometimes read by the cell as an instruction to insert the amino acids valine and serine in a protein but sometimes it signals the place to cut up and edit the genetic message; and sometimes it may be only a spacer, like 'do' in 'I do not know', that keeps other parts of the messages an appropriate distance from each other. Unfortunately we do not know how the cell decides among the possible interpretations.[43]

And just as one can never be sure what any triplet of nucleotides might mean, one can never be sure what the significance of a mutation in the nucleotides might be. Thus in sickle cell anaemia one defect in a sequence of nucleotides – GAG instead of GTG – leads to the insertion of the 'wrong' amino acid (valine instead of glutamic acid) in the haemoglobin protein and thus causes the red blood cell to sickle. But in cystic fibrosis, 200 or more such mutations of nucleotides have been identified that can cause the disease, and a further 200 that make no difference. Nor can one be confident that the same mutation causes the same disease, as illustrated by two sisters who both had the same mutation in the gene for the 'light-sensitive' protein rhodopsin in the retina that results in blindness from retinitis pigmentosa (a gradual destruction of the retinal cells at the back of the eye). The younger sister was indeed blind but the visual acuity of her older sibling – whose rhodopsin gene contained exactly the same mutation – was excellent and did not prevent her from working as a night-time truck driver. So, when, after prodigious efforts, the 'ultimate genetic cause' of retinitis pigmentosa was finally pinned down to a specific defect in a specific gene, it then emerged the 'ultimate cause' was apparently quite compatible with not having the disease at all. Such perverse complexities, inexplicable in the conventional understanding of the mechanism of gene action, abound. They lead to a situation of incomprehensible complexity, where precisely the same genetic disease can be caused by different mutations in several genes, while several different diseases can stem from mutations in a single gene.

These examples illustrate the fascinating but endlessly frustrating nature of The New Genetics.[44]

It could, of course, be argued that The New Genetics is currently in the same situation as The Old Genetics back in 1970 when, following the elucidation of the mechanism of gene action, most molecular biologists felt they had reached the limits of scientific understanding. Might it be that further technical innovations in the future, along with the completion of the Human Genome Project, may make genetic screening and gene therapy perfectly feasible? Perhaps, but both of these practical applications of The New Genetics rest on a concept of the nature of the gene – a unidirectional flow of information, DNA makes RNA makes protein – that is far too simplistic. Certainly the imagery of DNA as the 'master molecule, the blueprint from which everything flows' is vivid enough, but genes by themselves can do nothing without interacting with other genes operating within the context of the whole cell within which they are located. In the words of geneticist Philip Gell FRS, Emeritus Professor at the University of Birmingham: 'The heart of the problem lies in the fact that we are dealing not with a chain of causation but with a network that is a system like a spider's web in which a perturbation at any point of the web changes the tension of every fibre right back to its anchorage in the blackberry bush. The gap in our knowledge is not merely unbridged, but in principle unbridgable and our ignorance will remain ineluctable.'[45]

2

SEDUCED BY THE SOCIAL THEORY

(i) THE BEGINNING

There is, as has been suggested, a seductive familiarity in the symmetrical manner with which The New Genetics and The Social Theory sought to explain the causes of disease, evoking the separate contributions of nature (the gene) and nurture (upbringing) in human development. But the appeal of this complementarity can be misleading, as illustrated by the example of tuberculosis. In the mid-nineteenth century, tuberculosis was attributed to a combination of 'constitutional factors' (what would now be understood as 'the genes'), thus explaining its tendency to run in families, and also to the environment or 'the miasma', the putrid emanations from unhealthy places. It was only when Robert Koch looked down his microscope and observed the tubercle bacillus obtained from the lungs of consumptive patients that both these theories were seen for what they were – secondary explanations for a disease whose cause was a specific organism. We have seen in the preceding chapter how nature (the genes) is not after all a readily modifiable cause of disease; now we turn our attention to nurture, the 'miasma theory' of the late twentieth century, which attributes many diseases to social factors.

The great appeal of The Social Theory is not just that it provides an explanation for disease, but also opens the way to preventing them. And prevention, as everyone knows, is better than cure. From the 1950s onwards, the example of smoking had promised an entirely different approach to the problem of illness than that offered by the therapeutic revolution. It would be quite unnecessary to have to treat, not very successfully, lung cancer if only people abstained from smoking. Similarly there would be no need for most drugs and treatments were it possible to identify why people became ill in the first place and prevent their diseases in a similar manner. The problem was that up until the mid-1970s no one seemed to know what these other causes of disease might be. And then suddenly it seemed as if this ignorance was being swept away as, with increasing certainty, it was claimed they lay simply in people's lives and that most cancers, not to mention strokes and heart attacks, could be prevented by people changing their social habits in precisely the same way that lung cancer could be prevented by stopping smoking. The vision promised by The Social Theory is not just humane but also medicine on the grand scale of the great sanitary reforms of the nineteenth century when civil engineering, by providing a clean water supply, eradicated water-borne infectious diseases such as cholera. Now social engineering would, by encouraging people to adopt healthy lifestyles, have an equally beneficial effect.

The rise in the scope and ambition of The Social Theory is really quite extraordinary. Thus a booklet published by the British Medical Association in the late 1960s with the old-fashioned title 'Doctor's Orders' advised readers of the dangers of smoking, the merits of a 'sensible balanced diet', and particularly to avoid becoming overweight. It warned that drinking more than a bottle of wine a day (or its equivalent) could damage the liver. But that was all. By the 1990s, this sensible – if rather obvious – advice has escalated to encompass every aspect of people's lives. Now smokers harm not only themselves but innocent bystanders who are 'passively' exposed to an increased risk of lung cancer and heart disease. Medical advice about alcohol has been extended so now everyone is advised to drink no more than three glasses of wine a day – less than is required to become even slightly merry. Dozens of other quite unexpected hazards have been identified. In 1997 alone they included reports linking silicone breast implants with arthritis, computer screens with loss of memory and mobile phones with brain tumours. But much the most striking change from the 1960s is that advice on a 'sensible balanced diet' has metamorphosed into the claim that the specific diseases people die from – strokes, heart disease and cancer – are quite simply the outcome of specific foods they consume: salt overloads the circulation pushing up the blood pressure to cause paralysis or death from stroke; saturated 'fats' in dairy foods and meat fur up the arteries to cause untimely death from a heart attack, as well as being 'implicated' in causing many common cancers including those of the breast and bowel.

Clearly something has gone wrong. The Social Theory goes well beyond the commonsensical knowledge that those who eat sensibly, exercise regularly and abjure tobacco will be fitter and healthier than those who do not and are thus more likely to avoid or survive physical illness. Rather, it extrapolates such commonsensical knowledge *ad absurdum* to argue that most common diseases are caused by an 'unhealthy' lifestyle.

It is clearly impossible to evaluate all the relevant evidence in any detail. It is possible, however, to come to a reasoned judgement by examining its historical evolution, which takes us back first to 1976 when Thomas McKeown, Professor of Social Medicine at Birmingham University, launched an assault on the prevailing view of the time that the enormous improvement in health over the preceding 100 years had been brought about by the progress of medical science. On the contrary, argued McKeown, doctors might pride themselves on the modern drugs and technology they deployed in their shiny new palaces of disease, but in reality they have played only a minor role in reducing infant and maternal mortality and the substantial increase in life expectancy. These achievements could more readily be attributed to social changes: 'Medical science and its services are misdirected,' he said, 'because they rest on an indifference to the external influences and personal behaviour which are the predominant determinants of health.'

The essence of McKeown's argument is encompassed in a

single graph (see below) showing the decline in mortality from tuberculosis of the lungs in England and Wales, from a peak of 4,000 per million of the population in 1838, down to 350 per million in 1945 when the drugs streptomycin and PAS were introduced, and then almost to zero by 1960. Thus 92 per cent of the decline in tuberculosis could be attributed to 'social factors' and only 8 per cent to the great miracle of twentieth-century medicine – antibiotics. From this McKeown concluded that 'medical intervention can be expected to make a relatively small contribution to the prevention of sickness and health'. He conceded that there was 'no direct evidence' that social factors were primarily responsible; nonetheless it seemed plausible enough that better nutrition, improved hygiene and housing

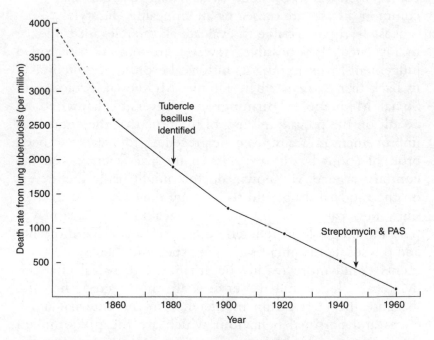

Respiratory tuberculosis: mean annual death rates (standardised to 1901 population: England and Wales)

(Adapted from Thomas McKeown, *The Role of Medicine*, Oxford: Blackwell, 1979.)

(and particularly the decline in overcrowding) could account for this massive decline of tuberculosis.[1]

Similar sentiments had been expressed before. If McKeown had merely limited his observations to the past, they would have had little impact, but, and this is the key to his subsequent influence, he used this example of the apparently limited contribution of antibiotics to the decline of tuberculosis to infer the same principles applied to contemporary medical problems in the 1970s – and this was a message that others were anxious to hear. Politicians and policy-makers, alarmed at the escalating costs of modern medicine, were impressed by this Birmingham professor's arguments that the emphasis on expensive hospital-oriented medical services was misdirected and that, were the emphasis to be shifted towards 'prevention', the health services would be not only much more effective but also a lot cheaper into the bargain. And certainly the parallel that McKeown was drawing seemed compelling enough. There were, he said, two broad categories of preventable illness: the 'Diseases of Poverty', which obviously included infectious diseases like tuberculosis, but also the 'Diseases of Affluence' which had become more prevalent with growing prosperity – cancer, strokes and heart disease. And just as the Diseases of Poverty became less common as society had become wealthier, so the Diseases of Affluence would diminish by adopting a more rigorous and ascetic lifestyle: 'The diseases associated with affluence are determined by personal behaviour, for example refined foods became widely available from the early nineteenth century . . . sedentary living dates from the introduction of mechanised transport, cigarette smoking on a significant scale has occurred only in recent decades.'

Almost immediately several developments in rapid succession strongly suggested McKeown was on the right track. Thus the following year, in 1977, the Assistant Secretary of Health to the US Government told a Congressional Sub-Committee: 'There is general agreement that the kinds and amounts of food we consume may be the major factor associated with the causes of cancer, circulatory disorders (heart disease and strokes) and other chronic disorders.' Acting on this 'general agreement' presidential candidate Senator Edward McGovern produced a report, 'Dietary Goals for the US', which called for massive reductions in the amount of meat and dairy foods consumed.[2] Soon afterwards Sir Richard Doll, former colleague of Sir Austin Bradford Hill and now Professor of Medicine at Oxford, provided his authoritative support. Following an extensive review of the relevant evidence, he had discovered that, leaving aside smoking, 70 per cent of all cancers were attributable to patterns of food consumption in Western society.[3] And there was more. Professor Samuel Epstein of the University of Illinois, writing in the journal *Nature* in 1980, argued that a further 20 per cent of cancers were caused by minute quantities of chemical pollutants in the air and water and were thus also theoretically preventable.[4] So, within four years of McKeown propounding his Social Theory, it seemed that he had been well and truly vindicated, and were attention paid to these 'social factors' then more deaths would be prevented every year than there were people dying.

It cannot be sufficiently stressed what a radical departure this Social Theory of disease was from the preceding thirty years. The achievements of the previous three decades had been hard won; the pursuit of the cure for leukaemia had taken the best part of twenty-five years, drawing on specialist scientific expertise from many disciplines and requiring the accidental discovery of no less than four different types of anti-cancer drugs. But now here were distinguished doctors and scientists arguing that the future direction of medicine lay in a completely different direction: get people to change their diets, control pollution and eradicate poverty, and many diseases would evaporate like snow on a sunny day. Could it be that simple? Why had no one conceived of the problems of disease in this way before? Certainly, had they done so much time and energy would have been saved trying to discover treatments for common diseases that now could so easily be prevented.

It might sound almost too good to be true, but The Social Theory was enthusiastically taken up by many intelligent observers, as reflected in the BBC's prestigious Reith Lectures for 1980, given by a young lawyer, Ian Kennedy, committed to the 'unmasking of medicine'. 'The elimination of the major infections has served as a star witness for the triumphs of modern medicine over illness,' he observed, 'but this has had the unfortunate consequence of creating a "mythology" where the doctor is portrayed as a crusader engaging in holy wars against the enemy of disease . . . The promise of more and more money to wage this war will not improve the quality of health care.' Rather 'the whole project' had to be reoriented towards 'prevention and health promotion' – and who could argue with that?[5] Since the war, 'the public health' had been very much the poor relation of medicine, marginalised by the glamorous successes of open-heart surgery and transplanting kidneys, with its only significant triumph being Bradford Hill's proof in 1950 of the hazards of tobacco. Here now was the opportunity to change all this and reassert the priority of preventive measures in the finest tradition of the nineteenth-century sanitary reformers. This 'new' public health movement, as it styled itself, was to move forward relentlessly from the early 1980s, warning people of the dangers lurking in their food supply and in the air and water. And it was a dynamic process that every year brought evidence of yet further unanticipated hazards of everyday life, while those responsible for health policy felt it necessary to proffer ever more precise advice on how the public should lead their lives.

And how much of it was true? I start and devote most space to the central pillar of The Social Theory, heart disease, whose rising incidence in the post-war years, it will be recalled, along with lung cancer and peptic ulcer, presented the major new challenge to medicine following the paradigm shift associated with the decline in infectious diseases. And just as the cause of lung cancer and peptic ulcer had been identified respectively as tobacco and (belatedly) the bacterium helicobacter, so there could be no more potent example of a Disease of Affluence than heart disease, where over-indulgence in 'high-fat' meat and dairy products should fur up the arteries to cause a heart attack. The self-evident veracity of this explanation made it much easier to accept the notion that other aspects of the

Western diet – salt, sugar, additives, and so on – might be equally harmful.

It is necessary to bear a few general points in mind. First, we are citizens of a society in which, utterly uniquely for the first time in history, most people now live out their natural lifespan to die from diseases strongly determined by ageing. Thus the putative gains from 'prevention' (if real) are likely to be quite small. Next, the human organism could not survive if its physiological functions such as blood pressure (implicated in stroke) or level of cholesterol (implicated in heart disease) varied widely in response to changes in the amount and type of food consumed. These functions rather are protected by a *milieu intérieur*, a multiplicity of different feedback mechanisms that combine to ensure 'a steady state'. Hence truly substantial changes in the pattern of food consumption are required to change them and thus influence the types of disease in which they have been implicated.

Next, man, as the end product of hundreds of millions of years of evolution, is highly successful as a species by virtue of this phenomenal adaptability. Humans can and do live and prosper in a bewildering variety of different habitats, from the plains of India to the Arctic wastes. No other species has the same facility, so it might seem improbable that for some reason right at the end of the twentieth century subtle changes in the pattern of food consumption should cause lethal diseases.

Finally, the evidence for The Social Theory is overwhelmingly statistical, based on the inference that the lives we lead and the food we eat cause disease in the same way that smoking causes lung cancer. Throughout this discussion it will be necessary to bear in mind Sir Austin Bradford Hill's insistence that such statistical inferences by themselves have no meaning unless they are internally coherent, that is to say, when the several different types of evidence for an association between an environmental factor and disease (such as tobacco and lung cancer) are examined, they all point to the same conclusion. Put another way, no matter how plausible the link between dietary fat and heart disease might seem, just one substantial inconsistency in the statistical evidence effectively undermines it.

We now turn to examine The Social Theory in more detail, but not before noting that McKeown's central argument, which was so important to his subsequent influence – that medical intervention could not take the credit for the decline in tuberculosis – has turned out to be incorrect. The bacillus that causes tuberculosis spreads itself around by the simple expedient of irritating the airways of the lungs of those infected, causing them to cough and sneeze. Thus millions of droplets of lung secretions are scattered into the atmosphere every time a patient with tuberculosis coughs, some of which will contain tubercle bacilli which, if inhaled by those nearby, will spread the infection. This dissemination of infection will clearly be interrupted if patients with tuberculosis are isolated in a sanatorium with others similarly infected until they either die, or, as happened to Bradford Hill, are cured by the admittedly crude methods available prior to the introduction of streptomycin. McKeown, it seemed, overlooked, presumably deliberately, this important point, for as a historian subsequently observed:

> McKeown mis-stated, or failed to understand, the point demonstrated with brilliant clarity in the classic book *The Prevention of Tuberculosis* published in 1908, namely that the effect of placing consumptive patients in poor law infirmaries was to separate them from the general populace and to restrict the spread of the disease – the proportion of consumptive patients thus segregated corresponded closely to the progressive rate of decline of tuberculosis in England and Wales.

Certainly, rising living standards and particularly improvements in housing with the decline in overcrowding contributed to tuberculosis's decline, but 'medical intervention' – the identification of those with tuberculosis by examining their sputum and their subsequent incarceration in a sanatorium – was also very important. This might not be a conventional view of 'medical intervention', but it was instigated and co-ordinated by doctors with the clear intention of reducing the spread of the disease, so medical intervention it must be.[6]

When the slightest breath of scepticism is sufficient to undermine McKeown's argument, perhaps a similar attitude will prove just as damaging to The Social Theory he instigated. We start with 'The Rise and Fall of Heart Disease', the bitterest intellectual controversy of post-war medicine that spans the last fifty years. Dauntingly it merits the greatest attention, but take courage, it is a fascinating story with a happy ending.

(ii) THE RISE AND FALL OF HEART DISEASE

The modern epidemic of heart disease started quite suddenly in the 1930s. Doctors had no difficulty in recognising its gravity because so many of their colleagues were among its early victims, apparently healthy middle-aged physicians who, for no obvious reasons, suddenly collapsed and died. Within a decade, heart disease had become much the commonest cause of death in the weekly obituary columns of the medical journals. This new disease clearly required a name. The cause, it seemed, was a clot of blood (or thrombus) in the arteries to the heart, which had been narrowed by a porridge-like substance, atheroma, made up of fibrous material and a type of fat called cholesterol. These are the 'coronary' arteries, for they form a 'crown' or corona at the top of the heart before passing over its surface to provide oxygenated blood to the heart muscle. Hence the blockage of one or other of these arteries with a thrombus became known as a 'coronary thrombosis' or simply 'a coronary', better known by the public as a 'heart attack'.

The novelty of this epidemic of coronary disease was emphasised in 1946 by Sir Maurice Cassidy, the King's physician, in the prestigious Harveian Oration. He first noted the numbers dying from heart disease had increased ten-fold in just over a decade, and then confirmed that, from his own clinical experience, 'coronary thrombosis is far more prevalent than it was. Looking through my notes of patients seen twenty or more years ago, I come across occasional cases where I failed to recognise it, which now appeared to be the obvious diagnosis, but such cases are exceptionally few.'[7] And what possibly could be the reason why apparently fit and healthy men in their forties and fifties should suddenly have their lives snuffed out in this way? Sir Maurice was puzzled. The presence of atheroma in the coronary arteries that appeared to predispose to a heart attack is almost universal, certainly in the elderly in Western societies, so one would naturally expect coronary thrombosis to have been a common disease in the past, but it was not. On the contrary, the first description in Britain of the characteristic severe crushing chest pain followed by sudden death of a heart attack had been reported just twenty years earlier in 1925: 'In sudden thrombosis of the coronary arteries, there may occur a very characteristic clinical syndrome which has attracted little attention in Britain and which receives scant attention in the text books.'[8] It seemed to Sir Maurice that the key to the epidemic must lie in the clot or thrombus, but what precipitated it, he admitted, 'is a problem I have failed to solve'.

Among those interested in 'solving the problem' was Ancel Keys, the forty-year-old Director of the Laboratory of Physiological Hygiene at the University of Minnesota. Keys had distinguished himself during the war by creating a high-calorie supplement for paratroopers, the K Ration, consisting of a piece of hard sausage, dried biscuits, a block of chocolate, a stick of chewing gum, matches and a couple of cigarettes, all in a waterproof package. 'I don't know how many K Rations were used by the paratroopers,' he subsequently recalled, 'but I do know that many thousands were issued when better food could have been provided; some soldiers lived on it for months on islands in the Pacific. "K Ration" became a synonym for awful food.'[9]

Keys had drive and imagination and, with the war ending, he turned his attention to investigating why so many middle-aged men were dying from heart attacks. His particular scientific interest was nutrition, and so naturally enough he focused his attention on the fat chemical cholesterol present in the atheroma of the arteries. The main source of cholesterol is the liver, from where it is released into the blood stream to fulfil its indispensable role as an integral part of the walls lining the cells, as well as being the precursor of many important hormones, including testosterone in the male and oestrogen in the female. Perhaps, Keys speculated, the other source of cholesterol in food — such as eggs and avocados — might, in combination with other fats, force up its level in the blood, which would then infiltrate the artery walls to form the atheroma that appeared to be implicated in heart attacks. It was not an original idea, but Ancel Keys was to pursue it so vigorously over the next years as essentially to make it his own.[10]

Firstly, it was necessary to know more about the predisposing factors for a coronary, so Keys set up a 'prospective' study, on the lines of Bradford Hill's famous doctors' study into smoking, involving almost 300 businessmen from his home town of Minneapolis. They were weighed and measured, their cholesterol levels monitored and their blood pressure recorded and their fate followed over the succeeding twenty-five years. From this it emerged there were three main 'risk factors' – smoking, raised blood pressure and a high cholesterol level – that together markedly increased the subsequent risk of a coronary.[11] Next he investigated the effect of different types of diet and this time he turned to the local mental asylum. Over a period of several years thirty patients with schizophrenia were subjected to a wide assortment of diets containing various amounts and types of fat: cocoa butter, corn oil, beef fat, rape seed oil, and so on.[12] From this it emerged that it was possible to lower the cholesterol level in the blood by lowering the amount of saturated fat (as in meat, milk and dairy products) and increasing the amount of polyunsaturated fat (as in vegetable oils), but it was not easy. Substantial changes were required because, as already pointed out, the survival of the human organism requires that the *milieu intérieur* – its physiological functions (such as the level of cholesterol in the blood) – should not be sensitive to modest changes in the *extérieur* such as the amount and type of food consumed. Rather, many 'feedback' mechanisms ensure the cholesterol levels stay at a steady state, so if the amount of fat in the diet is reduced, the liver compensates by increasing the amount of cholesterol it makes. There was another problem. The role of fat consumption in the heart disease epidemic would have been more straightforward had the Minnesota businessmen with high cholesterol levels been at 'greater risk' because they consumed more saturated fat. But this was not the case. Their dietary pattern was no different from that of anyone else.

It remained a puzzle until, almost inadvertently, Keys stumbled on what he believed must be the answer while on a trip to

Rome in 1951 to chair a United Nations committee. 'At the meeting all the discussion was about undernutrition in the underdeveloped countries, and when I asked about the problem of diet in coronary heart disease no one was interested,' he recalls, except for the Professor of Physiology at the University of Naples, who pointed out that heart disease was 'not a problem' in his city and this might be related to the typical Neapolitan diet. He invited Ancel Keys to come and see for himself. Keys was, at the time, based in Oxford, taking a sabbatical from his work in Minnesota but, come January of the following year, 'the thought of southern Italy and escape from the cold and food rationing was too alluring. My wife Margaret [a trained biochemist who specialised in measuring cholesterol levels in the blood] and I loaded the little Hillman with equipment and headed south.' In Naples they set up their cholesterol-measuring equipment and soon their Neapolitan friends were bringing in workers from the neighbourhood. Their cholesterol levels turned out to be one-third lower than those of the businessmen they had been studying back in Minnesota. The explanation had to be the Neapolitan diet:

> There is no mistaking the general picture – a little lean meat once or twice a week was the rule, butter was almost unknown, milk was never drunk except in coffee or for infants, 'colazione' on the job often meant half a loaf of bread crammed with baked lettuce or spinach. Pasta was eaten every day, usually also with bread (no spreads) and a fourth of the calories were provided by olive oil and wine. There was no evidence of nutritional deficiency but the working-class women were fat.

Keys's experience in Naples changed his life as, over the next few years, he travelled the world investigating the relationship between diet and coronary heart disease in different countries. These culminated in 1956 with his visits in the same year to the city of Fukuoka in Japan and the province of North Karelia in Finland. The Japanese famously enjoy a low-fat diet with little meat and dairy products but many fish and pickled foods, so the blood samples analysed by Margaret Keys from Japanese farmers, clerks and coalminers revealed, by now predictably enough, a low cholesterol level in the blood. Meanwhile a distinguished cardiologist, Paul White, who was accompanying them, 'spent weeks trying to find a case of coronary thrombosis in the big medical school hospital, district hospitals and private clinics'. The only pathological specimen of a heart exhibiting the typical changes of a coronary that could be found had belonged to a Japanese physician whose fatal coronary had occurred a few months after retiring from thirty years practising medicine in the United States. Later the same year Ancel Keys arrived with his entourage in North Karelia on the Finnish border with Russia:

> The first village had an infirmary with six beds for male patients. One was a young man who had been bitten by a bear. A second had cancer of the lung and the third was occupied by an old man wheezing with asthma. The other three patients had coronary heart disease. Later we went into the woods to have a sauna with some lumberjacks. Two of them confessed to being slowed up by angina, but even more interesting was a glimpse into the local eating habits, the favoured 'after-sauna' snack was a slab of full-fat cheese the size of a slice of bread on which was smeared a thick layer of 'that good Finnish butter'.[13]

There remained the possibility that the disparate difference in cholesterol levels and susceptibility to heart disease was a racial phenomenon because of genetic differences between the Finlanders and the Japanese. The following year Keys tackled the question in a typically ingenious way. In the 1950s the Japanese economy was still devastated by the effects of the Second World War, which encouraged many Japanese to migrate first to Hawaii – a sort of cultural halfway house – and then to Los Angeles. If the 'genetic' view was correct then if they moved from Japan to the United States their cholesterol levels would remain unchanged. Ancel and Margaret Keys proceeded to test Japanese migrants in Hawaii and Los Angeles and then compared the results with those they had obtained from the indigenous Japanese of Fukuoka the previous year. There was a clear gradient: as the Japanese became progressively more Westernised, so their cholesterol levels rose or, as Ancel Keys put it, 'the conclusion seemed to be inescapable – the proportion of calories provided by saturated fat (meat, milk and dairy products) is an important factor in the frequency of coronary heart disease'.[14] Thus was born the diet–heart thesis, the answer to the problem that Sir Maurice Cassidy admitted ten years previously 'I cannot solve': too much fat in the diet pushes up the cholesterol level in the blood, which infiltrates and narrows the walls of the coronary arteries, resulting in a heart attack.

Meanwhile two further and very evocative observations appeared to confirm Keys's theory. First, Axel Strom, Professor of Hygiene at the University of Oslo, reported a most unusual pattern of mortality statistics in Norway during the German occupation, when the population had suffered grievously from continual food scarcities. This serious and prolonged deprivation had, very surprisingly, been associated with a marked decrease in the overall death rate, including that from heart disease.[15] Two years later further powerful evidence of a very different kind emerged from the Korean War. The Pentagon, rather ruthlessly, perceived that the death of so many American soldiers offered an opportunity to examine the relative lethality of different types of bullets and despatched a team of pathologists to perform the necessary autopsy investigations on the spot. They were astonished to find that the coronary arteries of their young casualties showed obvious evidence of atheroma, varying from yellow patches to wart-like excrescences on the innermost surface. Though the average age of the soldiers who had been killed in battle was only twenty-two, in almost three-quarters 'gross evidence of coronary disease was present'. It seemed almost inevitable that many of their comrades lucky enough to survive the war would nonetheless be struck down by a coronary before the age of fifty.[16]

So, by the mid-1950s, Ancel Keys had become convinced for good reason that his original hypothesis of the epidemic of coronary heart disease as 'a nutritional disorder' – because of excess

Death rate from heart disease in the US rose dramatically from 1920 to 1960

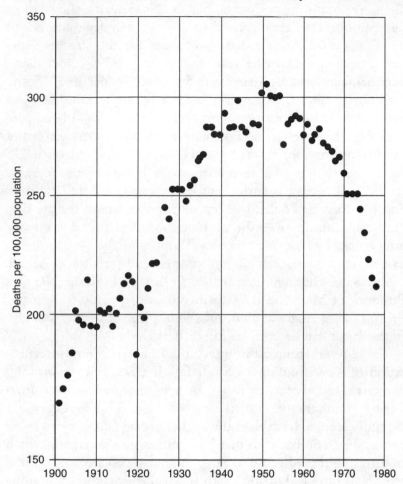

(From R. E. Stallones, 'The Rise and Fall of Ischaemic Heart Disease', *Scientific American*, 1980, Vol. 243, pp. 43–9.)

consumption of saturated fat – must be correct. But when, in 1957, the American Heart Association (AHA) invited a group of heart specialists to evaluate his theory they were unable to endorse it. They noted that within the United States an individual's food preferences neither predicted the level of cholesterol in their blood nor their subsequent risk of heart disease, hence food could scarcely be a determinant factor. They dismissed the wartime evidence from Norway on the grounds that many other illnesses, not just heart disease, had declined during the years of deprivation. They then turned to the two major weaknesses of Keys's theory. First, it failed to account for the striking 'epidemic' pattern of heart disease (see page 295), increasing exponentially year by year from the 1920s to become, by the early 1950s, much the commonest cause of death to middle-aged men. Clearly this dramatic rise in heart disease had not been paralleled by the necessary and substantive changes in the pattern of food consumption, for as the AHA report pointed out: 'US Army rations in the Western outposts in the late 1880s showed a fat content almost identical with current US Army rations.' Second, Keys had failed to account for the central feature of a coronary thrombosis – the clot or thrombus in the coronary artery that, by blocking the blood supply to the heart muscle, caused the sudden, dramatic symptoms of a heart attack. As one of Keys's most distinguished critics, Sir George Pickering, Regius Professor of Medicine at Oxford, was subsequently to observe: '[Keys's thesis] assigns a minor role, in fact almost an afterthought, to the event that determines life or death.'[17]

These reservations all pointed to a rather different interpretation of Keys's findings: a 'high-fat' diet along with smoking and raised blood pressure might be a *contributory* but not a *determinant* factor in the rise of heart disease. The Western diet certainly seemed to explain the higher average cholesterol levels in the West compared to other countries such as Japan, which in turn might predispose to both the narrowed arteries and the clot or thrombus. Further, within Western societies, individuals with a genetic predisposition to a higher cholesterol level, such as the Minnesota businessmen, would be at increased risk. But diet could not begin to explain the dramatic rise in heart disease as this would have required truly monumental increases in fat consumption in the United States that clearly had not happened. Keys's explanation, self-evident as it might seem, failed Bradford Hill's requirement that epidemiological evidence be 'internally coherent,' that it hangs together in such a way that from whatever angle the question is examined, it points to the same conclusion. Keys was half right — heart disease does have 'something to do' with cholesterol levels — but from the important point of view of prevention it was, regrettably, the wrong half. It would be quite unrealistic to expect people to make the major changes required in switching from a Western-style to a Mediterranean- or Japanese-style diet, when the resultant fall in cholesterol would only indirectly reduce the risk of a heart attack. A subtle point, perhaps, but sometimes subtlety can be important. And so the AHA committee concluded 'the evidence does not convey any specific implications for drastic dietary changes'.[18]

The verdict of the AHA was a serious blow. It conveyed the impression that Keys's scientific work over the previous ten years, impressive as it undoubtedly was, nonetheless could not sustain the interpretation he had placed on it. Keys, it would seem, was just one of many scientists who over the years had backed the wrong horse. Nor was he the only person to be discomfited. The careers of several other scientists who had rallied to his banner would similarly founder in the absence of official endorsement. The most prominent of these, and destined to become Keys's lifelong friend, was Jeremiah Stamler of Chicago University. In 1957, at the time of the publication of the AHA report, Stamler was about to launch the Coronary Prevention Evaluation Programme, whose purpose, as its name implies, was to demonstrate that heart disease was indeed preventable by encouraging people to take more exercise, stop smoking and change to a 'healthy' diet.[19] The AHA's failure to endorse the need for 'drastic dietary change' placed him in the same invidious position as Keys – vulnerable to the charge of dietary crankery, someone whose ideas were outside the mainstream of medical thinking.

Clearly the AHA had to be persuaded to change its mind. It took some time but within a couple of years the membership of the relevant committee had been reconstituted to include both Keys and Stamler. Its next report, predictably, was very different in tone and content from the first, running to a mere two pages, thus omitting any discussion of the substantial problems of Keys's thesis. Reversing the previous conclusion, it recommended that people should indeed reduce the amount of fat in their diet in anticipation of reducing the risk of heart disease while admitting there was, as yet, 'no final proof'.[20] The reversal of the original committee's conclusion might seem a trivial matter, and indeed was soon rapidly forgotten, never to be referred to again. But it was still one of the most important events in the history of post-war medicine, whose consequences would reverberate over the next four decades to profoundly influence public beliefs, government policy and the way in which medicine was practised.

Keys and Stamler then had a stroke of luck. The main contending explanation for heart disease – that the most important factor was the clot or thrombus in the coronary artery – collapsed with the publication in 1964 of an authoritative study evaluating the benefits of blood-thinning drugs (anticoagulants), which should, if the clot was the critical factor, have had a major impact on the risk of a heart attack. These drugs, it emerged, could indeed reduce the risk of a heart attack by reducing the 'clotability' of the blood, but this benefit was equally balanced by an increase in the numbers in whom the anticoagulants had also resulted – as they were likely to – in causing a fatal haemorrhage into the brain. 'The regime involves considerable sacrifice for a dubious gain,' observed Britain's leading cardiologist, Sir John McMichael of the Postgraduate Medical School, and that was the end of that. Over the years enormous time and energy had gone into trying to demonstrate that this form of treatment, which on theoretical grounds should have worked, would reduce mortality from heart attacks, but as one of those closely involved observed later, 'everyone was weary and felt alternative approaches must give more rewarding dividends . . . the coronary thrombosis–anticoagulant concept [that blood-thinning drugs would prevent a coronary thrombosis] was abandoned by most through apathy', though it was subsequently to be revived with dramatic effect in the late 1980s.[21]

The 'coronary thrombosis–anticoagulant concept' might have been abandoned, but medicine abhors a vacuum so an alternative had to be found. And it was at this crucial moment that Keys's thesis emerged, now endorsed (thanks to his efforts) by the American Heart Association and without a serious challenger, to become the central explanation of the coronary epidemic. The epidemic was now so severe that virtually any explanation would have served as a way of making sense of why for over thirty years the toll of young men dying from coronaries had increased exponentially year by year, with absolutely no sign it was coming to an end. Like the AIDS epidemic of the 1980s, coronary disease became an absolute priority for those engaged in promoting the public health. Virtually any research programme into heart disease was almost guaranteed to be funded, even if it was not particularly original. Ancel Keys had, after all, done it all but this did not discourage now well-funded researchers from doing it all over again but just on a grander scale. And the verdict reached was precisely the same. There were several important 'risk factors' associated with heart disease: smoking, raised blood pressure and a high cholesterol level in the blood. Therefore, logically, discouraging smoking, lowering blood pressure and reducing the cholesterol in the blood should reduce the risk of a heart attack. There was no difficulty with the first two, smoking and blood pressure, which were already well justified on other medical grounds in preventing lung cancer and strokes respectively. But if heart disease was also to be prevented then, in addition, the cholesterol level in the blood would also have to be lowered and that, as already indicated, was not going to be easy. By the early 1970s, the time had come to provide the incontrovertible proof that modifying these risk factors would prevent heart disease. To this end the protagonists in both the United States and Europe launched, in the early 1970s, the largest and most expensive scientific experiment ever conceived in the history of medicine, involving over 60,000 men and costing in excess of $200 million.

In the United States 360,000 middle-aged men were interviewed to find the 12,000 at highest risk. Most were smokers, had been diagnosed as having raised blood pressure while still young and had markedly elevated cholesterol levels. They were then randomly allocated into either an 'intervention' or a 'control' group and the Multiple Risk Factor Intervention Trial (MRFIT) was launched. The complexity and expense of this study lay in the need to change people's lives – to encourage them to give up one style of life and adopt another. There was little difficulty in ensuring that those with raised blood pressure were adequately treated by giving appropriate medication. Discouraging smoking was, as always, more difficult, and every conceivable way was deployed to encourage the men to quit, including monetary rewards, hypnosis and aversion techniques. But such practicalities were nothing when compared to what was required to achieve the dietary modifications necessary to lower the cholesterol level. Nothing other than monumental changes would do, so the participants were showered with nutritional information, taught how to shop for groceries, what to order in restaurants, given advice on how to rewrite their favourite recipes, asked to record everything they ate and sign contracts pledging to abstain from various foods. They were told to eat only low-fat cheese, restricted to two eggs a week and instructed to avoid all cakes, puddings and pastries and to reduce markedly the amount of meat consumed. These prodigious efforts were rewarded, the average amount of saturated fat in their diet fell by about a quarter, but disappointingly – if predictably because of the '*milieu intérieur*' already alluded to – their cholesterol level only fell by just over 5 per cent.

The dedication and energy of those involved in MRFIT was admirable, but it would be quite unrealistic to expect that such prodigious efforts would be readily applicable in the real world. Hence the interest in the second of the two studies launched at the same time and organised by Geoffrey Rose of the London School of Hygiene, the leading standard-bearer for Keys's hypothesis in Europe. Rose's predecessor-but-one as Professor of Epidemiology had been Sir Austin Bradford Hill, who had demonstrated so brilliantly the role of tobacco in lung cancer. The challenge for Geoffrey Rose as his successor was to demonstrate that another social habit – eating – was just as capable of causing a lethal disease. His project, co-ordinated under the auspices of the World Health Organisation and thus known as the 'WHO Trial', was much larger, involving almost 50,000 men in sixty-six factories in Britain, Belgium, Italy and Poland. The workers in the factories in the 'intervention' group were exposed to a blitzkrieg of health education to encourage them to change their lifestyle, backed up by evening meetings, floor shows, talks about heart disease and cookery demonstrations. Those in the 'control' factories were left in peace.

These two trials were doomed to failure from the moment of their inception for, if the rise in heart disease could not be explained by increasing amounts of saturated fat in the diet of Western nations, then the proposed dietary changes to reduce fat consumption would be ineffective in preventing it. There were some who perceived this central flaw in the enterprise, so before describing the outcome it is appropriate to hear what they have to say. The doubters were of two sorts – heart specialists and apostates. The cardiologists or heart specialists included Sir George Pickering, Regius Professor of Medicine at Oxford, and the architect of post-war British medicine, Sir John McMichael. They realised from their daily experience of dealing with patients that the role of diet explained very little, as those unfortunate enough to suffer a heart attack clearly consumed no more or less fat than anyone else. The apostates, by contrast, had at one time or another all been involved with Keys's thesis in the 1950s and 1960s but had subsequently become disillusioned. They included: Irvine Page, chairman of the crucial committee that included Keys and Stamler that had reversed the AHA's original verdict by endorsing Keys's thesis; George Mann, who had investigated the effects of feeding high-fat diets to monkeys; and Edward Ahrens, who had been one of the first to study the effect of different types of fats on blood cholesterol levels.[22] Throughout the late 1970s these dissidents conducted a guerrilla war against the diet-heart hypothesis in the pages of the medical journals. George Mann observed how Ancel Keys's 'fragile hypothesis' had been transformed into 'dogma' and lamented 'the lost generation of misguided and futile preoccupation with diet'.[23] Sir John McMichael drew attention to a survey of senior cardiologists conducted by the British Heart Foundation in which 80 per cent reported that they did not advise their patients to change their diet because 'they were not convinced it would be of benefit'. It was thus, he argued, 'deeply disturbing that some of our profession are stretching so much speculative and insecure evidence to support a theory no longer tenable'.[24]

The opinion of these critics, despite their eminence, could easily be ignored because they had no better or alternative explanation, and anyhow, the reputation of thousands of scientists and doctors – indeed, the very credibility of medicine's ability to provide answers – depended on Keys's thesis being vindicated. Then at the end of 1982 the juggernaut crashed. Despite the prodigious efforts of the MRFIT trial to cajole so many men into changing their lives and giving up the pleasures of meat and eggs and cakes and pastries and much else besides, they were no less likely to suffer from a heart attack than those in the 'control' group that had been left to lead their lives in peace.[25] Seven months later the WHO Trial delivered precisely the same verdict.[26]

The organisers seemed genuinely puzzled that they had failed to produce the 'correct' result and were not hesitant about coming forward with excuses. But as an informed commentator observed at the time, 'the best explanation for the failure to detect a beneficial effect is that no benefit accrued. No amount of wriggling on the hook alters the fact that for every 1,000 intervention subjects, 41 died, and for every 1,000 control subjects, 40 died. These statistics are the measure, and the only measure, of the benefit of the intervention programme.'[27]

Nor indeed were the negative results of the trials the only problem for Keys's thesis. There are only two ways in which it could be tested experimentally. The first, as represented by the trials, was to encourage people to change their diets and see the effect on heart disease. This, as has been noted, did not work. The alternative is to perform the experiment, as it were, the other way round and look to see whether the rising incidence of heart disease over several decades had been paralleled by major changes in what people eat. This, as has already been noted, was a central weakness of the thesis, as the twenty-fold rise in heart disease throughout the 1940s and 1950s had not been paralleled by increasing amounts of fat in the diet. By the early 1980s it was quite apparent that this original trend had been reversed and that the incidence of heart disease had gone into steep decline.[28] The decline, it must be appreciated, was universal, across all ages, classes and ethnic groups, and international, occurring simultaneously in the United States, Canada, New Zealand and Australia. Thus if the 'lifestyle' theory of heart disease were correct, people would have had to have made substantial changes in their diet at least ten years earlier, not just in the United States but in all these other countries as well. Clearly, this was impossible for, as shown in the graph on page 304, the precipitous rise and equally precipitous fall in heart disease occurs in different countries in parallel, while the proportion of fat in the diet hardly changes. Indeed, by the early 1980s, when this fall in heart disease was becoming ever more marked, the necessary dietary changes would have to have been monumental, much greater than those imposed on the 'intervention' group in the MRFIT trial. Rather, this pattern of 'the rise and fall' of heart disease resembled 'the rise and fall' of an infectious disease. It was not a 'social' but a 'biological' pattern, with the obvious implication that some unknown biological factor must be the culprit, either by influencing the severity of atheroma in the coronary arteries, or by precipitating the clot that causes the heart attack – or both. Thus, by the early 1980s, Keys's thesis had failed the two critical experimental tests of its validity.

This is an appropriate moment for a brief intermission as, amazing as it might seem, the events up till now are only half the story. In 1982, when the negative results of the MRFIT and WHO trials were reported, The Social Theory was just getting into its stride with its ambitious programme to realign medicine towards preventing the Diseases of Affluence. But now, and apparently quite unexpectedly, the central pillar of that strategy – the implication of the Western diet in the epidemic of heart disease – had been undermined. There were two powerful interested parties in particular who could not acknowledge defeat. The first were those like Keys, Stamler, Rose and many others who had invested a lifetime's work and hundreds of millions of pounds of research funds in trying to prove the thesis. The second were the drug companies who had made substantial capital investment in the development of cholesterol-lowering drugs for which, naturally, they needed a market. Now, choles-

The rise and fall of heart disease has not been paralleled by changes in the quantities of fat in the diet

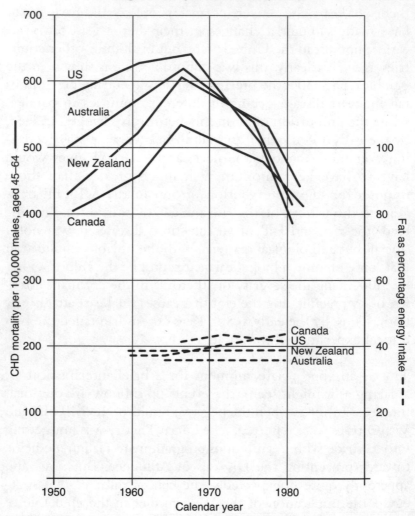

terol, as has been noted, was not entirely innocent, as, whatever might be the unknown 'biological' cause that explained the rise and fall of heart disease, it clearly was most likely to hit those with higher than average cholesterol levels and therefore more severe atheroma in their coronary arteries. Hence, both the drug companies and the dietary protagonists had a mutual interest in salvaging Keys's thesis. If the drug companies could show that their powerful cholesterol-lowering drugs reduced the chances of a heart attack in those 'at high risk' (which was probable), this would be evidence the disease was indeed 'preventable', which would then shore up the position of the proponents of the dietary theory like Stamler and Keys. On the other hand, if the dietary protagonists could convince the public that too much fat caused heart disease and that everyone should lower their cholesterol levels, this would markedly increase the market for cholesterol-lowering drugs way beyond the minority 'at high risk'. And that is precisely what happened.

We start with the dietary protagonists who, with some deft foot (or rather committee) work, were so successful that fifteen years after the débâcle of the trials the belief that 'high-fat' food was the 'cause' of heart disease, had acquired in the public mind the same self-evident veracity that smoking caused lung cancer.

Clearly the theory had to be shifted away from the scientific arena where it could be debated towards authoritative *ex cathedra* assertions that bacon and eggs (or their equivalent) really did cause heart attacks. The best way of ensuring this 'fact management' was through the medium of reports from 'expert committees' made up of the protagonists, precisely the same ploy by which Keys first had his thesis officially endorsed by the American Heart Association back in 1961. From the early 1980s onwards, these expert committees multiplied like rabbits, each claiming to have examined the entrails of the scientific evidence to come to precisely the same verdict that the Western diet caused heart disease (and strokes, diabetes, breast cancer and everything else). Their reports followed the same predictable pattern, opening with a consideration of the 'circumstantial' evidence: the comparisons of heart disease rates between different countries, and the changing pattern of heart disease of Japanese migrants. The practicalities and difficulties of lowering cholesterol levels by dietary means were ignored while, duplicitously, the falling rates of heart disease in the United States were cited as evidence that heart disease was indeed 'preventable'. They concluded with the apparently scientific recommendation that the amount of saturated fat in the diet should be reduced to '30 per cent of calorie intake' – a meaningless form of advice as there is no way anyone could tell (without having a formal degree in nutrition) how near or far off this desired target they might be.[29] It did not matter that no one read these reports; their function rather was to generate the impression that there was a widespread consensus on these matters and that scientists had all come to the same conclusion. So, like the steady drip-drip of water on a stone, the message could not but penetrate the public consciousness.

This was just the beginning of the Great Public Persuasion. The message of these reports was picked up by sympathetic journalists who passed it on to the wider public. Thus, in 1985, the readers of *The Times* were informed:

> Western food is the main single underlying cause of Western disease which leaders of the medical profession [describe] in apocalyptic terms as a holocaust, which medicine can do nothing to check.

This was clearly a very serious state of affairs, which naturally raised the important question of why so little was being done about it. Every good story requires a villain and, sure enough, the best intentions of the experts were being thwarted by powerful antagonistic forces in the form of the food industry and farmers – and their apologists, a small group of 'corrupt' scientists. 'There are some who, from a position of authority, assert the fat and salt in the quantities consumed in Britain today are harmless to health. As far as I know they are all employed, paid by or associated with the food industry.' The role of these scientific sceptics in condoning the food industry's attempts to peddle lethal foodstuffs to the public was 'the biggest scandal since the day 150 years ago when officials refused to act on the fact that cholera was caused by open sewers'.[30]

This splendid conspiracy theory proved perfectly suited to television, which commissioned many programmes extolling the virtues of a 'healthy diet', each replete with images of food and death, while omitting any reference to genuine scientific disagreement. Opening with a shot of an ambulance screeching through the night or more gruesomely a pathologist laying out his tools for a post-mortem, a voiceover would intone chilling statistics about how many people died from certain diseases every year. Then one of the experts, like Geoffrey Rose, would appear to link those diseases to food. 'The modern British diet is killing people in their thousands from heart attacks' or again 'modern Western food is the chief cause of our moden epidemic of heart disease'. And how were these discoveries made? 'It really turned out to be quite simple. All we had to do was look at the major national and international reports and they all came out with the same general message.' But might not there be some dissent? 'Most of those who are critical have no knowledge of the subject whatsoever . . . and many of them are self-serving' (Ancel Keys).

The programmes side-stepped the scale of dietary changes decreed by the experts to focus instead on those foods – cancer-causing chips, heart-stopping hamburgers – whose visual imagery could most powerfully sustain the message. The climax, against the backdrop of a cemetery, featured Geoffrey Rose intoning the warning: 'Behind each one of these statistics is a personal tragedy, each one has left a home without a breadwin-ner, a wife without a husband, children without parents. We know enough about the causes of these tragedies in relation to what we eat – if we could get the scientific information across to the public, then many of these tragedies would be avoided.'

The second interested party in salvaging the dietary theory was the pharmaceutical industry, anxious to promote its drugs. It was certainly very gratifying for all concerned when, in 1984, two years after the collapse of the MRFIT trial, it was announced that lowering the cholesterol in those at high risk with the drug cholestyramine had, as would have been pre-dicted, reduced the chances of dying from a heart attack by 25 per cent. This result, according to the chief organiser, offered 'conclusive proof' that heart disease could be prevented. Admittedly the participants had all been at 'very high risk', but 'the trial's implications could and should be extended to all age groups and those with more modest elevations of cholesterol'.[31]

The following week *Time*'s cover featured a plate of bacon and eggs arranged to resemble a doleful face with the headline 'CHOLESTEROL: AND NOW THE BAD NEWS . . .' 'Sorry, it's true, cholesterol really is a killer,' ran the story on the inside page. *Newsweek* pursued the same line, quoting an expert opinion that this was 'a milestone, with implications for all Americans'.

And how did the participants in this 'landmark study' fare? Cholestyramine has to be sprinkled directly on to food, rendering meals unpalatable and two-thirds of the participants reported moderate to serious side-effects of constipation, gas, heartburn and bloating. After seven years of this regime thirty out of the 1,900 taking cholestyramine had had a fatal heart attack compared to thirty-eight out of the similar number in the control group. This indeed can be interpreted as 'reducing the chances of dying from a heart attack by 25 per cent' (8 divided by 38 and multiplied by 100 equals almost 25). But put another way, almost 2,000 men took cholestyramine for seven years to increase their chances of not having a heart attack by less than half of 1 per cent (8 divided by 2,000 multiplied by 100). This seems a modest enough achievement, except that overall cholestyramine made no difference at all, as the total number of deaths in the 'intervention' and 'control' groups were exactly the same, with the modest reduction in heart disease mortality in those taking cholestyramine being balanced by an increased risk of death 'from other causes'.

These important matters were, for obvious reasons, not emphasised as it is much easier to promote a drug on the grounds that it reduces the 'risk of a heart attack by 25 per cent' than by pointing out that ruining one's meals with cholestyramine for seven years increases one's chances of not having a heart attack by 0.5 per cent, at the price of chronic bowel symptoms, depression and increased risk of death from other causes.

The gold mine of 'cholesterol-lowering for all' was much too enticing to be deflected by such considerations. After all, seven years' worth of cholestyramine for 2,000 men added up to £9 million, which worked out at over £1 million for each of the eight fatal heart attacks prevented and (as there was no difference in overall mortality) an infinite sum for every life saved.

Now for 'the sting'. It is only natural to be suspicious when a drug company extols the benefits of drug X, but an entirely different matter when the desirability of taking such a drug is endorsed by apparently 'independent' experts as part of an 'education' programme. And sure enough, in December 1984, just a few months after the cholestyramine trial (and *Time's* gloss upon it), the US National Institute of Health launched the National Cholesterol Education Program with the double message: 'The blood cholesterol level of most Americans is undesirably high' and should be reduced because 'it has been established beyond reasonable doubt' that this would reduce the subsequent risk of a heart attack.[32]

This education programme took the following form. First the fundamental message of the diet-heart thesis was asserted: all Americans (except children under the age of two years old) should make substantial reductions in the amount of meat, milk and dairy products they consumed so as to reduce the amount of fat in their diet by a quarter. Next, everyone needed to know their 'number' – their cholesterol level – by going to the doctor to have it checked, which would generate many more additional visits to the doctor every year. The millions whose 'number' was deemed too high would then require either dietary advice, which unless vigorously adhered to did not work, leaving no option other than the prescription of cholesterol-lowering drugs. The education programme was thus very useful to the drug companies, and their symbiotic relationship with its organisers was revealed very clearly when Merck launched a powerful new cholesterol-lowering drug, lovastatin. Its press release to journalists included the names and telephone numbers of doctors to contact for their comments on the benefits of the drug. In Dallas, the 'contact' was Scott M. Grundy, who had chaired the committee drawing up the education programme's recommendations; in San Diego it was Daniel Steinberg, who had developed the details of the education programme; while in Houston reporters could call no less than Antonio Gotto, president of the American Heart Association, which had its own Campaign Against Cholesterol (financed by Merck).[33]

The strategy worked brilliantly. The fear of premature death from a coronary was quite sufficient to propel the health-conscious to their doctor's surgery to 'learn their number'; a quarter of them would subsequently be started on drug therapy. Financially, everyone benefited (except for the unfortunate patient): the drug companies; those involved in testing for cholesterol; and, in private health-care systems such as that of the United States, the doctors who charged their patients for 'check-ups' on their cholesterol level. The total cost of this drug-company-inspired cholesterol obsession was phenomenal. By the mid-1990s hundreds of thousands of otherwise healthy men and women across the world were taking cholesterol-lowering drugs at a cost in excess of £3 billion a year.[34]

Together the drug companies and Social Theorists had triumphed. Snatching victory from the jaws of defeat of the verdict of the trials, dozens of expert committee reports had persuaded most people that 'Western food is the chief reason for our modern epidemic of heart disease'. This in turn had been the Trojan Horse by which millions had been prescribed cholesterol-lowering drugs. It is interesting to note how the 'lifestyle' explanation for heart disease had produced precisely the opposite effects to those that were promised. Its appeal lay in the promise of liberating people from their reliance on doctors, for by simply changing their diet they could reduce the risk of heart disease and thus the need for drugs and surgery. In practice the 'lifestyle' theory massively increased the influence of medicine, as medical experts now dictated what people should and should not eat. Further, it provided a context within which doctors could persuade otherwise healthy people that they needed to take drugs for life. And at the end of it all, Keys's thesis was no 'truer' than it had been back in 1957, when the first of the American Heart Association committees had observed how it failed to account for either the marked increase in heart disease or the thrombus in the coronary arteries.

Two final events finally undermined the apparently seamless litany of half-truths that sustained Keys's thesis by providing a much more satisfactory explanation of what was really going on. The first was the 'rediscovery' that the thrombus, not the levels of cholesterol in the blood, was the critical factor in causing heart disease. The second was the discovery of a bacterium, chlamydia, in the walls of the coronary artery, which helped to explain why the pattern of the rise and fall in heart disease resembled an infectious epidemic rather than a disease caused by social factors.

The critical role of the thrombus, it will be recalled, had been displaced in the mid-1960s after it was shown that blood-thinning drugs, though effective, had the unfortunate consequence of increasing the risk of haemorrhage into the brain. This failure, however, did not mean that the thrombus was unimportant, just that better ways had to be found of dissolving it, thus restoring the blood flow to the heart muscle. Ideally, two types of blood-thinning drug are required, a simple compound that will prevent the platelets from sticking together to form a thrombus in the first place, but also a more potent 'clot-busting' drug that could be administered in the aftermath of a heart attack.

Both types of drug had in fact already been around for a long time, in the case of the former − aspirin − for 200 years. Aspirin is a derivative of the bark of the willow tree, whose painkilling and fever-quenching properties had been reported in a letter to the Royal Society in 1763 by the Reverend Mr Edmund Stone of Chipping Norton in Oxfordshire.[35] Aspirin's further therapeutic property − the ability to prevent blood from clotting − was first noted in 1950 by a family physician from Cleveland, Lawrence Craven. The fashion for removing children's tonsils was then at its height, following which they naturally enough developed a sore throat, for which they were often given aspirin. 'For several years I have observed that haemorrhage following removal of tonsils occurs with noteworthy frequency when aspirin is administered for the relief of pain,' noted Dr Craven. He went on to suggest that if aspirin increased the risk of bleeding following tonsil removal, it might also reduce the tendency of the blood to clot in the new epidemic of 'coronary thrombosis'.[36] Dr Craven elaborated on this important observation in a series of papers until his death six years later.

Nobody took much notice as they appeared in an obscure medical journal, *The Annals of Western Medicine and Surgery*, and he was, after all, just a family doctor. The significance of Dr Craven's observation and the injustice of the lack of recognition of his important insight is emphasised by the fact that the next person to take an interest in the blood-thinning properties of aspirin, a British biochemist, John Vane, won the Nobel Prize. It is natural to presume that, as aspirin has so many therapeutic properties in reducing fever, relieving pain and thinning the blood, there must be some common underlying physiological process with which it interferes, and so there is. In 1971 Vane showed that aspirin blocked the action of a family of closely related chemicals – the prostaglandins – produced fleetingly in minute quantities by many different tissues in response to injury, one of which, thromboxane, encouraged platelets to stick together to plug a bleeding artery or vein.[37] This verified Dr Craven's original observation that aspirin, presumably by preventing the platelets from sticking together to form a clot, increased the subsequent risk of bleeding in children after they had had their tonsils out. What more could one ask for? Here was a very cheap drug that had been around for 200 years and in small doses discouraged platelets from sticking together and was thus capable of preventing the two terrible diseases associated with clotting – heart disease and strokes.[38]

Aspirin might prevent some, if not all, heart attacks, but for those who had just had one a different, albeit complementary, approach was needed, some method by which the clot could be dissolved after it has formed, thus restoring the blood flow to the heart muscle. Back in 1933, the streptococcus bacterium (responsible for dreadful illnesses such as puerperal fever following childbirth) was found to excrete an enzyme – streptokinase – that dissolved the fibrous material with which the body's defences tried to contain infection. Theoretically then, streptokinase should be capable of dissolving the clot of a heart attack. This was first demonstrated in 1958 with 'promising' results, though there were many problems associated with excess bleeding and other side-effects.[39]

It was not really until the introduction of the new X-ray technique of coronary angiography, where a dye is injected down the coronary arteries to demonstrate their degree of narrowing, that the full implications of the potential of strep-tokinase seemed to have been realised. In 1980 Dr Marcus de Wood of the University of Washington took the brave (or, as it was perceived at the time, foolhardy) decision to perform coronary angiograms on patients immediately following a heart attack. This was thought to be a very dangerous proce-dure, which was why no one had done it before, as it involved inserting a fine catheter directly into a blocked coronary artery to inject the X-ray dye. However, it turned out to be much less dangerous than had been anticipated and Dr de Wood clearly demonstrated an acute blockage of one or other of the coronary arteries in 110 out of the 126 patients he studied.[40] The sight of a blocked artery on the X-ray screen is a clear invitation to try and 'unblock' it. Very soon the prin-ciple of giving streptokinase immediately following a heart attack moved its status as 'a bold and exciting new technique to protect the heart muscle' into standard practice. When combined together aspirin and streptokinase have a truly astonishing effect on the outcome of a heart attack, reducing by over a half the numbers dying within the first four weeks.[41] It is possible now to get a sense of the enormous disparity in the practical application of the contending theories of heart disease. The application of Keys's dietary theory – in the form of the MRFIT trial – had required thousands of men to switch to a rigorous low-fat diet for seven years with no effect. By contrast, dissolving the thrombus – once the right combination of drugs had been found – saved tens of thousands of lives every year. And just in case this contrast needed emphasising, when a cholesterol-lowering drug that did seem to significantly influence survival after heart attack was finally introduced, its very effectiveness immediately raised the suspicion that its beneficial effect must result from some other means than lowering the cholesterol. It too turned out to work by thinning the blood and preventing it from clotting.[42]

The much neglected thrombus, marginalised by the baleful influence of the cholesterol obsession, may have turned out to be very important after all. But it still leaves unexplained the other limitation of Keys's theory: the epidemic pattern of the rise and fall of heart disease over the last fifty years. This pattern, as pointed out, is strongly suggestive of an underlying biological cause such as infection.

In 1986, quite unexpectedly, a probable culprit was found in the form of a new strain of the bacterium chlamydia, better known as the cause of psittacosis, a virulent form of pneumonia caught from parrots and ducks.[43] Soon after Thomas Grayston of the University of Washington had identified this novel strain of chlamydia, Finnish doctors reported that antibodies to the new organism were also present in nearly two-thirds of patients with heart attacks.[44] Next, one of Dr Grayston's colleagues – Dr Cho-chuo Kuo – used special staining techniques to look directly for the chlamydia itself in the walls of coronary arteries of recently deceased South African gold-miners. He found the organism to be present in all those whose arteries were narrowed by atheroma and absent in those without.[45] Then came the definitive test: if chlamydia was actively involved in narrowing the coronary arteries, which might be presumed to trigger off the thrombus, then antibiotics that killed off chlamydia should reduce the subsequent risk of a heart attack, which it does. Readers will have noted the instructive parallel with the discovery of the role of helicobacter in peptic ulcer, although it would be wrong to suggest that the evidence incriminating chlamydia in heart disease is anything as definitive.[46]

In retrospect it seems so obvious there had to be some biological explanation – such as a bacterium – to explain why, as Sir Maurice Cassidy had noted back in 1946, apparently healthy middle-aged men had suddenly started dying so unexpectedly. So how had Keys and Stamler and many others deceived themselves, and the public, for so long into believing that the victims really had only themselves to blame for eating the wrong sorts of food? They were lucky that the imagery of fat furring up the arteries and salt overloading the circulation was so evocative. They were lucky that their plausible story should coincide with the fitness enthusiasm of the 1980s, where a low-fat 'healthy' diet was perceived as part of a healthy living 'package' along with regular exercise, abstaining from tobacco and so on. They were lucky that heart disease fell so rapidly from the late 1960s, which could so readily be presented as showing that heart disease was indeed preventable were the public to follow their dietary recommendations. They were lucky their ideas came to fruition at a time that people were becoming disillusioned with 'high-technology medicine' and were thus open to the seductive message that social engineering – just as civil engineering a century earlier – could contribute more to the nation's health than expensive and often futile medical intervention.

None of this alters the fact they were wrong, and thus had no alternative other than to present their misleading version of events. They emphasised the comparisons between countries like Finland and Japan without pointing out that their validity was undermined by the failure of such 'cross-cultural' studies to demonstrate the recognised causative relationship between smoking and lung cancer. They glossed over the fact that the amount of fat in the diet predicted neither the cholesterol level nor the risk of heart disease in any single country. They masked the difficulty in influencing cholesterol levels in the blood unless extreme dietary measures were adopted. They failed to point out that the rising incidence of heart disease was not paralleled by changing patterns of food consumption and falsely claimed credit for its declining incidence. They rationalised the unpalatable results of the trials and continued to argue their case as if they had never happened. And finally, first in 1961 and many times subsequently, they exploited the device of the 'expert committee' to assert by fiat precisely what the scientific evidence had failed to demonstrate.

The natural world is, however, a hard task master. It does not readjust to fit in with the way that scientists believe it should behave and ultimately the inconsistency of erroneous theories becomes apparent. In the mid-1990s the cumulative evidence against the dietary theory had become overwhelming. An analysis in 1997 of nine MRFIT-type studies involving over 125,000 participants confirmed that admonishing people to adopt a 'healthy lifestyle' – no matter how desirable – and whatever benefits it might confer from promoting exercise and stopping smoking – had absolutely no effect on stopping them from dying from heart disease.[47]

Ancel Keys and Jeremiah Stamler are now retired and spend most of the year in adjoining houses in southern Italy, close to where their great adventure started almost fifty years ago monitoring the cholesterol levels of the Neapolitan working class. They might not admit that they have spent a lifetime promoting a theory that unfortunately for them was almost, but not sufficiently, right, but Ancel Keys is certainly defensive, portraying his critics as 'victims of their own vanity, ill-informed about the facts, unused to rigorous logic, ignorant of statistical theory or seduced by commercial interest. Unfortunately some of these disseminators of misinformation are prominent physicians or biologists so they readily find a speaking platform and publication.' How curious that these 'victims of their own vanity' just happened to include not just the most eminent clinical scientists of the post-war years but those who, as heart specialists, had practical experience of the inconsistencies of Keys's thesis.

The scale of the great cholesterol deception as outlined above might seem so extraordinary as to raise doubts about its veracity. But it was the inevitable consequence of the official endorsement of a false theory which, beyond a certain point, admits of no going back without destroying the professional reputations of its protagonists. Further, the chronology of these events cannot be emphasised too strongly. The experimental evidence refuting the diet-heart thesis emerged at precisely the moment in the early 1980s when the claims of The Social Theory to provide a new paradigm for medicine were in the ascendant. Its proponents therefore had no alternative other than to assert its validity by the means outlined above.

Before examining the other aspects of The Social Theory,

readers should now try to imagine themselves back in those
times when the link between food and heart disease and much
else besides was almost univerally accepted as being correct,
when distinguished professors such as Geoffrey Rose were
regularly appearing on television to assert that 'the modern
British diet is killing thousands from heart attacks'. They must
try to imagine how the apparent plausibility of Keys's thesis
gave credence to the notion that the causes of all common diseases lay simply in the manner that people lived their lives, in
their habits and their everyday environment, where the
Western diet was held responsible for virtually all cancers other
than those caused by smoking and where the presence of
minute concentrations of chemicals in the air and water apparently caused a bewildering variety of illnesses was allegedly
responsible for 75,000 deaths a year in Britain.

It is gratifyingly unnecessary to examine each of these other
aspects of The Social Theory in the same detail. It is quite sufficient merely to focus on the same cross as that on which Keys's
thesis was crucified – the cross of biology. It is a biological fact
that it is very difficult to influence the '*milieu intérieur*' of physiological functions such as cholesterol or blood pressure by
simple changes in the '*extérieur*', such as small changes in what
one eats. It simply cannot be done, and no matter how beautiful and plausible the statistics about heart disease mortality rates
in Finland compared to Japan, statistics cannot change the laws
of biology. And so now we turn to see how the statistics sustaining the three further instances of The Social Theory are
similarly crucified by biology. We start with the 'causes' of
cancer.

(iii) BEYOND TOBACCO: SIR RICHARD DOLL
AND THE 'CAUSES' OF CANCER

Cancer is a grievous illness that causes much misery not just to those who are afflicted but to their friends and relatives as well. It goes without saying that it would be very desirable to be able to identify its causes and thus prevent it but, with a handful of admittedly important exceptions (tobacco and lung cancer, asbestos exposure and mesothelioma), this goal has proved elusive mainly because for most there is no single cause. Rather, cancer is so strongly related to age – the risk increasing by a factor of ten with each passing decade – it is best seen as intrinsic to the ageing process itself. There are several reasons why this might be so. The replication and repair mechanisms of DNA become impaired with age, increasing the risk that individual cells might turn malignant. Similarly, the immune system loses the ability to identify and destroy potentially cancerous cells allowing them to 'escape' and multiply. Whatever the precise mechanism, the relationship between cancer and ageing is so powerful that it will be fair to infer that it could only ever be prevented were ageing itself to be preventable – which would seem unlikely.

Confronted by this admittedly harsh reality, the notion that cancer might simply be caused by the sorts of food we eat is strongly suggestive of quackery. Yet from 1980 onwards, for almost two decades, persistently and without equivocation, the Social Theorists have insisted that, excepting those cancers attributable to tobacco, virtually all the rest are caused by the Western diet. Why so?

By 1980 cancer had become vulnerable to the arguments of those, like McKeown, who maintained that social factors were the main cause of disease and hence prevention, by 'changing lifestyles', was a much better option than being treated, often unsuccessfully, with nasty anti-cancer drugs. Ten years earlier, in 1971, Dr Donald Pinkel of St Jude's Hospital had astonished the world with his news that a gruelling regime of four anti-cancer drugs given for two years combined with radiotherapy to the brain had increased the cure rate of childhood leukaemia from 0.07 per cent to over 50 per cent. But leukaemia and the other treatable cancers of childhood and young adult life represent only a small fraction of the total number of cases and so, fuelled by Richard Nixon's billion-dollar War Against Cancer, specialists took up the challenge of applying the same principles of treatment to the vastly greater numbers of age-related cancers – of the breast, bowel, brain and so on – that occur overwhelmingly in those aged sixty and over.

This approach, as we now know, did not work. With few exceptions these 'old-age' cancers failed to respond or became rapidly resistant to the anti-cancer drugs, whose main consequence was to make the last few months of patients' lives even more burdensome with their grievous side-effects. Thus by the end of the 1970s, despite the hundreds of millions of dollars a year being spent on cancer chemotherapy in the United States, the number of children and adults being cured – 5,000 a year – was dwarfed by the 700,000 a year with age-related cancers who were not.[48]

The futility of such massive and injurious overtreatment is obvious and provided the right climate for those who argued there 'must be a better way': '80–90 per cent of all cancers in Western nations are caused by environmental factors,' observed John Bailar III, in the *Journal of the National Cancer Institute*, and insisted it was time to switch attention to finding out what these might be.[49] The same argument would be restated many times over the next few years: the War on Cancer had failed, vast funds were being wasted and patients' lives were being made miserable by chemotherapy, to no good purpose. How much better it would be to prevent these cancers in the first place! It sounded plausible enough, but there was only one problem. Besides tobacco, no one knew what these causes of cancer might be until, in 1980, Sir Richard Doll, Emeritus Professor of Medicine at Oxford University, erstwhile collaborator with Sir Austin Bradford Hill back in the 1950s, and now one of the world's most eminent cancer epidemiologists, found the answer. After an exhaustive review of all the relevant evidence, he concluded that, besides tobacco, food was the other main culprit and so cancer could be avoided were people to switch to a 'healthier diet'.

It was all very astonishing. For years doctors and scientists had struggled to understand the causes of these diseases and it seemed that all along the explanation was staring them in the face every time they sat down to a meal. Indeed it was only curious how long it had taken Sir Richard himself to make his sensational discovery. Fourteen years earlier, in 1967, he had drawn attention in a prestigious lecture to the well-recognised causes of cancer such as tobacco and high-level exposure to certain chemicals in the workplace, but failed to mention the role of food at all.[50] Subsequently, it seemed, he had become persuaded by the evidence from international comparisons, which showed that common cancers in the West like that of the breast and colon were rare in Japan and – vice versa – stomach cancer was common in Japan but relatively rare in the West. It is of course precisely this type of evidence with which Ancel Keys had incriminated the Western diet in heart disease, so it shares its weaknesses. Even if it were true that the pattern of food consumption was the cause, then presumably switching to a Japanese diet would merely mean switching the risk of dying from the types of cancer common in the West to those common in Japan.[51]

Nonetheless, this notion that most cancers, not just those of the lung, might be 'preventable' had enormous appeal, especially for policy-makers and legislators apprehensive at the escalating costs of health care. In the late 1970s, they approached Sir Richard to produce a much more detailed review, duly published in 1981 as *The Causes of Cancer*, in which he makes the claim that, excluding tobacco, food caused 70 per cent of cases of cancer.[52]

The Causes of Cancer is an impressive document with an abundance of graphs and statistics, hundreds of references and no less than five appendices. The crucial argument centres on a comparison between the rates of specific cancers as recorded in the Connecticut Cancer Registry and the lowest recorded incidence of the same cancers elsewhere in the world. There are 60.2 cases per million of cancer of the pancreas in Connecticut, compared to 21 per million in India; presumably 'something' explains the difference. What could it be other than the fact that the citizens of Connecticut eat different sorts of food than the inhabitants of the Indian sub-continent? And that, astonishingly, is all there is to it.

The Causes of Cancer may look impressive, but appearances can be deceptive. The intellectual rigour required by Sir Richard Doll's mentor, Sir Austin Bradford Hill, for assessing the coherence of any hypothesised relationship between an environmental factor and disease – such as food and cancer – is conspicuous only by its absence. Thus the distinguishing feature between the Western diet, as eaten in Connecticut, and that of other countries, such as India, is the relatively high consumption of meat and dairy products. Hence cancers common in the West, such as those of the breast, colon and pancreas, are attributed to a 'high-fat' diet. True or false? The Mormons and Seventh-Day Adventists are identical in virtually every way: they lead sober lives, don't smoke or drink and go to church on Sundays. The only difference is that the Mormons eat meat and the Seventh-Day Adventists on the whole are vegetarians. If the 'high-fat' diet explanation for cancer was valid, then the meat-eating Mormons must *by definition* have a higher incidence of these cancers than the Seventh-Day Adventists. But they do not. Such an important observation in the context of a report in which diet is strongly incriminated in cancer requires serious consideration. There is none.[53]

But this omission fades into insignificance when compared to the manner in which Sir Richard Doll deals with the relationship between cancer and ageing. As pointed out, the likelihood of cancer is strongly age-determined, with an eighty-year-old having a thousand-times greater risk compared to when he was a teenager. This is fifty times *greater* than the twenty-fold increased risk of lung cancer in the smoker compared to the non-smoker.[54]

Ageing must therefore be right at the top of the list of 'causes of cancer', but Sir Richard dismisses it in the following manner:

'It is sometimes argued that because cancer is ten or a hundred times more likely to occur in the old rather than the young [the exact figure is, as has been noted, much higher even than this] then ageing per se might be thought of as an important determinant of cancer. We rather doubt whether this viewpoint is a scientifically fruitful one . . .' On the contrary it is scientifically very fruitful, for recognising the primacy of ageing as a powerful determinant of cancer is essential if one is not to fall into the trap of generating false notions about what else might be the cause.

Sir Richard Doll subsequently conceded the weaknesses of *The Causes of Cancer* but never publicly retracted his conclusions, and the claim that he had 'proved that food caused more than a third of cancers' was repeatedly cited by all those who had an interest – nutritionists, health educationists, food fanatics and others – in incriminating the Western diet as a major cause of death and disease. And so it was that without the slightest hint of irony Britain's Chief Medical Officer in 1998 advised that the recommended 'safe' levels of meat consumption for those wishing to avoid cancer should be raised from two lamb chops (or its equivalent) per day to three. Medical advice had become indistinguishable from quackery.

(iv) ENVIRONMENTAL ALARUMS

Those who may find it difficult to take seriously the proposition that the number of lamb chops they eat a day might influence the risk of getting cancer or heart disease must look elsewhere for 'causes'. The obvious other culprits are 'environmental' – the minuscule quantities of chemicals present in the air and water. At the beginning of the 1980s there was something of a turf war between these two contending theories, with the dietary protagonists such as Sir Richard Doll accusing (a bit richly perhaps) the environmentalists of 'bias, exaggeration and lack of balance'.[55] From the environmentalist camp Professor Samuel Epstein of the University of Illinois responded with the '*tu quoque*' argument: 'The scant scientific evidence for the dietary theory is contradicted by a substantial body of published evidence.'[56] There turned out to be room for both explanations and, over the next fifteen years, the public were exposed to a double whammy of health fears, with those of Sir Richard Doll's camp warning that bacon and eggs for breakfast were the culprits in heart attack, strokes and cancer, while those of Professor Epstein's persuasion arguing that chemicals and radiation were responsible for everything else: electricity pylons were implicated in leukaemia, hormonal chemicals in falling sperm counts and testicular cancer, and pesticides, mobile phones and even sewing machines were implicated in many other types.

The concern that environmental pollution might pose a threat to health started in 1962 with the publication of Rachel Carson's *Silent Spring*. The children of future generations, Carson argued, would never again hear the sound of birdsong in spring because pesticides thinned the shells of their eggs, resulting in a precipitous fall in their numbers. Carson's claims were at least partially vindicated, and following instructions on pesticide use the threat of a 'silent spring' was averted. This episode was so powerful a pointer to the possible harm of manmade chemicals that, inevitably, the question arose as to the dangers they might pose to human health. It certainly seems plausible enough that pesticides might be responsible for several diseases for which there is as yet no satisfactory explanation, including falling sperm counts which, if true, would mean that not just birds, but the human species, could soon be facing extinction.[57]

It is, of course, only sensible that the amounts of chemicals in the environment should be kept to the irreducible minimum, but the issue to be examined here is quite specific. Environmental pollution certainly posed a significant threat to health in the nineteenth century, when the all too readily detectable environmental pollution of our great industrial cities, with their stinking canals and rat-infested tenements, limited the average lifespan to little more than forty years. It certainly can matter in situations of high exposure, as experienced by workers in the asbestos industry or following major catastrophes such as the Bhopal accident in India that killed 2,000 people. The question rather is whether at the concentrations of these chemicals to which the general public is exposed – measured in parts per billion – they are injurious to health.

Many believe they are, including leading academics in Britain and America. Thus in a discussion on the effects of water pollution, Professor Howard Hu of Harvard University observes: 'The threat to health from water contamination remains high,' and goes on to cite examples – traces of arsenic could cause cancer 'in significant numbers'; nitrate residues from fertilisers have been linked to stomach cancer; pesticides have been linked with breast cancer; halogenated solvents 'with childhood leukaemia'; and so on. It certainly sounds scary enough, and this is just water pollution. Parallel litanies of hidden dangers apply to air pollution, food contamination and radiation.[58]

It should not be supposed that any of these allegations is scientifically proven for, as can be imagined, it is simply not possible to conduct the required scientific experiments of exposing large numbers of people for long enough to any pollutant in the minuscule quantities that are present in air and water to detect whether it is indeed harmful. Rather, the argument rests almost entirely on extrapolation from the consequences of high levels of exposure or toxicology tests in rodents. Certainly these chemicals in high doses can have adverse effects in rats, and so, the argument goes, even at a millionth of the dose they might, theoretically, adversely affect one in a million people.

The central assumption here, crucial to the environmental case, is that there is no 'threshold' of exposure below which even a scarcely measureable pollutant in the air or water can still be harmful to health. This 'no threshold' concept is best understood by analogy for, if it were correct, it would mean that not only the person drinking a bottle of whisky a day for five years is likely to damage his liver but also someone eating an alcohol-flavoured Christmas cake once a year for thirty years. This would seem unlikely and is contrary to the fundamental axiom expressed by the great French scientist Claude Bernard in the mid-nineteenth century: '*Tout est poison, rien n'est poison, tout est une question de dose*' – everything is poisonous, nothing is poisonous, it is all a matter of dose.[59]

It is clearly impossible to evaluate each and every alleged environmental threat to health. Some, such as global warming and the threat to the ozone layer from CFCs, are theoretical in that the putative harmful consequences have not yet occurred. Clearly no definitive verdict, one way or another, can be given on such predictions, and they will not be considered further. The focus rather is on the claims of those like Professor Hu who maintain that pollutants are responsible for contemporary health problems in the Western world. Here, though, we may come to some sort of conclusion, thanks to the banana.

It is customary to test the safety of chemicals such as pesticides by exposing experimental animals (such as rodents) to the Maximum Tolerated Dose (MTD), and if a substantial number develop cancer, the chemical could possibly be carcinogenic in humans. Vegetables and fruit – such as bananas – produce their own 'natural' pesticides to discourage bugs and weevils and other small creatures who might wish to eat them. In the mid-1980s, an eminent toxicologist, Dr Bruce Ames of the

University of California, began testing these 'natural' pesticides in precisely the same way as synthetic pesticides by giving the Maximum Tolerated Dose to rodents. He discovered, to his surprise, that half of these naturally occurring 'pesticides' were similarly carcinogenic:

> The twenty-seven natural pesticides that are rodent carcinogens are present in the following foods: annis, apple, apricot, banana, basil, broccoli, Brussels sprouts, cabbage, cantaloupe, caraway, carrot, cauliflower, celery, cherry, cinnamon, cloves, cocoa, coffee, collard greens, cumphrey herb tea, currants, dill, egg plant, endive, fennel, grapefruit juice, grapes, guava, honey, honeydew melon, horseradish, kale, lentils, lettuce, mango, mushrooms, mustard, nutmeg, orange juice, parsley, parsnip, peach, pear, peas, black pepper, pineapple, plum, potato, radish, raspberries, rosemary, sesame seeds, tarragon, tea, tomato and turnip. Thus it is probable that almost every fruit and vegetable in the supermarket contains natural plant pesticides that are rodent carcinogens.[60]

Dr Ames then calculated the average amount of the 'carcinogenic' natural pesticides in the diet to be 1,500mg a day, compared to only 0.09mg per day of synthetic chemical pesticides. Hence 99.9 per cent of the 'carcinogenic pesticides' to which we are exposed come from annis, apple, apricot, banana, etc. and, as fruit and vegetables are an essential part of a healthy balanced diet, the 0.01 per cent from manmade pesticides is unlikely to do much harm. Dr Ames's calculation points to the crucial weakness of the environmentalist argument. Every mouthful of food we eat contains thousands of different 'natural' chemicals in amounts greater by order of magnitude than any manmade chemicals we might be exposed to, thus when evaluating the potential of any such chemical to be harmful, its effects have to be viewed against the background of this much greater quantity of 'natural' chemicals that have similar biological effects.

The point is well illustrated by the claim, already alluded to, that the human species faces extinction from falling sperm counts. When in 1995 it was claimed that sperm counts were falling in Western Europe (though not apparently elsewhere), environmentalists claimed the culprits were chemical residues of PCBs (used in the manufacture of plastics) in the water supply, on the grounds they have biological properties similar to the female hormone oestrogen and are thus likely to depress sperm development. Now there are around forty types of vegetables that also contain small amounts of 'natural' oestrogenic chemicals, including garlic, pineapple, cabbage, coffee, carrots, fennel, olive oil, rice, potatoes and corn. The average daily consumption of these 'natural' oestrogenic chemicals is still enormously greater than the amount of oestrogenic PCB residues present in drinking water. Put another way, PCB residues constitute 0.00000025 per cent of the oestrogenic substances in the diet. Hence 'the suggestion that they contribute to male reproductive problems, such as low sperm counts, is not plausible'. The sensationalist claim that 'feminising chemicals' were threatening the survival of the human race simply cannot be true. Some other explanation must be found for the decline in sperm counts, if indeed they are declining.[61]

Precisely the same type of calculation applies to *all* the allegedly harmful chemicals on which Professor Hu of Harvard University based his claim that 'the threat to health from water contamination remains high'. Arsenic, nitrate residues and pesticides are all present as naturally occurring chemicals in fruit and vegetables in infinitely greater amounts than in manmade chemicals. Certainly everything can be poisonous and at high levels of exposure they can have adverse biological effects – but '*tout est une question de dose*'. The concentration of these chemicals to which the public are exposed is far below the level that could damage humans.

Similar arguments apply to allegations about the dangers of radiation. Thus, in the early 1980s, the link was easily made between the cluster of leukaemia cases in West Cumbria and the nearby nuclear reprocessing plant in Sellafield. But the levels of radiation exposure from the plant are only a small fraction of the 'natural' background radiation (from, for example, granite) to which everyone is exposed, which is itself only a minute fraction of the level of radiation exposure necessary to cause leukaemia. Indeed, radiation discharges from Sellafield would have to have been 400 times greater than those recorded by the National Radiation Protection Board to have caused leukaemia in children in the vicinity. Clearly, Sellafield cannot be the culprit and there must be some other explanation (which will be considered in the next chapter).[62,63]

Similarly, it is possible to dismiss the allegation that the electromagnetic fields created by electricity pylons might cause leukaemia as the strength of the field generated by the pylons is hundreds of times less than Earth's static magnetic field to which everyone is exposed every day.[64]

Finally, even the claims that air pollution is responsible for the threefold increased incidence in asthma over the last thirty years (though fumes can certainly exacerbate the condition) are almost certainly incorrect, as asthma is commonest in the least polluted parts of the kingdom, notably the Isle of Skye, and turns out to be much commoner in clean-aired Munich when compared to the similar, but heavily polluted town of Leipzig in former East Germany.[65] Rather it emerges that the rising incidence of asthma has occurred in parallel with other allergic diseases of childhood such as eczema and hayfever (which clearly are not related to air pollution), suggesting a common cause probably related to the declining incidence of common childhood infectious illnesses.[66]

It is an astonishing fact that not one of the numerous allegations of environmental threats to health of the last twenty years has ever been convincingly validated for the simple reason that they are all crucified on the one single biological fact that the scale of exposure is far below the threshold that could have physical effects on the human organism. The last word belongs to Aaron Wildavsky, author of much the most thorough and balanced analysis on this subject in recent years, *But is it True?*. And, is it true? 'Of all the subjects I have studied in over thirty years as a social scientist, environmental issues are the most extraordinary in that there is so little truth in them.'[67]

(v) THE END

And so, after this exhaustive review of The Social Theory we return again to the early 1980s when it seemed to offer so much. The Age of Optimism in scientific medicine was over, there was a Dearth of New Drugs, the clinical scientist was an Endangered Species and suddenly The New Genetics and The Social Theory emerged to provide an entirely new direction where the causes of disease would be elucidated in the interplay between the external world – people's social habits and their environment – and their genes. Together this opened up a whole new range of opportunities, where social engineering would eliminate the common causes of death, while genetic manipulation would fix everything else.

In 1980 the promise of The New Genetics still lay in the future, but there was already more than enough known about the social causes of disease for action to be taken. And how easy it.had turned out to be. Thirty years had elapsed since Sir Austin Bradford Hill had identified tobacco as the cause of lung cancer and now, in hardly any time at all, the other major pieces of the jigsaw had fallen into place. Sir Richard Doll in *The Causes of Cancer* revealed how the Western diet was just as important as tobacco in causing cancer. Professor Samuel Epstein had found that chemical pollutants in the air and water caused a further one in five of all cancers. And it had been proved 'beyond reasonable doubt' that milk and dairy foods were killing thousands a year from heart attacks and an excess of salt was equally implicated in strokes.

It was an extraordinary start to the decade, and called for extraordinary measures in the form of a massive programme, to deepen the scientific understanding about the links between everyday life and disease and also, more importantly, to do something about it – to get people to change their lives, to bring pressure to bear on industry to stop polluting the air and water. And as time passed the links between everyday life and disease became ever clearer as further investigations revealed many more previously unsuspected hazards. Alcohol was linked with cancer of the breast, coffee with cancer of the pancreas, yoghurt with cancer of the ovary, vaginal douching with cancer of the cervix, regular use of alcohol mouthwash with cancer of the mouth and red meat with cancer of the colon. Even the most innocent-seeming of inanimate objects, such as electricity pylons, mobile telephones and sewing machines, were all found to be full of menace. Thus, by the mid-1990s it is fair to say that every human pleasure – tobacco, alcohol, sex, smoking and food – had been anathematised, the air and water had been found to be packed with carcinogenic chemicals and the poor were poorer and sicker than ever.

But was any of it true? These hazards of everyday life might be a bit exaggerated but there can be no smoke without fire and so, one has to presume, they must contain an element of truth. Further, it would seem quite inconceivable that so many distinguished men of science over so many years could all have been wrong or that the deliberations of their expert committees should have conspired to mislead the public. Nonetheless the only sound verdict, hard as it might be to accept, is that The Social Theory, as discussed here, is in error *in its entirety*. It is possible to assert this without qualification because each of its four components either ignore or are contradicted by the inescapable laws of biology. The dietary theory of heart disease and strokes is invalidated by the biological imperative of maintaining the '*milieu intérieur*' so the important physiological functions such as the levels of cholesterol and blood pressure are kept in 'a steady state'. The dietary theory of cancer is invalidated by the contribution of biologically inevitable ageing to this age-determined disease. The environmentalist theory is invalidated by the biological necessity that the human organism be resilient and not readily injured by minuscule levels of pollutants in air and water.

Still, the façade of knowledge The Social Theory presents to the world appears so impressive that, before accepting its incompatibility with the laws of biology, it is necessary to understand a little more of the science that underpins it –

epidemiology – which, back in the 1940s, Sir Austin Bradford Hill had hoped would function as medicine's intellectual spring cleaner, dusting and hoovering away fallacious theories and treatments.

We start with the observation, already alluded to, that the post-war success of medicine was essentially empirical and technological, so that by the late 1970s therapeutic possibilities had been transformed, but medical science knew little more about what caused common diseases such as multiple sclerosis, diabetes and heart disease than forty years previously. This seeming inscrutability of the origins of disease extends to other phenomena, such as why they rise and fall over time and why they are common in some countries but rare in others. The one medical discipline most concerned with explaining these phenomena is epidemiology which, however, is constrained in its search for the causes of disease by only being able to measure that which is measurable in people's lives. It cannot, by definition, discover hitherto unknown biological phenomena, such as the new bacterium, helicobacter, implicated in peptic ulcer, even though the pattern of disease strongly pointed to the possibility that peptic ulcer must have an infectious cause. Put another way, epidemiologists can only find the causes of disease in everyday life, and if the cause is not a factor of everyday life – but a bacterium – then their explanation will be incorrect. Put a third way, most common diseases are either determined by ageing or caused by, it must be presumed, some unknown biological factor, hence the explanations that epidemiology provides are likely to be pseudo-explanations.

Nonetheless, epidemiological studies are easy to perform – take one group of people with a disease, another without, compare their lives and any differences can then be plausibly implicated as 'the cause' – and thus rapidly filled the vacuum of ignorance. But, and this is the crucial point, the human organism is very resilient and therefore on *prima facie* grounds 'everyday life' is unlikely to provide the correct explanation. Rather, the associations that do emerge from these studies are likely to be weak and contradictory, to the considerable confusion of the public. And, argues Professor Alvin Feinstein, editor of the *Journal of Clinical Epidemiology*, a scientific discipline that generates such conflicting findings (coffee does, or does not, cause bladder cancer or congenital defects or heart disease; alcohol does, or does not, cause breast cancer; keeping pets is, or is not, associated with multiple sclerosis, and so on) can hardly be considered 'scientific' at all, as its methods of investigation must be so clearly unreliable. 'In other branches of science substantial distress would be evoked by a conflicting result . . . authorities would clamour for special conferences or workshops intended to identify the [methodological] defect and to institute suitable repairs. No such conferences and no such workshops have occurred.' Professor Feinstein's inside observations are so important as to merit elaboration. A scientist in any serious scientific discipline, such as genetics, would be in serious trouble if his fellow scientists were unable to confirm or replicate his claim to have found the gene for fatness. He would gain a reputation as being 'unreliable' and universities would be reluctant to employ him. This self-imposed insistence on rigorous methodology is however missing from contemporary epidemiology; indeed the most striking feature is the insouciance with which epidemiologists announce their findings, as if they do not expect anybody to take them seriously. It would, after all, be a very serious matter if drinking alcohol really *did* cause breast cancer.[68]

In parallel with this lack of internal scrutiny, which arose from the failure to adhere to Bradford Hill's insistence that epidemiological evidence be internally coherent, there was the fear of external scrutiny by others who might ask questions about the apparent inconsistencies of their explanations. It is at this point that epidemiologists resorted (wittingly or not) to deceit to sustain their argument by presenting only the highly selected version of evidence that appeared to substantiate their case. And then they retired behind the closed doors of the committee room, where, under the guise of examining the entrails of the scientific evidence they could compile their reports – from which so many important facts were simply omitted. It worked back in the early 1960s when Stamler and Keys persuaded the American Heart Association to endorse their dietary theory of heart disease and has continued to work: Sir Richard Doll's *The Causes of Cancer* may appear to have rigorously examined the evidence, but clearly it does not.

Their motivation was simple enough – they had no alternative. By the 1970s, the rigorous epidemiological techniques developed by Sir Austin Bradford Hill had identified only a handful of causes of disease to add to tobacco – a few rare occupational illnesses relating to asbestos exposure and the effects of rubella infection in pregnancy.[69] This was quite insufficient to sustain the thesis that social factors caused common illnesses, so others had to be found, and as the protagonists had spent their professional lifetimes collecting the incriminating evidence they could scarcely be expected to turn around and admit they might be wrong. This, admittedly, required a certain degree of self-deception, but again there was no alternative.

The Social Theory was by the 1980s very influential. Its protagonists were powerful men and women who had spent enormous sums of state and charitable funds to prove their theories so their admission of error would not just be humiliating but could destroy their reputations. They did not even seem to acknowledge they might have been mistaken, but believed so passionately in the veracity of their theories that any minor blemish – such as negative results of the heart disease trials – could be brushed aside.

This collective self-delusion is not common and suggests the protagonists, in constructing their façade of knowledge, must in some way have been different from the mainstream of medicine. They were – being motivated by a shared set of ideological beliefs that might tactfully be described as idealist utopianism. They had a much grander, nobler vision than ordinary doctors in the surgery who spent their time treating the sick. They aspired to nothing less than the prevention of illness on a massive scale. There is nothing wrong with wanting to make the world a better place, but utopianism has its dangers. It presupposes a greater knowledge base than medicine possesses while, at the same time, it refuses to recognise the possibility of uncertainty – that some things might be unknown.

The utopians entranced by 'big' ideas tend to be dismissive

of small details that get in the way. They are forever producing plans and setting targets for how people should change their dietary habits or how wealth should be redistributed but have no model of human action, no understanding of how people do change. The inevitable consequence of this combination of a shallow knowledge base and the practical difficulties of making the world a better place is that their utopian plans end in a failure for which there is always a ready explanation: not enough money has been spent cajoling people into changing their lives, or alternatively their own brave efforts are being thwarted by the powerful vested interests of industry. Thus the cardinal feature of the Social Theorists is a lack of insight. With their eyes firmly fixed on the horizon and absolutely convinced of the rightness of their cause (and bolstered by their own personal sense of moral worthiness in pursuing it), they fail to appreciate the obvious explanation for their failure – that their theories are in error. Their understanding of disease is limited to the statistics that appear on their computer screens. It is theoretical rather than practical, so they miss out on the sobering experience of testing their theories against reality. It only takes contact with a few real patients with heart disease to appreciate that their dietary habits are no different from anyone else's. It only takes a short period as a family doctor to recognise how extraordinarily difficult it can be to get people to stop smoking, hence a 'public-health strategy' that requires doctors to encourage their patients to make substantial changes in what they eat – even if it were proven to be beneficial – is condemned by its own impracticality.

This utopian impracticality is epitomised by Sir Geoffrey Rose of the London School of Hygiene, the most prominent epidemiologist in Britain in the 1980s and already encountered as the organiser, under the auspices of the World Health Organisation, of the enormous trial involving tens of thousands of men in factories across Europe, in which intense efforts to encourage them to switch to a 'healthy lifestyle' had no effect on their subsequent risk of heart disease. This should have been a setback, but Professor Rose realised, after reflection, that the fault lay not in the theory but in the 'strategy' for preventing heart disease. It would be much better, he argued, rather than trying to get those with markedly elevated cholesterol levels to make substantial changes in the amount of fat they consumed, to try to persuade everyone to make small reductions. This became known as the 'population strategy' as it was directed, typically ambitiously, at the whole population. This concept might be difficult to grasp but is easier to understand in relation to another problem deemed suitable for the population strategy – preventing the harmful effects of heavy drinking. Within any society there will be a typical distribution of alcohol consumption, with a minority being teetotallers, most people drinking moderate amounts and at the other extreme another minority of heavy drinkers. Professor Rose's strategy requires that the moderate drinkers should slightly reduce their alcohol consumption, say by one glass of wine a day. This theoretically would shift the distribution of the pattern of alcohol consumption downwards, so that there would be fewer heavy drinkers at the top, thus reducing the problems associated with alcoholism. It sounds, and indeed is, a completely fantastical notion, but even more so when applied to preventing heart disease, as encouraging everyone to make small dietary changes has absolutely no effect on cholesterol levels. And yet, astonishingly, Geoffrey Rose's 'Big Idea', as it became known (without any ironic appreciation that 'Big Ideas' are precisely epidemiology's problem), now forms the basis of official health education policy, justifying the advice to everyone to change their lives in minute particulars. This disconnectedness from the real world, exemplified by the epidemiologists' espousal of Geoffrey Rose's population strategy, illustrates how they could believe in anything, even their own theories.[70]

The absurdities of utopian idealism did not prevent The Social Theory from being very popular. It certainly caught the zeitgeist of the times, plugging into the ethos of self-improvement associated with the re-emergence of free-market economics, which was readily translated into the pursuit of personal physical fitness and accounted for the surge in popularity of jogging and marathons, of being slim, not smoking and eating a 'healthy' diet. The Social Theory tuned into such sentiments and although its specific promise of preventing heart disease with a healthy low-fat diet was false, nonetheless the same diet, being low in calories, was effective for those 'self-improvers' who wished to lose weight and stay slim.

Further, The Social Theory was highly plausible. It exploited the powerful imagery of disease as suggested by the notion that fat furred up the arteries and salt overloaded the circulation; it provided, in the concept of the Diseases of Affluence, an explanation for the paradox that while everyone was becoming generally more prosperous and the standards of living ever higher, people still died. It seemed self-evident that life must have become too easy, as people could now afford to eat more than was good for them and drive around in cars instead of walk. Necessarily, they must pay the consequences. The wonder of it all was that it was all so simple, simple enough indeed to be encapsulated in a few powerful soundbites on television. It was certainly much easier for Professor Rose to say 'the modern British diet is killing people in their thousands from heart attacks' than to explain the complexities of why it is difficult to influence the cholesterol level in the blood by changing what one eats and, even if one were to make the effort, the evidence from the major trials showed that it conferred no benefit in protecting against heart disease. Finally, there was no ready way for others to test whether the claims of The Social Theory might be correct. When a surgeon introduces a new operation only for others to find it does not work, it falls into disrepute. But how could one tell whether the process of social engineering was actually preventing common diseases? If, for some unknown reason, the rate of heart disease started to fall, the Social Theorists were only too happy to accept the credit but if, as in other instances such as cancer, there was no change, this was only evidence that not enough money was being spent on health promotion or that their efforts to promote change were being set aside.

But biology does not readjust to accommodate the false theories of scientists, and by the mid-1990s the inconsistencies in The Social Theory started to become more generally recognised. In 1994 the editor of the prestigious *New England Journal of Medicine* inquired: 'What should the public believe? They substitute margarine for butter, only to learn that margarine may be worse for the arteries. They are told to eat oat bran to lower the cholesterol only to learn it is useless. They substitute saccharin for sugar only to hear that some research has found an association with bladder cancer, while others do not.'[71] A year later *Science*, in an article 'Epidemiology Faces Its Limits', observed 'the search for subtle links between diet, lifestyle or the environment and disease is an unending source of fear – but yields little certainty'. The public had been exposed to a 'mind-numbing array of potential disease-causing agents from hairdryers to coffee . . . the pendulum swings back and forth resulting in an "epidemic of anxiety".'[72]

By the mid-1990s, and in response to this greater scepticism, the main strands of The Social Theory underwent subtle, if unpublicised, changes. The warnings that milk, meat and dairy foods furred up the arteries became more muted, replaced by the less contentious recommendation that the public should eat five helpings of fruit or vegetables a day. The same dietary regime became the panacea for preventing cancer and Sir Richard Doll's implication of the Western diet was displaced by the equally unproven, if more positive, notion that lots of greens were protective. The environmentalists' concerns about the hidden dangers of minuscule pollutants in the air and water was deflected towards the much 'bigger' issues of global warming and holes in the ozone layer.[73]

There is a view that it has all been a good cause. Bacon and eggs may not cause heart attacks or cancer but the cult of a 'healthy lifestyle' is a good thing as it encourages people to go out and become fit. Health concerns about the environment may have been exaggerated but have led to ever stricter regulation, which again must be deemed a good thing.

But these alleged benefits must be set against a large debit account. The Social Theory is synonymous with victim-blaming because its logic requires that patients have only themselves to blame for persisting with their unhealthy habits and not heeding helpful advice. It has made people much more, rather than less, concerned about their health and an infinite variety of hidden dangers in their lives. The reality that now most live out their natural lifespans to succumb from complex diseases determined by ageing is transformed into the illusion that illness is ubiquitous, and its causes lie in the way that people lead their lives, and thus can be readily prevented. The Social Theory simultaneously manages to overemphasise the role of illness in people's lives while at the same time trivialising it. It generates the myth that the practice of medicine is futile, because the allegedly important factors in health are outside its control. Its apparently inexhaustible range of contradictory hazards of everyday life undermines the authority of medicine as a source of reliable knowledge, for if, as has been claimed, baked beans prevent cancer and children are to be discouraged from chewing plastic ducks lest their chemicals be carcinogenic, then anything goes. It has wasted hundreds of millions of pounds in futile research and health-education programmes while justifying the imposition of costly regulations to reduce yet further the minuscule levels of pollution in air and water. And to cap it all, it does not work. The promise of the prevention of thousands of deaths a year has not been fulfilled. Indeed, it is much more probable that, excepting the campaigns to discourage smoking, The Social Theory has had near enough zero effect on the nation's health over the last two decades.

3

THE UNSOLVED PROBLEM – THE
MYSTERIES OF BIOLOGY REVISITED

The failure of the two great projects of the last two decades – The New Genetics and The Social Theory – constitutes the fall of modern medicine. Their scientific basis – molecular biology and epidemiology respectively – could not have been more diverse, yet they shared the same aspiration. They sought to replace the chance discovery of new drugs and the empiricism of technological innovation by a new 'third' way – the elucidation of the causes of disease that would lead either to rational forms of treatment or the prevention of common illnesses. The lure of The New Genetics lay in its reductionism, the explanation of the phenomena of disease at the most fundamental level of the gene and its products. The allure of The Social Theory was its simple, readily understandable explanation of disease, which offered the prospect that they could be simply prevented. But it was not to be. Genes in general do not play an important role in disease and when they do – as in the single-gene defect cystic fibrosis – the genome turns out to be so complex and elusive that there is not much can be done about it. As for The Social Theory, it has been invalidated by the mundane biological fact that the human organism is – as it has to be – impervious to minor changes in its external environment.

The main reason why these two projects have failed is that

the causes of common disease are neither genetic nor social, but rather are either age-determined or biological and (for the most part) unknown. The time has come to switch from contemplating the failures of the past to gaze into the crystal ball, to see how near, or far, medicine might be from identifying these unknown determinant, biological causes of disease. We start by reiterating the nature of this great unsolved problem of contemporary medicine.

Medicine's post-war success, built on the chance discovery of drugs and technological innovation, concealed the fact that its impressive achievements have been won without the necessity to understand the nature or causation of disease. And now, fifty years on, medicine still knows the cause of only a fraction of the diseases in the textbooks: the bacterial and viral infections, those resulting from a defect in a single gene (like cystic fibrosis), tobacco and lung cancer and a handful of occupational diseases and those primarily determined by ageing: arthritis, cataracts, the majority of cases of cancer and the circulatory disorders. But everything else – all the neurological diseases such as multiple sclerosis, and all the rheumatological diseases such as rheumatoid arthritis, and all the dermatological diseases like psoriasis, and all the gut disorders like Crohn's disease, and so on – their causes, quite simply, are not known. Contemporary medicine is thus in a situation directly analogous to that of the mid-nineteenth century when, too, there were a whole series of recognisable diseases whose causes were unknown – anthrax, gonorrhoea, typhoid fever, suppuration, cholera, diphtheria, tetanus, pneumonia, meningitis, food poisoning, gas gangrene, plague, botulism, dysentery, paratyphoid, syphilis and whooping cough. Then, Robert Koch and his colleagues in less than two decades, armed only with their microscopes and a few simple stains, discovered the precise bacteria responsible for each and every one. Similarly, it has to be presumed that some types of as yet elusive biological agents must explain why one person gets multiple sclerosis, another rheumatoid arthritis and a third schizophrenia. But what are they?

The probability that these unknown biological agents must be some form of infectious organism emerges quite clearly from examining the evidence of causation of two very different illnesses – multiple sclerosis and childhood leukaemia. Multiple sclerosis is an episodic illness where the fatty sheath that insulates the nerves become inflamed, causing acute episodes of weakness and incoordination followed by partial (or sometimes complete) recovery. It is much commoner among Northern Europeans than other racial groups, affecting 1 in 1,000 people in Britain between the ages of twenty and forty. Why? There is, as always, a genetic element. The risk of MS rises to one in fifty for those who have an affected sibling and one in two for those with an affected identical twin. In well over 90 per cent of cases, however, MS just comes 'out of the blue', so the genetic component presumably increases susceptibility to whatever causes MS but cannot be the determining factor. The proponents of The Social Theory, needless to say, believe the cause to be the Western diet, because of the high incidence among Western nations and the observation that MS, like so many other illnesses, became less common during the war years in occupied Holland and Denmark. By now it has become quite unnecessary to even refute such speculation (though it will come as no surprise that the diet of those unfortunate enough to have MS is no different from anyone else), so it is possible to turn immediately to considering the evidence that MS has a biological cause.[1]

The pattern of MS over the last fifty years conforms to that of an infectious disease: its incidence has increased ten-fold in Britain over the last fifty years, while simultaneously (as happens with infections) becoming less severe over time. MS was a much more aggressive and rapidly progressive disease in the past, with the average period from its onset to debilitating paralysis and death being a mere eight years. Nowadays MS is almost compatible with a normal lifespan and most survive at least twenty-five years with the disease.[2]

But the most persuasive evidence for a biological cause for MS comes from several 'epidemics' of the disease, of which the best described was in the Danish Faroe Islands in the North Atlantic, related both in time and exposure to the islands' occupation by 7,000 British troops during the war. Prior to 1943 there had been not a single recorded case of MS on the Faroe Islands. Then, between 1943 and 1949, sixteen cases were diagnosed in a population of less than 30,000 and a further sixteen followed over the subsequent twenty years. Twenty-five of the thirty-two cases had never left the islands. 'There is no question the British troops introduced multiple sclerosis into the Faroe Islands during their occupation,' observed Dr John F. Kurtzke of Georgetown University School of Medicine in Washington in 1986. 'We also conclude that affected Faroese later [transmitted] the illness to other Faroese. It seems inescapable that a transmissible agent is the cause of MS. We think it is a single, specific, widespread systemic infection which in only a small proportion of those affected ever involves the central nervous system.'[3]

We now turn to the second example, acute leukaemia in childhood, where the malignant proliferation of white blood cells infiltrates the brain, the bone marrow and other organs and which, prior to 1971, was incurable. There is already one well-known cause of leukaemia, radiation, as revealed by the increased incidence among survivors from Hiroshima and Nagasaki, so when in the early 1980s a cluster of cases was identified in Seascale near the nuclear reprocessing plant of Sellafield in West Cumbria, it was only logical to presume the radioactive discharges from Sellafield must be responsible. This assumption, as observed earlier, proved to be incorrect, as it would have required levels of radiation 400 times greater to have caused the cases of leukaemia. There had to be another explanation. The 'clustering' of cases of leukaemia that occurred in Seascale is a well-recognised phenomenon, having been first thoroughly documented back in 1963 with an 'outbreak' in eight children from the suburban community in the town of Niles in Illinois. 'Seven of the eight children were from Roman Catholic families and each attended or had older siblings who attended the single Parochial Grade School in the parish. The eight cases occurred in a typical time pattern and were accompanied by the parallel appearance of a "rheumatic-like" illness amongst other children attending the school.'[4]

This clustering pattern was no more than suggestive of an

infectious cause (and could indeed have occurred by chance) until Dr Leo Kinlen of Oxford University conducted an extended and inspired series of studies. He noted how, as with MS in the Faroe Islanders, the cluster of leukaemia cases in Seascale occurred in a previously isolated and small community exposed to the influx of a large group of outsiders, the construction workers involved in the massive civil-engineering project of constructing the Sellafield plant. If leukaemia, like MS, was related to an isolated population's exposure to some infectious agent 'from outside' to which they had no natural immunity, then, speculated Dr Kinlen, there should be similar clusters of leukaemia around other major civil-engineering sites in remote areas and in other situations where there was large-scale 'mixing' of populations – around military camps and the building of new towns in rural areas.

And so it has turned out. The excess number of cases is not great, but is certainly present wherever Dr Kinlen has looked: 'The magnitude and consistency of the increases of childhood leukaemia found in population-mixing studies effectively rules out the operation of chance. Overall the findings point strongly to the transmission of some unidentified, possibly viral, infection and provides the most likely explanation for the Sellafield cases.'[5]

It is not usual to think of diseases such as MS or leukaemia as being 'infectious' illnesses, but, unlikely as it may seem, the pattern of their occurrence is strongly suggestive of some contagious biological agent that passes from one person to another, either damaging the insulating material around the nerves or stimulating the massive over-production of white blood cells. It seems likely, on reflection, that the same must apply to all the other hundreds of illnesses that appear 'out of the blue' and are not determined by ageing – like rheumatoid arthritis, Crohn's, schizophrenia or diabetes – and where, like multiple sclerosis and leukaemia, the responsible biological agent is not known. If one tries to imagine what difference it would make to the treatment and prevention of these diseases were those biological agents known, it is easy to appreciate why this is the concrete ceiling against which medical research has been banging its head for the last twenty years.

It is, of course, not possible to predict where the biological explanations for these illnesses will come from, or indeed what form they will take (or indeed whether they will ever be elucidated), but there would seem to be three possible ways in which they might be found.

Firstly, the cause might be a bacterium or virus that has been overlooked or has proved difficult to isolate. Here, Dr Barry Marshall's discovery in 1984 of helicobacter as the cause of peptic ulcer is the classic example, and it is interesting to note how the same organism has subsequently been implicated in other gut disorders, including stomach cancer and tumours of the small intestine.[6] Dr Thomas Grayston's identification two years later of a new strain of the chlamydia bacterium falls into the same category, though its precise role in coronary heart disease has still not been clarified.[7] There are other examples ranging from the mundane, like dandruff (now known to be caused by a fungus, pityrosporum ovale) to the exotic, such as tick-born Lyme disease (caused by an organism similar to that which causes syphilis).[8,9] And, rather more circuitously, rheumatoid arthritis is now believed by some rheumatologists to be induced by the bacterium proteus.[10]

There is a second and particularly fruitful method of identifying the putative but unknown biological agents of disease: a technique known as Polymerase Chain Reaction (PCR), which can detect the genes of a virus in the cells it has infected. PCR was discovered by molecular biologist Kari Mullis who, to put it (very) simply, realised how, starting with a single molecule of DNA, he could generate millions of others in an afternoon. It was, enthused the journal *Scientific American*, one of 'the century's greatest scientific breakthroughs' and subsequently earned its young discoverer the Nobel Prize for chemistry. Now if that single molecule of DNA comes from a virus, then clearly multiplying it in this way makes it much easier to identify what it is. Thus, the droopy face of Bell's palsy has long been presumed to result from a viral inflammation of the facial nerve. But which virus? In 1996 Dr Shingo Murakami, a Japanese virologist, with the help of PCR found traces of the genes of the herpes simplex virus (responsible for

cold sores) in the fluid surrounding the facial nerve of patients
with Bell's palsy, but not in the fluid taken from patients with
other forms of facial paralysis. Hence Bell's palsy must be
caused by the herpes virus.[11] Similarly, another variant of the
herpes virus has been incriminated, with the PCR technique,
in the lethal cancer, Kaposi's sarcoma, particularly prevalent
among AIDS patients, and the human wart virus has been
incriminated in cancer of the cervix.[12,13] Similarly again, the
acute onset of diabetes in childhood is highly suspicious of an
acute viral infection attacking the insulin-producing cells in
the pancreas, but it was not until the advent of PCR that the
precise virus – coxsackie B – was identified.[14]

Finally, it must be presumed that forms of biological agents,
as yet undreamed of, hold the key to the understanding of
some diseases, or as Hamlet tells Horatio: 'There are more
things in heaven and earth, than are dreamt of in your philosophy.' The biological world, it cannot be stressed enough, is full
of mysteries. We have encountered many along the way. Why
do bacteria produce antibiotics? Why are plants medicinal factories? We do not, and probably cannot, answer these questions
because, as Einstein once famously observed, nature is 'damned
weird'. And perhaps somewhere in this 'damned weirdness'
will be found the as yet unanswered explanations for the causes
of disease. Two examples must suffice. Every living organism
from amoeba to man shares the one common feature that the
DNA of their genes makes the messenger RNA that codes for
the construction of the proteins that make up their cells. Or
that was at least the dogma until the discovery in 1970 of the
one solitary exception to this rule, a retrovirus that takes RNA
and turns it back into DNA. The discovery of this utterly
unique biological organism proved to be enormously significant on two counts. The enzyme produced by the retrovirus –
reverse transcriptase – was the crucial step that allowed the
New Geneticists to identify the genes for haemoglobin and
insulin. Then, in 1984, Robert Gallo of the National Cancer
Institute discovered that one species of retrovirus – human
immunodeficiency virus – was responsible for the most lethal
new infection to have emerged in the Western world over the

last one hundred years, AIDS, which again utterly uniquely, wreaked its havoc by destroying the immune system of those infected.[15]

Or again, the notion that a non-living organism, a protein, could cause a transmissible disease would until recently have been inconceivable – until, that is, Stanley Prusiner discovered a special type of protein (or prion). Prions, it subsequently emerged, could be transmitted from the brain of sheep to that of cattle to cause mad cow disease, and then to the brains of humans to cause the variant of the lethal dementing illness Creuzfeldt-Jakob disease. Prions are, in the words of Chief Medical Officer McCoy of the starship *Enterprise*, 'life, but not as we know it'. Prusiner duly received the Nobel Prize for medicine in 1997 'for his pioneering discovery of an entirely new genre of disease-causing agent'.[16]

There is no precedent in the whole of biology for either retroviruses or prions, but that does not prevent them from having an enormous influence on human disease. Perhaps it is in such mysterious niches of the natural world that the last great intellectual problem facing medicine – the causes of disease – will be found. Or perhaps they never will be.

PART 4

The Rise and Fall –
Causes and Consequences

LEARNING FROM THE PAST

The pattern of the Rise and Fall identified in the Introduction is clear enough. For thirty years from the mid-1940s onwards, the combination of clinical science, fortuitous drug discovery and innovative technology – together with the human virtues of imagination, perseverance and hard work – impelled medicine forward. By the late 1970s, these dynamic forces had become exhausted, creating the intellectual vacuum that was filled by the two radical but ultimately unsuccessful approaches of The Social Theory and The New Genetics. Further, as promised in the Introduction, this pattern of a Rise and Fall helps to explain the paradox that, despite medicine's staggering success, doctors are increasingly discontented and the public is increasingly neurotic about its health. It would be reasonable to infer that doctors' discontents may be related to the fact that medicine is not quite as exciting as in the past, while increasing public neuroticism may be related to the anxiety-mongering of the proponents of The Social Theory. It is necessary, however, to dig a bit deeper than this.

First we must satisfy ourselves – for the last time – that the pattern of a Rise and Fall is indeed correct. There can be no doubting the concentration of major discoveries prior to 1975, while other evidence for the decline in innovation around this time, such as the Dearth of New Drugs is clear enough.

349

This interpretation of events is admittedly difficult to accept, primarily because the belief in the limitless possibilities of medical progress is so pervasive, but it is a common historical observation that such things do happen. Every field of human knowledge has its Golden Age, which is followed by a decline in creativity and new ideas.[1] Geology's 'finest hour' was the mid-nineteenth century, with the startling discovery that the world was billions of years old. Then it was the turn of natural history, with the Darwinian theory of evolution. The glory days of theoretical physics were between the wars, grappling with quantum physics and Einstein's Theory of Relativity. The 1960s were the heyday of space exploration, and so on. Medicine's Golden Age lasted longer than most and had a greater impact, but there is no reason why it should be an exception to this rule, for just as the nineteenth-century European explorers eventually found there was no more left of Africa to explore so, once hearts are being transplanted and childhood cancer cured, the potential for further progress in these areas is clearly constrained. Medicine, like any field of endeavour, is bounded by its concerns – the treatment of disease – so success necessarily places a limit on further progress. Indeed, according to the 'Law of Acceleration' proposed by the American historian Henry Adams, it is precisely at the moment that a scientific discipline is at its most apparently successful, as medicine was in the 1960s and early 1970s, that it will be approaching its apotheosis.

But there are also specific reasons why medicine should conform to this pattern of a Rise and Fall. First, it is limited to doing what is 'do-able', and by the 1970s much of what was 'do-able' had been done. The main burden of disease had been squeezed towards the extremes of life. Infant mortality was heading towards its irreducible minimum, while the vast majority of the population was now living out its natural lifespan to become vulnerable to diseases strongly determined by ageing. Second, these age-determined diseases, which are far and away the dominant preoccupation of Western medicine, are of two sorts. Some, like arthritis of the hips and furred-up arteries, can be markedly improved with drugs and operations, while others, like cancer and the circulatory disorders, can be palliated though not postponed indefinitely. In neither is there much scope for further medical progress. Thirdly, and very importantly, the rate of medical innovation was inevitably bound to decline because so many of its important discoveries had depended on luck. The bountifulness of nature in providing the extremely potent but entirely unanticipated antibiotics and cortisone is unlikely to be repeated, while sooner or later research chemists will find they are scraping the bottom of the barrel of chemical compounds that can be synthesised and screened for their therapeutic potential. And finally, medical research is, in Peter Medawar's memorable phrase, 'the art of the soluble'. As of this moment, it is not at all clear whether or how the last challenge left – the discovery of the causes of diseases like multiple sclerosis and leukaemia – is indeed 'soluble'.

Now this contention that science has 'reached its limits' has been expressed many times in the past, only to be repeatedly disproved. Famously Lord Kelvin, at the close of the nineteenth century, insisted that the future of the physical sciences were to be looked for in 'the sixth place of decimals' (that is, futile refinements of the then present state of knowledge). Within a few years Einstein had put forward his Theory of Relativity and the certainties of Lord Kelvin's classical physics were eclipsed. Perhaps predictions about medicine 'having reached its limits' will be similarly overthrown in the coming years. Perhaps, but the brick wall blocking further medical progress is solidly built being no less than four layers thick. The readily do-able has been done, the chronic diseases of ageing have been ameliorated, the bottom of the barrel of lucky drug discoveries has been scraped and the causes of the common diseases of mid-life remain a mystery.

The epochs of the Rise and Fall of medicine do not just follow each other chronologically, but are dynamically related. The Fall from the late 1970s onwards is best understood as a set of false strategies by which the express train of medical advance, fuelled by the successes of the Rise, sought to variously hammer away at, pole-vault over, circumvent or undermine this four-layered brick wall impeding further progress.

The essence of 'hammering away' is to do the same things but at greater intensity. We encountered this in Technology's Failings with the excessive use of new investigative techniques for straightforward medical problems: an endoscopy for everyone with a stomach ache, a CT scan for everyone with a headache, and complex studies of urine flow for every male with symptoms of an enlarged prostate. The potential for expanding the use of these diagnostic techniques is virtually limitless, especially if the age group being investigated is pushed upwards to include those in their eighties and nineties. There was also considerable scope for hammering away in the pursuit of marginal treatment benefits as in the massive over-use of cancer chemotherapy in the palliation of age-determined cancers or futile attempts to prolong life, as illustrated by the description of General Franco's final illness. A quarter of all health expenditure in the United States, it will be recalled, is now spent on patients during the last six months of their lives.

The pharmaceutical industry has also had no alternative, in the absence of new and lucky drug discoveries, other than to keep hammering away. This takes several forms of which the most obvious is the 'better mousetrap' – new and more costly variants of drugs already available. These may well be 'better' in the sense of being easier to take and having fewer side-effects, but they are no more effective therapeutically. Alternatively, when there is no effective remedy for a disease the drug companies have adopted the 'useless mousetrap' strategy on the grounds that patients and relatives want to be doing 'something'. Thus new drugs for Alzheimer's and multiple sclerosis are increasingly widely prescribed even though their efficacy is scarcely detectable.

The second response to the brick wall was to try and pole-vault over the lack of effective treatments with complex and expensive strategies. The saga of foetal monitoring introduced in the 1970s in the hope of preventing cerebral palsy belongs in this category, as do the national screening programmes for the early detection of cancers of the breast and cervix. Screening certainly can work. There is no simpler and more effective medical intervention than screening every newborn baby to detect those at risk of mental deficiency from an underactive thyroid. A spot of blood obtained from a heel prick can be automatically processed at virtually zero cost to establish the diagnosis while treatment – thyroxine replacement – is 100 per cent effective. By contrast the principle behind screening for cancer may be the same, the detection of disease at an early enough stage for it to be curable, but that is all. Cancer screening is logistically very complex to organise, the techniques of diagnosis – cervical smears and mammography – require considerable skill, while the distinction between the normal and pathological is uncertain. Finally, even though cancer screening involves the dedicated skills of nurses, radiologists, pathologists, gynaecologists and surgeons, the impact is marginal, because the most aggressive cancers that need to be caught early arise so rapidly.[2]

The third option, circumventing the brick wall, sought to bypass the dearth of new treatments by preventing disease in the first place. This was The Social Theory. Its approach, if not examined overcritically, certainly appeared plausible enough and indeed was widely perceived as representing a further stage in the evolution of medicine, where prevention was a more sophisticated response to the problem of illnesses such as cancer and heart disease than an attempt to 'cure' them with relatively ineffective medical therapies. Enormous sums of money have been expended on 'health promotion' to achieve these ends. Its drawback is that it does not work. The Social Theory fulfilled another important function by expanding the influence of medicine beyond the traditional confines of the consultation between doctor and patient to reach out to the healthy too. It provided apparently authoritative advice to the public on how they should lead their lives, instructing them in what they should and should not eat, while alerting them to previously unsuspected hazards in their everyday lives.

Finally, The New Genetics sought to undermine the wall by illuminating the workings of the human organism at its most fundamental level with the promise that at some indefinable point in the future the brick wall would come tumbling down, leaving a long straight road to health and happiness for all.

The perverse consequence of all these unsuccessful attempts to hammer, pole-vault, circumvent and undermine the brick wall is that medicine has sustained, even enhanced, its dominant position within Western society. Medicine has never been so powerful, and yet its success is seriously compromised by another 'Rule of Four', the four-fold paradox noted in the Introduction.

First, doctors themselves are dispirited, the proportion 'regretting' their decision to enter medicine rising from 15 per cent in 1966 to 50 per cent in 1988.[3] Second, the public's attitude to health shows precisely the same pattern: despite the prodigious medical advances of the post-war years the proportion claiming to be 'worried' about their health has also risen from 15 per cent to almost 50 per cent over the same period.[4] Third comes the paradox that despite the fact that modern medicine clearly works, a startling number of adults are sufficiently dissatisfied with its style or what it has to offer to seek out and pay for the attentions of alternative practitioners.[5] Finally there is the paradox of the explosion in costs (in Britain a doubling of health service expenditure in under ten years) with precious little to show for it.

The causes of these four paradoxes are diverse and complex ranging from the dominance of authoritarian, managerialist attitudes in medical practice to the increasing litigiousness of patients. Nonetheless, as was suggested in the Introduction, an historical perspective shows they can also be seen as the multi-faceted side of the singular phenomenon of medicine's Rise and Fall.

Paradox 1: Disillusioned Doctors

Medicine is, sadly, no longer as satisfying as in the past. Many of the most interesting diseases that tested the doctor's clinical acumen have simply disappeared, and a family doctor is lucky to see a patient with a serious acute medical problem from one week to the next. This lack of satisfaction has been compounded by the rise of specialisation, so the cardiac surgeon who in the early days of the pump was faced by the challenge of repairing many different complex anatomical defects of the heart now spends all his time routinely doing coronary artery bypass grafts. Further, the dearth in therapeutic innovation now means that doctors are doing much the same as they were twenty years ago and what seemed very exciting in the 1960s and 1970s, such as transplantation and CT scans, has become routine. In short, medicine is duller, as can readily be ascertained by contrasting the sparkle and interest of medical journals from two or three decades ago with those of today, where impenetrable genetics and improbable epidemiology jostle for space and no one is any the wiser. Further, doctors are now, on average, much brighter than in the past because entry to medical school has become so much more competitive, and they are thus likely to be more intolerant or less accepting of the humdrum nature of most medical practice.

Paradox 2: The Worried Well

It is most peculiar that as medicine has become more successful, the proportion of the public who apparently are 'worried' about their health has increased. This could be because people 'don't know when they are well off', certainly when compared to their parents' generation, who lived through the privations of the Depression and war. But equally importantly they have been encouraged by the falsehoods of The Social Theory to become more neurotic. If it were correct that so innocent a pleasure as eating bacon and eggs for breakfast can lead to an untimely demise from a heart attack, then there is no reason to doubt the myriad other hazards of everyday life that have been identified over the last decade. It would be most surprising if sections of the public did not, as a result, become more alarmed about their health. This in turn has compounded the professional discontent of Paradox 1 as an excessive concern about 'health' can only too obviously encourage people to see their doctors unnecessarily. They in turn become frustrated at the time they have to spend dealing with the 'Worried Well'.[6]

Paradox 3: The Soaring Popularity of Alternative Medicine

The 'alternatives' – in their various different guises of home-opathy, naturopathy, acupuncture and so on – are now so popular, being used by one-third of adults in any one year, that it is difficult to appreciate that prior to the 1980s they were very much a minority interest and widely perceived as quackery. The surging popularity of these alternatives might be explained by the undivided attention and the physical manipulation offered by its practitioners which, to many, might seem prefer-able to being expensively overinvestigated and overtreated in a hospital bed.

But these alternatives are more than just 'feel-good thera-pies'. The effectiveness of the modern drugs that came tumbling out of the drug companies in the 1960s and 1970s led to the neglect of simpler, more traditional remedies and the dis-missal of anything that did not fit the 'scientific' ideas of the nature of disease. Thus, following the discovery of cortisone and other anti-inflammatory agents, the skills of rheumatolo-gists devolved around juggling various toxic regimes of drugs in the hope that the benefits might outweigh the sometimes grievous side-effects. Meanwhile, all the other therapies for rheumatological disorders – such as massage, manipulation and dietary advice – were abandoned virtually wholesale, only to be 'rediscovered' by alternative practitioners in the 1980s.

Paradox 4: The Spiralling Costs of Health Care

The more that medicine can do, the greater will be the demand and thus the greater the cost. But it is incorrect, as is often asserted, that the demands for health care are potentially limit-less. On the contrary, it is quite easy to spend too much on health. The negligible cost of the consultation for a tension headache becomes substantial when a brain scan is thrown in for good measure. Such examples could be multiplied a thou-sand times.

Further, the pattern of a Rise and Fall indicates that the

future scope of medicine will primarily be directed at ameliorating the chronic degenerative diseases of ageing, such as hip
replacements and cataract operations. The rising numbers of
those needing such procedures will certainly push up the cost,
but this is finite and measurable. The paradox of the rise of
medical expenditure rather lies in the magnitude of the
increased funds allocated to health, which in the United States
have almost doubled in the last ten years from $391 billion to
$668 billion without there being any measurable or subjective
impression of improvements on a scale to justify such an
increase. It is rather accounted for by the processes already
described of hammering away, pole-vaulting and circumventing
the obstacles to further medical progress that have already been
outlined. These escalating costs are an enormous cause for concern, as the state has many other responsibilities just as, or
indeed more, deserving than health, such as education and the
arts.

In summary the four paradoxes of the success of modern medicine can all be understood as different aspects of medicine's
Rise and Fall. By now it will be clear there is more to the Fall
than a sloping-off in the rate of medical innovation. Medicine's
moral and intellectual integrity has also been eroded over the
last two decades, as revealed by the obvious contrast between,
for example, the protracted engagement with the profound
problems posed by transplantation or curing childhood cancer
and the illusory promises of The Social Theory and The New
Genetics. The distinguished social historian Roy Porter elaborates on the consequences:

> The irony is that the healthier Western society becomes,
> the more medicine it craves . . . Immense pressures are
> created – by the medical profession, by the media, by the
> high pressure advertising of pharmaceutical companies – to
> expand the diagnosis of treatable illnesses. Scares are cre-
> ated, people are bamboozled into lab tests, often of dubious
> reliability. Thanks to diagnostic creep or leap, ever more
> disorders are revealed, extensive and expensive treatments

are then urged . . . [This] is endemic to a system in which an expanding medical establishment, faced with a healthier population, is driven to medicalising normal events, converting risks into diseases and treating trivial complaints with fancy procedures . . . The law of diminishing returns necessarily applies. Extending life becomes feasible, but it may be a life exposed to degrading neglect as resources grow overstretched. What an ignominious destiny if the future of medicine turns into bestowing meagre increments of unenjoyed life![7]

And yet the everyday practice of medicine belies this gloomy interpretation because, despite everything, it delivers and, thanks to the therapeutic revolution, much more so than fifty years ago. Consequently doctors do find their work satisfying and their patients do get better. The public is probably less concerned about the alleged hazards of everyday life than surveys would suggest and, when the crunch comes, most would put their trust in the orthodox rather than the alternatives. Still, this analysis of the past certainly makes sense of present discontents, which, if confronted and corrected, are the best guarantees of medicine's continuing success in the future.

2

LOOKING TO THE FUTURE

For I dip't into the future, far as human eye could see
Saw a vision of the world, and all the wonders that would be.
Alfred, Lord Tennyson

At the mid-point of the century, a few years after this historical account opens, Lord 'Tommy' Horder addressed a
meeting on the theme 'Whither Medicine?'. The miraculous
effect of cortisone had just been described, there were encouraging signs that children with leukaemia were responding to
anti-cancer drugs, both the cure of tuberculosis and the implication of tobacco in lung cancer were imminent. In the midst
of such momentous events, Lord Horder suggested, a visitor
from Mars would have thought the subject of his address
incomprehensible: '"Whither Medicine?" the Martian would
say, "Why, whither else than straight ahead; forging still more
weapons with which to conquer disease."' And, as we have
seen, the Martian would have been absolutely right.[1]

But the burden of the history of post-war medicine that
emerges from this book is that such genuine and unbridled
optimism is no longer possible. The race has been run, the
Golden Age is over and so for a contemporary Martian the
most likely scenario for the future would seem to be at best a
continuation of the present. Medicine will continue to be a

359

powerful and immensely successful enterprise, ameliorating the chronic diseases associated with ageing and, where possible, saving the lives of the acutely ill. But, equally, medicine's discontents are also likely to continue. The next surveys will reveal a yet higher proportion of doctors 'with regrets', and a yet higher proportion of the public who are neurotically concerned about their health. Yet more unanticipated hazards of everyday life will be identified and the cost of medical care will continue to spiral upwards.

That is what the future *will* be, but it is legitimate to speculate what the future *might* be, if the present discontents were to be addressed. The preliminary and essential step must be to recognise and discard error, just as the great seventeenth-century British physiologist William Harvey, prior to his description of the circulation of the blood, felt it necessary to discard 'those things that up till now have been written, but are by no means true'. In contemporary medicine this means discarding the intellectual falsehoods of The Social Theory and the intellectual pretensions of The New Genetics. The Social Theory has so undermined the authority of medicine as a source of reliable knowledge that urgent remedial action must be taken. It will not be easy to admit that much current medical advice is quackery, but it must be done. Meanwhile the simple expedient of closing down most university departments of epidemiology could both extinguish this endlessly fertile source of anxiety-mongering while simultaneously releasing funds for serious research.

The problem posed by the pretensions of The New Genetics is rather different. This, at least, has the merit of being genuine science, which will keep legions of molecular biologists happy for decades working out, to the last point of decimals, the infinite complexity of the genes and the proteins for which they code. This is interesting enough for those who are interested in that sort of thing, if rather tedious for everyone else. The danger of The New Genetics, as is now widely perceived, is that it threatens to sideline medical research down the blind alley of reductionist explanations, where all biological questions are reduced to the most fundamental level of the gene, when it should be looking upwards and outwards – and sideways – probing the 'mysteries of biology' to find the causes of disease.[2] Under the banyan tree nothing grows, and the banyan tree of genetics and epidemiology now casts such long shadows that the fresh green shoots of medical research are stifled.

The benefits of blowing away this smoke screen of false illusions and millenarian promises would be to liberate medicine to concentrate on its legitimate task of, in William Blake's memorable phrase, 'Doing Good in Minute Particulars'.

There is, however, a further dragon that must be slain and its name, surprisingly, is Progress, or rather the ideology of progress. At first sight it is hard to imagine a more unlikely dragon as the remarkable achievements of post-war years were fuelled by the two most progressive of ideologies – science and capitalism. Further, life would be a dreary thing were it not for the optimistic search for new ideas with which to push forward the boundaries of knowledge. All this is indisputable, yet it is obvious, at least on reflection, that medicine is not, or should not be (as it has become), synonymous with scientific progress. Its knowledge base may increase, as it has spectacularly over the last fifty years, but its concerns – what doctors do – remain the same as in ancient Greece. 'No other profession can boast of the same unbroken continuity of ideals [that stretch back to] the critical sense [as established by] the Hippocratic school,' observed the magnificent Sir William Osler. 'We may indeed by justly proud of our apostolic succession. *These are our methods* – to carefully observe the phenomena of life in all its stages, to cultivate the reasoning faculty so as to be able to know the true from the false. *This is our work* – to prevent disease, to relieve suffering and to heal the sick.'[3]

There is a false antithesis in posing tradition against progress, but Osler's inspirational perspective on the historical continuity of medicine's 'methods and work' provides the appropriate context within which to view medicine's current 'almost exclusive homage to the shock of the new [with its] central emphasis on novelty'.[4] We start with the progressivist ideology of science. At its simplest, this 'obsession with the new' ignores the wisdom of the past. This could be lived with during the

Rise, when the new was genuinely new and important. But when this is no longer the case, this preoccupation with progress takes on a different guise, becoming a decoy, concealing from the public and indeed the profession itself the current intellectual state of medicine. The focus on medicine's future possibilities discourages people from looking back when they might too readily be dazzled by the scale of past achievements and thus legitimately wonder at the reasons for the lack of genuine developments in recent years. Caught between ignoring the past and fantasising about the future, it is easy for medicine to lose its grip on reality and what it should be trying to do.

This loosening hold on reality is compounded by a second feature of scientific progressivism: the belief that it can explain everything. This intellectual hubris of not recognising what is not known opens the door to false explanations where, as with The Social Theory, people are blamed for their illnesses and are deceived into believing their everyday lives are full of hazards.

Nor is that the end of it. For medical science now recognises only one source of knowledge, that which has 'been proven' by statistics, and this too is a potent source of error. There are many ways of knowing and among the most powerful is the tacit knowledge that comes from experience and is best described as 'judgement'.[5] Sir Austin Bradford Hill's legacy, albeit unintentionally on his part, has been to marginalise this tacit form of knowledge, so it is deemed less reliable and inferior to that which can be objectively and explicitly demonstrated with statistical techniques and clinical trials.

But, as has been observed repeatedly, the reverse is the case. It is this statistically derived knowledge that has consistently been shown to be unreliable, promoting the patently absurd as proven fact. Further, clinical trials cannot answer the sort of complex questions that frequently crop up in medical practice and when many are aggregated together, 'incomplete data is run through computer programs of bewildering complexity to produce results of implausible precision'. This form of knowledge, when subjected to critical scrutiny, has been shown to result in the adoption of an ineffective treatment in 32 per cent of cases and the rejection of a useful treatment in 33 per cent of cases. It is only of moderate consolation to realise that in the remaining third, it must have produced the 'right' answer.[6]

Perversely, then, scientific progressivism has undermined medicine's most important asset – knowledge based on practical experience, allied with 'a reasoning faculty' that can distinguish the true from the false.

We turn now to the second dynamic force of progress of the post-war years, capitalism, as represented by the pharmaceutical companies whose 'obsession with the new' exerts a very different, but equally destructive, influence on contemporary medicine. The reason for this 'obsession with the new' is obvious enough as new drugs, and the prospect of windfall profits while they remain under patent, are the life blood that drives the industry forward. This worked very well in the years of cornucopia, but when the rich stream of accidental drug discoveries began to dry up, the drug companies have had to resort to other means to maintain their profitability. This, as has been seen, has taken the form of 'better (but more expensive) mousetraps' or indeed 'useless mousetraps', promoted on the grounds that they are better than no mousetraps at all.

It is, of course, up to doctors whether or not to prescribe these new drugs, but therein lies the problem. The drug companies are very rich but they are also desperate, because marketing their wares is now so costly. By contrast, academic doctors are poor, or at least always relatively short of funds for their research, and one way of acquiring those funds is to agree, for a fee, to investigate whether the latest wonder drug is indeed wonderful. They thus become, wittingly or not, the respectable front for the drug companies while, as was seen with the example of cholesterol-lowering drugs, providing the rationale for their almost universal prescription. In these circumstances, patients have become overmedicalised and the nation's drugs bill continues to escalate. Who is to know whether the alleged efficacy of these new drugs is as claimed, when the head of an academic unit of a teaching hospital spends two months of the year away from his post travelling in the United States, Europe and the Far East at the behest of a drug company? When a medical academic's 'commercial involvement reaches this level,' observes the disapproving editor of *The Lancet*, 'the very independence of research and opinion is put at risk'.[7]

This unhealthy situation is the inevitable reverse side of the dynamic and progressive nature of the pharmaceutical industry that was so intrinsic to the Rise, for, self-evidently, the drug companies as capitalist enterprises cannot escape from the imperative to innovate, they cannot impose restraints upon themselves, and thus must pursue every legitimate avenue in promoting the drugs up to, and including, subverting the integrity of the medical profession.

It is possible from these reflections on medicine and progress to make a very clear distinction. Genuine progress, optimistic and forward-looking, is always to be welcomed, but progress as an ideological necessity leads to obscurantism, falsehood and corruption. The question as to how to maximise the possibilities of the former, while rejecting the latter, is best resolved by accepting at face value the version of events as revealed by this historical account, where the last fifty years are best seen as one episode, albeit a very glorious one (indeed a culminating one), in a historical tradition that stretches back over the past 2,500 years. The time has come to relocate medicine back within that tradition so eloquently evoked by Sir William Osler. The timeless virtues of judgement and good sense might then triumph over the shallow restlessness of the present through a reaffirmation of the personal human relationship between doctor and patient. The personal doctor listens carefully to what he is being told. He (or she) performs the irreducible minimum of investigations necessary to establish a diagnosis. He confines himself to the matter in hand and does not stray beyond to give impudent or gratuitous advice. He recognises the intellectual limits of human understanding and the practical limits of what medicine can legitimately be expected to achieve.[8] This reaffirmation of the central tenet of medical practice may, or may not, mean that doctors in the future will be less inclined to 'regret' their chosen career, but the public will certainly have less reason to be unduly concerned about their health or to look elsewhere for help with their medical problems. Meanwhile, the limited prospects of future medical advance should by now be well recognised, so there is no need for the cost of medical care to continue to spiral upwards. Thus, the present discontents of medicine may be resolved and its future guaranteed.

References

ABBREVIATIONS

AJM	*American Journal of Medicine*
AJOG	*American Journal of Obstetrics and Gynaecology*
BJHH	*Bulletin of the Johns Hopkins Hospital*
BMJ	*British Medical Journal*
JAMA	*Journal of the American Medical Association*
JRSM	*Journal of the Royal Society of Medicine*
MRC	*Medical Research Council*
NEJM	*New England Journal of Medicine*
PSMMC	*Proceedings of the Staff Meetings of the Mayo Clinic*

The place of publication is London unless otherwise stated.

Introduction

1. Richard Horton, 'A Manifesto for Reading Medicine', *The Lancet*, 1997, Vol. 349, pp. 872–4.
2. Isobel Allen, *Doctors and Their Careers* (Policy Studies Institute, 1988); Isobel Allen, *Doctors and Their Careers: A New Generation* (Policy Studies Institute, 1994).
3. Anthony King, *Daily Telegraph*, 3 June 1996.
4. Peter Skrabanek, *The Death of Humane Medicine and the Rise of Coercive Healthism* (Social Affairs Unit, 1994).
5. David Eisenberg, 'Unconventional Medicine in the United States:

Prevalence Costs and Patterns of Use', *NEJM*, 1993, Vol. 328, pp. 246–52.

6. Office of Health Economics, *Compendium of Health Statistics*, 1999.

A Lengthy Prologue: Twelve Definitive Moments

1. Lewis Thomas, 'Biomedical Science and Human Health', *Yale Journal of Biology and Medicine*, 1978, Vol. 51, pp. 133–42.
2. H. H. Dale, 'Advances in Medicinal Therapeutics', *BMJ*, 7 January 1950, pp. 1–7.

1: Penicillin

GENERAL READING

R. Hare, *The Birth of Penicillin* (Allen & Unwin, 1970)

G. Macfarlane, *Howard Florey: The Making of a Great Scientist* (Oxford: OUP, 1979)

——, *Alexander Fleming: The Man and the Myth* (Chatto & Windus, 1984)

John C. Sheehan, *The Enchanted Ring* (Cambridge, MA: MIT Press, 1982)

Wesley W. Spink, *Infectious Diseases: Prevention and Treatment in the Nineteenth and Twentieth Centuries* (Folkestone: Dawson, 1979)

Milton Wainwright, *Miracle Cure* (Oxford: Blackwell, 1990)

REFERENCES

1. Charles Fletcher, 'First Clinical Use of Penicillin', *BMJ*, 1984, Vol. 289, pp. 1721–3.
2. E. P. Abraham, E. Chain, H. W. Florey *et al.*, 'Further Observations on Penicillin', *The Lancet*, 16 August 1941, pp. 177–88.
3. Ronald Hare, *The Birth of Penicillin*. See also John Henderson, 'The Yellow Brick Road to Penicillin: A Story of Serendipity', *PSMMC*, 1997, Vol. 72, pp. 683–7; Alexander Fleming, 'Discovery of Penicillin', *British Medical Bulletin*, 1944, Vol. 2, pp. 4–5.
4. Alexander Fleming, 'On the Antibacterial Action of Cultures of a Penicillium, With Special Reference to Their Use in the Isolation of B. Influenzae', *British Journal of Experimental Pathology*, 1929, Vol. 10, pp. 226–36.
5. E. Chain, 'Thirty Years of Penicillin Therapy', *Proceedings of the Royal Society of London: Series B*, 1971, Vol. 179, pp. 293–319.
6. E. Chain, H. W. Florey *et al.*, 'Penicillin as a Chemotherapeutic Agent', *The Lancet*, 24 August 1940, pp. 226–8.

7. G. Macfarlane, *Alexander Fleming: The Man and the Myth*.
8. G. Macfarlane, *Howard Florey: The Making of a Great Scientist*.
9. H. W. Florey, 'Penicillin', *Nobel Lectures: Physiology or Medicine, 1940–62* (New York: Elsevier, 1964).
10. Table 1: Lawrence Garrod and Francis O'Grady, *Antibiotics and Chemotherapy* (E & S Livingstone, 1971).
11. E. F. Gale *et al.*, *The Molecular Basis of Antibiotic Action* (Chichester: John Wiley & Sons, 1981).
12. S. A. Waksman, 'The Role of Antibiotics in Nature', *Perspectives in Biology and Medicine*, Spring 1961, pp. 271–87.
13. L. C. Vining, 'Role of Secondary Metabolites from Microbes', *Secondary Metabolites: Their Function and Evolution*, ed. D. Chadwick and J. Whelan, Ciba Foundation Symposium 171 (Chichester: John Wiley & Sons, 1992).

2: Cortisone

GENERAL READING

E. G. L. Bywaters, 'The History of Paediatric Rheumatology', *Arthritis and Rheumatism*, 1977, Vol. 20, pp. 145–52

David Canton, 'Cortisone and the Politics of Drama, 1949–55', *Medical Innovations in Historical Perspective*, ed. John V. Pickstone (Macmillan, 1992)

George D. Kersley and John Glyn, *A Concise International History of Rheumatology and Rehabilitation* (Royal Society of Medicine Press, 1992)

Albert Q. Maisel, *The Hormone Quest* (New York: Random House, 1965)

Harry M. Marks, 'Cortisone, 1949: A Year in the Political Life of a Drug', *Bulletin of the History of Medicine*, 1992, Vol. 66, pp. 419–39

REFERENCES

1. Philip S. Hench *et al.*, 'The Effect of a Hormone of the Adrenal Cortex on Rheumatoid Arthritis', *PSMMC*, 1949, Vol. 24, pp. 181–97.
2. Albert Maisel, *The Hormone Quest*.
3. Philip S. Hench, 'Analgesia Accompanying Hepatitis and Jaundice in Cases of Chronic Arthritis', *PSMMC*, 1933, Vol. 8, pp. 430–37.
4. Philip S. Hench, 'Effect of Spontaneous Jaundice on Rheumatoid Arthritis: Attempts to Reproduce the Phenomenon', *BMJ*, 1938, Vol. 2, pp. 394–8.
5. Philip S. Hench, 'The Reversibility of Certain Rheumatic and Non-rheumatic Conditions by the Use of Cortisone', *Nobel Lectures: Physiology or Medicine, 1942–62* (New York: Elsevier, 1964).

6. F. A. Hartman *et al.*, 'The Hormone of the Adrenal Cortex', *Science*, 1930, Vol. 72, p. 76.

7. H.L. Mason *et al.*, 'The Chemistry of Crystalline Substances Isolated from the Suprarenal Gland', *Journal of Biological Chemistry*, 1936, Vol. 114, pp. 613–31.

8. H. Selye, 'Thymus and Adrenals in the Response of the Organism to Injuries and Intoxications', *British Journal of Experimental Pathology*, 1936, Vol. 17, p. 234.

9. See Note 2. See also Edward Kendall, 'The Development of Cortisone as a Therapeutic Agent', *Nobel Lectures: Physiology or Medicine, 1942–62* (New York: Elsevier, 1964).

10. *The Times*, 5 July 1949.

11. Philip S. Hench, 'A Reminiscence of Certain Events Before, During and After the Discovery of Cortisone', *Minnesota Medicine*, July 1953, pp. 705–10.

12. W. S. C. Copeman (ed.), *Cortisone and ACTH in Clinical Practice* (Butterworth, 1953).

13. The initial reaction to Hench's paper had been very enthusiastic. See 'A New Treatment for Rheumatoid Arthritis', *BMJ*, 7 May 1949, p. 812, and 'Cortisone in the Treatment of Rheumatism', *BMJ*, 2 July 1949, p. 24. Hench's results were replicated in Britain in a trial reported in the *BMJ* the following year: 'A Study of Cortisone and Other Steroids in Rheumatoid Arthritis', 14 October 1950, pp. 847–55 – 'the dramatic clinical effects of cortisone were immediately obvious'.

14. Harvey A. McGhee *et al.*, 'Introduction to a Series of Papers on Studies on ACTH and Cortisone', *BJHH*, 1950, Vol. 87, pp. 349–507.

15. The main papers describing the effect of cortisone in diseases other than rheumatoid arthritis include: Philip S. Hench *et al.*, *PSMMC*, 1949, Vol. 24, pp. 277–97 (rheumatic fever); L. A. Brunsting *et al.*, *PSMMC*, 1950, Vol. 25, pp. 479–82 (lupus erythematosis); R. A. Carey, *BJHH*, 1950, Vol. 87, pp. 425–60 (polyarteritis nodosa); T. W. Oppel, *Annals of Internal Medicine*, 1950, Vol. 32, pp. 318–24 (dermatomyositis); R. R. Kierland *et al.*, *Archives of Dermatology and Syphilology*, 1951, Vol. 64, pp. 549–54 (scleroderma); R. A. Carey *et al.*, *BJHH*, 1950, Vol. 87, pp. 354–414 (drug hypersensitivity and asthma); A. C. Woods, *American Journal of Ophthalmology*, 1950, Vol. 33, pp. 1325–49 (ocular inflammatory disease); B. J. Kennedy *et al.*, *AJM*, 1951, Vol. 10, pp. 134–55 (silicosis); M. Gladstone *et al.*, *AJM*, 1951, Vol. 10, pp. 166–81 (pulmonary fibrosis); L. E. Shulman, *BJHH*, 1952, Vol.

91, pp. 371–415 (sarcoidosis); W. H. Deering *et al.*, *PSMMC*, 1950, Vol. 25, pp. 486–8 (ulcerative colitis); T. E. Machella *et al.*, *AJM*, 1951, Vol. 221, pp. 501–7 (Crohn's); E. R. Sulzberg *et al.*, *JAMA*, 1953, Vol. 151, pp. 468–72 (dermatological disease); E. P. Farnsworth, *Proceedings of the Society for Experimental Biology and Medicine*, 1950, Vol. 74, pp. 60–2 (nephrotic syndrome); M. M. Wintrobe *et al.*, *AMA Archives of Internal Medicine*, 1951, Vol. 88, pp. 310–36 (haematological disorders); H. Ducchi *et al.*, *Gastroenterology*, 1952, Vol. 21, pp. 357–74 (hepatitis).

3: Streptomycin, Smoking and Sir Austin Bradford Hill

GENERAL READING

Richard Doll, 'Sir Austin Bradford Hill and the Progress of Medical Science', *BMJ*, 1992, Vol. 305, pp. 1521–6

Edmund A. Gehan and Noreen Lemak, *Statistics in Medical Research: Developments in Clinical Trials* (New York: Plenum, 1994)

Sir Austin Bradford Hill, *Statistical Method in Clinical and Preventive Medicine* (E & S Livingstone, 1962) – a collection of his important papers

International Agency for Research on Cancer (IARC), *Statistical Methods in Cancer Research, Vol. 1: The Analysis of Case-Control Studies* (IARC, 1987)

——, *Statistical Methods in Cancer Research, Vol. 2: The Design and Analysis of Cohort Studies* (IARC, 1987)

David E. Lillienfeld and Abraham M. Lillienfeld, 'Epidemiology: A Retrospective Study', *American Journal of Epidemiology*, 1977 Vol. 106, pp. 445–59

J. Rosser Matthews, *Quantification and the Quest for Medical Certainty* (Princeton, NJ: Princeton University Press, 1995)

Theodore M. Porter, *The Rise of Statistical Thinking, 1820–1900* (Princeton, NJ: Princeton University Press, 1986)

——, *Trust in Numbers: The Pursuit of Objectivity in Science and Public Life* (Princeton, NJ: Princeton University Press, 1995)

Statistics in Medicine, 1982, Vol. 1, pp. 1–375 – a series of essays exploring different aspects of Bradford Hill's life

Mervyn Susser, 'Epidemiology in the United States After World War II: The Evolution of Technique', *Epidemiologic Reviews*, 1985, Vol. 7, pp. 147–77

Peter Taylor, *Smoke Ring: The Politics of Tobacco* (Bodley Head, 1986)

Lisa Wilkinson, 'Sir Austin Bradford Hill: Medical Statistics and the Quantitative Approach to Prevention of Disease', *Addiction*, 1997, Vol. 92, pp. 657–66

REFERENCES

1. Sir Henry Dale, 'Advances in Medicinal Therapeutics', *BMJ*, 7 January 1950, pp. 1–7.
2. A. Bradford Hill, 'The Life of Sir Leonard Erskine-Hill FRS, 1866–1952', *Proceedings of the Royal Society of Medicine*, 1968, Vol. 61, pp. 307–16. See also I. D. Hill, 'Austin Bradford Hill: Ancestry and Early Life', *Statistics in Medicine*, 1982, Vol. 1, pp. 297–300.
3. A. Bradford Hill, 'A Pilot in the First World War', *BMJ*, 1983, Vol. 287, pp. 1947–8.
4. Major Greenwood, 'Medical Statistics', *The Lancet*, 1921, Vol. 1, pp. 985–8. See also Major Greenwood, *Some British Pioneers of Social Medicine* (Oxford: OUP, 1948).
5. Edmund A. Gehan and Noreen Lemak, *Statistics in Medical Research: Developments in Clinical Trials*.
6. A. Bradford Hill, 'Memories of the British Streptomycin Trial', *Controlled Clinical Trials*, 1990, Vol. 11, pp. 77–9.
7. F. H. K. Green, 'The Clinical Evaluation of Remedies', *The Lancet*, 1954, Vol. 2, pp. 1085–91. See also J. P. Bull, 'The Historical Development of Clinical Therapeutic Trials', *Journal of Chronic Diseases*, 1959, Vol. 10, pp. 218–48.
8. Peter M. Dunn, 'James Lind of Edinburgh and the Treatment of Scurvy', *Archives of Disease in Childhood*, 1997, Vol. 76, pp. 64–5. See also Duncan P. Thomas, 'Sailors, Scurvy and Science', *JRSM*, 1997, Vol. 90, pp. 50–4.
9. A. Bradford Hill, 'The Clinical Trial', *NEJM*, 1952, Vol. 247, pp. 113–19.
10. MRC, 'Streptomycin Treatment of Pulmonary Tuberculosis', *BMJ*, 30 October 1948, pp. 769–82.
11. John Crofton and D. A. Mitchison, 'Streptomycin Resistance in Pulmonary Tuberculosis', *BMJ*, 11 December 1948, pp. 1009–15.
12. M. E. Florey, *The Clinical Application of Antibiotics, Vol. 2: Streptomycin* (Oxford: OUP, 1961), p. 133.
13. Jorgen Lehmann, 'Para-amino Salicylic Acid in the Treatment of Tuberculosis', *The Lancet*, 1946, Vol. 1, pp. 15–16.
14. MRC, 'Treatment of Pulmonary Tuberculosis With PAS and Streptomycin: Preliminary Report', *BMJ*, 31 December 1949, p. 1521.
15. MRC, 'Treatment of Pulmonary Tuberculosis With Streptomycin and Para-amino-salicylic Acid, *BMJ*, 11 November 1950, pp. 1074–85. See also: MRC, 'The Prevention of Streptomycin Resistance by Combined Chemotherapy', *BMJ*, 31 May 1952, pp. 1157-64.

16. MRC, 'Isoniazid in the Treatment of Pulmonary Tuberculosis', *BMJ*, 7 March 1953, pp. 551–63.
17. Bernard Crick, *George Orwell: A Life* (Secker & Warburg, 1980).
18. Richard Doll, 'Clinical Trials Retrospect and Prospect', *Statistics in Medicine*, 1982, Vol. 1, pp. 337–44.
19. W. Grant Waugh, 'A Blast of the Trumpet Against the Monstrous Regiment of Mathematics', *BMJ*, 3 November 1951, p. 1088.
20. Andrew Wilson *et al.*, *Clinical Trials: Symposium, 5 April 1962* (Pharmaceutical Press, 1962).
21. Joan Austoker, *History of the Imperial Cancer Research Fund, 1902–86* (Oxford: OUP, 1988).
22. J. R. Bignell, 'Bronchial Carcinoma: Survey of 317 Patients', *The Lancet*, 1955, Vol. 1, pp. 786–8.
23. Conversation with Sir Richard Doll, *British Journal of Addiction*, 1991, Vol. 86, pp. 365–77. See also A. Bradford Hill, 'Mortality from a Malignant Disease', *The Practitioner*, 1945, Vol. 155, pp. 27–34.
24. Franz Muller, 'Tabakmissbrauch und lungencarcinom', *Zeitschrift für Krebsforschung*, 1940, Vol. 49, p. 57. See also G. Davey Smith, 'Smoking and Health Promotion in Nazi Germany', *Journal of Epidemiology and Community Health*, 1994, Vol. 48, pp. 220–3; Johannes Clemmesen, 'Lung Cancer from Smoking: Delays in Attitude, 1912–65', *American Journal of Industrial Medicine*, 1993, Vol. 23, p. 941; Colin White, 'Research on Smoking in Lung Cancer: A Landmark in the History of Chronic Disease Epidemiology', *Yale Journal of Biology and Medicine*, 1990, Vol. 63, pp. 29–46.
25. Richard Doll and A. Bradford Hill, 'Smoking and Carcinoma of the Lung', *BMJ*, 30 September 1950, pp. 740–9.
26. Ernest L. Wynder and E. A. Graham, 'Tobacco Smoking as a Possible Aetiologic Factor in Bronchiogenic Carcinoma', *JAMA*, 1950, Vol. 143, pp. 329–37.
27. A. Bradford Hill, 'Do You Smoke?', *BMJ*, 10 November 1951, p. 1157.
28. Richard Doll and A. Bradford Hill, 'Mortality of Doctors in Relation to Their Smoking Habits', *BMJ*, 26 June 1954, pp. 1451–5.
29. Richard Doll *et al.*, 'Mortality in Relation to Smoking: Forty Years' Observation on Male British Doctors', *BMJ*, 1994, Vol. 309, pp. 901–9. See also David Sharp, 'Cancer Prevention Tomorrow', *The Lancet*, 1993, Vol. 341, p. 486.
30. A. Bradford Hill, 'Heberden Oration, 1965: Reflections on the Controlled Trial', *Annals of the Rheumatic Diseases*, 1966, Vol. 25, pp. 107–13.

31. A. Bradford Hill, 'The Environment and Disease: Association or Causation?', *Proceedings of the Royal Society of Medicine*, 1965, Vol. 58, pp. 295–300.

32. Alvin R. Feinstein, 'Limitations of Randomised Trials', *Annals of Internal Medicine*, 1983, Vol. 99, pp. 544–50. See also Brian Cromie, 'The Feet of Clay of the Double-blind Trial', *The Lancet*, 1963, Vol. 2, pp. 994–7; H. A. F. Dudley, 'The Controlled Clinical Trial and the Advance of Reliable Knowledge: An Outsider Looks In', *BMJ*, 1983, Vol. 287, pp. 957–60; correspondence, M. Baum *et al.*, *BMJ*, 1983, Vol. 287, pp. 1216–18; Bruce G. Charlton, 'The Future of Clinical Research: From Mega-trials Towards Methodological Rigour and Representative Sampling', *Journal of Evaluation in Clinical Practice*, 1996, Vol. 2, pp. 159–69; John C. Bailar, 'The Promise and Problems of Meta-analysis', *NEJM*, 1997, Vol. 337, pp. 559–61; S. Blinkhorn, 'Meta Better', *Nature*, 1998, Vol. 392, pp. 671–2.

4: Chlorpromazine and the Revolution in Psychiatry

GENERAL READING

Arvid Carlsson, *Annual Review of Neuroscience*, 1978, Vol. 10, pp. 19–40

David Healy, 'The History of British Psychopharmacology', *150 Years of British Psychiatry, Vol. 2: The Aftermath*, ed. Hugh Freeman and German E. Berrios (Athlone Press, 1996)

'History of Psychopharmacology', *Journal of Psychopharmacology*, 1990, Vol. 4 (Special Issue)

Edward Shorter, *A History of Psychiatry* (Chichester: John Wiley & Sons, 1997)

REFERENCES

1. Brian Barraclough in conversation with David Clark, *Bulletin of the Royal College of Psychiatrists*, 1986, Vol. 10, pp. 42–9.

2. J. Elkes and C. Elkes, 'Effect of Chlorpromazine on the Behaviour of Chronically Overactive Psychotic Patients', *BMJ*, 4 September 1954, pp. 560–5.

3. F. Peters, *The World Next Door* (New York: Farrar, Straus & Giroux, 1949).

4. Barbara Freedman, 'The Subjective Experience of Perceptual and Cognitive Disturbances in Schizophrenia', *Archives of General Psychiatry*, 1974, Vol. 30, pp. 333–40. See also Robert Sommer, 'A Bibliography of Mental Patients' Autobiographies, 1960–82', *American Journal of Psychiatry*, 1983, Vol. 140, pp. 1051–4; Clare Creer and John Wing, 'Living With a Schizophrenic Patient', *British Journal of Hospital Medicine*, July 1975, pp. 73–85.

5. Giuseppe Epifanio in *Rivista di Patologia Nervosa e Mentale*, 1915, Vol. 20, pp. 273–308.
6. M. Sakel in *Wiener Medizinische Wochenschrift*, 1934, Vol. 84, pp. 112–13.
7. L. von Meduna in *Zeitschrift für die Gesante Neurologie*, 1935, p. 237.
8. Ugo Cerletti in *Archivio Generale di Neurologia*, 1938, Vol. 19, pp. 266–8.
9. E Moniz, 'Prefrontal Leucotomy and the Treatment of Mental Disorders', *American Journal of Psychiatry*, 1937, Vol. 93, pp. 1379–85.
10. Aubrey Lewis, 'On the Place of Physical Treatment in Psychiatry', *British Medical Bulletin*, 1945, Vol. 3, p. 614.
11. H. Rollin, 'Festina Lente: A Psychiatric Odyssey', The Memoire Club, *BMJ*, 1990.
12. H. Laborit in *Acta Chirurgica Belgica*, 1949, Vol. 48, pp. 485–92.
13. A comprehensive account of Laborit's discovery of chlorpromazine is to be found in Judith P. Swazey, *Chlorpromazine in Psychiatry: A Study of Therapeutic Innovation* (Cambridge, MA: MIT Press, 1974). See also Anne E. Caldwell, *Origins of Psychopharmacology from CPZ to LSD* (Charles C. Thomas, 1970).
14. Paul Charpentier and Simone Courvoisier in the *Journal of Clinical Experimental Psychopharmacology*, 1956, Vol. 17, p. 25.
15. Jean Delay, Pierre Deniker and J.-M. Harl, 'Utilisation en Therapeutique psychiatrique d'une phenothiazine d'action centrale élective', *Annales Medico-Psychologiques*, 1952, Vol. 110, pp. 112–20. See also E. Shorter, *A History of Psychiatry*.
16. Heinz Lehmann, 'The Introduction of Chlorpromazine to North America', *Psychiatric Journal at the University of Ottawa*, 1989, Vol. 14, pp. 263–5. See also interview with Heinz Lehmann by David Healey quoted in E. Shorter, *A History of Psychiatry*; Frances Frankenberg, 'The History of the Development of Antipsychotic Medication', *Psychiatric Clinics of North America*, 1994, Vol. 17, pp. 3531–40; H. E. Lehmann and G. E. Hanrahan, 'Chlorpromazine', *Archives of Neurology and Psychiatry*, 1954, Vol. 71, pp. 227–37; Douglas Goldman, 'Treatment of Psychotic States with Chlorpromazine', *JAMA*, 1955, Vol. 157, pp. 1274–8.
17. Roland Kuhn in *Schweizerich Medizinisch Wochenschrift*, 1957, Vol. 87, pp. 1135–40. See also G. E. Crane, 'Psychiatric Side-effects of Iproniazid', *American Journal of Psychiatry*, 1956, Vol. 112, pp. 494–501; John Cade, 'Lithium Salt in the Treatment of Psychotic Excitement', *Medical Journal of Australia*, 3 September 1949, pp. 349–51; L. H. Steinbach, 'The Benzodiazipene Story', *Progress in Drug Research*, 1978, Vol. 22, pp. 229–66.

18. J. Delay and P. Deniker, 'Neuroleptic Effects of Chlorpromazine in Therapeutics of Neuropsychiatry', *International Record of Medicine and GP Clinics*, May 1955, pp. 318–26.
19. Arvid Carlsson, 'Antipsychotic Agents: Eludication of Their Mode of Action', *Discoveries in Pharmacology, Vol. 1*, eds M. J. Parnham and J. Bruinvens (New York: Elsevier, 1983). See also T. J. Crow, 'Molecular Pathology of Schizophrenia: More Than One Disease Process?', *BMJ*, Vol. 280, pp. 66–8; 'Discussion: Positive and Negative Schizophrenic Symptoms and the Role of Dopamine', *British Journal of Psychiatry*, 1980, Vol. 127, pp. 379–86; Brenda Costall and Robert Naylor, 'Neurotransmitter Hypothesis of Schizophrenia', *The Psychopharmacology and Treatment of Schizophrenia*, eds P. B. Bradley and S. H. Hirsch (Oxford: OUP, 1986); G. W. Ashcroft *et al.*, 'Modified Amine Hypothesis for the Aetiology of Affective Disorders', *The Lancet*, 1972, Vol. 2, pp. 573–7; D. Healey, 'Schizophrenia: Basic, Release, Reactive and Defect Processes', *Human Psychopharmacology*; D. Healey, 'D1, D2 and D3', *British Journal of Psychiatry*, 1991, Vol. 159, pp. 319–24.
20. M. Shepherd in the *Journal of Psychopharmacology*, 1990, Vol. 4, pp. 131–5.

5: Open-Heart Surgery – The Last Frontier

GENERAL READING

Louis J. Acierno, *The History of Cardiology* (Carnforth: Parthenon, 1994)

Richard J. Bing (ed.), *Cardiology: The Evolution of the Science and the Art* (Reading: Harwood Academic, 1992)

Raymond Hurt, *The History of Cardiothoracic Surgery from Early Times* (Carnforth: Parthenon, 1996)

Stephen L. Johnson, *The History of Cardiac Surgery, 1896–1955* (Baltimore, MD: Johns Hopkins University Press, 1970)

Harris B. Shumacker, *The Evolution of Cardiac Surgery* (Bloomington, IN: Indiana University Press, 1992)

H. A. Snellen, *History and Perspectives of Cardiology* (Leiden: Leiden University Press, 1981)

REFERENCES

1. L. Eloesser, 'Milestones in Chest Surgery', *Journal of Thoracic and Cardiovascular Surgery*, 1970, Vol. 60, pp. 157–165.
2. Christian Barnard, *One Life* (Harrap, 1970).
3. H. B. Taussig and Alfred Blalock, 'Surgical Treatment of Malformation of the Heart', *JAMA*, 1945, Vol. 128, p. 189.

4. Letters from Lord Brock to Mark Ravitch (September 1965), cited by Raymond Hurt in *The History of Cardiothoracic Surgery*.

5. Lord Brock in H. A. Snellen (ed.), *History and Perspectives of Cardiology*.

6. R. C. Brock, 'Pulmonary Valvulotomy for the Relief of Congenital Pulmonary Stenosis', *BMJ*, 12 June 1948, p. 1121.

7. T. H. Sellors, 'Surgery of Pulmonary Stenosis', *The Lancet*, 1948, p. 998.

8. E. C. Cutler, 'Cardiotomy and Valvulotomy for Mitral Stenosis', *Boston Medical and Surgical Journal*, 1923, Vol. 188, pp. 1023–7.

9. H. S. Souttar, 'The Surgical Treatment of Mitral Stenosis', *BMJ*, 1925, Vol. 2, pp. 603–7.

10. W. P. Cleland, 'The Evolution of Cardiac Surgery in the United Kingdom', *Thorax*, 1983, Vol. 38, pp. 887–96.

11. D. E. Harken, 'Techniques for Approaching and Removing Foreign Bodies from Chambers of the Heart', *Surgery, Gynaecology and Obstetrics*, 1946, Vol. 83, pp. 117–25.

12. D. E. Harken *et al.*, 'The Surgical Treatment of Mitral Stenosis', *NEJM*, 1948, Vol. 239, pp. 891–909.

13. D. E. Harken, 'The Emergence of Cardiac Surgery', *Journal of Thoracic and Cardiovascular Surgery*, 1989, Vol. 98, pp. 805–13.

14. J. H. Gibbon, 'The Development of the Heart/Lung Apparatus', *American Journal of Surgery*, 1978, Vol. 135, pp. 608–19.

15. J. H. Gibbon, 'Medicine's Living History', *Medical World News*, 1972, Vol. 13, p. 47.

16. Quoted in Stephen L. Johnson, *The History of Cardiac Surgery, 1896–1955*.

17. J. H. Gibbon, 'Artificial Maintenance of the Circulation During Experimental Occlusion of the Pulmonary Artery', *Archives of Surgery*, 1937, Vol. 34, p. 1105. See also J. H. Gibbon, 'The Maintenance of Life During Experimental Occlusion of the Pulmonary Artery Followed by Survival', *Surgery, Gynaecology and Obstetrics*, 1939, Vol. 69, p. 602.

18. John W. Kirklin, 'The Middle 1950s and C. Walter Lillehai', *Journal of Thoracic and Cardiovascular Surgery*, 1989, Vol. 98, pp. 822–4.

19. J. H. Gibbon, 'Application of a Mechanical Heart and Lung Apparatus to Cardiac Surgery', *Minnesota Medicine*, 1954, Vol. 37, p. 171.

20. C. Walter Lillehai, 'A Personalised History of Extra Corporeal Circulation', *Transactions of the American Society for Artificial Organs*, 1982, Vol. 28, pp. 5–16.

21. H. E. Warden, 'C. Walter Lillehai: Pioneer Cardiac Surgeon',

Journal of Thoracic and Cardiovascular Surgery, 1989, Vol. 98, pp. 823–45.

22. Hugh McLeave, *The Risk Takers* (Frederick Miller, 1962).
23. C. Walter Lillehai, 'The Results of Direct Vision Closure of Ventricular Septal Defects in Eight Patients by Means of Controlled Cross-circulation', *Surgery, Gynaecology and Obstetrics*, 1955, pp. 147–465. See also C. Walter Lillehai, 'Direct Vision Intracardiac Surgical Correction of the Tetralogy of Fallot', *Annals of Surgery*, 1955, Vol. 142, pp. 418–45. (Lillehai subsequently reviewed the long-term results in 'The First Open-heart Repairs: A Thirty-year Follow-up', *Annals of Thoracic Surgery*, 1986, Vol. 41, pp. 4–21.)
24. Richard A. DeWall *et al.*, 'Simple Expendable Artificial Oxygenator for Open-heart Surgery', *Surgical Clinics of North America*, 1956, Vol. 36, pp. 1025–34.
25. C. Walter Lillehai, 'Cardio-pulmonary Bypass in Surgical Treatment of Congenital Acquired Cardiac Disease: Use in 305 Patients', *AMA Archives of Surgery*, 1957, Vol. 75, pp. 928–45. See also C. Walter Lillehai, 'Direct Vision Intracardiac Surgery in Man Using a Simple Disposal Artificial Oxygenator', *Diseases of the Chest*, 1956, Vol. 29, p. 128; John W. Kirklin *et al.*, 'Intracardiac Surgery With the Aid of a Mechanical Pump/Oxygenator System (Gibbon Type), Report of 8 Cases', *PSMMC*, 1955, Vol. 30, pp. 201–6; John W. Kirklin *et al.*, 'Surgical Treatment for the Tetralogy of Fallot', *Journal of Thoracic and Cardiovascular Surgery*, 1959, Vol. 37, pp. 22–51.
26. John W. Kirklin, 'The Middle 1950s and C. Walter Lillehai', *Journal of Thoracic and Cardiovascular Surgery*, 1989, Vol. 98, pp. 822–4.
27. Harris B. Shumacker, *The Evolution of Cardiac Surgery*.
28. Donald Longmore, *Towards Safer Cardiac Surgery* (MTP Press, 1981).
29. Christian Barnard, 'The Operation', *South African Medical Journal*, 1967, Vol. 41, pp. 1271–4.

6: Transplanting Kidneys

GENERAL READING

Leslie Brent, 'Transplantation: Some British Pioneers', *Journal of the Royal College of Physicians*, 1997, Vol. 31, pp. 434–41

Sir Roy Calne, *The Ultimate Gift* (Headline, 1998)

Francis D. Moore, *A Miracle and a Privilege: Recounting a Half-Century of Surgical Advance* (Washington, DC: Joseph Henry, 1995)

Joseph E. Murray, 'Human Organ Transplantation: Background and Consequences', *Science*, 1992, Vol. 256, pp. 1411–16

Tony Stark, *Knife to the Heart: The Story of Transplant Surgery* (Macmillan, 1996)

Thomas Starzl, 'Personal Reflections in Transplantation', *Surgical Clinics of North America*, 1978, Vol. 58, pp. 879–93

——, *The Puzzle People: Memoirs of a Transplant Surgeon* (Pittsburgh, PA: University of Pittsburgh Press, 1992)

REFERENCES

1. Peter Medawar, *Memoir of a Thinking Radish* (Oxford: OUP, 1986).
2. T. Gibson and P. Medawar, 'The Fate of Skin Homografts in Man', *Journal of Anatomy*, 1942/3, Vol. 77, p. 299.
3. R. E. Billingham, L. Brent and P. Medawar, '"Actively Acquired Tolerance" of Foreign Cells', *Nature*, 1953, Vol. 172, p. 603. See also P. Medawar, 'A Biological Analysis of Individuality' (reprinted from the *Times Science Review*), *Clinical Orthopaedics and Related Research*, 1996, No. 326, pp. 5–10; P. Medawar, 'Immunological Tolerance', *Nobel Lectures: Physiology or Medicine, 1942–62* (New York: Elsevier, 1964).
4. R. Y. Calne, 'Organ Transplantation: From Laboratory to Clinic', *BMJ*, 1985, Vol. 291, pp. 1751–4.
5. W. J. Kolff and H. J. Berk, 'The Artificial Kidney: Dialysis With a Great Area', *Acta Medica Scandanavica*, 1944, Vol. CXVII, pp. 121–34. See also W. J. Kolff, 'First Clinical Experience With the Artificial Kidney', *Annals of Internal Medicine*, 1965, Vol. 62, pp. 608–19; Patrick McBride, *The Development of Haemodialysis and Peritoneal Dialysis, in Clinical Dialysis*, ed. Allen R. Nissenson (New York: Prentice Hall, 1990).
6. Tony Stark, *Knife to the Heart.*
7. Alexis Carrell, letter to Theodore Cocher, 9 May 1914, quoted in Theodore Malinin, *Surgery and Life.* See also Note 6.
8. Joseph E. Murray, 'Reflections on the First Successful Kidney Transplantation', *World Journal of Surgery*, 1982, Vol. 6, pp. 372–6.
9. Frank Parsons, 'Origins of Haemodialysis in Great Britain', *BMJ*, 1989, Vol. 299, pp. 1557–60.
10. J. P. Merrill, J. E. Murray *et al.*, 'Successful Homotransplantation of the Human Kidney Between Identical Twins', *JAMA*, 1956, Vol. 160, p. 277.
11. See Note 8.
12. Human Kidney Transplant Conference, *Transplantation Proceedings*, 1964, Vol. 2, pp. 147–65, 581–600.
13. Willard E. Goodwin *et al.*, 'Human Renal Transplantation', *Journal of Urology*, 1963, Vol. 68, pp. 13–24.
14. J. H. Burchenal *et al.*, 'Clinical Evaluation of 6 mercaptopurine in the Treatment of Leukaemia and Other Diseases', *Blood*, 1953,

Vol. 8, pp. 966–99. See also Gertrude B. Elion, 'The Purine Path of Chemotherapy', *Science*, 7 April 1989, pp. 41–47; George Hitchings, 'Chemotherapy and Comparative Biochemistry', *Cancer Research*, 1969, Vol. 29, pp. 1895–903.

15. Robert Schwartz and William Dameshek, 'Drug-induced Immunological Tolerance', *Nature*, 1959, Vol. 183, pp. 1682–3. See also Robert Schwartz, 'Design and Achievement in Chemotherapy', *A Symposium in Honour of George Hitchings* (Burroughs-Wellcome, 1976).

16. See Note 6.

17. John Hopewell, 'Witness Seminar on the History of Early Renal Transplantation', Wellcome Institute for the History of Medicine, 13 September 1994.

18. R. Calne, 'The Rejection of Renal Homografts Inhibition in Dogs by 6 mercaptopurine', *The Lancet*, 1960, pp. 417–18.

19. John Hopewell *et al.*, 'Three Clinical Cases of Renal Transplantation', *BMJ*, 5 November 1964, pp. 411–13.

20. See Note 12.

21. Joseph E. Murray *et al.*, 'The Long Survival of Human/Kidney Homografts by Immunosuppressive Drug Therapy', *NEJM*, 1963, Vol. 268, pp. 1315–23.

22. Thomas E. Starzl, *The Puzzle People*.

23. See Note 6.

24. Thomas E. Starzl, 'Reversal of Rejection in Human Renal Homografts with Subsequent Development of Homograft Tolerance', *Surgery, Gynaecology and Obstetrics*, 1963, Vol. 117, pp. 385–95. (The theoretical potential of steroids as immunosuppressant drugs was first identified by Medawar in 1951. See R. E. Billingham *et al.*, 'Effect of Locally Applied Cortisone Acetate on Survival of Skin Homografts in Rabbits', *BMJ*, 3 November 1951, pp. 1049–53.)

25. Thomas E. Starzl *et al.*, 'Long-term (25-year) Survival After Renal Homo-transplantation: The World Experience', *Transplantation Proceedings*, 1990, Vol. 22, pp. 2361–5.

26. J. F. Borel, 'Effect of the New Anti-lymphocytic Peptide Cyclosporine A in Animals', *Immunology*, 1977, Vol. 32, pp. 1017–25.

7: The Triumph of Prevention – The Case of Strokes

GENERAL READING

William S. Fields and Noreen Lemak, *A History of Stroke: Its Recognition and Treatment* (Oxford: OUP, 1989)

Nicholas Postel-Vinay (ed.), *A Century of Arterial Hypertension, 1896–1996* (Chichester: John Wiley & Sons, 1996)

REFERENCES

1. M. Hamilton and E. N. Thompson, 'The Role of Blood Pressure Control in Preventing Complications of Hypertension', *The Lancet*, 1964, Vol. 1, pp. 235–9.
2. VA Co-operative Study Group, 'Effects of Treatment on Morbidity in Hypertension', *JAMA*, 1967, Vol. 202, pp. 1028–33.
3. Franz Messerli, 'This Day Fifty Years Ago', *NEJM*, 1995, Vol. 332, pp. 1038–9.
4. J. Hart, 'While America Slept', *National Review*, 15 September 1989, p. 32.
5. J. W. Norris, 'Stalin's Stroke', *Neurology*, 1994, Vol. 44, pp. 765–6.
6. W. Kempner, 'Treatment of Hypertensive Vascular Disease With Rice Diet', *AJM*, 1948, Vol. 4, pp. 545–77.
7. G. W. Pickering, *High Blood Pressure* (Churchill-Livingstone, 1968).
8. Herbert Chasis, 'Salt and Protein Restriction: Effects on Blood Pressure', *JAMA*, 1950, Vol. 142, p. 711.
9. R. H. Smithwick, 'Splanchnicectomy for Essential Hypertension: Results in 1,266 cases', *JAMA*, 1953, Vol. 152, pp. 1501–4.
10. William B. Schwartz, 'The Effect of Sulfanilamide on Salt and Water Excretion in Congestive Heart Failure', *NEJM*, 1949, Vol. 240, p. 173.
11. Karl H. Beyer, 'Discovery of the Thiazides: Where Biology and Chemistry Meet', *Perspectives in Biology and Medicine*, Spring 1977, pp. 410–20.
12. Edward D. Freis *et al.*, 'Treatment of Essential Hypertension With Chlorothiazide', *JAMA*, 1958, Vol. 166, pp. 137–41.
13. Raymond P. Ahlquist, 'A Study of the Adrenotropic Receptors', *American Journal of Physiology*, 1948, Vol. 153, pp. 586–98.
14. J. W. Black and J. S. Stephenson, 'Pharmacology of a New Adrenergic Beta-receptor Blocking Compound', *The Lancet*, 1962, Vol. 2, pp. 311–15.
15. B. N. C. Pritchard and P. M. S. Gillam, 'Treatment of Hypertension With Propranolol', *BMJ*, 4 January 1969, pp. 7–15. See also B. N. C. Pritchard, 'Beta Adrenergic Receptor Blockage in Hypertension: Past, Present and Future', *British Journal of Clinical Pharmacology*, 1978, Vol. 5, pp. 379–99.
16. Nicholas Postel-Vinay (ed.), *A Century of Arterial Hypertension*.
17. J. D. Swales, *Platt Versus Pickering: An Episode of Recent Medical History* (Keynes Press, 1985).
18. Jeremiah Stamler *et al.*, 'Hypertension Screening of One Million Americans', *JAMA*, 1976, Vol. 235, p. 229.
19. R. Brian Haynes *et al.*, 'Increased Absenteeism from Work after

Detection and Labelling of Hypertensive Patients', *NEJM*, 1978, Vol. 229, pp. 741–5.

20. MRC, 'Adverse Reactions to Bendrofluazide and Propranolol for the Treatment of Mild Hypertension', *The Lancet*, 1981, Vol. 2, pp. 539–43.

21. MRC, 'MRC Trial of Mild Hypertension: Principal Results', *BMJ*, 1985, Vol. 291, pp. 97–103.

22. N. M. Kaplan, *Clinical Hypertension* (Philadelphia, PA: Williams & Wilkins, 1994).

23. Morris J. Brown, 'The Causes of Essential Hypertension', *British Journal of Clinical Pharmacology*, 1996, Vol. 42, pp. 21–7.

8: Curing Childhood Cancer

GENERAL READING

J. H. Burchenal, 'Historic Development of Cancer Chemotherapy', *Seminars in Oncology*, 1977, Vol. 4, pp. 135–47

A. H. Calvert (ed.), 'A Critical Assessment of Chemotherapy', *Cancer Surveys*, 1989, Vol. 3

George J. Hill, 'Historic Milestones in Cancer Surgery', *Seminars in Oncology*, 1979, Vol. 6

Henry S. Kaplan, 'Historic Milestones in Radiobiology', *Seminars in Oncology*, 1979, Vol. 6

Irwin Krakoff, 'Progress and Prospects in Cancer Treatment', *Journal of Clinical Oncology*, 1994, Vol. 12, pp. 432–8

James S. Olson, *The History of Cancer: An Annotated Bibliography* (Westport, CT: Greenwood Press, 1989)

Grant Taylor (ed.), *Pioneers of Paediatric Oncology* (Austin, TX: University of Texas Press, 1990)

Maxwell M. Wintrobe, *Haematology: The Blossoming of a Science* (Lea & Febiger, 1985)

C. Gordon Zubrod, 'Historic Milestones in Curative Chemotherapy', *Seminars in Oncology*, 1979, Vol. 6

REFERENCES

1. David Galton, Sir Eric Sharp lecture (unpublished).

2. R. J. Araur *et al.*, 'Central Nervous System Therapy and Combination Chemotherapy of Childhood Lymphocytic Leukaemia', *Blood*, 1971, Vol. 37, pp. 272–81.

3. F. N. Hersh, 'Causes of Death in Acute Leukaemia', *JAMA*, 1965, Vol. 193, pp. 99–103. See also Joseph V. Simone, 'Fatalities During Remission of Childhood Leukaemia', *Blood*, 1972, Vol. 39, pp. 759–69.

4. M. L. Murphy *et al.*, 'Long-term Survival With Acute

Leukaemia', *Proceedings of the American Association for Cancer Research*, 1963, p. 46.

5. Wolf Zuelzer, 'Therapy of Acute Leukaemia in Childhood', *Proceedings of the International Conference on Leukaemia Lymphoma*, ed. Chris Zarafonetis (Lea & Febiger, 1968).

6. Donald Pinkel, *Treatment of Acute Lymphocytic Leukaemia* (Leukaemia Research Fund, 1973).

7. Editorial, 'Radical Treatment of Acute Leukaemia in Childhood', *The Lancet*, 1972, Vol. 2, p. 910.

8. E. B. Kurmbahaar, 'The Blood and Bone Marrow in Yellow Gas (Mustard Gas Poisoning)', *Journal of Medical Research*, 1919, Vol. 40, pp. 497–507.

9. Stewart F. Alexander, 'Medical Report of the Bari Harbour Mustard Casualties', *Military Surgeon*, 1947, Vol. 101, p. 1216.

10. Louis S. Goodman *et al.*, 'Nitrogen Mustard Therapy', *JAMA*, 1946, Vol. 132, p. 12. See also Alfred Gilman, 'The Initial Clinical Trial of Nitrogen Mustard', *American Journal of Surgery*, 1963, Vol. 105, pp. 574–8.

11. See Note 1.

12. Cornelius P. Rhoads, 'The Sword and the Ploughshare', *Journal of the Mount Sinai Hospital*, 1946, Vol. 13, pp. 299–309.

13. Lucy Wills, 'The Nature of the Haemopoetic Factor in Marmite', *The Lancet*, 1933, Vol. 2, pp. 1283–4.

14. R. B. Angier *et al.*, 'The Structure and Synthesis of the Liver', *Science*, 1946, Vol. 103, pp. 667–9.

15. Sidney Farber *et al.*, 'The Action of Pterolyglutamic Conjugates on Man', *Science*, 19 December 1947, pp. 619–21.

16. Sidney Farber *et al.*, 'Temporary Remissions in Acute Leukaemia in Children Produced by Folic Acid Antagonist Aminopterin', *NEJM*, 1948, Vol. 238, pp. 787–93.

17. Sidney Farber *et al.*, 'The Effect of ACTH in Acute Leukaemia in Childhood', *Proceedings of the First Clinical ACTH Conference*, ed. J. A. Churchill, 1950.

18. Sidney Farber *et al.*, 'Chemotherapy in the Treatment of Leukaemia and Wilm's Tumour', *JAMA*, 1966, Vol. 198, pp. 154–64.

19. Ronald Bodley Scott, 'Cancer Chemotherapy: The First Twenty-five Years', *BMJ*, 31 October 1970, pp. 259–64.

20. J. H. Burchenal, 'Clinical Evaluation of a New Anti-metabolite, 6 mercaptopurine in the Treatment of Leukaemia and Other Diseases', *Blood*, 1953, Vol. 8, pp. 965–96.

21. J. D. Broome, 'Evidence that the L-Asparaginase Activity of Guinea Pig Serum is Responsible for Anti-lymphoma Effect',

Nature, 1961, Vol. 181, p. 1114. See also Joseph M. Mill *et al.*, 'L-Asparaginase Therapy for Leukaemia and Other Malignant Neoplasms', *JAMA*, 1967, Vol. 202, pp. 116–22.

22. M. E. Hodes *et al.*, 'Vincaleukoblastine Preliminary Clinical Studies', *Cancer Research*, 1960, Vol. 20, p. 1041.

23. Barnett Rosenberg, 'Inhibition of Cell Division in E.Coli by Electrolysis Products from a Platinum Electrode', *Nature*, 1965, Vol. 205, p. 698. See also J. M. Hill, 'Cisplatinous Therapy of Various Malignant Diseases', *Proceedings of the American Association of Cancer Research*, 1972, p. 20.

24. 'History of the Cancer Chemotherapy Programme', *Cancer Chemotherapy Reports*, 1966, Vol. 50, pp. 349–81. See also Alfred Gelhorn, 'Invited Remarks on the Current Status of Research in Clinical Cancer Chemotherapy', *Cancer Chemotherapy Reports*, 1959, Vol. 5, p. 1217.

25. Min C. Li, 'Effect of Methotrexate Therapy Upon Choriocarcinoma', *Proceedings of the Society for Experimental Biology and Medicine*, 1956, Vol. 93, p. 361. See also Min C. Li, 'Historical Background of Successful Chemotherapy for Advanced Gestational Tumours', *AJOG*, 1979, Vol. 135, pp. 266–72; Min C. Li, 'Effects of Combined Drug Therapy on Metastatic Cancer of the Testes', *JAMA*, 1960, Vol. 174, pp. 145–53.

26. Margaret P. Sullivan, 'Intra-cranial Complications With Leukaemia in Childhood', *Paediatrics*, 1957, Vol. 20, pp. 757–81.

27. James A. Whiteside, 'Intrathecal Amethopterin in Neurological Manifestations of Leukaemia', *Archives of Internal Medicine*, 1958, Vol. 101, pp. 279–85. See also Ralph Johnson, 'An Experimental Therapeutic Approach to Leukaemia in Mice: Combined Chemotherapy and Central Nervous System Irradiation', *General National Cancer Institute*, 1964, Vol. 32, pp. 1333–9.

28. A. Spiers, personal communication, 1997.

29. Emil Frei III *et al.*, 'Studies of Sequential and Combination Therapy in Acute Leukaemia: 6-MP and Methotrexate', *Blood*, 1961, Vol. 18, pp. 431–54. See also Emil Frei III *et al.*, 'The Effectiveness of Combinations of Anti-leukaemic Agents in Inducing and Maintaining Remission in Children With Acute Leukaemia', *Blood*, 1965, Vol. 26, pp. 642–56.

30. Sidney Farber *et al.*, 'Advances in Chemotherapy of Cancer in Man', *Advances of Cancer Research*, ed. Jessie P. Greenstein (New York: Academic Post, 1956).

31. Howard Skipper, 'On the Criteria and Kinetics Associated with "Curability of Experimental Leukaemia"', *Cancer Chemotherapy Reports*, 1964, No. 34, pp. 65, 328.

32. William S. Wilcox, 'The Last Surviving Cancer Cell: The Chances of Killing It', *Cancer Chemotherapy Reports*, 1966, Vol. 50, pp. 541–2.
33. P. George and D. Pinkel, 'CNS Radiation in Children with Acute Lymphocytic Leukaemia in Remission', *Proceedings of the American Association for Cancer Research*, 1965, p. 22.
34. See Note 2.
35. Gaston K. Revera, 'Treatment of Acute Lymphoblastic Leukaemia: Thirty Years' Experience at St Jude's Children Research Hospital', *NEJM*, 1993, Vol. 329, pp. 1289–94.
36. Donald Pinkel, 'Treatment of Acute Lymphocytic Leukaemia', *Cancer*, 1979, Vol. 43, pp. 1128–37.
37. K. D. Bagshawe, 'Successful Drug Therapy in Cancer', *Modern Trends in Oncology*, ed. Ronald Raven (Butterworth, 1973).
38. Wolf Zuelzer, 'Therapy of Acute Leukaemia in Childhood', *Proceedings of the International Conference on Leukaemia Lymphoma*, ed. Chris Zarafonetis (Lea & Febiger, 1968).
39. James T. Patterson, *The Dread Disease: Cancer and Modern American Culture* (Cambridge, MA: Harvard University Press, 1987).
40. C. Gordon Zubrod, 'Historic Milestones in Curative Chemotherapy', *Seminars in Oncology*, 1979, Vol. 6, pp. 490–506.
41. Emil Frei III, 'Clinical Cancer Research: An Embattled Species', *Cancer*, 1982, Vol. 50, pp. 1979–92.
42. A. H. Lang *et al.*, 'Treatment of Inoperable Carcinoma of the Bronchus', *The Lancet*, 1975, Vol. 2, pp. 1161–4.
43. Colin P. Beg, 'Clinical Trials and Drugs Toxicity in the Elderly', *Cancer*, 1983, Vol. 52, pp. 1896–92.
44. J. S. Malpas, 'Are We All Oncologists?', *Journal of the Royal College of Physicians of London*, 1984, Vol. 18, p. 82.
45. Everett Vokes, 'Combined Modality Therapy of Solid Tumours', *The Lancet*, 1997, SII, pp. 4–5.

9: The First 'Test-Tube' Baby

GENERAL READING

Serena Chen and Edward E. Wallach, 'Five Decades of Progress in Management of the Infertile Couple', *Fertility and Sterility*, 1994, Vol. 62, pp. 665–85

R. G. Edwards and I. Craft, 'Development of Assisted Conception in Assisted Human Conception', *British Medical Bulletin*, 1990, Vol. 46, pp. 565–80

Robert Edwards and Patrick Steptoe, *A Matter of Life* (Sphere, 1981)

Roy Greep, 'Gonadotrophins', *Endocrinology: People and Ideas*, ed. S. M. McCann (New York: American Physiological Society, 1988)

Maureen McCall, 'Pursuing Conception', *Canadian Medical Association Journal*, 1996, Vol. 154, pp. 1075–9 (a personal account of undergoing In Vitro Fertilisation)

V. C. Medvei, *The History of Medical Endocrinology* (Carnforth: Parthenon, 1993)

Michael J. O'Dowd and Elliot E. Philipp, *A History of Obstetrics and Gynaecology* (Carnforth: Parthenon, 1994)

Nicola Perone, 'In Vitro Fertilisation and Embryo Transfer: A Historical Perspective', *Journal of Reproductive Medicine*, 1994, Vol. 39, pp. 695–700

REFERENCES

 1. Robert Edwards and Patrick Steptoe, *A Matter of Life*.
 2. Editorial, 'Conception in a Watch Glass', *NEJM*, 1937, Vol. 217, p. 678.
 3. G. Pincus and E. V. Enzmann, 'Can Mammalian Eggs Undergo Normal Development In Vitro?', *Proceedings in the National Academy of Science*, 1934, Vol. 20, pp. 121–2.
 4. Gregory Pincus and Barbara Saunders, 'The Comparative Behaviour of Mammalian Eggs In Vivo and In Vitro', *Anatomical Record*, 1939, Vol. 75, pp. 537–42.
 5. John Rock and Miriam Menkin, 'In Vitro Fertilisation and Cleavage of Human Ovarian Eggs', *Science*, 1944, Vol. 100, pp. 105–7. See also Miriam Menkin and John Rock, 'In Vitro Fertilisation and Cleavage of Human Ovarian Eggs', *AJOG*, 1948, Vol. 55, pp. 440–51.
 6. Margaret Marsh and Wanda Ronner, *The Empty Cradle: Infertility in America* (Baltimore, MD: Johns Hopkins University Press, 1996).
 7. M. C. Chang, 'Fertilising Capacity of Spermatazoa Deposited into the Fallopian Tubes', *Nature*, 1951, Vol. 168, pp. 697–8.
 8. R. G. Edwards, 'Meisos in Ovarian Oocytes of Adult Mammals', *Nature*, 1962, Vol. 196, pp. 446–50.
 9. See Note 1.
 10. Ibid.
 11. Ibid.
 12. R. G. Edwards, 'Maturation In Vitro of Human Ovarian Oocytes', *The Lancet*, 1965, Vol. 2, pp. 926–9. See also R. G. Edwards, 'Maturation In Vitro of Mice, Sheep, Cow, Pig, Rhesus Monkey and Human Ovarian Oocytes', *Nature*, 1965, Vol. 208, pp. 349–51.
 13. R. G. Edwards, Roger Donohue *et al.*, 'Preliminary Attempts to Fertilise Human Oocytes Matured In Vitro', *AJOG*, 1966, Vol. 96, pp. 192–200.

14. R. G. Edwards, B. D. Bavister, 'Early Stages of Fertilisation In Vitro of Human Oocytes Matured In Vitro', *Nature*, 1969, Vol. 221, pp. 632–5.

15. Dorothy Price, 'Feedback Control of Gonadal Hormones: Evolution of the Concept', *Pioneers in Neuro Endocrinology*, ed. Joseph Meites (New York: Plenum, 1975).

16. R. Borth and B. Lunenfield, 'Activitie Gonadotrope d'un extrait d'urines de femmes en menopause', *Experientia*, 1954, Vol. X, pp. 266–8.

17. J. K. Butler, 'Clinical Results With Human Gonadatrophins in Anovulation', *Postgraduate Medical Journal*, 1972, Vol. 48, pp. 27–32. See also B. Lunenfield, 'Historic Aspects of Gonadotropins in the Induction of Ovulation', *Ovulation*, ed. Robert Greenblatt (Philadelphia, PA: Lippincott, 1966).

18. Editorial, 'Pituitary Gonadatrophins and Multiple Pregnancy', *The Lancet*, 1965, Vol. 2, p. 276.

19. P. C. Steptoe, 'Laparoscopy and Ovulation', *The Lancet*, 1968, Vol. 2, p. 913. See also R. G. Edwards, 'Tribute to Patrick Steptoe: Beginnings of Laparoscopy', *Human Reproduction*, 1989, Vol. 4 (supplement), p. 129.

20. Patrick Steptoe, *Laparoscopy in Gynaecology* (E & S Livingstone, 1967).

21. See Note 1.

22. R. G. Edwards and Ruth Fowler, 'Human Embryos in the Laboratory', *Scientific American*, 1997, Vol. 223 (6), pp. 45–54. See also P. C. Steptoe and R. G. Edwards, 'Laparoscopic Recovery of Pre-ovulatory Human Ovocytes, After Priming of Ovaries With Gonadatrophins', *The Lancet*, 1970, Vol. 1, pp. 683–5; R. G. Edwards, P. C. Steptoe and J. M. Purdy, 'Fertilisation and Cleavage In Vitro of Pre-ovulator Human Oocytes', *Nature*, 1970, Vol. 227, pp. 1307–9; P. C. Steptoe, R. G. Edwards and J. M. Purdy, 'Human Blastocysts Grown in Culture', *Nature*, 1971, Vol. 229, pp. 132–3.

23. See Note 1.

24. Ibid.

25. R. G. Edwards, 'Studies on Human Conception', *AJOG*, 1973, Vol. 117, pp. 587–601. See also R. G. Edwards and P. C. Steptoe, 'Control of Human Ovulation, Fertilisation and Implantation', *Proceedings of the Royal Society of Medicine*, 1974, Vol. 67, pp. 932–6.

26. P. C. Steptoe and R. G. Edwards, 'Reimplantation of a Human Embryo With Subsequent Tubal Pregnancy', *The Lancet*, 1976, Vol. 1, pp. 880–2.

27. P. C. Steptoe and R. G. Edwards, 'Birth After the Reimplantation of a Human Embryo', *The Lancet*, 1978, Vol. 2, p. 366. See also R. G. Edwards, P. C. Steptoe and J. M. Purdy, 'Establishing Full-term Human Pregnancy Using Cleaving Embryos Grown In Vitro', *British Journal of Obstetrics and Gynaecology*, 1980, Vol. 87, pp. 737–68.

28. A. O. Trounson *et al.*, 'Pregnancies in Humans by Fertilisation In Vitro and Embryo Transfer in the Controlled Ovulatory Cycle', *Science*, 1981, Vol. 212, pp. 681–2. See also Howard W. Jones *et al.*, 'Three Years of In Vitro Fertilisation', *Fertility and Sterility*, 1984, Vol. 42, pp. 826–34; R. Fleming and J. R. T. Coutts, 'Induction of Multiple Follicular Development for IVF Assisted Human Conception', *British Medical Bulletin*, 1990, Vol. 46, pp. 596–616.

29. P. C. Steptoe, R. G. Edwards and D. E. Walters, 'Observations of 767 Clinical Pregnancies and 500 Births After Human In Vitro Fertilisation', *Human Reproduction*, 1986, Vol. 1, pp. 89–94.

10: Helicobacter – The Cause of Peptic Ulcer

GENERAL READING

Basil Hirschowitz, 'History of Acid-peptic Diseases', *The Growth of Gastroenterological Knowledge During the Twentieth Century*, ed. Joseph Kirsner (Lea & Febiger, 1994)

C. S. Goodwin, 'Historical and Microbiological Perspectives', *Helicobacter Pylori Infection*, eds T. C. Northfield *et al.* (Dordrecht: Kluwer Academic, 1993)

Robert J. Hopkins, 'Helicobacter Pylori: The Missing Link in Perspective', *AJM*, 1994, Vol. 97, pp. 265–77

Howard M. Spiro, 'Peptic Ulcer: Moynihan's or Marshall's Disease', *The Lancet*, 1998, Vol. 352, pp. 645–6

REFERENCES

1. Barry J. Marshall *et al.*, 'Attempt to Fulfil Koch's Postulates for Pyloric Campylobacter', *Medical Journal of Australia*, 1985, Vol. 142, pp. 436–9.

2. Lawrence K. Altman, *Who Goes First?* (Thorsons, 1988).

3. R. A. Giannela *et al.*, 'Gastric Acid Barrier to Ingested Micro-organisms in Man', *Gut*, 1972, Vol. 13, pp. 251–6.

4. F. Alexander, 'Influences of Psychological Factors upon Gastrointestinal Disturbances', *Psychoanalytical Quarterly*, 1935, Vol. 3, p. 501.

5. F. Goldberg, *Family Influences in Psychosomatic Illness* (Tavistock Press, 1958).

6. S. Wolff and H. G. Wolff, *Human Gastric Function* (Oxford: OUP, 1943).

7. W. Porter *et al.*, 'Some Experimental Observations on the Gastrointestinal Lesions in Behaviourally Conditioned Monkeys', *Psychosomatic Medicine*, 1958, Vol. 20, p. 379.

8. Albert Mendeloff, 'What Has Been Happening to Duodenal Ulcers?', *Gastroenterology*, 1974, Vol. 67, pp. 1020–2.

9. J. Robin Warren, 'Unidentified Curved Bacilli in Gastric Epithelium in Active Chronic Gastritis', *The Lancet*, 1983, Vol. 1, pp. 1273–5.

10. B. J. Marshall, 'History of the Discovery of C.Pylori', *C.Pylori in Gastritis and Peptic Ulcer Disease*, ed. M. J. Blaser (New York: Igaku-Shoin, 1989).

11. B. J. Marshall and J. Robin Warren, 'Unidentified Curved Bacilli in the Stomach of Patients With Gastritis and Peptic Ulceration', *The Lancet*, 1984, Vol. 1, pp. 1311–14.

12. C. S. Goodwin, 'Historical and Microbiological Perspectives', *Helicobacter Pylori Infection*, eds T. C. Northfield *et al.*

13. K. T. Wormsley, 'Relapsed Duodenal Ulcer', *BMJ*, 1986, Vol. 293, p. 150.

14. E. A. J. Rauws and G. N. J. Tytgat, 'Cure of Duodenal Ulcer Associated With Eradication of H.Pylori', *The Lancet*, 1990, Vol. 335, pp. 1233–5.

15. Eurogast Study Group, 'An International Association Between H.Pylori Infection and Gastric Cancer', *The Lancet*, 1993, Vol. 341, pp. 1359–62. See also J. Parsonnet *et al.*, 'Helicobacter Pylori Infection and the Risk of Gastric Carcinoma', *NEJM*, 1991, Vol. 4325, pp. 127–31.

16. M. Stolte, 'Healing Gastric Malt Lymphomas by Eradicating H.Pylori', *The Lancet*, 1993, Vol. 2, p. 568.

17. Bruce E. Dunne, 'Pathogenic Mechanisms in H.Pylori Infection', *Gastroenterology Clinics of North America*, 1993, Vol. 22, pp. 43–59. See also G. N. J. Tytgat *et al.*, 'H.Pylori Infection and Duodenal Ulcer Disease', *Gastroenterology Clinics of North America*, 1993, Vol. 22, pp. 127–41.

18. J. V. Joossens, 'Diet and the Environment in the Etiology of Gastric Cancers', *Frontiers of Gastrointestinal Cancer*, ed. R. H. Riddle (New York: Elsevier, 1984), pp. 167–283.

19. David Forman and Richard Doll, 'Nitrates and Nitrites in Gastric Cancer in Great Britain', *Nature*, 1985, Vol. 313, pp. 620–5.

Part 1: The Rise

2: Clinical Science – A New Ideology for Medicine

GENERAL READING

Christopher C. Booth, 'Clinical Research', *Historical Perspectives on the Role of the MRC*, ed. J. Austoker and L. Bryder (Oxford: OUP, 1989)

Irving Ladimer (ed.), *Clinical Investigation in Medicine: Legal, Ethical and Moral Aspects* (Oxford: OUP, 1960)

REFERENCES

1. Christopher C. Booth, 'Medical Science and Technology at the Royal Postgraduate Medical School: The First Fifty Years', *BMJ*, 1985, Vol. 291, pp. 1771–9.
2. E. G. L. Bywaters, 'Crush Injuries With Impairment of Renal Function', *BMJ*, 22 March 1941, pp. 427–35.
3. J. H. Dible, John McMichael and S. P. V. Sherlock, 'Pathology of Acute Hepatitis: Aspiration Biopsy Studies of Epidemic, Arseno-therapy and Serum Jaundice', *The Lancet*, 1943, Vol. 2, pp. 402–8.
4. Henry Barcroft and John McMichael, 'Post-haemorrhagic Fainting: Study by Cardiac Output and Forearm Flow', *The Lancet*, 1944, Vol. 1, pp. 489–90.
5. Sir Thomas Horder, *Munk's Roll* (Royal College of Physicians, 1968).
6. Mervyn Horder, *The Little Genius: A Memoir of the First Lord Horder* (Duckworth, 1966).
7. Paul White, *My Life in Medicine: An Autobiographical Memoir* (Boston, MA: Gambit, 1971), quoted in Arthur Hollman, *Sir Thomas Lewis* (Berlin: Springer-Verlag, 1996).
8. Arthur Hollman, 'Sir Thomas Lewis: Clinical Scientist and Cardiologist, 1881–1945', *Journal of Medical Biography*, 1994, Vol. 2, pp. 63–70.
9. Christopher C. Booth, 'Clinical Research', *Historical Perspectives on the Role of the MRC*, ed. J. Austoker and L. Bryder.
10. Renée C. Fox and Judith P. Swazey, *The Courage to Fail: A Social View of Organ Transplants and Dialysis* (Chicago, IL: University of Chicago Press, 1978).
11. Hugh McLeave, *A Time to Heal: The Life of Ian Aird, Surgeon* (Heinemann, 1964).
12. See Note 1.
13. M. H. Pappworth, *Human Guinea Pigs* (Routledge & Kegan Paul, 1966).
14. M. H. Pappworth, *A Primer of Medicine* (Butterworth, 1963).

15. W. H. Ogilvie, 'Whither Medicine?', *The Lancet*, 1952, Vol. 2, p. 820.

3: A Cornucopia of New Drugs

GENERAL READING

Karl H. Beyer, *The Discovery, Development and Delivery of New Drugs* (SP Medical & Scientific Books, 1978)

Frank H. Clarke, *How Modern Medicines are Discovered* (Futura, 1973)

R. D. Mann, *A Textbook of Pharmaceutical Medicine* (Carnforth: Parthenon, 1993)

M. J. Parnham and J. Bruinvels, *Discoveries in Pharmacology, Vols 1–3* (New York: Elsevier, 1986)

David Schwartzman, *Innovation in the Pharmaceutical Industry* (Baltimore, MD: Johns Hopkins University Press, 1976)

Walter Sneader, *Drug Discovery* (Chichester: John Wiley & Sons, 1985)

——, *Drug Prototypes and Their Exploitation* (Chichester: John Wiley & Sons, 1996)

M. Weatherall, *In Search of a Cure* (Oxford: OUP, 1990)

REFERENCES

1. Paul E. Beeson, 'Changes in Medical Therapy During the Past Half-century', *Medicine*, 1980, Vol. 59, pp. 79–99.

2. William Paton, 'The Evolution of Therapeutics: Osler's Therapeutic Nihilism and the Changing Pharmacopoeia', *Journal of the Royal College of Physicians*, 1979, Vol. 13, pp. 74ff.

3. Gerhard Domagk, 'Ein Beitrag zur Chemotherapie der bakteriellen infektionen', *Deutsche Medizinische Wochenschrift*, 1936, Vol. 61, pp. 250–3.

4. J. Trefouel et al., *Comptes Rendus de la Société de Biologie*, 1937, Vol. 120, pp. 756–8.

5. L. Colebrook et al., 'Treatment of Human Puerperal Infections With Prontosil', *The Lancet*, 1936, Vol. 2, pp. 1279–85. See also Irvine Loudon, 'Puerperal Fever, the Streptococcus and the Sulphonomides, 1911–45', *BMJ*, 1987, Vol. 295, pp. 485–91.

6. L. B. Garrod, 'The Eclipse of the Haemolytic Streptococcus', *BMJ*, 16 June 1979, pp. 1607–8. See also Floyd W. Denny, 'A 45-Year Perspective on Streptococcus and Rheumatic Fever', *Clinical Infectious Diseases*, 1994, Vol. 19, pp. 110–22. For an account of someone dying from rheumatic fever, see Burton Korelitz, 'A Harvard Medical Student Chronicles Its Fatal Illness', *Mount Sinai Journal of Medicine*, 1995, Vol. 62, pp. 226–34.

7. D. D. Woods, 'The Relation of PABA to the Mechanism of Action of Sulphanilamide', *British Journal of Experimental Pathology*,

1940, Vol. 21, pp. 74–90. See also D. D. Woods, 'The Biochemical Mode of Action of the Sulphonamide Drugs', *Journal of General Microbiology*, 1962, Vol. 29, pp. 687–702.

8. Gertrude B. Elion, 'The Purine Path to Chemotherapy', *Science*, 7 April 1989, pp. 41–7. See also George H. Hitchings, 'Chemotherapy and Comparative Biochemistry', *Cancer Research*, 1969, Vol. 29, pp. 1895–903; D. W. Woolley, 'The Antimetabolite Revolution in Pharmacology', *Clinical Pharmacology and Therapeutics*, 1959, pp. 556–69.

9. R. O. Roblin and J. W. Clapp, *Journal of the American Chemistry Society*, 1950, Vol. 72, p. 4890.

10. Carl H. Beyer, 'Discoveries of Thiazides: Where Biology and Chemistry Meet', *Perspectives in Biology and Medicine*, Spring 1977, pp. 410–19.

11. G. W. Anderson *et al.*, *Journal of the American Chemistry Society*, 1945, Vol. 67, p. 2197.

12. R. C. Cochrane, 'The Chemotherapy of Leprosy', *BMJ*, 1952, Vol. 2, p. 1220.

13. J. C. Henquin, 'The Fiftieth Anniversary of Hypoglycaemic Sulphonamides', *Diabetologia*, 1992, Vol. 25, pp. 907–12.

14. Walter Sneader, *Drug Prototypes and Their Exploitation*.

15. Leonard Engel, *Medicine Makers of Kalamazoo* (New York: McGraw-Hill, 1961).

4: Technology's Triumphs

GENERAL READING

James M. Edmonson, 'History of the Instruments for Gastrointestinal Endoscopy', *Gastrointestinal Endoscopy*, 1991, Vol. 37, pp. S27–54.

Charles J. Filipi, 'Historical Review: Diagnostic Laparoscopy and Beyond', *Surgical Laparoscopy*, ed. Karl A. Zucker (St Louis, MO: Quality Medical Publishing Inc., 1991)

William S. Haubrick, 'Gastrointestinal Endoscopy', *The Growth of Gastroenterologic Knowledge During the Twentieth Century*, ed. Joseph B. Kirsner (Lea & Febiger, 1994)

Bryan Jennett, *High Technology Medicine: Benefits and Burdens* (Oxford: OUP, 1986)

W. Y. Lau, 'History of Endoscopic and Laparoscopic Surgery', *World Journal of Surgery*, 1997, Vol. 21, pp. 444–53.

Grzegorz Litynski, *Highlights in the History of Laparoscopy* (Berlin: Barbara Bernert-Verlag, 1996)

Stanley Reiser, *Medicine and the Reign of Technology* (Cambridge: CUP, 1978)

David Rosin (ed.), *Minimal Access General Surgery* (Abingdon: Radcliffe Medical Press, 1994)

James W. Smith, 'Microsurgery: Review of the Literature and Discussion of Microtechniques', *Plastic and Reconstructive Surgery*, 1966, Vol. 37, pp. 227–43.

Susumu Tamai, 'History of Microsurgery', *Microsurgery*, 1993, Vol. 14, pp. 6–13

J. E. A. Wickham, 'Future Developments in Minimally Invasive Surgery', *BMJ*, 1994, Vol. 308, pp. 193–6.

REFERENCES

1. Bryan Jennett, *High Technology Medicine: Benefits and Burdens*.

2. J. Anthony Seibert, 'One Hundred Years of Medical Diagnostic Imaging Technology', *Health Physics*, 1995, Vol. 69, pp. 695–719. See also G. N. Handsfield, 'Computerised Transverse Axial Scanning', *British Journal of Radiology*, 1973, Vol. 46, pp. 1016–22; F. H. Doyle *et al.*, 'Imaging of the Brain by Nuclear Magnetic Resonance', *The Lancet*, 1981, Vol. 2, pp. 53–7.

3. See Notes on Open-Heart Surgery and Hip Replacement.

4. Susumu Tamai, 'History of Microsurgery', *Microsurgery*, 1993, Vol. 14, pp. 6–13. See also James W. Smith, 'Microsurgery: Review of the Literature and Discussion of Microtechniques', *Plastic and Reconstructive Surgery*, 1966, Vol. 37, pp. 227–43.

5. Howard P. House, 'The Evolution of Otosclerosis Surgery', *Otolaryngologic Clinics of North America*, 1993, Vol. 26, pp. 323–33. See also C. O. Nylen, 'The Microscope in Aural Surgery: Its First Use and Later Development', *Acta Oto-laryngolica Supplement*, 1954, Vol. 116, pp. 226–40.

6. Harold Ridley, 'Intra-ocular Acrylic Lenses', *Transactions of the Ophthalmological Society of the United Kingdom*, 1951, Vol. 71, pp. 617–21. See also Harold Ridley, 'Intra-ocular Acrylic Lenses', *British Journal of Ophthalmology*, 1952, Vol. 36, pp. 113–22; Harold Ridley, 'The Story of Acrylic Lenses, 1949–62', *Transactions of the Ophthalmological Society of Australia*, 1962, Vol. 15, pp. 53–61.

7. Daniel Albert, *The History of Ophthalmology* (Oxford: Blackwell, 1996).

8. Ch'en Chung-Y *et al.*, 'Salvage of the Forearm Following Complete Traumatic Amputation', *Chinese Medical Journal*, 1963, Vol. 82, pp. 632–8.

9. Julius S. Jacobson *et al.*, 'Microsurgery as an Aid to Middle Cerebral Artery Endarterectomy', *Journal of Neurosurgery*, 1962, Vol. 19, pp. 108–15. See also W. M. Lougheed, 'The Diploscope in Intracranial Aneurysm Surgery: Results in Forty Patients',

Canadian Journal of Surgery, 1969, Vol. 12, pp. 75–82; Eugene S. Flamm, 'Cerebral Aneurysms and Subarachnoid Haemorrhage', *A History of Neurosurgery*, ed. Samuel H. Greenblatt (Oxford: Blackwell/ American Association of Neurosurgeons, 1997); Steven T. Onesti, 'Cerebral Revascularization: A Review', *Neurosurgery*, 1989, Vol. 25, pp. 618–23; J. Lawrence Pool, 'The Development of Modern Intracranial Aneurysm Surgery', *Neurosurgery*, 1977, Vol. 1, pp. 233–7.

10. Antony F. Wallace, *The Progress of Plastic Surgery: An Introductory History* (Oxford: Wilhelm A. Meeuws, 1982). See also Sir Archibald McIndoe, 'Total Reconstruction of the Burnt Face', *British Journal of Plastic Surgery*, 1983, Vol. 36, pp. 410–20; Y. Godwin, 'Time is the Healer: McIndoe's Guinea Pigs Fifty Years On', *British Journal of Plastic Surgery*, 1997, Vol. 50, pp. 88–98.

11. Rollin K. Daniel and G. Ian Taylor, 'Distant Transfer of an Island Flap by Macrovascular Anastomoses', *Plastic and Reconstructive Surgery*, 1973, Vol. 52, pp. 1111–17. See also Bernard M. O'Brien *et al.*, 'Successful Transfer of a Large Island Flap from the Groin to the Foot by Microvascular Anastomoses', *Plastic Reconstructive Surgery*, 1973, Vol. 52, pp. 271–6.

12. James G. Gow, 'Harold Hopkins and Optical Systems for Urology: An Appreciation', *Journal of Urology* (to be published).

13. H. H. Hopkins and N. S. Kapany, 'A Flexible Fibrescope, Using Static Scanning', *Nature*, 1954, Vol. 173, pp. 39–40. See also Steven F. Dierdorf, 'The Physics of Fibreoptic Endoscopy', *Mount Sinai Journal of Medicine*, 1995, Vol. 62, pp. 1–9; William S. Haubrich, 'The Advent and Evolution of Endoscopy', *Gastroenterology*, 1997, Vol. 117, pp. 591–3.

14. Basil Hirschowitz, 'A Personal History of the Fibrescope', *Gastroenterology*, 1979, Vol. 76, pp. 864–9. See also Basil Hirschowitz, 'Endoscopic Examination of the Stomach and Duodenal Cap With a Fibrescope', *The Lancet*, 1961, Vol. 1, pp. 1074–7; Basil Hirschowitz, 'Fibreoptics and Research in the Last Twenty-five Years', *Endoscopy*, 1980 (supplement), pp. 13–18.

15. Christopher B. Williams, 'Flexible Endoscopy at St Mark's', *Contributions from St Mark's Hospital, London*, ed. Charles Mann (Nymphenburg, 1988). See also J. Loren Pritcher, 'Therapeutic Endoscopy and Bleeding Ulcers: A Historical Overview', *Gastrointestinal Endoscopy*, 1990, Vol. 36, pp. S2–S7.

16. J. Gow, personal communication, 1997.

17. H. H. Hopkins, 'The Modern Urological Endoscope', *Handbook of Urological Endoscopy*, eds J. G. Gow and H. H. Hopkins (Churchill-Livingstone, 1978).

18. K. Semm, 'History', *Operative Gynaecologic Endoscopy*, ed. J. S. Sanfilippo (Berlin: Springer-Verlag, 1989).
19. Patrick C. Steptoe, *Laparoscopy in Gynaecology* (E & S Livingstone, 1967).
20. W. Y. Lau, 'History of Endoscopic and Laparoscopic Surgery', *World Journal of Surgery*, 1997, Vol. 21, pp. 444–53.
21. Brereton B. Strafford, 'A Historical Review of Shoulder Arthroscopy', *Orthopaedic Clinics of North America*, 1993, Vol. 24, pp. 1–3.
22. H. Stammberger, 'The Evolution of Functional Endoscopic Sinus Surgery', *ENT Journal*, 1994, Vol. 73, pp. 451–5. See also Steven S. Sachs, 'Fibreoptics in Otolaryngology', *Mount Sinai Journal of Medicine*, 1995, Vol. 62, pp. 47–9.
23. 'Advances in Laparoscopic Urology: History and Development of Procedures', *Urology*, 1994, Vol. 43, pp. 420–7.
24. M. L. Clark, 'Upper Intestinal Endoscopy', *The Lancet*, 1985, Vol. 1, p. 629. See also Howard M. Spiro, 'My Kingdom for a Camera: Some Comments on Medical Technology', *NEJM*, 14 November 1974, pp. 1070–2.

5: The Mysteries of Biology

REFERENCES
1. Selman Waksman, 'The Role of Antibiotics in Nature', *Perspectives in Biology and Medicine*, 1961, Vol. 4, No. 3, pp. 271–2.
2. Ronald Bentley, 'Secondary Metabolites Play Primary Role in Human Affairs', *Perspectives in Biology and Medicine*, 1997, Vol. 40, pp. 197–219. See also Ronald Bentley, 'Microbial Secondary Metabolites Play Important Roles in Medicine: Prospects for Discovery of New Drugs', *Perspectives in Biology and Medicine*, 1997, Vol. 40, pp. 365–93; D. Chadwick (ed.), *Secondary Metabolites: Their Function in Evolution*, Ciba Foundation Symposium 171 (Chichester: John Wiley & Sons, 1992).
3. D. J. Ingle, 'From A–F', *Pharos*, July 1964, pp. 77–80.
4. Michael Denton, *Evolution: A Theory in Crisis* (Bethesda, MD: Adler & Adler, 1986).

Part 2: The End of the Age of Optimism

1: The Revolution Falters

REFERENCES
1. Office of Health Economics, *Compendium of Health Statistics*, 1984.

2. Colin Dollery, *The End of an Age of Optimism* (Nuffield Provincial Hospitals Trust, 1978).
3. James B. Wyngaarden, 'The Clinical Investigator as an Endangered Species', *NEJM*, 1979, Vol. 301, pp. 1254–9.
4. Editorial, 'A Dearth of New Drugs', *Nature*, 1980, Vol. 283, p. 609.
5. Fred Steward and George Wibberley, 'Drug Innovation: What's Slowing It Down?', *Nature*, 1980, Vol. 284, pp. 118–20.

2: The Dearth of New Drugs

REFERENCES
1. Richard J. Wurtman and Robert L. Bettiker, 'The Slowing of Treatment Discovery, 1965–95', *Nature Medicine*, 1995, Vol. 1, pp. 1122–5. See also Joseph DiMasi, 'New Drug Development in the United States, 1963–90', *Clinical Pharmacology and Therapeutics*, 1991, Vol. 50, pp. 471–86.
2. A. Willman, 'Thalidomide and Foetal Abnormalities', *BMJ*, 17 February 1962, p. 477. See also Editorial, 'Thalidomide's Long Shadow', *BMJ*, 13 November 1976, pp. 1155–6.
3. M. Weatherall, 'An End to the Search for New Drugs?', *Nature*, 1982, Vol. 296, pp. 387–90. See also Max Tishler, 'Drug Discovery: Background and Foreground', *Clinical Pharmacology and Therapeutics*, 1973, Vol. 14, pp. 479–86.
4. J. W. Black and J. S. Stephenson, 'Pharmacology of a New Adrenergic Beta Receptor Blocking Compound', *The Lancet*, 1962, Vol. 2, pp. 311–15. See also J. W. Brimblecombe *et al.*, 'Cimetidine: A Non-thiourea H2 Receptor Antagonist', *Journal of International Medical Research*, 1975, Vol. 3, pp. 86–92.
5. Alan S. Perelson *et al.*, *Nature*, 1997, Vol. 387, pp. 188–91. See also Editorial, 'New Hope in HIV Disease', *Science*, 1996, Vol. 279, pp. 1988–90; Mei-hwei Chang *et al.*, 'Universal Hepatitis B Vaccination in Taiwan and the Incidence of Hepato-cellular Cancer in Children', *NEJM*, 1997, Vol. 336, pp. 1855–60.
6. The top-ten pharmaceutical products in 1993 were as follows: Zantac, Renitec, Ciproxin, Voltaren, Zovirax, Capoten, Augmentin, Mevacor, Procardia and Prozac.
7. Roger S. Rittmaster, 'Finasteride', *NEJM*, 1994, Vol. 330, pp. 120–4. See also G. J. Gormley *et al.*, 'The Effect of Finasteride in Men With Benign Prostatic Hyperplasia', *NEJM*, 1992, Vol. 327, p. 1185.
8. Richard Appleton, 'The Anti-epileptic Drugs', *Archives of Disease in Childhood*, 1996, Vol. 75, pp. 256–62. See also Gilles Mignot,

'Drug Trials in Epilepsy: New Drugs Have Been Poorly Assessed', *BMJ*, 1996, Vol. 313, p. 1157.

9. W. I. McDonald, 'New Treatments for Multiple Sclerosis', *BMJ*, 1995, Vol. 310, pp. 345–7. See also Peter Harvey, 'Why Interferon Beta 1B Was Licensed Is a Mystery', *BMJ*, 1996, Vol. 313, pp. 297–8; Cornelius Kelly, 'Drug Treatments for Alzheimer's Disease', *BMJ*, 1997, Vol. 314, pp. 693–4; Nicholas Wagner, 'Local Committee Has Declined to Approve NHS Hospital Prescription of Donepezil', *BMJ*, 1997, Vol. 314, p. 1555.

10. Jill Rafuse, 'US Industry Hurt by Rising Research Costs and Slump in Prices', *Canadian Medical Association Journal*, 1994, Vol. 150, p. 130.

11. John Griffin, 'The Madness of Industry's Mega Mergers', *Scrip Magazine*, May 1996, pp. 10–11. See also Editorial, 'Bigger Companies for Better Drugs', *The Lancet*, 1995, Vol. 346, p. 585.

12. James R. Broach and Jeremy Thorner, 'High-Throughput Screening for Drug Discovery', *Nature*, 1996, Vol. 384, pp. 14–16.

3: Technology's Failings

GENERAL READING

John Bunker, 'Artificial Organs and Life-support Systems', *Encyclopaedia of Bioethics, Vol. 1*, ed. Warren Thomas Reich (New York: Macmillan, 1978)

Bryan Jennett, *High Technology Medicine: Benefits and Burdens* (Oxford: OUP, 1986)

Tim Chard and Martin Richards, 'Benefits and Hazards of the New Obstetrics', *Clinics in Developmental Medicine*, 1977, No. 64

Anne Oakley, *The Captured Womb* (Oxford: Blackwell, 1984)

REFERENCES

1. J. A. Seibert, '100 Years of Diagnostic Imaging Technology', *Health Physics*, 1995, Vol. 69, pp. 695–719.

2. Katherine Petre *et al.*, 'PTCA in 1985–86 and 1977–81', *NEJM*, 1998, Vol. 318, pp. 265–70.

3. W. Y. Lau, 'History of Endoscopic and Laparoscopic Surgery', *World Journal of Surgery*, 1997, Vol. 21, pp. 444–53. See also P. J. Treacy and A. G. Johnson, 'Is the Laparoscopic Bubble Bursting?', *The Lancet*, 1995, Vol. 346, p. 23.

4. M. E. Abrams, 'Cost of Tests', *Journal of the Royal College of Physicians*, 1979, Vol. 13, pp. 217–18. See also Bruce R. Smoller, 'Phlebotomy for Diagnostic Laboratory Tests in Adults', *NEJM*, 1986, Vol. 314, pp. 1233–5; John F. Burnum, 'Medical Vampires', *NEJM*, 1986, Vol. 314, p. 1250.

5. Editorial, 'Reducing Tests', *The Lancet*, 1981, Vol. 1, pp. 539–40. See also Jonathan Showstack, 'Changes in the Use of Medical Technology, 1972–77', *NEJM*, 1982, Vol. 306, pp. 706–13; Paul F. Griner, 'Misuse of Laboratory Tests and Diagnostic Procedures', *NEJM*, 1982, Vol. 307, pp. 1336–9.

6. M. L. Clark, 'Upper Intestinal Endoscopy', *The Lancet*, 1985, Vol. 1, p. 629. See also Howard M. Spiro, 'My Kingdom for a Camera: Some Comments on Medical Technology', *NEJM*, 1974, pp. 1070–2.

7. Edward J. Quilligan and R. H. Paul, 'Foetal Monitoring: Is It Worth It?', *Obstetrics and Gynaecology*, 1975, Vol. 45, pp. 96–100.

8. Ronald E. Miers, 'Two Patterns of Perinatal Brain Damage and Their Conditions of Occurrence', *AJOG*, 1972, Vol. 112, pp. 246–60.

9. R. W. Beard *et al.*, 'The Significance of Changes in the Continuous Foetal Heart Rate in the First Stage of Labour', *Journal of Obstetrics and Gynaecology of the British Commonwealth*, 1971, Vol. 78, pp. 865–81. See also R. W. Beard *et al.*, 'Intensive Care of the High-risk Foetus in Labour', *Journal of Obstetrics and Gynaecology of the British Commonwealth*, 1971, Vol. 78, pp. 882–93; Raymond Kennedy, 'Electronic Foetal Heart Rate Monitoring: Retrospective Reflections on a Twentieth-century Technology', *JRSM*, 1998, Vol. 91, p. 244.

10. William Arney, *Monitoring and Surveillance in Power and the Profession of Obstetrics* (Chicago, IL: University of Chicago Press, 1982).

11. Compare Editorial, 'Is Foetal Monitoring Worthwhile?', *BMJ*, 6 March 1971, pp. 515–16 with G. S. Sykes *et al.*, 'Foetal Distress in the Condition of New-born Infants', *BMJ*, 1983, Vol. 287, pp. 943–5; also correspondence, *BMJ*, 1984, Vol. 288, pp. 567–9 and Editorial, 'Foetal Monitoring During Labour', *BMJ*, 3 December 1983, pp. 1649–50.

12. Dermot Macdonald, 'Cerebral Palsy and Intrapartum Foetal Monitoring', *NEJM*, Vol. 334, pp. 659–60. See also Adrian Grant *et al.*, 'Cerebral Palsy Among Children Born During the Dublin Randomised Trial of Intrapartum Monitoring', *The Lancet*, 1989, Vol. 2, pp. 1233–5; Fiona Stanley, 'Cerebral Palsy: The Courts Catch Up With Sad Realities', *Medical Journal of Australia*, 1994, Vol. 161, p. 236; David Hall, 'Birth Asphyxia and Cerebral Palsy', *BMJ*, 1989, Vol. 299, pp. 279–83; Eve Blair, 'Intrapartum Asphyxia: A Rare Cause of Cerebral Palsy', *Journal of Paediatrics*, 1988, Vol. 112, pp. 5125–519; Editorial, 'Cerebral Palsy, Intrapartum Care and a Shot in the Foot', *The Lancet*, 1989, Vol. 2, pp. 1251–2; Fritz K. Beller,

'The Cerebral Palsy Story: A Catastrophic Misunderstanding in Obstetrics', *Obstetrical and Gynaecological Survey*, 1995, Vol. 50, p. 83.

13. R. S. Illingworth, 'Why Blame the Obstetrician? A Review', *BMJ*, 1979, Vol. 1, pp. 797–801.

14. Quoted in Roy Porter, *The Greatest Benefit to Mankind* (HarperCollins, 1997).

15. Muriel Gillick, 'The High Cost of Dying', *Archives of Internal Medicine*, 1994, Vol. 154, pp. 2134–7.

16. David P. Schapira, 'Intensive Care: Survival and Expense of Treating Critically Ill Cancer Patients', *JAMA*, 1993, Vol. 269, pp. 783–6.

4: The Clinical Scientist as an Endangered Species

REFERENCES
1. James Wyngaarden, 'The Clinical Investigator as an Endangered Species', *NEJM*, 1969, Vol. 301, pp. 1254–9.

2. JAMA, 1970, Vol. 211, pp. 289–360

3. Jonathan M. Glass. The proportion of the *BMJ*'s editorials on medical subjects is decreasing: *BMJ*, 1996, Vol. 313, pp. 1403–4. See also Bruno Simini, 'Randomised Control Trials', *The Lancet*, 1998, Vol. 351, p. 682.

4. JAMA, 1999, Vol. 281, pp. 297-394.

5. Christopher C. Booth, 'Clinical Research', *Historical Perspectives on the Role of the MRC*, ed. Joan Austoker and Linda Bryder (Oxford: OUP, 1989). See also Editorial, 'Brave New Hospital', *BMJ*, 5 September 1970, p. 538; 'Northwick Park Hospital and Clinical Research Centre', *BMJ*, 5 September 1970, pp. 576–80.

6. Editorial, 'The Future of Clinical Research in Britain', *BMJ*, 1986, Vol. 292, pp. 416–17. See also 'A Boost for Clinical Research', *BMJ*, 1986, Vol. 292, p. 362 and correspondence: Christopher Booth, *BMJ*, 1986, Vol. 292, p. 556; Richard Edwards, *BMJ*, 1986, Vol. 292, p. 619; Victor Hawthorne, *BMJ* 1986, Vol. 292, p. 830.

7. Everett Vokes, 'Combined Modality Therapy of Solid Tumours', *The Lancet*, 1997, Vol. 349 (supplement II), pp. 4–6.

Part 3: The Fall

1: The Brave New World of The New Genetics

GENERAL READING
Walter Bodmer and Robin McKie, *The Book of Man* (Little, Brown, 1994)

Stephen S. Hall, *Invisible Frontiers: The Race to Synthesise a Human Gene* (Sidgwick & Jackson, 1988)

Horace Freeland Judson, *The Eighth Day of Creation: Makers of the Revolution of Biology* (Penguin, 1979)

Evelyn Fox Keller, *Refiguring Life: Metaphors for Twentieth-Century Biology* (New York: Columbia University Press, 1995)

Daniel J. Kevles and Leroy Hood, *The Code of Codes* (Cambridge, MA: Harvard University Press, 1992)

Dorothy Nelkin and M. Susan Lindee, *The DNA Mystique: The Gene as a Cultural Icon* (New York: W. H. Freeman, 1995)

Robert Shapiro, *The Human Blueprint: The Race to Unlock the Secrets of Our Genetic Script* (Cassell, 1992)

James D. Watson, *The Double Helix* (Weidenfeld & Nicolson, 1997)

David Weatherall, *The New Genetics and Clinical Practice* (Oxford: OUP, 1991)

——, *Science and the Quiet Art* (Oxford: OUP, 1993)

Tom Wilkie, *Perilous Knowledge* (Faber & Faber, 1993)

Christopher Wills, *Exons, Introns and Talking Genes: The Science Behind the Human Genome Project* (Oxford: OUP, 1992)

REFERENCES

1. John Saville, 'Prospecting for Gold in the Human Genome', *BMJ*, 1997, Vol. 314, pp. 43–9.

2. J. D. Watson and F. H. C. Crick, 'Molecular Structure of Nucleic Acids: A Structure for Deoxyribose Nucleic Acid', *Nature*, 1953, Vol. 171, p. 737.

3. J. D. Watson and F. H. C. Crick, 'Genetic Implications of the Structure of DNA', *Nature*, 1953, Vol. 171, pp. 964–6.

4. F. H. C. Crick, 'On Protein Synthesis', *Symposia of the Society for Experimental Biology* (Cambridge: CUP, 1958), pp. 138–53.

5. Joshua Lederberg, 'What the Double Helix Has Meant for Basic Medical Science', *JAMA*, 1993, Vol. 269, pp. 1981–5. See also Victor McKusick, 'Medical Genetics: A Forty-year Perspective on the Evolution of a Medical Specialty from a Basic Science', *JAMA*, 1993, Vol. 270, pp. 2351–6; Irwin Chargaff, 'Preface to a Grammar of Biology: 100 Years of Nucleic Acid Research', *Science*, 1971, Vol. 172, pp. 637–42; Gunther S. Stent, 'That Was the Molecular Biology That Was', *Science*, 1968, Vol. 160, pp. 390–5.

6. Christopher Wills, *Exons, Introns and Talking Genes*.

7. David Weatherall, *Science and the Quiet Art*.

8. Maxim Frank-Kamenetskii, *Unravelling DNA* (New York: Wiley-VCH, 1993).

REFERENCES 401

9. Hamilton O. Smith, 'Nobel Lectures: Physiology or Medicine, 1971–80', *World Scientific*, 1992, pp. 523–43.
10. Stanley N. Cohen *et al.*, 'Construction of Biologically Functional Bacterial Plasmids In Vitro', *Proceedings of the National Academy of Science*, 1973, Vol. 70, pp. 3240–4. See also Stanley N. Cohen, 'The Manipulation of Genes', *Scientific American*, 1975, pp. 25–33.
11. David Baltimore, 'RNA-dependent DNA Polymerase in Virions of RNA Tumour Viruses', *Nature*, 1970, Vol. 226, pp. 1209–11; Howard M. Temin, 'RNA-dependent DNA Preliminaries in Virions of Rouse Sarcoma Virus', *Nature*, 1970, Vol. 226, pp. 1211–13; David Baltimore, 'Nobel Lectures: Physiology or Medicine, 1971–80', *World Scientific*, 1992, pp. 215–29.
12. Axel Ullrich, 'Rat Insulin Genes: Construction of Plasmids Containing the Coding Sequences', *Science*, 1977, Vol. 196, pp. 1313–17. See also D. L. Kacian *et al.*, 'Decreased Globin Messenger RNA in Thalassaemia Detected by Molecular Hybridization', *Proceedings of the National Academy of Science*, 1973, Vol. 70, pp. 1886–90.
13. Frederick Sanger, 'Determination of Nucleotide Sequences in DNA', *Science*, 1981, Vol. 214, p. 1205. See also F. Sanger *et al.*, 'Nucleotide Sequence of Bacteriophage x174 DNA', *Nature*, 1977, Vol. 265, p. 687.
14. Walter Gilbert, 'DNA Sequencing and Gene Structure', *Science*, 1981, Vol. 214, p. 1305.
15. David E. Comings, 'Prenatal Diagnosis and the "New Genetics"', *American Journal of Human Genetics*, 1980, Vol. 32, p. 453. See also D. J. Weatherall, *The New Genetics and Clinical Practice*; Tony Smith, 'How Will the New Genetics Work?', *BMJ*, 1983, Vol. 286, pp. 1–2.
16. Stephen S. Hall, *Invisible Frontiers*.
17. Walter Bodmer and Robin McKie, *The Book of Man*.
18. James Erlichman, *Guardian*, 15 September 1982.
19. John Pickup, 'Human Insulin', *BMJ*, 1989, pp. 991–3. See also A. Teuscher, 'Hypoglycaemia Unawareness in Diabetics Transferred from Beef/Porcine Insulin to Human Insulin', *The Lancet*, 1987, Vol. 2, pp. 382–5; Simon P. Wolf, 'Trying Times for Human Insulin', *Nature*, 1992, Vol. 356, pp. 375–6; Edwin A. M. Gale, 'Hypoglycaemia and Human Insulin', *The Lancet*, 1989, Vol. 2, pp. 1264–6.
20. Joseph Eschbach, 'Correction of the Anaemia of End-stage Renal Disease With Recombinant Human Erythropoietin', *NEJM*, 1987, Vol. 316, pp. 73–8.

21. Martin Gore et al., 'Tumour Marker Level During Marimastat Therapy', The Lancet, 1996, Vol. 348, p. 263. See also W. Wayt Gibbs, 'State of Shock: Sepsis Can Be Fatal to Firms As Well As to Patients', Scientific American, October 1994, pp. 107–8; Editorial, 'Biotech's Uncertain Future', The Lancet, 1996, Vol. 347, p. 1497.
22. Judy C. Chang and Yuet Wai Kan, 'A sensitive new prenatal test for sickle cell anaemia', NEJM, 1982, Vol. 307, pp. 30–31. See also Henry M. Kronenberg, 'Looking at Genes', NEJM, 1982, Vol. 307, pp. 50–2.
23. E. M. Southern, 'Detection of Specific Sequences Among DNA Fragments Separated by Gel Electrophoresis', Journal of Molecular Biology, 1975, Vol. 98, pp. 503–51.
24. David Botstein, 'Construction of a Genetic Linkage Map in Man Using Restriction Fragment-length Polymorphisms', American Journal of Human Genetics, 1980, Vol. 32, pp. 314–31.
25. John R. Riordan, 'Identification of the Cystic Fibrosis Gene', Science, 1989, Vol. 245, pp. 1066–73. See also Leslie Roberts, 'The Race for the Cystic Fibrosis Gene', Science, 1988, Vol. 240, pp. 141–5, 282–5; Francis S. Collins, 'Positional Cloning Moves from Perditional to Traditional', Nature Genetics, 1995, Vol. 9, pp. 347–50; Huntington's Disease Collaborative Research Group, Cell, 1993, Vol. 72, pp. 971–83.
26. Michael Angastiniotis et al., 'How Thalassaemia Was Controlled in Cyprus', World Health Forum, 1986, Vol. 7, pp. 291–7.
27. David J. H. Brock, 'Prenatal Screening for Cystic Fibrosis: Five Years' Experience Reviewed', The Lancet, 1996, Vol. 347, pp. 148–50. See also Editorial, 'Screening for Cystic Fibrosis', The Lancet, 1992, Vol. 340, pp. 209–10; Matthew John Smith, 'An Evaluation of Population Screening for Carriers of Cystic Fibrosis', Journal of Public Health Medicine, 1992, Vol. 14, pp. 257–63; M. E. Mennie et al., 'Prenatal Screening for Cystic Fibrosis: Psychological Effect on Carriers and Their Partners', Journal of Medical Genetics, 1993, Vol. 30, pp. 543–8; John Burn, 'Screening for Cystic Fibrosis', Primary Care, 1993, Vol. 306, pp. 1558–9; Nicholas J. Wald, 'Couples Screening for Cystic Fibrosis', The Lancet, 1991, Vol. 338, pp. 1318–19.
28. Reed Edwin Pyeritz, 'Family History and Genetic Risk Factors', JAMA, 1997, Vol. 278, pp. 1284–5. See also Angus Clark, 'Population Screening for Genetic Susceptibility to Disease', BMJ, 1995, Vol. 311, pp. 35–7; Karol Sikora, 'Genes, Dreams and Cancer', BMJ, 1994, Vol. 308, pp. 1217–20.
29. Amelia A. Langston, 'BRCA1 Mutations in a Population-based Sample of Young Women With Breast Cancer', NEJM, 1996, Vol.

334, pp. 137–42. See also Francis S. Collins, 'BRCA1: Lots of Mutations, Lots of Dilemmas', *NEJM*, 1996, Vol. 334, pp. 186–8; Rachel Nowak, 'Many Mutations May Make Tests Difficult', *Science*, 1994, Vol. 266, p. 1470; Jean Marx, 'A Second Breast Cancer Susceptibility Gene is Found', *Science*, 1996, Vol. 271, pp. 30–1.

30. Peter S. Harper, 'Genetic Testing, Common Diseases and Health Service Provision', *The Lancet*, 1995, Vol. 346, pp. 1645–6. See also Editorial, 'Have You Had a Gene Test?', *The Lancet*, 1996, Vol. 347, p. 133; correspondence: *The Lancet*, 1996, Vol. 347, p. 685; Ehsan Masood, 'Gene Tests: Who Benefits from Risks', *Nature*, 1996, Vol. 379, pp. 389–92.

31. R. Michael Blaese, 'T. Lymphocyte: Directed Gene Therapy for ADA-SCID – Initial Trial Results After Four Years', *Science*, 1995, Vol. 270, pp. 475–9.

32. W. French Anderson, 'Human Gene Therapy', *Science*, 1992, Vol. 256, pp. 808–13. See also Theodore Friedmann, 'A Brief History of Gene Therapy', *Nature Genetics*, 1992, Vol. 2, pp. 93–8; Manal A. Morsy, 'Progress Towards Human Gene Therapy', *JAMA*, 1993, Vol. 270, pp. 2338–46; A. Dusty Miller, 'Human Gene Therapy Comes of Age', *Nature*, 1992, Vol. 357, pp. 455–9.

33. Eliot Marshal, 'Less Hype, More Biology Needed for Gene Therapy', *Science*, 1995, Vol. 270, p. 1751. See also Eliot Marshal, 'Gene Therapy's Growing Pains', *Science*, 1995, Vol. 269, pp. 1050–5.

34. Michael R. Knowles *et al.*, 'A Controlled Study of Adenoviral-Vector-Mediated Gene Transfer in the Nasal Epithelium of Patients With Cystic Fibrosis', *NEJM*, 1995, Vol. 333, pp. 823–31.

35. Jerry R. Mendell, 'Myoblast Transfer in the Treatment of Duchenne's Muscular Dystrophy', *NEJM*, 1995, Vol. 333, pp. 832–8.

36. Jeffrey M. Leiden, 'Gene Therapy: Promise, Pitfalls and Prognosis', *NEJM*, 1995, Vol. 333, pp. 871–3.

37. Theodore Friedman, 'Human Gene Therapy: An Immature Genie But Certainly Out of the Bottle', *Nature Medicine*, 1996, Vol. 2, pp. 144–7.

38. Meredith Wadman, 'Review Panel Cancels Meeting as Gene Therapy Proposals Fall', *Nature*, 1996, Vol. 379, p. 66.

39. Tom Wilkie, *Sunday Telegraph*, 7 December 1997.

40. Peter J. Morris, 'Pig Transplants Postponed', *BMJ*, 1997, Vol. 314, p. 242.

41. Dorothy Nelkin, *The Genome Mystique* (Basingstoke: W. H. Freeman, 1997).

42. Ruth Hubbard and R. C. Lewontin, 'Pitfalls of Genetic Testing', *NEJM*, 1996, Vol. 334, pp. 1192–3.

43. R. C. Lewontin, 'The Dream of the Human Genome', *New York Review of Books*, 28 May 1992.

44. David Papermaster, 'Necessary but Insufficient', *Nature Medicine*, 1995, Vol. 1, pp. 874–5. See also Nicholas Short, 'A Dose of Molecular Medicine', *Nature*, 1993, Vol. 366, p. 505.

45. P. G. H. Gell, *Destiny and the Genes: The Encyclopaedia of Medical Ignorance*, eds R. Duncan and M. Weston-Smith (Kidlington: Pergamon, 1984).

2: Seduced by The Social Theory

GENERAL READING

Peter Skrabanek and James McCormick, *Follies and Fallacies in Medicine* (Newton Stewart: Tarragon Press, 1989)

Peter Skrabanek, *The Death of Humane Medicine and the Rise of Coercive Healthism* (Social Affairs Unit, 1994)

James Le Fanu, *Eat Your Heart Out* (Macmillan, 1987)

Aaron Wildavsky, *But is it True? A Citizen's Guide to Environmental Health and Safety Issues* (Cambridge, MA: Harvard University Press, 1995)

REFERENCES

1. Thomas McKeown, *The Role of Medicine: Dream, Mirage or Nemesis?* (Oxford: Blackwell, 1979).

2. *Dietary Goals for the United States* (Washington, DC: US Government Printing Office, 1977).

3. Richard Doll and Richard Peto, *The Causes of Cancer* (Oxford: OUP, 1981).

4. Samuel S. Epstein and Joel B. Swartz, 'Fallacies of Lifestyle Cancer Theories', *Nature*, 1981, Vol. 289, pp. 127–9.

5. Ian Kennedy, *The Unmasking of Medicine* (Allen & Unwin, 1981).

6. Simon Szreter, 'The Importance of Social Intervention in Britain's Mortality Decline', *Social History of Medicine*, 1988, Vol. 1, pp. 1–19. See also Leonard G. Wilson, 'The Historical Decline of Tuberculosis in Europe and America: Its Causes and Significance', *Journal of the History of Medicine and Allied Sciences*, 1990, Vol. 45, pp. 366–96; Johan P. Mackenbach, 'The Contribution of Medical Care to Mortality Decline: McKeown Revisited', *Journal of Clinical Epidemiology*, 1996, Vol. 49, pp. 1207–13.

7. M. Cassidy, 'Coronary Disease: The Harveian Oration', *The Lancet*, 1946, Vol. 2, pp. 587–90.

8. J. W. McNee, 'The Clinical Syndrome of Thrombosis of the Coronary Arteries', *Quarterly Journal of Medicine*, October 1925, pp. 44–51.

9. Ancel Keys, 'Recollections of Pioneers in Nutrition: From Starvation to Cholesterol', *Journal of the American College of Nutrition*, 1990, Vol. 9, pp. 288–91.

10. I. Snapper, 'Chinese Lessons in Medicine', *Interscience* (New York: n.p., 1941).

11. Ancel Keys *et al.*, 'Mortality and Coronary Heart Disease Among Men Studied for Twenty-three Years', *Archives of Internal Medicine*, 1971, Vol. 128, pp. 201–14. See also Ancel Keys *et al.*, 'The CVD Research Programme of the Laboratory of Physiological Hygiene: The Journal', *The Lancet*, July 1961, pp. 291–5.

12. Ancel Keys *et al.*, 'Prediction of Serum Cholesterol Responses of Man to Changes in Fat in the Diet', *The Lancet*, 1957, Vol. 2, pp. 959–66.

13. Ancel Keys, 'From Naples to Seven Countries: A Sentimental Journey', *Progress in Biochemical Pharmacology*, 1983, Vol. 19, p. 130.

14. Ancel Keys *et al.*, 'Lessons from Serum Cholesterol Studies in Japan, Hawaii and Los Angeles', *Annals of Internal Medicine*, 1958, pp. 83–93.

15. Axel Strom, 'Mortality from Circulatory Disorders in Norway, 1940–45', *The Lancet*, 1951, Vol. 1, pp. 126–8. See also H. O. Bang, 'Personal Reflections on Incidence of Ischaemic Heart Disease in Oslo During the Second World War', *Acta Medica Scandinavica*, 1981, Vol. 210, pp. 245–8.

16. William J. Enos *et al.*, 'Coronary Disease Among the United States Soldiers Killed in Action in Korea', *JAMA*, 1955, Vol. 152, pp. 1090–3.

17. George Pickering, 'Pathogenesis of Myocardial Infarction', *BMJ*, 29 February 1964, pp. 517–29.

18. Irvine H. Page *et al.*, 'Atherosclerosis and the Fat Content of the Diet', *Circulation*, 1957, Vol. 16, pp. 163–78.

19. Jeremiah Stamler *et al.*, 'Diet and Serum Lipids in Atherosclerotic Coronary Heart Disease', *Medical Clinics of North America*, 1963, Vol. 47, pp. 3–28.

20. 'Ad hoc Committee on Dietary Fat and Atherosclerosis; Dietary Fat and Its Relation to Heart Attack and Strokes', *Circulation*, 1961, Vol. 23, pp. 133–6.

21. J. R. A. Mitchell, 'Come Back, Anticoagulants, All May Yet Be Forgiven', *Advance Medicine, Vol. 17*, ed. D. Jewell (Pitman Medical, 1981). See also George Pickering *et al.*, 'An Assessment of Long-term Anticoagulant Administration After Cardiac Infarction', *BMJ*, 3 October 1964, pp. 837–43; J. McMichael, 'Anticoagulants: Another View', *BMJ*, 17 October 1964, p. 1007.

22. E. H. Ahrens, 'Dietary Fats in Coronary and Heart Disease: Unfinished Business', *The Lancet*, 1979, Vol. 2, pp. 1345–8.

23. George Mann, 'Diet-Heart: End of an Era', *NEJM*, 1977, Vol. 297, pp. 644–50.

24. J. McMichael, 'Dietetic Factors in Coronary Disease', *European Journal of Cardiology*, 1977, Vol. 5, pp. 447–52. See also J. McMichael, 'Fats and Atheroma: An Inquest', *BMJ*, 1979, Vol. 1, p. 173.

25. Mr Fit Research Group, 'Multiple-risk Factor Intervention Trial', *JAMA*, 1982, Vol. 248, pp. 1465–77.

26. WHO European Collaborative Group, 'Multi-factorial Trial in Prevention of Heart Disease Incidence and Mortality Results', *European Heart Journal*, 1983, Vol. 4, pp. 141–7.

27. Reuel Stallones, 'Mortality and the Multiple-risk Factor Intervention Trial', *American Journal of Epidemiology*, 1983, Vol. 117, pp. 647–9. See also George D. Lundberg, 'Mr Fit and the Goals of the Journal', *JAMA*, 1982, Vol. 248, p. 1501; Gina Kolata, 'Heart Study Produces a Surprise Result', *Science*, 1982, Vol. 218, pp. 31–3.

28. Weldon J. Walker, 'Coronary Mortality – What is Going On?', *JAMA*, 1974, Vol. 227, pp. 1045–6. See also Reuel Stallones, 'The Rise and Fall of Ischaemic Heart Disease', *Scientific American*, 1980, Vol. 243, pp. 43–9.

29. NACNE, *Proposals for Nutritional Guidelines for Health Education in Britain* (Health Education Council, 1983). See also HEC, *Coronary Heart Disease Prevention Plan: Plans for Action* (HEC, 1984); DHSS, *Diet and Cardiovascular Disease: Report on Health and Social Subject No. 7* (HMSO, 1984); British Medical Association, *Diet, Nutrition and Health* (BMA, 1986); JACNE, *Eating for a Healthy Heart* (HEC, 1986); European Atherosclerosis Society, 'Strategies for the Prevention of Coronary Heart Disease', *European Journal of Cardiology*, 1987, Vol. 8, pp. 77–88.

30. G. Cannon and C. Walker, *The Food Scandal*, London

31. LRC-CPPT, 'Reduction in Incidence of Coronary Heart Disease', *JAMA*, 1984, Vol. 251, pp. 351–73. See also Editorial, 'Is Reduction of Blood Cholesterol Effective?', *The Lancet*, 1984, Vol. 1, pp. 317–18; Leon Simons, 'The Lipid Hypothesis is Proven', *Medical Journal of Australia*, 1984, Vol. 410, pp. 316–17.

32. Consensus Conference, 'Lowering Blood Cholesterol to Prevent Heart Disease', *JAMA*, 1985, Vol. 253, pp. 2080–7. See also 'Campaign Seeks to Increase US Cholesterol Consciousness', *JAMA*, 1986, Vol. 255, pp. 1097–1102.

33. Thomas J. Moore, *Heart Failure: A Critical Inquiry into American*

Medicine and the Revolution in Heart Care (New York: Random House, 1989).

34. George Davey Smith *et al.*, 'Should There Be a Moratorium on the Use of Cholesterol-lowering Drugs?', *BMJ*, 1992, Vol. 304, pp. 431–4.

35. John R. Vane, 'History of Aspirin and Its Mechanism of Action', *Stroke*, 1990, Vol. 21 (supplement 4), pp. 12–23. See also David B. Jack, 'A Hundred Years of Aspirin', *The Lancet*, 1997, Vol. 350, pp. 437–9.

36. Lawrence Craven, 'Acetyl Salicylic Acid: Possible Preventive of Coronary Thrombosis', *Annals of Western Medicine and Surgery*, 1950, Vol. 4, pp. 95–9. See also James Dalen, 'An Apple a Day or an Aspirin a Day', *Archives of Internal Medicine*, 1991, Vol. 151, pp. 1066–9.

37. John R. Vane, 'Inhibition of Prostaglandin Synthesis as a Mechanism of Action for Aspirin-like Drugs', *Nature: New Biology*, 1971, Vol. 231, pp. 230–5. See also J. B. Smith and A. L. Willis, 'Aspirin Selectively Inhibits Prostaglandin Production in Human Platelets', *Nature: New Biology*, 1971, Vol. 231, pp. 235–7; John R. Vane, 'Prostacyclin: A Hormone With a Therapeutic Potential', *Journal of Endocrinology*, 1982, Vol. 95, pp. 3–43.

38. Valentine Fuster, 'Aspirin in the Prevention of Coronary Disease', *NEJM*, 1986, Vol. 321, pp. 183–5. See also John A. Mills, 'Aspirin, the Ageless Remedy', *NEJM*, 1991, Vol. 325, pp. 1303–4; R. Peto *et al.*, 'Randomised Trial of Prophylactic Daily Aspirin in British Male Doctors', *BMJ*, 1988, Vol. 296, pp. 313–21; Steering Committee Preliminary Report, 'Findings from the Aspirin Component of the Ongoing Physician's Health Study', *NEJM*, 1988, Vol. 318, pp. 262–4; M. J. Underwood, 'The Aspirin Papers', *BMJ*, 1994, Vol. 308, pp. 71–2.

39. Saul Sherry, 'The Origin of Thrombolytic Therapy', *Journal of the American College of Cardiology*, 1989, Vol. 14, pp. 1085–92.

40. Marcus de Wood *et al.*, 'Prevalence of Total Coronary Occlusion During the Early Hours of Transmural Myocardial Infarction', *NEJM*, 1980, Vol. 303, pp. 897–902.

41. ISIS 2, 'Randomised Trial of Intravenous Streptokinase, Oral Aspirin, Both or Neither Among 17,187 Cases of Suspected Acute Myocardial Infarction', *The Lancet*, 1988, Vol. 2, pp. 349–59.

42. James Shepherd, 'Prevention of Coronary Heart Disease With Pravastatin in Men With Hypercholesterolemia', *NEJM*, 1995, Vol. 333, pp. 1301–7. See also Carl J. Vaughan, 'Statins Do More Than Just Lower Cholesterol', *The Lancet*, 1996, Vol. 348, pp. 1079–82.

43. J. Thomas Grayston, 'A New Chlamydia Strain Isolated in Acute Respiratory Tract Infection', *NEJM*, 1986, Vol. 315, pp. 161–7.

44. P. Saikku, 'Serological Evidence of an Association of a Novel Chlamydia With Chronic Heart Disease and Acute Myocardial Infarction', *The Lancet*, 1988, Vol. 2, pp. 983–5.

45. A. Shor *et al.*, 'Detection of Chlamydia in Coronary Arterial Fatty Streaks and Atheromatous Plaques', *South African Medical Journal*, 1992, Vol. 82, pp. 158–61.

46. Sandeep Gupta *et al.*, 'Elevated Chlamydia Antibodies, Cardiovascular Events and Azithromycin in Male Survivors of Myocardial Infarction', *Circulation*, 1997, Vol. 96, pp. 404–6. See also Enrique Gurfinkel, 'Randomised Trial of Roxithromycin in Non-acute Wave Coronary Syndromes', *The Lancet*, 1997, Vol. 350, pp. 406-408; Michael Mendall, 'Inflammatory Responses in Coronary Heart Disease', *BMJ*, 1998, Vol. 316, pp. 953–4; Gregory H. Lip, 'Can We Treat Coronary Heart Disease With Antibiotics?', *The Lancet*, 1997, Vol. 350, pp. 378–9; Sandeep Gupta, 'Chlamydia and Coronary Heart Disease', *BMJ*, 1997, Vol. 314, pp. 1778–9; Phyllida Brown, 'Can You Catch a Heart Attack?', *New Scientist*, 8 June 1996, pp. 38–42.

47. Shah Ebrahim, 'Systematic Review of Randomised Control Trials of Multiple-risk Factor Interventions for Preventing Coronary Heart Disease', *BMJ*, 1997, Vol. 314, pp. 1666–73.

48. G. M. Mead, 'Chemotherapy for Solid Tumours: Routine Treatment Not Yet Justified', *BMJ*, 1995, Vol. 310, pp. 146–7. See also Albert S. Braverman, 'Medical Oncology in the 1990s', *The Lancet*, 1991, Vol. 337, pp. 901–2; John Cairns, 'Cancer Chemotherapy', *Science*, 1983, Vol. 220, pp. 252–4.

49. John C. Bailar III, 'The Case for Cancer Prevention', *Journal of the National Cancer Institute*, 1979, Vol. 62, pp. 727–31. See also John Cairns, 'The Treatment of Diseases and the War Against Cancer', *Scientific American*, 1985, Vol. 253 (5), pp. 31–9; Mary M. Cohen, 'Are We Losing the War on Cancer?', *Nature*, 1986, Vol. 323, pp. 488–9; N. J. Temple and D. P. Burkitt, 'The War on Cancer: Failure of Therapy and Research', *JRSM*, 1991, Vol. 84, pp. 95–6; John C. Bailar III and Elaine Smith, 'Progress Against Cancer?', *NEJM*, 1986, Vol. 314, pp. 1226–32; correspondence: *NEJM*, 1986, Vol. 315, pp. 963–8; Tim Beardsley, 'A War Not Won', *Scientific American*, 1994, Vol. 1, pp. 118–26.

50. Richard Doll, *Prevention of Cancer: Pointers from Epidemiology* (Nuffield Provincial Hospitals Trust, 1967).

51. Bruce Armstrong and Richard Doll, 'Environmental Factors and Cancer Incidence and Mortality in Different Countries With

Special Reference to Dietary Practices', *British Journal of Cancer*, 1975, Vol. 15, pp. 617–31.

52. See Note 4.

53. J. Lyon *et al.*, 'Cancer Incidence in Mormons and Non-Mormons in Utah During 1967–75', *Journal of the National Cancer Institute*, 1980, Vol. 65, pp. 1055–71. See also R. L. Phillips *et al.*, 'Mortality Among California Seventh-Day Adventists for Selected Cancer Sites', *Journal of the National Cancer Institute*, 1980, Vol. 65, pp. 1097–1107.

54. Gary M. Williams and George T. Baker, 'The Potential Relationships Between Ageing and Cancer', *Experimental Gerontology*, 1992, Vol. 27, pp. 469–76. See also Douglas Dix, 'The Role of Ageing and Cancer Incidence: An Epidemiological Study', *Journal of Gerontology, Biological Sciences*, 1989, Vol. 44, pp. 10–18; Richard A. Miller, 'Gerontology as Oncology', *Cancer*, 1991, Vol. 68, pp. 2496–501.

55. R. Peto, 'Distorting the Epidemiology of Cancer: The Need for a More Balanced Overview', *Nature*, 1980, Vol. 284, pp. 297–300. See also Editorial, 'Two Views of the Causes of Cancer', *Nature*, 1981, Vol. 289, pp. 431–2.

56. See Note 5.

57. Gino J. Marco (ed.), *Silent Spring Revisited* (Washington, DC: American Chemical Society, 1987).

58. Eric Chivian *et al.* (eds), *Critical Condition: Human Health and the Environment* (Cambridge, MA: MIT Press, 1993).

59. M. Tubiana, 'The Carcinogenic Effect of Exposure to Low Doses of Carcinogens', *British Journal of Industrial Medicine*, 1992, Vol. 49, pp. 601–5. See also Ronald L. Kathren, 'Pathway to a Paradigm: The Linear Non-threshold Dose-response Model in Historical Context', *Health Physics*, 1996, Vol. 70, pp. 621–35.

60. Bruce N. Ames and Lois Gold, 'Chemical Carcinogenesis: Too Many Rodent Carcinogens', *Proceedings of the National Academy of Science*, 1990, Vol. 87, pp. 7772–6. See also Editorial, 'Testing for Carcinogens With Rodents', *Science*, 1990, Vol. 249, P1357; correspondence: *Science*, 1990, Vol. 250, pp. 1644–6.

61. Stephen Safe, 'Environmental and Dietary Oestrogens in Human Health: Is There a Problem?', *Environmental Health Perspectives*, 1995, Vol. 103, pp. 346–51.

62. 'Investigation of Possible Increased Incidence of Cancer in Western Cumbria', HMSO, 1984. See also David Sumner, 'Low-level Radiation: How Dangerous Is It?', *Medicine and War*, 1990, Vol. 6, pp. 112–19; NRBP, 'Risk of Radiation-induced Cancer at Low Doses', 1995, Vol. 6, No. 1; Paula Cook Mozaffari, 'Cancer

Near Potential Sites of Nuclear Installations', *The Lancet*, 1989, Vol. 2, pp. 1145–7.

63. J. W. Stather *et al.*, 'The Risk of Childhood Leukaemia Near Nuclear Establishments', NRPB-R215 (HMSO, 1988).

64. Edward Campion, 'Powerlines, Cancer and Fear', *NEJM*, 1997, Vol. 337, pp. 45–7.

65. Erica von Mutius, 'Prevalence of Asthma and Allergic Diseases in Children in United Germany: A Descriptive Comparison', *BMJ*, 1992, Vol. 305, pp. 1395–7.

66. J. B. Austin, 'Prevalence of Asthma and Wheeze in the Highlands of Scotland', *Archives of Disease in Childhood*, 1994, Vol. 71, pp. 211–16. See also Michael L. Burr, 'Pollution: Does it Cause Asthma?', *Archives of Disease in Childhood*, 1995, Vol. 72, pp. 377–87.

67. Aaron Wildavsky, *But is it True?*.

68. Alvan R. Feinstein, 'Scientific Standards in Epidemiologic Studies of the Menace of Daily Life', *Science*, 1988, Vol. 242, pp. 1257–63. See also Linda C. Mayes *et al.*, 'A Collection of Fifty-six Topics With Contradictory Results in Case Control Research', *International Journal of Epidemiology*, 1988, Vol. 17, pp. 680–5.

69. Mervyn Susser, 'Epidemiology in the United States After World War II: The Evolution of Technique', *Epidemiologic Reviews*, 1985, Vol. 7, pp. 147–77.

70. Geoffrey Rose, 'Sick Individuals and Sick Populations', *International Journal of Epidemiology*, 1985, Vol. 14, pp. 32–8. See also Geoffrey Rose, 'The Population Mean Predicts the Number of Deviant Individuals', *BMJ*, 1990, Vol. 301, pp. 1031–5; Geoffrey Rose, *The Strategy of Preventive Medicine* (Oxford: OUP, 1992); Bruce Charlton, 'A Critique of Geoffrey Rose's "Population Strategy for Preventive Medicine"', *JRSM*, 1995, Vol. 88, pp. 607–8.

71. Marcia Angell, 'Clinical Research: What Should the Public Believe?', *NEJM*, 1994, Vol. 331, pp. 189–90.

72. Gary Taubes, 'Epidemiology Faces Its Limits', *Science*, 1995, Vol. 269, pp. 164–6.

73. Anthony J. McMichael, 'Global Climate Change: Potential Effects on Health', *BMJ*, 1997, Vol. 315, pp. 805–9. See also Gregory Gardner, 'Many Climate Change Scientists Do Not Agree That Global Warming is Happening', *BMJ*, 1998, Vol. 316, p. 116.

3: The Unsolved Problem – The Mysteries of Biology Revisited

REFERENCES

1. Y. Ben-Shlomo, 'Dietary Fat and Epidemiology of Multiple Sclerosis', *Neuroepidemiology*, 1992, Vol. 11, pp. 214–25.

2. D. A. S. Compston, 'The Dissemination of Multiple Sclerosis', *Journal of the Royal College of Physicians of London*, 1990, Vol. 24, pp. 207–19. See also Bernard Souberbielle *et al.*, 'Is There a Case for a Virus Etiology in Multiple Sclerosis?', *Scottish Medical Journal*, 1995, Vol. 40, pp. 55–6.

3. John F. Kurtzke *et al.*, 'Multiple Sclerosis in the Faroe Islands', *Neurology*, 1986, Vol. 36, pp. 307–32.

4. Clark W. Heath and R. J. Hasterlik, 'Leukaemia Among Children in a Suburban Community', *AJM*, 1963, Vol. 34, pp. 796–812.

5. L. J. Kinlen, 'Epidemiological Evidence for an Infective Basis in Childhood Leukaemia', *British Journal of Cancer*, 1995, Vol. 71, pp. 1–5. See also M. F. Grieves, 'Aetiology of Acute Leukaemia', *The Lancet*, 1997, Vol. 1, pp. 344–9.

6. Martin J. Blaser, 'Helicobacter Pylori and Gastric Diseases', *BMJ*, 1998, Vol. 316, pp. 1507–10.

7. Thomas Grayston, 'A New Chlamydia Psittaci Strain Isolated in Acute Respiratory Tract Infections', *NEJM*, 1986, Vol. 315, pp. 161–4.

8. S. Shuster, 'The Aetiology of Dandruff and the Mode of Action of Therapeutic Agents', *British Journal of Dermatology*, 1984, Vol. 111, pp. 235–42.

9. Allen Steere *et al.*, 'The Spirochetal Aetiology of Lyme Disease', *NEJM*, 1983, Vol. 308, pp. 731–40.

10. J. S. H. Gaston, 'The Role of Infection in Inflammatory Arthritis', *Quarterly Journal of Medicine*, 1984, Vol. 87, pp. 647–51. See also R. A. Hughes, 'The Microbiology of Chronic Inflammatory Arthritis: An Historical View', *British Journal of Rheumatology*, 1994, Vol. 33, pp. 361–9; W. W. Buchanan, 'That Rheumatoid Arthritis Will Disappear?', *Journal of Rheumatology*, 1979, Vol. 6, pp. 324–6; R. J. McKendry, 'Is Rheumatoid Arthritis Caused by an Infection?', *The Lancet*, 1995, Vol. 1, pp. 1319–20; A. Ebringer, 'Klebsiella Antibodies in Ankylosing Spondilitis and Proteus Antibodies in Rheumatoid Arthritis', *British Journal of Rheumatology*, 1988, Vol. 27 (supplement 2), pp. 72–85; J. S. H. Gaston, 'Proteus: Is it a Likely Aetiological Factor in Chronic Polyarthritis?', *Annals of the Rheumatic Diseases*, 1995, Vol. 54, pp. 157–8.

11. S. Murakami *et al.*, 'Bell's Palsy and Herpes Simplex Virus: Identification of Viral DNA in Endoneurial Fluid and Muscle', *Annals of Internal Medicine*, 1996, Vol. 124, pp. 27–30.

12. D. Whitby *et al.*, 'Detection of Kaposi Sarcoma Associated Herpes Virus in Peripheral Blood of HIV-infected individuals and Progression to Kaposi's Sarcoma', *The Lancet*, 1995, Vol. 346, pp. 799–802.

13. J. D. H. Morris, 'Viral Infection and Cancer', *The Lancet*, 1995, Vol. 346, pp. 754–8.
14. G. B. Clements *et al.*, 'Coxsackie B Virus Infection and Onset of Childhood Diabetes', *The Lancet*, 1995, Vol. 346, pp. 221–3. See also M. Horwitz *et al.*, 'Diabetes Induced By Coxsackie Virus: Initiation by Bystander Damage and Not Molecular Mimicry', *Nature Medicine*, 1998, Vol. 4, pp. 781–5.
15. R. Gallo *et al.*, 'Frequent Detection and Isolation of Cytopathic Retroviruses from Patients With AIDS and at Risk for AIDS', *Science*, 1984, Vol. 224, pp. 500–3. See also Jean L. Mar, 'Strong New Candidate for AIDS Agent', *Science*, 1984, Vol. 224, pp. 475–7.
16. Stanley B. Prusiner, 'Novel Proteinaceous Infectious Particles Cause Scrapie', *Science*, 1982, Vol. 216, pp. 136–43. See also Stanley B. Prusiner, 'Prion Diseases of Humans and Animals', *Journal of the Royal College of Physicians*, 1994, Vol. 28, 2S; Roger Rosenberg, 'Nobel Prize in Physiology or Medicine for 1997 Awarded to Stanley B. Prusiner', *Archives of Neurology*, 1997, Vol. 54, p. 1456.

Part 4: The Rise and Fall – Causes and Consequences

1: Learning from the Past

REFERENCES
1. John Horgan, *The End of Science* (Little, Brown, 1996). See also Bentley Glass, 'Science: Endless Horizons or Golden Age?', *Science*, 1971, Vol. 171, pp. 23–9.
2. M. Baum, 'Screening for Breast Cancer: Time to Think – and Stop', *The Lancet*, 1995, Vol. 346, pp. 436–7.
3. Isobel Allen, *Doctors and Their Careers* (Policy Studies Institute, 1988) and *Doctors and Their Careers: The New Generation* (Policy Studies Institute, 1994).
4. *Daily Telegraph*, 3 June 1996.
5. David M. Eisenberg, 'Unconventional Medicine in the United States', *NEJM*, 1993, Vol. 328, pp. 246–52.
6. Arthur J. Baskey, *Worried Sick: Our Troubled Quest for Wellness* (New York: Little, Brown, 1988).
7. Roy Porter, *The Greatest Benefit to Mankind* (HarperCollins, 1998).

2: Looking to the Future

REFERENCES
1. Lord Horder, 'Whither Medicine?', *BMJ*, 2 April 1949, pp. 557–60.

2. Gail Vines, 'Starvation Diet', *New Scientist*, 4 July 1998, p. 50.
3. Sir William Osler, quoted in Horder, 'Whither Medicine?', *BMJ*, 2 April 1949, pp. 557–60.
4. Richard Horton, 'A Manifesto for Reading Medicine', *The Lancet*, 1997, Vol. 349, pp. 872–3.
5. Sandra J. Tanenbaum, 'What Physicians Know', *NEJM*, 1993, Vol. 329, pp. 1268–71. See also Gilbert M. Goldman, 'The Tacit Dimension of Clinical Judgement', *Yale Journal of Biology and Medicine*, 1993, Vol. 63, pp. 47–61.
6. Editorial, 'Meta-analysis Under Scrutiny', *The Lancet*, 1997, Vol. 350, p. 675. See also Samuel Shapiro, 'Meta-analysis/Schmeta-analysis', *American Journal of Epidemiology*, 1994, Vol. 140, pp. 771–8.
7. Editorial, 'A Meeting Too Many', *The Lancet*, 1998, Vol. 352, p. 1161.
8. James McCormick, 'Death of the Personal Doctor', *The Lancet*, 1996, Vol. 2, pp. 667–8.